Informatik aktuell

Herausgeber: W. Brauer
im Auftrag der Gesellschaft für Informatik (GI)

Subreihe Künstliche Intelligenz
Mitherausgeber: C. Freksa
in Zusammenarbeit mit dem Fachbereich 1
„Künstliche Intelligenz" der GI

G. Barth   A. Günter   B. Neumann (Hrsg.)

KI-94

Anwendungen der Künstlichen Intelligenz

18. Fachtagung für Künstliche Intelligenz
Saarbrücken, 22./23. September 1994
(Anwenderkongreß)

Springer-Verlag
Berlin Heidelberg New York
London Paris Tokyo
Hong Kong Barcelona
Budapest

Herausgeber

Gerhard Barth
Daimler Benz AG
Forschungszentrum Ulm
Wilhelm-Runge-Str. 11, D-89081 Ulm

Andreas Günter
Bernd Neumann
Universität Hamburg
FB Informatik, Labor für Künstliche Intelligenz
Vogt-Kölln-Str. 30, D-22527 Hamburg

CR Subject Classification (1993): I.2.1, I.2.5

ISBN-13:978-3-540-58464-3   e-ISBN-13:978-3-642-79283-0
DOI: 10.1007/978-3-642-79283-0

CIP-Eintrag beantragt.

Satz: Reproduktionsfertige Vorlage vom Autor/Herausgeber

SPIN: 10476651   33/3140-543210 – Gedruckt auf säurefreiem Papier

Vorwort

Der vorliegende Band enthält Beiträge, die auf dem KI-Anwenderkongreß in der 18. Deutschen Jahrestagung für Künstliche Intelligenz vorgetragen wurden. Der Kongreß hatte das Ziel, den Informationsaustausch zwischen KI-Forschern, Entwicklern und Anwendern zu fördern und zur Umsetzung von Forschungsergebnissen in praktische und wirtschaftlich erfolgreiche Anwendungen beizutragen.

Die Beiträge verdeutlichen das breite Anwendungs- und Methodenspektrum der KI. Künstliche Intelligenz ist ein lebendiges Fachgebiet, das neue Entwicklungen aufnimmt und neue Anwendungsbereiche erschließt. Dabei kommt es vielfach zu fruchtbaren Begegnungen mit anderen Disziplinen, insbesondere den Ingenieurwissenschaften. Dieser Band wendet sich deshalb auch bewußt an Leser, die ihre Hauptinteressen nicht unbedingt in der KI sehen. Er will innovative Lösungen und interessante Anwendungen aufzeigen, die durch KI-Methoden ermöglicht werden. Damit trägt er nicht nur zu einem Brückenschlag zwischen Forschern und Anwendern, sondern auch zu interdisziplinärer Verständigung bei.

Nach einer in den letzten Jahren spürbaren Zurückhaltung von Anwendern gegenüber KI-Methoden kann festgestellt werden, daß die KI ein beträchtliches und kontinuierlich wachsendes Potential für wirtschaftlich interessante Anwendungen besitzt. Dies ist auch eines der Ergebnisse einer kürzlich von Arthur D. Little für den BMFT erstellten Evaluierung. Jedoch ist der Weg zu erfolgreichen Anwendungen nicht so einfach wie früher vielfach angenommen.

Wichtig für die Diskussion um das KI-Anwendungspotential scheint uns folgendes zu sein:

- KI bietet durch die wissensbasierte Methodologie Vorteile, die bisher weder von der klassischen Informatik noch von Ingenieurwissenschaften angeboten werden. Diese Vorteile sind, wenn richtig genutzt, unmittelbar relevant für leistungsfähige, durchschaubare, leicht modifizierbare und damit ökonomisch vorteilhafte Lösungen komplexer Probleme in vielen Bereichen der Wirtschaft.

- In den letzten Jahren konnten wirtschaftlich nützliche KI-Anwendungen realisiert werden durch Anwendungsnähe, eine verstärkte Auseinandersetzung mit konventionellen Lösungen, Integration in die jeweilige DV-Umgebung, bessere Durchschaubarkeit des repräsentierten Wissens, Aussagen über die Korrektheit der Lösungen, Modifizierbarkeit und Adaptierbarkeit.

- Eine weitere Qualitätsverbesserung von KI-Anwendungen kann im wesentlichen durch Fortschritte in zwei Richtungen erreicht werden:
  (i) Konsequent anwendungsorientierte Problemlösungen unter Berücksichtigung der Anwendungsumgebung und, wo erforderlich und nützlich, unter Einbeziehung erprobter Methodik des Anwendungsbereiches sowie konventioneller Informatik-Methoden;
  (ii) Entwicklung validierter und wiederverwendbarer Software-Bausteine, mit denen effektive KI-Methoden wirtschaftlich zur Anwendung gebracht werden können.

Wir meinen, daß die Beiträge dieses Bandes nicht nur eine Momentaufnahme heutiger KI-Anwendungen darstellen, sondern auch wichtige anwendungsorientierte Entwicklungstrends der KI aufzeigen.

Die Herausgeber

Inhaltsverzeichnis

Neural Robot Control

A. Kellner
Deutsche Aerospace AG
Raumfahrt-Infrastruktur
Huenefeldstr. 1-5
28199 Bremen, Germany
Tel 421 539 4987   Fax 421 539 5726

INTRODUCTION

Current concepts of robot-supported operations for Space Laboratories (payload servicing, inspection, repair and ORU exchange) are mainly based on the concept of "interactive autonomy" which implies autonomous behaviour of the robot according to predefined timelines, predefined sequences of elementary robot operations and within predefined world models supplying geometrical and other information for parameter instantiation on the one hand, and the ability to override and change the predefined course of activities by human intervention on the other hand.

Although in principle a very powerful and useful concept, in practice the confinement of the robot to the abstract world models and predefined activities appears to reduce the robot's stability within real-world uncertainties and its applicability to non-predefined parts of the world, calling for frequent corrective interaction by the operator, which in itself may be tedious and time-consuming.

In this paper methods are presented to improve this situation by incorporating "robotic skills" based on Neural Nets into the concept of interactive autonomy.

CONTROL FUNCTIONS AND INFORMATION BASES FOR INTERACTIVE AUTONOMY

The control and information architecture associated with the concept of interactive autonomy can be conceived as a three-layered structure, where the top-layer (the system layer) reads in the timeline of robot, payload and subsystem tasks driving the whole system, checks the tasks for consistency and delegates them to the different recipients (robot, payloads, subsystems), the middle layer (subsystem layer) breaks down the tasks into robot- and payload-specific action sequences, instantiates their parameters and delegates them to the bottom layer (equipment layer) where the final control execution is performed.

Associated with each control layer is a database of *predefined* operational knowledge (timelines, action sequences, control strategies, as well as failure handling methods) and a database containing *predefined* environment representations (e.g. geometrical world-model for the robot) updated according to *predefined* transitions after action execution.

To support interaction with the real world, *predefined* expected sensor values (e.g. forces and torques) may be supplied with the predefined actions.

Moreover, associated with each control layer there is an MMI which allows operator interaction on the respective layer at any time during the autonomous execution of the timelines, thus providing for *interactive* autonomy.

NEED FOR OPERATIONAL ENHANCEMENTS

First analyses and practical experience with prototypes realizing the a.m. control and information architecture show both the power of this concept of interactive autonomy and its shortcomings.

The power of the concept is particularly apparent on system level in the case of payload servicing operations. By a suitable MMI, the coordinated, interactive robot-payload operations can easily be monitored, and whenever a change in robot-payload interaction is necessary, this can easily be achieved by changing the task sequences accordingly.

However, on subsystem-level problems can occur when there is a mismatch between predefined world-model and real-world data, e.g. due to erroneous input or update, deformation in the environment, or miscalibration of the robot, or when objects need to be handled which have not been foreseen in the world-model or which are not amenable to modelling, e.g. hoses and cables.

Operator intervention on subsystem-level in this case implies selection of robot action sequences and action parameter tuning, which can be extremely tedious and time-consuming.

Of course, operator intervention on equipment level, i.e. by telemanipulation (joystick control) seems more appropriate in these cases.

However, if the control is performed from the ground, the command-feedback round-trip time of several seconds again leads to tedious and time-consuming operations, not to speak of the problems inherent per se in fine-manipulation using video feedback.

The same applies to problems which may occur on equipment-level during control execution, such as jamming in insert/extract operations.

Obviously, some type of sensor-based control algorithms would be required to eliminate these problems.

However, in general these cannot only be of the type providing closed-loop sense-act cycles (e.g. for force/torque-based compliant motion) but need to provide strategies based on general knowledge, e.g. how to grasp objects which are not amenable to modelling in a world-model, such as hoses or cables.
This leads to the concept of "robotic skills" as an additional, essential ingredient of the concept of interactive autonomy.

ROBOTIC SKILLS

As examples, in the following two skills are presented: the "grasping skill" and the "insert/extract-skill".

In the first case, the robot is provided with the ability to grasp an a priori unknown object indicated by placing the cursor on its 3D-video image generated by a pair of gripper cameras - certainly an enhancement of the a.m. concept of interactive autonomy, which would otherwise require action sequence selection and parametrization "by hand", or telemanipulation as explained above.

In the second case, the skill provides for a general jamming-free insertion/extraction capability.

Grasping Skill

This skill comprises an image preprocessing function which segments out the object indicated by the cursor, and a "sensomotory mapping" which incorporates generic knowledge for mapping object images onto robot commands such that the gripper can grasp the objects. In the following, only these sensomotory mappings are discussed further:

Since they represent generalized "grasping knowledge" which is not easily amenable to explicit (algorithmic) coding, the approach taken was to encode them in Neural Nets trained on a set of samples and to investigate the generalization capability of these mappings.

In the first, straightforward analysis a 3-layered backpropagation net was trained on a large number of objects, each in various orientations, together with the corresponding correct grasping poses of the robot, thus providing mappings from object shape and orientation to robot commands. Essentially these commands are joint angle increments which improve the gripper pose relative to the "graspable" area of the object. After each increment execution, the sensomotory mapping is performed again, thus providing a "servoing" on the object's shape. However, training times appear to be quite prohibitive and, in particular, the generalization capabilities to non-trained shapes is not satisfactory.

In a second approach the image of the indicated object is scanned for grasping areas by means of a filter realized by a 3-layered backpropagation net which has learned the human (!) assessment of a large number of object-partitions which can be grasped and partitions which cannot be grasped by the robot. This method produces excellent results in acceptable computation times.

Surprisingly, a third method also proved very promising: in this case both architecture and synaptic weights of a Neural Net were designed "by hand" such that as soon as an area fitting between the gripper fingers is detected by the first layer of neurons as the robot slowly rotates (by default) the gripper cameras over the object, the shape of the area generates robot commands such that the area's line of gravity is aligned with the symmetry line between the gripper fingers. Grasping is performed when the width of the aligned area is identified by the net as large enough for the robot's gripper. However, this method only applies for objects with not too complex structures of the grasp surfaces.

Of these three approaches, the first was analyzed by simulation only. In the latter two cases both simulation and subsequent testing on a 6 DOF commercial robot with gripper cameras were performed.

Insert/extract-Skill

In this case the "sensomotory mapping" is given by the mapping of force/torque-histories typical for imminent jamming (measured by suitable sensors in the robot's wrist) onto appropriate corrective robot commands to avoid the jamming situation in insert or extract operations.

Input signals are the 6 components of the force/torque signals and the current position of the robot. In order to incorporate the temporal evolution of the input signals, backpropagation nets with tapped delays are used. The difficulty lies in the training procedure: the only possibility is to record a large number of examples of a human operator performing jamming-free inserts/extracts or remedies in case jamming is imminent, and to train the net on this human behaviour.

First tests already showed promising results. However, further investigation is necessary to provide a truly general insert/extract-skill module.

CONCLUSIONS

The current concept of interactive autonomy for robot operations in Space Laboratories can be enhanced by robotic skills. Since these imply complex sensomotory mappings not easily amenable to explicit representations, encoding these mappings by Neural Nets trained on a set of representative samples seems to be an appropriate approach.

First tests with such Neural-Net-based skills for grasping and insert/extract operations provided promising results and clearly undergird the feasibility of the method of neural control.

Artificial Intelligence in Economics and Finance
a State of the Art 1994

L. F. Pau
Digital Equipment Europe, European Center, POBox 27
F 06901 Sophia Antipolis, France
e-mail: pau@azur.enet.dec.com

1. Introduction
1. 1. Historical perspective

It is time to look back, and forward, into the applications and the research challenges ahead for artificial intelligence in economics and finance. This broad area had in the late 1970's been labelled as "the one" field where AI would "with certainty and brilliance" make the deepest inroads, owing to the relatively high proportion of simple formalized heuristic knowledge and low labor productivity. Until about 1990 a large number of banks, insurance or finance companies embarked on internal developments, hiring a few key AI specialists for overall software architectural design and prototyping. Some specialist companies also emerged, offering generic approaches using mostly knowledge based or natural language based tools tailored to special needs of these generic areas (like insurance, asset allocation, formatted message understanding). It is estimated that more than 2000 prototypes were developed in industry worldwide, most with standard "shells", and defined as a commercial effort of more than 6 man. months. For rather strange reasons, "open" AI applications in economics and finance was never a prime area for academic researchers in their academic capacities, and economics/management science by and large never showed any interest at that time.

Already in the late 1980's some pragmatic voices had incisive remarks on the above phenomenon, stressing altogether low integration, poor tools, and above all lack of trust by management mostly for lack of exhaustive or "accepted" knowledge. A thorough verification as to the actual use of these prototypes and later ones [3, 27] led to at most 350 systems deployed, and this often on a trial basis, leaving today in 1994 less than 80 "survivors", meaning solutions used in an operational context (separate from development) and including identifiable AI technologies in the deployed solution. These survivors shared a few recognizable characteristics:
- very narrow and focussed functionalities
- non-strategic, but identified and measureable usefulness
- developed by conventional software engineering methodologies and by mostly internal staff having had a dual training/experience in banking and software, with only limited exposure to AI research
- heavy use of database systems, and AI represents less than 20% of the total solution (and is often not the critical p art, as opposed to database engineering)
- growing use of "complementary" techniques, such as object oriented problem specification, machine learning and neural networks
- PC target platforms combined with networking and possibly client-server architectures

Another major trend of the early 1990's has been growing awareness and use of AI techniques amongst management science and some economics academics, although they tend in turn to "bypass" AI and embrace "newer" techniques such as constraint programming or neural networks.

1. 2. Plan of the paper

This paper will not describe any AI techniques, but relate them and further research to applications, and give the views on each from a user point of view. To illustrate this approach, a unifying case problem will be considered, i. e. real estate pricing and credit (Section 3), not because it is a dominating one, but because it is both a good illustration of the analysis performed around the usefulness of AI and because it leads directly to some key areas of further research common to the whole field. Sections 2 and 4 reflect concerns in the business community about the use of AI techniques, and offer a systematic goal-driven methodology for selection of solution approaches combining AI and other techniques. Section 5, 6, 7 present basic approaches, their advantages/disadvantages and examples linked to the common real estate case, covering respectively conventional AI approaches (knowledge based systems, natural language, qualitative modeling), machine learning (including induction, concept learning and neural processing), and the very promising case-based reasoning. A conclusion describes in Section 8 new and important research and application areas.

2. Motivations for the Use of AI in Economics and Finance

In the areas of banking, financial services, insurance, economics, accounting, and related industries, the main operational motivations for initiating, and eventually fielding systems solutions using some significant portions of AI techniques, are the following:

$M1$: development of computer based solutions allowing for the handling of tasks of a high relative complexity, as measured vs. operator skills or combinatorics, thus leveraging skills/staff and reducing risks; the complexity involves achieving a compromise between: providing a consistent level of information, a wide range of capabilities around some specific goals, and providing training capabilities; Example: lending advisors.

$M2$: setting up computer and communications based information services, with user specific interfaces and dialogue functions, offering a time- and/or competitive edge over the other actors operating in the same domain, and pooling knowledge for the preparation of time critical decisions. Example: bond trading and allocation system.

$M3$: replacing paperwork, information consolidation and cumbersome control procedures in routine operations involving usually distributed agents/information sources, and where a high consistency is needed reflecting a common policy or legal/tax rules. Example: real estate appraisal for credit.

$M4$: outright labor, quality, time and money savings in centralized routine tasks, with reduced errors. Example: money transfer telex conversion into verified standard formats

$M5$: ability to upgrade a solution software incrementally with a higher software cost productivity. Example: cash point machines network management and fault diagnosis

Table 1: Motivations

These classes of motivations may be further related to the location (Lx) of the need in terms of the organizational element where this solution is needed; this is very important as the "cultures" and "business performance metrics"are very different between these locations:

$L1$: front-office services facing the end customer

$L2$: general support functions including dealing rooms

$L3$: product or service specific support functions

$L4$: internal policy making and related information analysis

$L5$: auditing, compliance and security functions

Table 2: Locations

3. Real Estate Pricing and Lending

This case [32] offers a very nice example of mix of techniques, of integration, and of multi-level analysis (domains Dx) (from household economics, demographics [50] to macroeconomics) with different information sources/constraints. This combination of characteristics is certainly and fundamentally what makes the use of AI in economics and finance so challenging. This case is pedagogically a nice one, as many people will understand it.

LEVEL	Goals	Information	Approaches
D1:National	Acceptable monetary aggregates, inflation and employment	Demographics Sectoral economic activity Money and bond markets Tax and investment laws	Macroeconomic models Neural networks Qualitative simulation Inductive logic
D2:Mortgage bank	Assets and liabilities allocation Profitability Risk control	Balance sheet structure Credit policies Branch policies Competition	Optimization Constraint programming Spreadsheet
D3:Housing	Detect quality trends Real estate taxation Public valuations	Local government policies Environment Supply/demand of housing Land use structure/age	Optimization Constraint programming Spreadsheet
D4:Individual	Quality and risk assessment Private valuation	Household finances Taxation Visual observations Historical/credit records	Expert systems Machine learning Probability estimation

<u>Table 3</u>: Levels of the Real Estate Pricing and Credit Case

In the above, information is normally collected and analyzed at one level Dx, whereas the AI approaches in the rightmost columns must provide outputs fed upwards and downwards (Dx+1, Dx-1), for the techniques selected at those levels to be able to achieve their specific goals listed in the second column. It should also be noticed that there is conflict between some of the goals at the different levels; for example risk minimization in property valuation at level D4 will reduce profits at level D2 and increase long term interest rates at level D1. The motivations and locations (Table 4, 5) are different too; assuming the actor is just the mortgage bank (other actors would lead to different combinations).

4. Generic Tasks

The analysis of the motivations, in relation to the types of information sources and to the AI (or other) approaches is essential to allow the users select AI techniques for testing and later deployment, and also for researchers to identify which features are still missing in a given context (formalized here by the triplet Mx, Ly, Dz)). Most users do not care about a specific approach, but for the ability to carry out certain generic tasks (noted Tn) linked to the motivations, and constrained by the locations and information types. Much energy goes precisely in identifying and assessing whether a given technique, in a given operational environment, can or cannot perform a task well understood by the "user". It is often regretted that AI research ignores such categorization issues, which are on the contrary well practised for example in statistics or operations research, thus implicitly inducing these "users" to select such approaches initially.

In the first Table 6 below, a the motivations Mx are linked to specific generic tasks Tn. In the second Table 7 below, which is not exhaustive vs. the range of AI approaches, a relation is established between these generic tasks Tn and AI approaches & others, in that the sign "+" means that a given approach can perform a given task. Whereas these two tables are general, the final selection candidates for a solution architecture combining several techniques to meet the goals of a specific application case, will require the Table 5 above, which is case specific.

LEVEL	LOCATIONS
D1:National level	L4 (economic analysis)
D2:Mortgage bank	L3 (assets and liability management) L3 (treasury) L4 (commercial lending policy) L5 (auditing)
D3:Housing district/branch	L2 (mortgage payments) L4 (marketing)
D4:Individual home	L1 (bank desk) L1 (valuation expert)

Table 4: Locations in the Real Estate Pricing and Credit Case

GOAL/LEVEL	MOTIVATION
Acceptable monetary aggregates, inflation and employment/D1	M3
Assets and liabilities allocation/D2	M2
Profitability/D2	M2
Risk control/D2	M4
Detect quality trends/D3	M1
Real estate taxation/D3	M2, M5
Quality and risk assessment/D4	M1
Private valuation/D4	M3

Table 5: Goals in Relation to Motivations in the Real Estate Pricing and Credit Case

Of course, at this level, the specific techniques under a given approach cannot be specified. The more important issue here in economics and finance, because of the strong influence of statistics, econometrics, operations research, and control theory, is whether any AI approach can supplement these established approaches (besides database and integration techniques), and not the other way around. Spreadsheet are mentioned here on purpose, because it should be recognized that current spreadsheet products (which include conditional IF_THEN_ELSE jumps, as well as mathematical programming) offer most of the functionalities end users are looking for, including real-time data feeds. Likewise economics formulae used in models are very important [30], and many tools exist for user friendly quantitative modelling [45].

GENERIC TASKS	M1	M2	M3	M4	M5
T1:Declarative heuristic knowledge	+	+	+	+	+
T2:Formal/model/procedural knowledge	+		+	+	+
T3:Adaptive learning		+			+
T4:Dynamics		+	+		
T5:Constraint based search or classification	+		+	+	
T6:Optimization	+			+	
T7:Quantitative estimation		+			
T8:Explanation	+		+	+	
T9:Commands and control		+	+	+	

Table 6: Generic Tasks in Relation to Motivations for the use of AI

Such as systematic screening process is fully representing state-of-the art goal driven thinking around AI approaches in economics and finance. It goes beyond the relative enhanced interest in one given approach at any one point in time, by showing why new approaches become relevant as they serve to fulfill some very explicit goals. Such a screening fails however at highlighting the importance of efficiency related techniques, such as knowledge representation, knowledge acquisition methodologies, search/matching algorithm efficiency, conflict resolution strategies, semantic d disambiguation, terminology data bases, etc. . which are all extremely important, but only once the solution architecture is defined meeting user goals.

	T1	T2	T3	T4	T5	T6	T7	T8	T9
Qualitative simulation		+		+			+		+
Constraint programming	+	+			+	+		(+)	
Expert systems	+	+			+			+	
Induction	+		+						
Case based reasoning	+	+	+		+			+	
Parsing	+	+						+	
Neural processing		+	+	+	(+)		+		+
Dynamic modeling		+					+		+
Mathematical programming		+				+	+		+
Spreadsheets		+		+		+	+		
Genetic algprithm [42]	+	+				+			

<u>Table 7</u>: AI & other Approaches in Relation to Generic Tasks

Irrespective of all motivations Mx and tasks Tz, there is always in economics and finance a set of permanent constraints to be satisfied about risks. The Federal Reserve Board, FDIC and the Office of the Comptroller of the currency have defined seven categories of risks in all economic transactions, all of which must be bounded:
• (counterparty) credit risk
• market price risk in view of price variations
• settlement risk
• operating risk, i. e. having people, means and methods to engage in activities
• liquidity risk, i. e. risk of not being able to replace a non-marketable good
• legal risk
• interconnection risk between instruments
Probabilistic or uncertainty reasoning is far from enough to deal with these risks.

5. Conventional AI Approaches

This Section will briefly define and evaluate the more conventional AI approaches, taken among those most frequently tested in prototyping in economic and financial applications.

5. 1. Knowledge based systems
A conventional knowledge based system/expert system will consist of:
    • heuristic knowledge, stored in a knowledge base, formalized as stored via a knowledge representation scheme (such as IF_THEN_ELSE rules, logic predicates, frames with nested slots (and class-instance object oriented variations hereof).
    • a conflict resolution strategy (first found, least recently used, antecedent ordered, consequent ordered, etc. .) [10, 28]
    • one or several inference engines implementing search algorithms on the chosen knowledge representation data structures (such as forward chaining, backward chaining,

truth maintenance, breadth-first, etc. .) possibly specialized to different knowledge base segments
• a goal seeking and querying facility, which will allow the user to enter his requests, and decode them into a data structure compatible with the knowledge representation, thus activating the search and letting alternative answers be evaluated by the conflict resolution strategy
• possibly: an explanation facility to justify the reasoning path from query to conclusion
• possibly: interfaces to external call facilities, or from other software modules

Table 8: Typical Knowledge Based System Structure

Example: The mortgage bank valuator / real estate assessor will visit the property and inspect it and the surroundings, entering qualitative attributes about it. This goes into the same fact base as another part of the same knowledge based system who will evaluate the loan applicant's household finances, tax situation, and the ability to pay back the mortgage. The property valuation by the assessor will be adjusted by heuristic knowledge specific for the district and for the bank's commercial policy. The output will be: a loan granting decision, a loan size, a loan interest rate, and possibly some tax advice to the applicant [35].

Advantages: Thanks largely to the widespread use of expert systems shells, or of libraries of basic elements hereof, many users have tried out expert systems, this approach representing in 1994 about 85% of all prototypes in the data base [27]. Provided the knowledge exists or can be acquired, validated and "accepted" it is a simple and efficient route, and integration facilities exist today which did not exist 5 years ago.

Disadvantages: Expert systems/ knowledge based systems "fail" almost always to get into real exploitation, say with an average 80% likelihood, because the knowledge was either not available already in a documented and agreed form, so that the knowledge acquisition effort is either too costly or risky. Another reasons for failures in the past were oversophistication, lack of integration facilities, lack of knowledge representation standardization, and management control issues.

5. 2. Natural language parsing

A typical natural language module will either serve as a natural language interface for querying a knowledge based system or a database (or several), or to automatize the screening for correctness of formatted forms. It will typically consist of:
- a terminology database containing, besides general language dictionaries, domain specific terms, with linked pointers to acronyms, synonyms, validity periods, etc., and possibly other languages
- a formal syntactic, grammatical and semantic description of the correct sentences and layouts
- a parser who matches, possibly by search, a given piece of text with its formal description and the root instances in the terminology database, and which labels each item in the text with a whole range of attributes
- possibly a limited form of discourse analysis
- almost always a document layout language obeying the ODA/CDA or SGML, made specific to the specific text layout, so that contents is spatially tagged
- possibly an optical character reading (OCR) module

Table 9: Typical Natural Language Module

Example: The granted loan contracts are scanned and particulars about the specific properties or loan conditions are parsed for storage in a database and subsequent aggregation of loan data. It also serves the periodic audit and review of the specific loans, and to "pool"/"securitize" packages of mortgages having similar properties.

Example: Using the methodology developped in [49] one can in limited cases build a semantic causal model from a text description of the real estate market behavior, and link the endogeneous nodes in the semantic net to external quantitative models.

Advantages: If the terminology data base is small, if the semantic ambiguity is minimal, and if the document layout structure is pretty fixed, good results have been obtained by banks and securities companies using natural language techniques.

Disadvantages: The costs of just the terminology management, and of the natural language technology are a deterrent to wider use, not to speak of those cases where semantic ambiguity or shear text size make impossible any robust routine exploitation.

Natural languague theory and terminology databases also rely on ontologies, especially domain ontologies, which are essential e. g. to structure any object oriented software in finance.

Example: An ontology for developping any software in personal finances, is:
- "linguistic/terminology object instances " include: checks, checkbooks, ledgers, paying agents, bank accounts, bank statements, budgets, tax forms, . .
- "actions" include:writing a check, depositing a payemt, balancing the ledger, preparing a budget, preparing a tax return
- "standard practices" include: check writing, depositing, withdraing, paying bills, balancing the books, filing out tax forms, . . .
- "institutions" include: banks, payment agents, merchants, IRS
- "tools" include: checks, checkbooks, ledgers, data management systems
- "faults " include:improperly filed out checks, errors in checkbook, late payments, missed deposits, negative cash flows, inability to prepare tax reports
- "concerns" include: financial solvency, timeliness of payments, creditworthiness, payment of taxes.

5. 3 Qualitative simulation

In almost all economic and financial applications, dynamics, forecasting and model identification are systematic requirements. Needless to say there is a wide range of very powerful and widely spread techniques to do this, both on numeric data, but also on graphical trends. This last remark is about so-called "technical analysis" which is essentially a parsing of temporal curve shapes by syntactic pattern recognition which, combined with a knowledge base of market behavior, leads to powerful trend analysis [3, Chapter 5]. But needless to say also, there is no Delphi Oracle, and where AI comes in is with qualitative simulation, where both the underlying model structure and its dynamic behavior are based on causal links and trends. The ambition is here to bypass the quantitative model identification and parametric estimation, to achieve robust qualitative long term forecasts. A typical qualitative simulation environment would consist of:
- interval logic to relate quantitative data and quantitative derivatives, to trend labels (such as high growth, low growth, strong decrease, etc. .)
- fuzzy membership relations to measure the interaction between two variables
- a temporal logic, which is a kind of a clock timer, with possibly time interval logics

* aggregation functions, spelling out how and when exogeneous and endogeneous variables are combined
* a temporal causal graph, spelling out explicitly how the variables interact over time, with strengths set up by the interval logic, and aggregated by the fuzzy membership relations.

<u>Table 10</u>: Typical Qualitative Simulation Structure

Example in relation to the case: To model quantitatively the housing demand/supply at the macroeconomic level D1 is very difficult. Qualitative simulation then attempts at model over time the decision making psychology of investors, owners, and buyers vis- -vis macroeconomic and demographic aggregates, to be able to predict robustly cycles and basic trends in the housing supply, demands, and used property price levels.

Advantages: There is great potential in just having robust qualitative forecasts, possibly filtered by heuristic knowledge.

Disadvantages: The modeling effort is very high, and the sensitivity of the results in the economic/financial field to any of the parameters of the technique is very high, so there is a risk of only being able to achieve robust forecasts at such an aggregate levels that the usefulness is only very limited or the delay to obtain them is too long.

6. Machine Learning Approaches
6. 1. Introduction to alternative approaches
In an economic world, there are intelligent economic agents who must be able to change over time as they interact Introduction with the markets, as well as through the experience of their own internal states and processes. Machine learning is relevant in such a changing world, because it is likely that econometric modeling may fail due to unexpected changes, and that new economic relations are not known explicitly in a timely fashion.

Learning is important as a partial countermeasure to the "knowledge acquisition/engineering bottleneck" which refers to the cost and difficulty of obtaining knowledge and afterwards maintaining the knowledge base up to date and consistent. The solution, as evidenced in most attempted uses in economics and finance, is therefore to begin with a minimal amount of knowledge and learn from examples, advice, or explorations of the domain. These techniques of partly automating knowledge acquisition is known as machine learning. The research field of machine learning has been fruitful enough to yield many different problems and solutions. These algorithms vary in their goals, in their training data types, and in the learning strategies and knowledge representation. However, all of these algorithms learn by searching through a space of possible concepts to find an acceptable generalization.

The primary learning task is induction, which is to learn a generalization from a set of examples, such as concept learning in the ID3 algorithm, which produces IF_THEN rules from examples. Given examples of some concept, such as for example "high bankruptcy risk", the learning system can infer a formal knowledge based definition that will allow itself to correctly recognize future instances of that concept. Logic induction is especially important in economics and management, as it will produce logic predicates from structure t-uples of examples, thus allowing for immediate validation against e. g. legal /procedural knowledge expressed in logic or PROLOG. It should also be noted that logic induction can be speeded up by stating economic "impossibility theorems" [28] as negative t-uples; for example, in our application case of mortgage credit, mortgage interest rates cannot be very different from long term bond interest rates.

The algorithms are data driven (thus appealing to many economists. .), do not use prior knowledge of the learning domain, and rely on a large number of examples to define the essential properties of a general concept. Algorithms that generalize on the basis of patterns in training data are referred to as similarity-based learning.

In contrast, explanation-based learning uses analogy and other techniques to utilize prior knowledge and learn from a limited amount of training data. Case-based reasoning, for example, stores solutions to problems in their original or slightly modified form. On addressing a new problem, a case-based reasoning system retrieves a case it deems sufficiently similar and uses that case as a basis for solving the new problem. Although similarity-based and explanation-based learning differ in search strategies, representation languages and amount of prior knowledge used, they all assume that training data are classified by a "teacher". The learning system is told whether an instance is a positive example, which belongs to the target concept, or a negative example, which does not. This reliance on training instances of known classification defines the task of supervised learning. In unsupervised learning, an intelligent learning system can acquire useful knowledge in the absence of correctly classified data. For example, in conceptual clustering, the system has to divide a given set of objects, such as households or companies, into homogeneous categories. We will examine CLUSTER/2, an approach to the problem of category formation.

Parallel distributed learning refers to a family of learning models, including neural networks, which examine the way in which intelligent behavior can arise from the interactions of large numbers of small, individually simple elements. Whereas the learning techniques previously mentioned work on symbolic knowledge, neural networks operate usually on numeric or categorized input data, but they also represent knowledge in the large number of interconnections among nodes, which are abstractions of biological nerve cells.

In machine learning, the maturity of learning methods varies from one part of the field to another. Supervised inductive learning of classification rules is a well understood technology; although we shall below only give one example ID3 of such methods, many exist and are turned into tools [34]. At least one company (Westinghouse) reports substantial cost savings resulting from knowledge discovered through inductive learning [40, 44]. Scaling up inductive methods to handle more complex inductive learning tasks remains a formidable challenge. Unsupervised learning and discovery techniques are much less mature, partly because the goals and criteria for success in these areas are still ill-defined. It has been demonstrated that unsupervised learning algorithms can contribute to new scientific discoveries [18].

Neural network techniques are generating much interest in real world applications recently, although there are associated problems of "black boxes" (not able to explain the decision). Furthermore, it is our guess that much work remains to be done before practical neural network systems can be deployed. A few of these techniques will be introduced and evaluated below, while case based reasoning will be dealt with specifically in a following Section.

6. 2. Tree induction: ID3
The ID3 algorithm [22, 23] represents concepts as decision trees, a representation that allows to determine the classification of an object by testing its attribute value for certain properties. The ID3 algorithm partitions examples with respect to combinations of attribute values of the examples, a set of positive and negative examples, such that it classifies cor-

rectly the given cases. The decision tree algorithm builds the tree so that all training samples on a leaf of the tree belong to the same class. It adopts an information theoretic approach, by generating splits in the tree each time there is information gained from it about some specific attribute.

Advantages: Tree based induction, and most other induction algorithms offer the capability to generate incremental knowledge tied to dynamic and changing situations, for example in trading situations, or in risk evaluation cases. If indeed limited to small to medium training sets, and validation, this gives a significant performance edge over other economic actors who must stick to one case instead of seeing the implications.

Disadvantages: Although the ID3 algorithm produces simple decision trees, it is not obvious that such trees will be effective in predicting the classification of unknown examples. Variations of ID3 have been developed to deal with such problems as noise and excessively large training sets. For more details, see [23, 24].

6. 3 Unsupervised learning: conceptual clustering
The clustering techniques begin with a collection of unclassified objects and some means of measuring the similarity of objects, say for example securities or individual accounts. Its goal is to organize these objects into a hierarchy of classes that meet some standard of homogeneity, such as maximizing the similarity of objects in the same class; this is typical of marketing research.

Numeric taxonomy is one of the most ancient approaches to the clustering problem. Numerical methods rely upon the representation of objects as a collection of features, each of which may have some numerical value. A reasonable similarity metric treats each object (a vector of n feature values) as a point in n-dimensional space. The similarity of pwo objects is the Euclidean distance between them in this space. We may extend this numeric taxonomy to objects represented as sets of symbols, rather than numeric features. A reasonable way to define the simiharity of two objects is the proportion of features they have in common. However, similarity-based clustering algorithms do not adequately capture the underlying role of semantic knowledge in cluster formation, for example, certain of an object's features might be more important than others.

Example in relation to the case: At level D3 it is of the utmost importance to analyze portofolios of mortgaged properties as to homogeneity in terms of quality vs. price, to avoid risks which are either too large or too small. Conceptual clustering is applied to such spatially close mortgaged properties, and/or to bank client groups (i. e. those which have an account just because of the loan, and those who also buy financial products, or who cover living expenses and cash flow the same place)

Advantages: Conceptual clustering offers objective means to categorize the data across operators, and thus help target marketing, back-office and other operations.

Disadvantages: The selection of the seeds and the interpretation can be delicate. It is till a too sophisticated method for many users in banking and insurance.

6. 4 Neural processing
6. 4. 1 Neural network architectures
A neural network appears more attractive than traditional statistical or times-series modeling approaches for certain problem domains due to its ability to learn from large

number of different input data sources, and from the execution speed once training is completed. This is especially relevant in finance and risk assessment where clearly identifiable dominant problem features often do not exist, as opposed to a wide array of useful data with little explicit and formally modeled interactions. The neural network is able to abstract and generalize from past experience quantified from the problem domain, and apply it to new problems.

A typical simple neural network can be visualized as a multi-layered interconnection of nodes. input nodes accept data, the hidden nodes extract features/generalizations from the data, and the output nodes present the verdict of the network to the user (i. e. either a forecast, a classification, a parameter estimation, and even a sub-optimum).

A neural network learns from examples by modifying by some training algorithm the strength of its connections, represented by the eights of all arcs linking the nodes at the different levels. The most popular model used in practical applications is the backpropagation network with its corresponding training algorithm. The mechanism in a backpropagation network is simple: training data is fed to the input layer of the network, and is passed on to the hidden layer, weighted by the interconnection strengths. The neurons at the hidden layer sum the incoming values, transform this value (nonlinearly) into their output value, and pass it on to the output layer. Likewise, neurons at the output layer sum the weighted incoming values. The error is determined as the difference between the computed output and the desired output (target), and this error is "back propagated" from the output layer to the input layer. Based on the propagated error, the connection strengths of the neural network, also called weights, are being modified. After repeated presentation of training data (drilling), the network gradually learns the underlying distribution of the data, and is able to generalize to unknown data.

There are many kinds of neural networks, each classified according to their architecture and training algorithms. For different problem domains, the performance of these networks vary. A list of introductory references is provided for interested readers to explore neural networks on their own [17, 19, 25, 26].

6. 4. 2 Neural network applications in economics and finance

Some typical examples are given below:
• Classification of firms
Consider the problem of determining whether a firm, based on its financial performance, is likely to go bankrupt. This is a straight-forward classification problem, as the goal is to classify a firm as either bankrupt or non-bankrupt (output class) on the basis of its financial characteristics (inputs).
Assume that a neural model has been trained, i. e., the neural network has been presented with both bankrupt and non-bankrupt firms and adequately discriminates between them. To determine the classification of a specific firm, its financial ratios are input to the trained network, and the network will in turn provide the user with a classification of this firm.
• Forex forecasting
Time series forecasting is perhaps the most exciting application of neural networks. The objective is to discover the underlying "structure" of the mechanism generating the data, i. e. to discover the relationship between present, past, and future observations. Conventional time series analysis restricts attention to cases where this relationship is expressed linearly. The nonlinear nature of neural networks extends their power in modeling this relationship. Very good short term predictions are often produced with little effort.
• Abnormal trading pattern detection

The detection of abnormal trading patterns in certain financial activities may require much effort from the auditor. For example, the fraudulent use of ATM cards may be detected by looking for certain withdrawal or spending patterns. These patterns, once quantified, can be used for training neural networks. A trained network is able to screen huge amount of transaction data for abnormal activities.
- Example in relation to the case: A simple neural network using data about:
  - volumes of mortgages issued, and by whom
  - liquidity positions in deposit banks vs. national/federal bank
  - interest rate time structure for money markets and bond markets
  - interest rate time structure for mortgages
  - global data on disposal income with households
  - price indexes for apartments and houses can produce excellent forecasts up to one year ahead for price indexes for apartments and houses, for risk exposure by mortgage banks, and profit margins for the mortgage banks.

6. 4. 3. Backpropagation neural network

The backpropagation training algorithm is an iterative gradient algorithm designed to minimize the mean square error between the actual output of a multilayer feed-forward perceptron and the desired output. It requires continuous differentiable non-linearities.

Advantages: Neural networks are highly flexible, in that they can be trained in any problem domain, as long as the data is well quantified, and sufficient historical data is available. Areas where neural networks work best include data classification, modeling and forecasting, and signal processing which includes generating control outputs (such as generate a trading position). Neural networks are also of high appeal in finance for their real-time capability once trained to process data from real-time data feeds and generate trades or estimates. The choice of the training algorithm is only of secondary importance as long as the computer platform is powerful enough.

Disadvantages:Neural networks offer almost no explanation capability to justify how the input nodes where exploited for the generation of the output node results. Also the statistical performance generally underscores statistical methods, such as projection pursuit [33]; computation architectures exist however allowing for parallel implementations.

7. Case Based Reasoning in Economics and Finance

7. 1 Introduction

If you look up Case based reasoning (CBR) in any of the standard textbooks in Artificial Intelligence or Economics, or both (e. g. [3, 8]) you won't see CBR listed in the tables of contents; the topic first emerged in 1990-91 although its premises have been researched for some while [1, 2]. Very little, if anything at all, has yet been published to show its very direct relevance to economic analysis and its extensions which are the focus of this paper.

From an analysis point of view, case based reasoning refers to reasoning in which a human problem-solver relies on previous cases, or examples that have been encountered, to tackle a new problem. The problem-solver recalls previous cases and decides how they are similar or dissimilar to the present issue being considered. If any of the previous cases provides any insight, the problem solver tries to solve the present case using strategies that have been proven to be actually effective in the previous ones. On the other hand, if the problem-solver finds that the new problem is different from the previous cases, the new problem and its proposed solution are stored;in other words, learning occurs when a new type of case is dealt with.

From a theoretical perspective, CBR refers to a number of concepts and techniques (e. g. data structures and algorithms) that can be used to record and index past cases, and then search them to identify the ones that might be useful in solving a new case. In addition, techniques are required to modify earlier cases to better match the new cases, and still other techniques to synthesize new cases when they are needed.

In view of the motivations and goals in the previous Sections, CBR in economics and finance is clearly only of emerging interest, but it offers what is closest to the motivations M1, M2 and M3, while being also closest to the operating traditions in locations L1, L3, L4 and L5. It is also typical of the "mixing" of different techniques, this time within one single AI approach, thus supplementing also the integration described in the real estate pricing and lending case, where there was an integration across levels by letting different techniques be nested together via results and data. The primary reason for this special strong interest for CBR in economics and finance, is indeed that both economic data, economic model structures, and even reasoning, can be rather heterogeneous from case to case, while one or several of these three dimensions were usually fixed in the three sets of techniques just mentioned. Also, there are many problems in reasoning just in terms of rules, since rules that embody the exceptional cases are often hard to induce and write, and even harder to modify when new cases come up.

Example: For example, how can we benefit from experiences with a given monetary policy in a given country in terms of selecting the instrument variables to be manipulated and their amplitudes for another country, while of course some of the data may be different and the economic structures/models even more so ? Likewise in financial analysis, how can we devise a sectoral trend and sectoral correction factors, when analyzing as cases data from a number of companies from that sector, with heterogeneous sizes, product structures and accounting methods ?

The secondary reason why CBR is, even when imperfect, highly relevant in economic analysis is that it does derive solutions when querying solution goals, instead of just, like machine learning providing some best match of a prior set of goals and measures, and eventually some elementary reasonings valid in the average sense over the case data taken jointly.

In summary, CBR is an attempt at fulfilling needs such as: -for the economists and financial analysts:simple tools that can represent cases and can be modified quickly -for the model builders and knowledge engineers:simplifying the problems involved in representing knowledge and rules, and in updating systems Needless to say, CBR has been heavily influenced by learning by analogy [4]: here one set of information is compared with another, and a decision is made about whether they are similar. One such technique is the derivational-analogy method.

Section 7.2 reviews the basic CBR approaches and concepts, illustrated by examples of suggested applications to economics, and gives a step-by-step decomposition of the case based reasoning implementation and use. In Section 7.3, we shall identify the subjects of early CBR projects in economics and finance.

7. 2 Implementation of case based reasoning in economics

All CBR systems include two key ingredients: -a case representation: as groups of features with associated values;some of the features(typically:collections of objects, rules or predicates) may be actions that have been taken in the past -algorithms for indexing, searching for, and modifying cases, as just described. Thus a CBR implementation is an environment that allows a developer to represent knowledge in terms of cases. Consequently, first generation type CBR tools are often a collection of search algorithms that sit on top of an existing hybrid expert systems tool.

7. 2. 1 Case representation

In several domains the initially available information is called "surface" features and has two characteristics:it covers real situations sparsely and does not allow the system to reliably discriminate between cases. As a result, the retrieval operations may return a number of inappropriate cases along with the relevant ones. However in many domains the retrieved cases provide a CBR system with the means of obtaining additional more discriminating features called "deep features", through so-called "probes". These are data structures which include means to acquire data, and domain-specific interpretation knowledge which is used on this data to pmoduce the deep features. The knowledge about probes is encoded in a structure called a validation model.

Thus, case representation is still the least tested area of work on CBR, in that no general guidelines yet exist for the selection of case features and their attributes. Whereas the focus on rules, frames, predicates or objects only is certainly not correct, a mixture may be slightly better. The proposed IEEE Standard P1032 for frame based knowledge representation and management of knowledge assets, also called IMKA, is a step in that direction but as yet untested in relation to other CBR steps. Therefore we propose for the time being the following formal, probably more powerful and flexible case representation, as tested out in other fields [6, 7].

A CBR environment should be able to store thousands of cases. Therefore the essence is as a result good case library development, but with identifiers for typical or representative cases. The representation CR) above seems a bit complex but is intended to force the identification of the constituents of the "case space" into segments, and then in entering typical cases from each segment of the overall domain of cases. Another remark is that frame systems allow instances to have unique attributes, while conventional object systems require a unique class to serve as the template for any instance that is created. Both are insufficient for CBR, hence the proposed representation CR) above.

7. 2. 2 Indexing of cases

There are several ways to organize or index the cases;this is detailed in some detail here, especially as in Section 1 there was a remark about a lack of use of database technology in many AI solutions to problems in economics and finance. The four common case indexing ways are:
1) Simple case-based inductive indexing: The CBR system will here dynamically develop a tree using an inductive algorithm like ID3 (see [3] for economic applications). The end nodes of the CBR tree represent sets of cases rather than specific conclusions. The steps along the way involve tests for the presence or absence of features. This indexing also can support the retrieval of cases that are similar but not exact matches.
2) Nearest neighbor indexing: If each attribute in each case has a value, matching between a new case and a set of pre-existent ones can be done by standard nearest-neighbor information retrieval criteria. They calculate the degree to which the new case matches the existing ones, attribute by attribute. Fuzzy natural language matching, and thesauri equivalence are used. Thus with the type text, a partial match occurs if any individual word is used in the description of the feature of the presented case and the feature of the stored case. The

character type is even more flexible and provides in effect spell-checking capabilities that achieve partial matches even when the feature being described contains misspelled words.
3) Hierarchical indexing: A hierarchy tree is developed from the cases;this tree can be used to quickly screen any new case and then match it with only those cases in the case library that have characteristics similar to the prototype that is most like the new case. The algorithm calculates a score for the presented case and each of the cases in the case library and selects those with the closest score and presents them for indexing. This approach exploits the layers of abstract classes between the root case class and the specific graphs of instances of cases derived from the causal graphs.
4) Knowledge guided indexing: If the CBR is built on top of an hybrid expert system shell, one can use the rules in $N(j, G(i, j))$ to reason about which subset of cases is most like the new case one tries to match.
5) Combination of indexing techniques: One can finally combine 1-4 to provide efficient full indexing for large applications. This can be formalized by having an indexing script saying which indexing technique is applied to which set of cases and in which order. Normally in this event, nearest neighbor indexing comes last as it applies weightings to attributes.

These weights are match and mismatch weights. The match weight indicates the importance of the presence of a feature while the mismatch weight indicates how important it would be if the feature were not present in the case being examined. These default absent-present weights can be inherited from the root class case to handle situations in which there is a feature in the new case that is not present in a stored case. All these weights must be specified exogeneously.

7. 2. 3 Case retrieval
There are also several techniques for retrieving cases from the case library when the user presents a new case. All possible matches are identified and possibly ranked in case the technique uses weights.
1) Template retrieval: Here one looks for a case in the case library that exactly matches the new case. This is what database retrieval implements. Each attribute of the new case must exactly match the attributes of one or more cases otherwise nothing is returned.
2) Hierarchical retrieval: Whenever the cases have been indexed with either inductive or hierarchical techniques, one will search the tree structure, making decisions at each node until one can go no further. If a leaf-node is reached, then the set of cases found there is returned. If the retrieval stops short of a leaf-node, then all the sets of cases that lie beyond that point are returned.
3) Associative retrieval: Associative retrieval is used with nearest neighbor indexing. The associative retrieval algorithm [9] examines the attributes of the new case in the case library, using weights assigned to each attribute of each stored case.
4) Knowledge based retrieval: In this case the user can write a small set of rules to guide or filter the search for appropriate cases. This approach relies on a conventional search algorithm such as forward search or beam-search or constraint satisfaction [3].

The effectiveness of the retrieval is measured by recall and precision [12]. Recall measures the percentage of the relevant information that is retrieved from the database in response to a particular query. Precision measures the retrieved information that is relevant.

7. 2. 4 Learn and adopt new cases
In many situations, a good match cannot be found in Step 7.2.3.4), and one must provide formulas, procedural code, or rules that will allow the system to adopt an existing case so

that it will better match the new case. Also, the end user may adopt and store new cases that are unique and should be included in the case library in the future. This process is sometimes called case adaptation.

7. 3 Potential applications of CBR in economics and finance

This Section in no way pretends to describe full or solved CBR problems in economics or finance. It proposes rather precisely a solution's implementation (Section 7.2), and provides pointers to some possible, yet untested, applications. We list such potential applications below.

1) Example: Property valuation in a district As individual mortgage applications are being processed by a bank branch, it uilds up a library of cases. These cases are not independent in that property assessment criteria, zoning infrastructure, municipal real estate taxation rules link them together. CBR can indeed help carry out a "calibration" of property valuations, with the case retrieval providing a very pragmatic explanation and justification [32, 47].

2) Explanation in relation to the case: Securitization of mortgage portofolio By the introduction of suitable similarity measures, eventually explored before by conceptual clustering, the case based retrieval can both provide a rule base as to the characteristics a given candidate pool of mortgages, and give a means to retrieve mortgages to be allocated to pools with given characeristics. It also provides a documentation feature to the buyer/seller of the securitized mortgage pool.

3) Example: mergers and acquisitions There have been very few formal approaches to this area, for very good reasons. Nevertheless an ex-post case based analysis of M&A, based on later performances, would prove to be an interesting testing ground both for CBR and for financial analysis.

4) Example: marketing research For targeting selected groups, there is a still unsolved problem in selection of representative elements, and to evaluate whether a new case (that is a new completed survey questionnaire) falls in this or that action category. Whereas statistical clustering, and neural networks show some promise they are poor at handling qualitative and causality aspects, which CBR should be able to [38].

8. Conclusions: Areas for further Research

In the real world of economic analysis, there will be many cases, some with more features and some with less, some with more or less qualitative attributes or different causal structures, and also with more or less legal/procedural consraints. AI approaches must be able to scalable and tunable to these changing characteristics without changing the underlying techniques or algorithms as now.

Also, and essential to economic applications, a better explanation based interfaces are necessary between user and system, in that the discussion around a set of solutions generated by a system will invariably turn around features or problems (and not just "knowledge"), while being supported with lots of examples retrieved with varying degrees of match. It is essential to learn from the evolution in economic analysis that feature-centered discussions are key to the debates although sometimes hidden behind modeling issues [10]. The selection of instrument variables and policies is a feature selection. Reference [5] adds to this the potential dimension of introducing the behavioral elements of the economic agents.

Still from the point of view of business, almost no AI research adresses econmic competition theories, either with reference to game theory [28, 31], or to disequilibrium theories. AI search theory has much to gain from revisiting both ecomic theories and game theory, especially as computer supported cooperative work environments [29] pop-up in AI solutions.

On a more fundamental level, the business communities have over the past 5-10 years developped strong understandings for the value of knowledge assets, thse being people based skills, intellectual property, information, trademarks, process/design knowledge. However, even when restricted to such a lear issue as interoperable and exchangeable knowledge bases, to be derived from the standardization of some of the basic knowledge representations, the academic AI community prefers to push for many unproven concepts. Banking, finance, services and administrations are tired of this, and want quickly accepted knowledge representation standards they can stake their survival and competitivity on. In this relation, knowledge acquisition is a far les important issue.

Economic and financial processes are extremely "brittle", and so are the technique sused to analyze them. The choice is always between flexible techniques and accurate ones, but AI can contribute to both, provided it is supplemented by learning and adaptation to face changing behaviors, experiments, etc. . This brittleness and compromise suggest that genetic algorithms [42] combined with heuristic knowledge, are worth exploring, to address fundamentally different systems than conventional symbolic AI. Genetic algorithms allow for gaming, competition and optimization, as work on double auction tournaments in economics has shown.

But the one and yet little explored strongest potential of some AI techniques lie in their data/information fusion capability [6, 28]; this holds especially for neural networks, case based reasoning, and of course knowledge representation standards. In many of the above trends, final success will ultimately depend on a subtle balance between letting some AI techniques be implemented alongside and like other mainstream techniques, while also exploring thoroughly challenging fields, such as machine learning and explanation.

REFERENCES

1. Proc. Case based reasoning workshops, DARPA, 1988-1991, Morgan Kaufman, Menlo Park, 1991

2. R. Shank, C. Riesbeck, Inside case-based reasoning, Lawrence Erlbaum Assoc., Hillsdale, NJ, 1989

3. L. F. Pau, C. Gianotti, Economic and financial knowledge-based processing, Springer Verlag, Heidelberg/NY, 1990

4. S. J. Russell, The use of knowledge in analogy and induction, Research notes in AI, Pitman, London, 1989

5. L. F. Pau, Behavioral knowledge in sensor/data fusion, Special issue "Multisensor fusion", J. Robotic systems, Vol 7, no 3, june 1990, 295-308

6. L. F. Pau, Sensor and data fusion, Academic Press, London, in print, 1992

7. L. F. Pau, Knowledge representation approaches in sensor fusion, Automatica, Vol 25, no 2, feb. 1989, 207-214

8. Handbook of artificial intelligence, Morgan Kaufman Publ., Palo Alto, 1985

9. Y. H. Pao, Adaptive pattern recognition and neural networks, Addison Wesley, 1989

10. L. F. Pau, Artificial intelligence in financial services, Special issue "AI in management", IEEE Trans. Data and knowledge engineering, fall 1991

11. L. F. Pau, Feature extraction in the time domain:application to the analysis of financial data in strategies over time, in K. S. Fu, A. Whinston (Eds), "Pattern recognition theory and applications", NATO ASI Series, Vol E-22, Noordhoff Publ., Leyden, NL, 1977, 75-90

12. G. Salton, Another look at automatic text retrieval systems, Comm. of the ACM, Vol 29, 1986, 648-656

13. D. Fisher, P. Langley, Conceptual clustering and its relation to numerical taxonomy, in:W. Gale (Ed), "Artificial intelligence and statistics", Addison Wesley, 1988, 77-116

14. J. L. Kolodner, R. L. Simpson, The mediator:analysis of an early case-based problem solver, Cognitive Science J., Vol 13, 1989, 507-549

15. W. G. Lehnert, Case -base problem solving with a large knowledge base of learned cases, Proc. National Conf. on AI, 1988, 301-306

16. C. K. Riesbeck, R. C. Schank, Inside case-based reasoning, Lawrence Erlbaum Assoc. Publ., 1989

17. Aleksander, I. and Morton, H., "An introduction to Neural Computing", Chapman and Hall, 1990.

18. Cheeseman, P., Kelly, J., Self, M., Stutz, J., Taylor, W., Freeman, D. "Autoclass: a bayesian classification system", Proceedings of the Fifth International Conference on Machine Learning, 1988, p 54-64.

19. Maren, A, Harston, C., Robert, R., Handbook of neural computing applications, Academic Press, 1990.

20. Michalski, R. S., Carbonell, J. G., Mitchell, T. M., Machine intelligence: an artificial intelligence approach. Vol 1, 1983.

21. Michalski, R. S., Stepp, R. E., "Learning from observation: conceptual clustering", in Michalski, Carbonell, and Mitchell, [20].

22. Quinlan, J. R., "Learning efficient classification procedures and their application to chess endgames", In Michalski, Carbonell, and Mitchell [20].

23. Quinlan, J. R., "Induction of decision trees", Machine Learning Vol 1, no 1, 1986, p. 81-106.

24. Quinlan, J. R., "The effect of noise on concept learning", in Michalski et. al. [20]

25. Trippi, R. and Turban, E., "Neural networks in finance and investing", Probus., 1993

26. Wasserman, P., "Neural computing: theory and practice", Van Nostrand-Reinhold, 1989.

27. L. F. Pau, Database of 400+ financial and economic fielded applications of AI with their solution architecture (only available commercially), continuously updated

28. L. F. Pau, A survey of reasoning procedures in knowledge based systems for economics and management, J. Computer science in economics and management, Vol 3, 1990, p 3-22

29. S. M. Easterbrook (Ed), CSCW: cooperation or conflict, NATO ASI Proc., Springer Verlag, 1992

30. P. Berck, Economist's mathematical manual, Springer Berlag, 1993

31. B. Dutta (et al)(Eds), Game theory and economic applications, Lecture notes in economics and mathematical systems Vol 389, Springer Berlag, 1992

32. AI-ECON project, SPES Program, European community, Brussels, 1992-1995 (with the participation of Heriot Watt University, ABN-AMRO Bank, Digital Equipment Europe, Tilburg University, AIS Spa)

33. STATLOG Project, ESPRIT project no 5170, European Community, 1990-1993, on the comparison of neural networks, machien learning and statistics

34. MLT Machine learning toolbox, ESPRIT project 2154, coordinated by ALCATEL Research, 1989-1993

35. L. F. Pau, T. Tambo, Knowledge based mortgage loan credit granting and risk assessment, J. economic dynamics and control, Vol 14, 1990, 255-262

36. M. M. Richter, et al (Eds), Proc. EWCBR-93 1st European workshop on case based reasoning, Univ. Kaiserslautern, 1-5 Nov. 1993

37. R. Koselka, Businessman's dilemma: latest developments in game theory, FORBES, 11 october 1993, p 107-114

38. D. E. O'Leary, Case based reasoning and multiple agent systems for accounting regulation systems, J. Intelligent systems in accounting, finance and management, Vol 1, 1992, p. 41-52

39. J-P Aubin, Optima and equilibria, Springer Verlag, 1993

40. B. P. Allen, Case based reasoning: business applications, Communications of the ACM, Vol 37, no 3, march 1994, 40-44

41. F. Hayes Roth, N. Jacobstein, The state of the art of knowledge based systems, Communications of the ACM, Vol 37, no 3, march 1994, 27-39

42. R. J. Bauer, Genetic algorithms and investment strategies, Wiley, 1993

43. D. Sleeman, Towards a technology and a science of machine learning, J. AICOM, Vol 7, no 1, march 1994, 29-38

44. A. Aamodt, E. Plaza, Case based reasoning: foundation issues, J. AICOM, Vol 7, no 1, march 1994, 39-59

45. H. Varian, Economic and financial modeling with MATHEMATICA, Springer Verlag, 1993

46. R. J. Aumann, S. Hart (Eds), Handbook of game theory, North Holland, 1992

47. A. J. Gonzalez, R. Laureano-Ornz, A case based reasoning approach to real-estate property appraisal, J. expert systems with applications, Vol 4, no 2, 89-

48. J. L. Kolodner, An introduction to case based reasoning, Artificial intelligence Review, 1992, no 4

49. L. F. Pau, Inference of the structure of economic reasoning from natural language analysis, Int. J. Decision support systems, Vol 1, no 4

50. N. G. Mankiw, D. N. Weil, The baby boom, the baby bust, and the housing market, J. Regional science and urban economics, Vol 19, no 2, 1989

BUILDING SUCCESSFUL APPLICATIONS: THE WRONG WAY AND THE RIGHT WAY

Robert Milne
Intelligent Applications Limited
Kirkton Business Centre
Livingston Village
West Lothian EH54 7AY
Scotland UK

Abstract

Over the past year or two, artificial intelligence technology has made a transition to a new era. Previously, there was a wide spread exploration of AI techniques and their possible applications, now companies are very impatient with long-term research and exploration and are very keen to see more successful applications deployed.

Based on my perspective of building applications for many years, I propose that the only way to build really successful AI applications is to focus on narrow, vertical application areas and deliver complete solutions to users embedding artificial intelligence technology.

1   Introduction

In order to understand the issues facing artificial intelligence applications today, its useful to consider a story of two pioneers. Many, many years ago when mountaineering was still young and many of the mountains in Europe had not been climbed, two mountaineering pioneers got together to try and climb a difficult looking mountain. From the valley they were in, it was difficult to see all the sides of the mountain but it was obvious that the part of the mountain rising directly above them was sheer and precipitous. Clearly a direct attack on the summit was going to prove very difficult. However, the valley itself rose gently around the sides of the mountain, although it was heavily forested.

The two pioneers had a long argument as to the best way to approach the top. The first pioneer wanted to go in a vertical line straight for the summit. The second pioneer wanted to explore horizontally through the forest and around the sides in easier terrain. They agreed to separate and pursue their own approach. The pioneer who decided to work through the valley made rapid progress initially. He moved quite high up the sides of the mountain and continued around, avoiding the most difficult vertical sections. He was able to progress many kilometres quite quickly and felt optimistic that his was the right approach. Whenever one line of advancement became difficult, he retreated slightly and always found another way around to move to a different area.

Every now and then however he became lost in the forest and had difficulty finding his way through all the undergrowth and confusing paths that existed. Sometimes he would come back to where he started, other times he would retreat from difficult situations only to find other difficult situations around the next corner. For many years he continued his exploration, but the mountain itself was difficult on all sides and there was no easy way to the top.

After many years the horizontal explorer started to give up. Although he made rapid initial progress, he was now finding it very difficult to gain any altitude. He had circled the mountain had come back to the initial problem, to go higher would require considerable effort.

The pioneer trying the vertical approach made very slow progress initially. He could examine the vertical landscape and note that there were lines of weaknesses. In some places there were obvious great cracks and chimneys rising and he could make rapid progress, but often there were small difficult barriers that slowed or stopped him completely. He made several attempts and got quite high up the mountain. However, in each case he realised that he needed better equipment and tools and better training.

He decided to return to the valley and go to a practise area and develop his climbing skills much better. He also developed much better tools to attack the specific problems of the vertical cliffs. In many cases what looked like an easy starting path got much more difficult higher up. In some situations he discovered difficult beginning sections that became easier further up the mountain. It took considerable exploration to determine which of the vertical paths of the mountain gave the best chance of reaching the top.

Although he did not make much progress initially, he eventually got much more experience and improved his skills and his tools, and was able to make considerable progress. Each time there was a major barrier to overcome he persisted in his efforts until he was able to move higher.

The higher he got on the mountain the more pronounced the effects were of the regular winters. In these cold and freezing conditions he was able to persist for a time before having to retreat, but each time he suffered the winter he gained more experience on how to deal with the cold.

Finally, he was able to approach the very summit of the mountain. It was a hostile environment and seemed like winter all the time, but his experiences carried him through, he finally achieved the summit. Standing in the sunshine on top, he felt it was all worthwhile. Once he had made the top many others followed exploiting these vertical lines of weakness and many possible routes to the top were made.

They are only open to people with considerable skill and experience who persisted in overcoming the barriers.

This story is presented as an analogy to the work in the artificial intelligence field over the past ten years. Most people involved are like the pioneer exploring the horizontal way. They developed generic toolkits and explored easy approaches to the problems. When they encountered difficulty they would backtrack and try another approach. They seemed to make rapid progress, but in fact this was just a confusion.

What is needed today is people like the second pioneer who focused on vertical solutions to specific problems. By developing the appropriate tools and increasing their skills in other areas, they were able to solve complete specific problems. If AI wants to reach the summit and develop many applications, then this is the approach that must be followed.

2 Background

Before we discuss further the approaches necessary for developing artificial intelligence applications, I believe it is useful to provide a summary of my experience and the viewpoint from which I am coming. For the past eight years, my company Intelligent Applications, has focused on applications of artificial intelligence. We never explored the area of developing tools or providing generic technology, we always focused on building complete solutions for end users. It is from these experiences that these comments are based.

We have now developed more working expert system based applications than any other UK company [5]. All of our work has been focused in the area of manufacturing and process industry and virtually all of our systems are diagnostic systems. Among the systems we have developed include the following;

- A large scale real-time on-line diagnostic system for a British Steel plant.

- A monitoring and diagnosis system to detect faults in equipment controlled by programmable logic controllers for British Steel.

- A monitoring and diagnostic system using gas chromatography data for a Nuclear Power Station.

- A diagnostic system to interpret vibration data in support of vibration based condition monitoring. This system *Amethyst* has over 600 users in more than 30 countries. It is one of the most widely used expert systems in engineering.

- A gas turbine condition monitoring system in daily use at Exxon Chemical in Scotland. It is instrumental at finding the cause of a major fault [7]. Finding the cause was worth an extra £1.2 million in production at Exxon. The company were also so pleased with finding the fault that they bought all 400 employees a bottle of Malt Whiskey!

- A diagnostic system that identifies causes of energy wastage in building heating systems.

- Several electronic troubleshooting diagnostic systems in use by companies such as Compaq Computers.

It is generally acknowledged that Intelligent Applications have built more working expert system diagnostic systems in the UK than any other company. In addition, I have been involved with the organisation and evaluation of the UK Department of Trade & Industry's Manufacturing Intelligence Competition. This presents an award for the best expert system in use in manufacturing each year. This has given us experience of a wide range of applications that have been successful within the UK.

3   Where Is Artificial Intelligence Today?

The artificial intelligence field is at a critical stage just now. Many years ago the field was dominated by people exploring the technology and searching for good applications. The tool vendor market thrived as many companies bought tools in order to experiment with the technology and explore possible applications. This caused a great surge in growth in the market.

Today many of the companies that explored new technologies have moved their attention to other technical areas. This has also greatly reduced the market and demand for AI tools. The net result is that there seems to have been a major downturn in the artificial intelligence market (also called an AI winter). Many companies have either greatly reduced in size or gone bust.

Many people involved in the field have moved to other areas. In some areas, government funding has shifted away from AI to newer technologies. After many years of exploring the technology, there are relatively few successful applications. There are a large number of hard core AI types who are very interested in working with AI and continuing to evolve the field. However, they are finding funding more difficult. This is partly because of the resources for funding have moved to new technical areas and partly because of the lack of applications has slowed down the investment in the field.

Many of the people involved in AI over the past ten years could not have been expected to develop applications. They were researchers involved in exploring the technology, not experts in vertical application areas. Many of them did not persist long enough or were not provided with enough resources to build successful applications.

The AI field is also relatively new. When I started in AI 20 years ago, the term 'expert system' had not been invented. When you compare with other fields and new technologies, it is not expected to have produced significant results on a wide spread basis in such a short timescale. But these early horizontal explorations are now completed. We are perhaps at a time when the pioneer exploring the horizontal approach realised that he would not be successful. Now is the time to focus on more vertical solutions.

The technology has now become very confusing. One of the major strengths of the artificial intelligence area is the object oriented approach to problem solving and programming of solutions. Now object oriented programming has become an accepted and integral part of the software community. This has resulted in an identity crisis with AI, where we are not quite sure whether they are a separate technology or part of the object oriented world. In fact, many tool vendors are now promoting themselves as object oriented programming environments rather than artificial intelligence technologies.

From my viewpoint this is not a major crisis or problem. The key realisation is that there is nothing special or unique about artificial intelligence from other software technologies. In the early days of the AI field there was a strong belief that you could do things differently because it was AI. Gradually it has emerged that the same rules of software that applied to traditional systems apply to AI. The requirements must be clear, the specification must be clearly defined so that it is obvious how to build the system, the system must be properly designed and modularised.

Testing is a difficult problem, but not any different for AI approaches than traditional software. In fact, the conclusion is that there really is nothing special about artificial intelligence technology. The same rules and ideas of standard software apply. This is an important realisation and understanding how AI fits with the rest of the technology community. AI does have to follow the same rules of good system development. The leverage over other approaches is slight, although it does exist. At the same time this means there is no disadvantage to artificial intelligence technologies. It is traditional software. There is no reason for a business manager to be worried about AI approaches. There is nothing different than the traditional software approaches. I can think of no argument against AI technology that is not also a problem with any other software approach.

Because AI technology is no different from any other software approaches there is nothing to be afraid of and it should be just as successful as the new approaches. There is no reason to abandon the technology or change course. It also means that it is one element of the broader software solutions area and should be considered as such.

If there is one area to be unhappy with, it is that the powerful and strong technology that is available has not really found their way into many applications. This is the subject of the rest of the paper.

4   Amethyst : A Vertical Solution

It is helpful to consider a specific example of a successful application and also understand its limitations. Probably the most widely used diagnostic expert system in the engineering area is *Amethyst* [2,4,6]. *Amethyst* is very specific in what it does. It performs diagnostics based on fast fourier transforms of vibration data collected by hand-held data collector from IRD Mechanalysis in support of vibration based condition monitoring. Although this focus seems very narrow there are over 600 users in more than 30 countries, and the product is available in four languages.

Condition monitoring is an essential element of most plant and equipment maintenance. The idea is to perform maintenance when it is needed rather than on a routine or calendar basis. The goal is to monitor the condition of the equipment. As a problem develops the condition of the equipment changes and maintenance actions can then be planned. *Amethyst* works in the domain of rotating machinery such as pumps, fans, compressors, gear boxes and bearings. Rotating machinery always produces a small level of vibration. When a fault develops, vibration at specific frequencies increases. Hence, the most appropriate way to perform condition monitoring of rotating machinery is by monitoring the vibration patterns.

The large scale industrial plant, the most common and cost effective way to collect vibration is to use a hand-held data collector. This is a battery powered data acquisition and fast-fourier transform analyser. The user would tour his plant taking vibration signatures from each item of rotating machinery. On a large plant on a typical day, an end user might collect over 100 vibration patterns. The problem for the end user then is to interpret these vibration patterns and perform a diagnosis as to what is wrong with each machine.

The task of *Amethyst* is to automate this interpretation and diagnostic step. *Amethyst* is integrated with one supplier of vibration data collectors and data management database. Hence, it is very well integrated with the system. There are several reasons *Amethyst* is successful;

One of which is that it provides very detailed expert knowledge about a specific problem.

Another reason is that it is very well integrated with the data acquisition and the way that the user works in his daily activities.

The third reason is that although *Amethyst* sounds very narrow in its application, it is in fact very generic. It is able to diagnose faults on most types of rotating machinery making it applicable across the wide variety of industries.

The last, and perhaps the most important reason, is that it is well integrated with a company already established into the market place with easy access to a large customer base.

For the businessman they will appreciate the benefit of having a product that you can sell to the same customer on the same visit. The major point is that *Amethyst* fits right in with the existing infrastructure and is easy to sell as an additional product by the same salesman. This is an example of the type of vertical solution that leads to successful applications.

Because of the success of *Amethyst*, Intelligent Applications received a Queen's Award for Technology. This was the first time this prestigious award had been given to the use of knowledge based systems in technology.

5   The Limitation Of Amethyst

Although *Amethyst* has a very large customer base, it turns out not surprisingly, that many of the users are not successful in using *Amethyst* [1]. After extensive customer feedback it was discovered that you could divide the *Amethyst* customers into two groups; those using the system successfully and those not using the system. It was established that all those using the system successfully had performed the proper setup and configuration of *Amethyst*. More importantly, it was established that all those not using *Amethyst* had not performed the configuration and setup.

Although the diagnostics for *Amethyst* are generic, it requires certain information about the machine to diagnose such as what type of machine - an electric motor or a fan for example. What is it's rotating speed? Does it have a gear drive, a belt drive or a direct drive? What type of bearings does it have, etc? It is this configuration information that helps *Amethyst* adopt to a wide variety of machines.

One can also make a case that it is impossible to properly perform vibration diagnostics without knowing this information. The important point, is that *Amethyst* users must perform a certain amount of setup and configuration. This should be information that they have readily available and they could not properly perform the task without this information. This information is entered through a table driven database. So we argue that it is a simple process of entering the setup information. Hence, it is very remarkable that so many users have problems in providing this information. Rather than spend more time on the problem however, I would like to concentrate on the lesson.

The lesson is that even when a system is almost completely self contained, end users do not perform the minimal setup and configuration needed. If they do not perform this type of minimal setup then what chance do they have to configure or acknowledge to a generic knowledge base system? The answer based on our experience is that they have no chance.

Today most end users are under tremendous pressure. They must achieve more work, in more complex environments with less time and a minimal of training. Any task that you ask them to perform is too much because they are already over loaded. Clearly for a good benefit people can invest more time and money, although it is a risk, but they have the time to make this decision.

Even though *Amethyst* is very successful it would be approximately twice as successful in terms of successful end users if no setup was required.

6   End Users Do Not Write Knowledge Bases

The implication of the limitations of *Amethyst* is that, if the end user must do anything at all to deploy and construct an application, then he won't. This is an important assumption because it is counter to the original ideas of the knowledge based systems field. Many years ago the emphasis was on developing easy to use expert system shells. The major thrust was that if the tools were adequately easy to use, then end users would develop their own diagnostic systems or other applications.

Dupont in the United States was very successful for a time by giving many end users a simple to use shell. They then built small, but effective applications very quickly. This strategy was successful because of the breadth of applications that were deployed. However, it did not succeed in wide scale replication of developed systems. Instead, each person developed their own little system. Unfortunately, there are very few examples of other corporations being so successful and having end users write knowledgebases.

At Intelligent Applications we have been involved with many companies where we develop the first version of a diagnostic system and then the end users would take over the improvements and advancement of the knowledgebase. Almost without exception, the end users had failed to improve the knowledgebase after the hand-over [3]. They are always too busy or had too little experience on how to improve the system. Most of the time they required additional consulting effort to help maintain the system. I have heard of many example systems where the research group built the first prototype then hoped the end users would extend the knowledgebase. Virtually all of these systems failed. There are many reasons for it, but the conclusion is that end users do not write knowledgebases and do not extend expert systems. It is accepted that there are a group of end users able to do this. However, our interest is in achieving the mass market and wide scale deployment of applications. From this viewpoint it is not practical for end users to develop systems.

7 Developing Vertical Applications

The approach we followed at Intelligent Applications for the past few years, and the approach that I think should be adopted by those wanting to develop artificial intelligence applications, is to focus on developing vertical solutions. *Amethyst* is a classic example where it performs a complete solution to one problem. Setup should be minimised although it will always be present.

Many years ago we worked in the area of building air conditioning alarm diagnostics. The idea was to diagnose the cause of an alarm in a building heating system to assist the maintenance staff in rapidly repairing it. We have long since abandoned the generic approach to this. We have now built a very specific system that identifies causes of energy wastage in a type of building. The major strength of the system is an extensive and detailed knowledgebase that has knowledge about most types of problems and how they manifest themselves. The end user only does a basic setup and configuration of the system to describe his building.

We are doing a lot of work in machine tool diagnostics. After trying to help end users build diagnostic systems it became obvious that the only area where we get the scale and efficiency to pay back the development of a diagnostic system, is by working with machine tool manufacturers. For one end user to get a pay-back from a diagnostic system is almost impossible. But for the manufacturer to be able to sell the diagnostic system to several hundred users, makes the economics very attractive.

Another example of our vertical solution is our work in gas turbine condition monitoring. There are many tools available today for the development of real-time knowledge based systems. However the uptake in the heavy industries have been relatively small.

In the ESPRIT Project TIGER [8], we are developing a complete condition monitoring system for a gas turbine. This builds on existing real-time tools, but includes a complete set of diagnostics for the gas turbine. We expect a much bigger uptake of the TIGER system within the gas turbine market than the uptakes of real-time tools. This is quite simply because it has a complete set of diagnostics.

At AAAI'83, Ed Fiegenbaum, one of the founders of the artificial intelligence field gave a keynote lecture on the same topic of applications. His main thrust was also to focus on vertical solutions. He discussed the idea of knowledge publishing where knowledge based systems were an integral part of a wide spread task that is distributed in software form. For example, a tax advisory system in the US is by far the most widely used expert system, although many users do not realise that they are using an expert system.

This approach is similar to our pioneer exploring the vertical way. You must identify the lines of weakness and head straight for the top trying to provide a complete solution. There are many barriers and winters on the way, but you must persist and overcome these with the same approaches as traditional software in order to reach the top.

8 New Directions

In spite of the progress being made in developing vertical oriented application solutions there are still many problems and difficulties. Many of these relate to the task of building the diagnostics and knowledgebase. In this section, I touch on a few important technologies to assist with these problems in the future.

Writing knowledgebases is still a very difficult and time consuming task. Although methodologies help to ensure a thorough and complete development. There are many applications for which it is just too much work to build a good diagnostic system.

8.1 Building Systems From Existing Descriptions

One approach that I feel has tremendous potential and will be very important in the future, is the ability to build diagnostic systems directly from information already existing in other computer systems. For example, many years ago we worked in the area of automatically developing electronic troubleshooting systems [9]. Given an electronic form of a schematic description of a printed circuit board, we were able to derive much of the tests and the fault isolation procedures. This model based approach [10] did not require the end user to write rules, but rather the system was intelligent enough to derive the diagnostic procedure from the connectivity information.

Given that electronic circuits are all designed in CAD systems, and also given that recently the interchange of data between systems has become practical, then I would expect electronic troubleshooting systems will be developed automatically from existing circuit descriptions. Its this type of approach that will be needed in many areas long-term. In this case, not only does the end user do very little to use the system, but the knowledge base system developer does not do very much either.

As part of the TIGER project we have been working on the problem of diagnosing faults or stoppages in machines controlled by programmable logic controllers. These devices control the sequence of events and check for interlocks. Very often when there is a problem the system stops. Although it is difficult for the engineer to understand why, the task for the engineer is to trace slowly through the logic sequence and find at which point the interlock sequence was stopped.

As part of TIGER we have developed an automatic model based system to diagnose faults in alarms generated by the gas turbine controller. This system takes its input from existing computer descriptions of the programmable ladder logic code. It automatically processes this into a dependency network and then automatically generates a set of rules for the diagnostics. What is important is that you are able to build a diagnostic procedure fully automatically from the existing system description. There are many domains where extensive computer descriptions of the system exist already. For these domains it is highly desirable and probably required to build diagnostic systems directly from this information. This is particularly important where the specific details of the diagnostic system will vary from user to user.

8.2   Constraint Programming

For many years artificial intelligence has been associated with expert systems and a particular diagnostics. Planning and scheduling has always been an active research area that has previously seen relatively little application. In the past few years the tools for constraint programming have evolved rapidly. This has caused a revolution in the scheduling industry and the applications of scheduling systems are growing quite rapidly. Although constraint programming is not to be undertaken by the novice or faint hearted, the vendors are now developing scheduling packages to make this easier for the end user. This is another example of focusing on vertical solutions. Although the scheduling system still requires some work from the end user. Hopefully over the next few years the scheduling system will be able to integrate with other factory systems and perform its work for a wide variety of users with very little user input.

8.3   Case Based Reasoning

From my viewpoint Case Based Reasoning is perhaps the most important new technology to facilitate the development of knowledge based systems. Rather than write rules to explicitly define how to solve a problem, a system is developed that gathers past situations and their solutions. These cases are then used to guide the end user in developing a solution. This is particularly attractive when defining the precise rules in detail is too difficult. A heuristic mapping can be made between the description of a problem situation and the desired solution.

Also in many domains, an exact solution is not practical, but a hint or indication of the possible solution is very helpful in finding the solution. Rather than provide a solution to a problem, the Case Based Reasoning approach provides 10 suggestions of near solutions for example. The end user must then solve the problem but this greatly expands the areas for which artificial intelligence techniques can be applied.

One vertical application area has already been very successful using Case Based Reasoning technology, that's the use of Case Based Reasoning for help desks. In a situation such as this where problems occur very frequently, the problem descriptions are always a little bit different and it is impossible to enumerate all the solutions. By understanding the process used to support a help desk it is possible to package a Case Based Reasoning tool so that it is easy for end users to evolve Case Based Reasoning systems.

Within the past two years a number of good Case Based Reasoning tools have emerged on the market and I see a great growth in the applications of this. Although it will not eliminate the problem of developing knowledgebases it will greatly reduce the demands on this task in some areas.

8.4   Learning

Ten years ago if I was asked about the use of learning in an application, I would tell people to forget it. It was too difficult and there were too many problems. Now my view is different, learning has become an integral part of many artificial intelligence based solutions. Neural networks have shown they can be very effective in a well defined class of problems. Some of the Case Based Reasoning tools use rule induction techniques to help build the indexes and retrieve the most similar cases. This also opens up the area of data mining, looking for hidden knowledge in databases.

We have already performed a number of successful data mining applications using the induction techniques of the Case Based Reasoning tools. The implementation and availability of learning techniques is now suitable for a variety of application areas. In addition, they are an essential element in helping deliver vertical solutions to end users and reducing the setup that is needed. We now considered learning techniques to be essential as part of the setup process so that the system can automatically learn the appropriate configuration for an end user.

9   SUMMARY

There is a strong similarity to the recent history of the artificial intelligence area with our two pioneers. The early explorations were similar to the horizontal pioneer; he avoided the hard problems and seemed to make rapid progress but in fact never found the easy way to the top, because there was no easy way.

The vertical pioneer persisted, sometimes stopping for additional training and improving the tools, but always trying to push higher up the mountain. By staying very focused in a narrow vertical way, he was ultimately successful. End users of artificial intelligence systems do not want or do not have the time to do anything more than use the system, hence we must deliver a complete vertical solutions in order to achieve wide spread applications. This is one of the key elements of delivering successful applications.

REFERENCES

[1] R. Milne. *'Amethyst: The Development Experience'.* Industrial Applications of Knowledge-Based Diagnosis. Editors G. Guida and A. Stefanini. Elsevier Science Publishers B.V., P115-141.

[2] R. Milne. *'Amethyst: Automatic Diagnosis of Rotating Machinery Faults'.* Operational Expert System Applications in Europe. Edited: Gian Piero Zarri, Pergamon Press, p244 - 258.

[3] R. Milne. *'Petroleum Applications: How Do We Realise The Potential?'* Revue De l' Institut Francais Du Petrole, May-June 1992, Vol. 47. No. 3.

[4] R. Milne. *'Amethyst: Vibration Based Condition Monitoring'.* The Handbook of Expert Systems Applications In Manufacturing, Jessica Keyes, Rex Maus, Editors, McGraw Hill Inc, Publishers, 1990.

[5] R. Milne. *'Case Studies in Condition Monitoring'.* Knowledge-Based Systems for Industrial Control, IEE Control Engineering Series 44. J McGhee, M.J. Grimble and P. Mowforth, Editors, Peter Peregrinus Ltd Publications, p255-266, 1990.

[6] R. Milne. *'Amethyst: An Expert System for the Diagnosis of Rotating Machinery'.* Proceedings of Comadem 90 Conference on Condition Monitoring and Diagnostic Engineering Management, Brunel University, England, p287-292, 16th-18th July, 1990.

[7] R. Milne. *'On-Line Diagnostic Expert System For Gas Turbines'.* Tooldiag'93, Toulouse, France. 5-7 April 1993.

[8] R. Milne. *'TIGER First Annual Report'.* ESPRIT Project TIGER. September 1993.

[9] R. Milne. *'Synergist: From Design to Manual Test'.* Electronic Design & Automation Conference, London, England, 27th-30th June 1988.

[10] R. Milne. *'Strategies for Diagnosis'.* IEEE Transactions on Systems, Man, and Cybernetics, Vol. SMC-17, No. 3, May/June 1987

Optimales Scheduling mit Hilfe von Constraint-Netzen

Susanne Heipcke[1+2], Josef Kallrath[1], Matthias Bücker[3] und Stefan Brode[1]

[1] BASF-AG, ZXA/ZC, Kaiser-Wilhelm-Str. 52, 67056 Ludwigshafen
[2] Katholische Universität Eichstätt, Math.-Geogr. Fakultät, 85071 Eichstätt
[3] Georg Heeg, Objektorientierte Systeme, Baroper Str. 337,44227 Dortmund

Zusammenfassung Constraint-Netze sind eine aus der KI Forschung entliehene Technik, die verwendet werden kann, um auch komplizierte Lösungsräume auf natürliche Art und Weise durch lokale Beschreibung der Beziehungen zwischen Variablen (Constraints) darzustellen. Es gibt keinerlei prinzipielle Beschränkung auf bestimmte, z.B. lineare Beziehungen. Die Constraints sind durch lokale Propagierungs- Mechanismen bei der Suche nach optimalen Lösungen eine wertvolle Hilfe, da durch die Propagierung einzelner Werte und Wertebereiche der Variablen in einem Constraint-Netz die Menge der noch zu untersuchenden Lösungen erheblich eingeschränkt werden kann.

In diesem Beitrag wird die Darstellung von zwei Optimierungsproblemen und ihre Zerlegung in einzelne Komponenten zur Erstellung eines "computertauglichen Modells" vorgestellt. Durch Rezepturbedingungen verknüpfte Aufträge werden chemischen Anlagen unter Berücksichtigung detaillierter Personalanforderungen zugeordnet, wobei die Gesamtbearbeitungsdauern minimiert werden. Eine gemischt-ganzzahlige Formulierung dieses Problems und der Versuch, es mit einem auf LP-Relaxierung beruhenden Branch & Bound Verfahren zu lösen, liefert bei restriktiven Personalressourcen infolge eines signifikanten *duality gaps* in vertretbarer Zeit keine zulässige Lösung. Mit Hilfe der Constraint-Netz-Propagierung konnten jedoch Lösungsmannigfaltigkeiten effizient untersucht werden und zum Beispiel die Konsequenzen kurzdauernder Überauslastungen diskutiert werden.

Abschließend wird als weitere industrielle Anwendung der beschriebenen Technik ein Modell zur optimalen Reihenfolgeplanung quantenmechanischer Berechnungen mehrerer Moleküle auf einem Cluster aus parallel arbeitenden Workstations diskutiert. Diese Rechnungen zerfallen in mehrere Teilschritte mit unterschiedlichem Parallelisierungsgrad. Mathematisch führt dieses Modell auf ein nicht-lineares, beschränktes, gemischt-ganzzahliges Optimierungsproblem.

1   Einleitung

Auf mathematischen Modellen basierende Optimierung kann in fast allen Bereichen der Industrie wertvolle Beiträge leisten, beginnend mit der Anregung und Bewertung neuer Ideen in Forschung und Entwicklung über Prozeßoptimierung,

Steuerung in Produktion und Logistik, Erstellung von Marktprognosen, optimale Preisfindung bis zur strategischen Planung. Die **mathematische Optimierung** kann garantieren, daß eine gefundene Lösung sämtliche Randbedingungen erfüllt und die bestmögliche Lösung überhaupt unter diesen Bedingungen ist. Erst durch den Einsatz mathematischer Optimierung wird es möglich, auch komplexe Systeme optimal zu steuern, zu konfigurieren oder in ihnen optimale Entscheidungen zu treffen. Der Begriff der **Optimierung** — im mathematischen Sinne verwendet— bedeutet die Bestimmung des Maximums oder Minimums einer bestimmten Funktion, die auf einem (beschränkten) Bereich S oder Zustandsraum definiert ist. Die klassische Optimierungstheorie (Differentialrechnung, Variationsrechnung, Optimale Steuerung) behandelt die Fälle, in denen S kontinuierlich ist. Die **gemischt-ganzzahlige, kombinatorische**, oder kurz **diskrete Optimierung**, bis vor wenigen Jahren noch ein Randgebiet der mathematischen Optimierung, spielt eine zunehmend wichtige Rolle [6] und bietet Algorithmen [11], wie z.B. auf LP-Relaxation beruhende Branch&Bound Verfahren, die inzwischen auch in kommerziellen Produkten implementiert sind. Der Definitionsbereich S ist teilweise *diskret*, d.h. einige Variablen sind auf ganze Zahlen beschränkt. Die Ganzzahligkeit der Problemstellungen rührt z.B. daher, daß sogenannte Null-Eins-Entscheidungen — etwa die Entscheidung ob ein Arbeitsschritt von einem bestimmten Mitarbeiter zu einem Zeitpunkt bearbeitet wird oder nicht — zu treffen sind oder Größen — z.B. Standort, Stufenzahl einer Kolonne, Containergröße — nur ganzzahlige oder nur bestimmte Werte annehmen können. Ein Überblick über den Einsatz diskreter Optimierungsverfahren in der chemischen Industrie findet sich bei [9]. Im Rahmen des von der Europäischen Gemeinschaft geförderten ESPRIT-Projektes "PAMIPS", bei dem die BASF Mitglied in einem aus 4 Industriepartnern und 3 Universitäten bestehenden Konsortium ist, werden parallele Algorithmen zur Lösung gemischt-ganzzahliger Formulierungen von Scheduling-Problemen behandelt. Die Notwendigkeit paralleler Hardware und Software deutet schon den enormen Rechenaufwand an, der mit der Lösung von Scheduling-Problemen ([3],[4]) verbunden ist; in der Tat gehören sie zu den NP-schweren Problemen; oft ist die Bestimmung einer Lösung oder der Nachweis der Optimalität in vertretbarer Zeit nicht möglich. Wie in Kapitel 3 beschrieben und in [8] ausführlicher gezeigt wird, läßt sich für das hier aufgeführte Problem bei niedriger Personalkapazität mit einem auf LP-Relaxierung basierenden Branch&Bound Verfahren (siehe z.B. [11]) in vertretbarer Zeit keine Lösung der gemischt-ganzzahligen Formulierung des in Kapitel 2 dargestellten Problems gewinnen. Ein Ansatz ganz anderer Art, welcher der KI Forschung entliehen ist, beruht auf Constraint-Netzen (siehe z.B. [5] oder [7]). Diese Technik kann verwendet werden, um auch komplizierte Lösungsräume einfacher, auf natürliche Art und Weise durch lokale Beschreibung der Beziehungen zwischen Variablen (Constraints) darzustellen. Es gibt dabei keinerlei prinzipielle Beschränkung auf bestimmte, z.B. lineare Beziehungen. Constraints sind durch lokale Propagierungs-Mechanismen bei der Suche nach optimalen Lösungen eine wertvolle Hilfe, da durch die Propagierung einzelner Werte und Wertebereiche der Variablen in einem Constraint-Netz die

Menge der noch zu untersuchenden Lösungen erheblich eingeschränkt werden kann, was ausführlicher in Kapitel 4 beschrieben wird. Recht effizient lassen sich "Constraints" im Zusammenhang mit objektorientierten Darstellungen nutzen; das eingesetzte Werkzeug basiert auf Smalltalk-80 mit der Klassenbibliothek COME ([5]). Dieses Werkzeug wird seit einigen Jahren erfolgreich bei CIBA-GEIGY in Basel zur Modellierung, Simulation und Optimierung kontinuierlicher Prozesse genutzt.

Die Anwendung dieses Ansatzes auf das im folgenden beschriebene personalbeschränkte Scheduling-Problem führt wie in Kapitel 5 dargestellt zu zufriedenstellenden Resultaten. Als Ergebnis der Untersuchung wird auf drei Punkte besonders eingegangen: Qualität der Lösungen (Zeitbedarf zur Abarbeitung sämtlicher Kampagnen bei Planung mit mit Constraint-Netz-Propagierung - im folgenden mit *CNP* abgekürzt), erforderliche Rechenzeit und quantitative Auswirkungen kurzzeitiger Personalüberauslastungen. In Kapitel 6 wird noch kurz ein weiteres zur Zeit in Arbeit befindliches schwieriges Scheduling-Problem vorgestellt. Dabei handelt es sich um ein Reihenfolgeplanungsproblem quantenmechanischer Berechnungen mehrerer Moleküle auf einem Cluster aus parallel arbeitenden Workstations. Diese Rechnungen zerfallen in mehrere Teilschritte mit unterschiedlichem Parallelisierungsgrad. Mathematisch führt dieses Modell auf ein nicht-lineares, beschränktes, gemischt-ganzzahliges Optimierungsproblem. Kapitel 7 faßt schließlich die Ergebnisse dieser Arbeit zusammen.

Variablen/Unbekannte sind mit kleinen Buchstaben gekennzeichnet, wobei kleine griechische Buchstaben auf binäre, d.h. (0,1)-Variablen hinweisen, die in der Regel als Entscheidungs- oder Belegungsvariablen verwendet werden. Mit großen Buchstaben werden die vor der Optimierung bekannten Größen (direkte Eingabedaten oder aus Eingabedaten ableitbare Daten) bezeichnet.

2 Problembeschreibung: Personalbeschränktes Scheduling-Problem

Im Rahmen dieser Untersuchung soll eine Planung zur optimalen Personalauslastung für einen Gesamtzeitraum von $N_T = 840$ Stunden (5 Wochen) auf Stundenbasis erstellt werden. Betrachtet werden hierbei $N_K = 10$ Kampagnen, die jeweils auf einer fest bestimmten von 9 Anlagen bearbeitet werden sollen; für die Kampagnen 6 und 7 steht nur eine Anlage zur Verfügung. Die Kampagnen bestehen aus je $N_{c(k)}$, ($N_{c(k)} \approx 3 - 30$), Chargen (Ansätze), die jeweils 1 bis 6 Arbeitsschritte mit unterschiedlichem, bekanntem Personalbedarf und unterschiedlicher Dauer erfordern. Ferner ist gegeben, wann die letzte Charge einer Kampagne fertiggestellt sein muß (= *Liefertermin*) sowie die Dauer (Tabelle 1). Zur Verfügung stehen bis zu 4 Mitarbeiter in kontinuierlicher Wechselschicht. Die Zuordnung von bestimmten Arbeitskräften zu bestimmten Anlagen oder Arbeitsschritten ist nicht vorgesehen, Pausenzeiten und Schwankungen des Personalstandes (Urlaub, Krankheit) werden nicht berücksichtigt. Die verfügbare Personalzahl N_P wird über den gesamten Zeitraum als konstant angenommen. Alternativ zu untersuchende Optimierungsziele sind die möglichst frühe Fertigstellung der letzten (oder auch aller) Chargen bzw. eine Personalauslastung, die möglichst nahe bei 100% liegt. Die Produktion der Kampagnen 2-6 und 9-10 ist

Tabelle1. Die Tabelle gibt für die Kampagnen k die gewünschten Fertigstellungstermine Z_k sowie die Attribute $a_{ks} - e_{ks} : p_{ks}$ eines einzelnen Arbeitsschritt, d.h. Startzeit-Endzeit: Personalbedarf in Einheiten von 1/6 Arbeitskraft

k	Z_k	$a_{ks} - e_{ks} : p_{ks}$					
1	264	1- 2:12	3 : 6	4- 9:2	10-11:6	12-24:3	25-28:12
2	762	1 :12	2- 7: 2	8:6			
3	432	1- 2:12	3-19:12	20-21:2	22-23:9		
4	552	1- 2:12	3- 9: 2	10-11:6	12-24:2	25-26:12	
5	624	1- 2: 6	3- 9: 6	10-12:2	13-24:2		
6	744	1-12: 6					
7	840	1- 2: 6	3- 9: 3	10-12:6			
8	840	1- 2:12	3 : 6	4-24:2	25-27:6	28-34:3	35-37:12
9	744	1- 2:12	3-19: 3	20-24:6	25-29:3	30-31:6	
10	840	1- 5: 6	6 :12	7-15:2	16-21:6		

durch ein *Rezepturgefüge* verkettet, d.h. der Output einer Kampagne wird als Vorprodukt für die nächste Kampagne benötigt. Für alle übrigen Kampagnen bestehen keine Restriktionen bezüglich der Ausgangsprodukte. Die Produktion einer Charge c_{k_1} von Kampagne k_1 erfordert $p = p(k_1, k_2)$ Chargen c_{k_2} von Kampagne k_2, symbolisch $(k_1 \leftarrow p \cdot k_2)$. Im vorliegenden Fall wird das Rezepturgerüst durch $\{(3 \leftarrow 2.5 \cdot 2), (4 \leftarrow 3 \cdot 3), (5 \leftarrow 1 \cdot 4), (6 \leftarrow 1 \cdot 5), (10 \leftarrow 0.3 \cdot 9)\}$ repräsentiert. Aus Rezepturgerüst und Aufträgen ergibt sich der Vektor der zu produzierenden Chargen (7,30,12,4,4,4,10,4,3,10), d.h. insgesamt $Nc = 88$ Chargen. Eine Charge besteht aus einer Zahl von Verfahrenschritten s, die durch Personalbedarf P_{cs} und Dauer D_{cs} charakterisiert sind.

Aus der Dauer $D_c := \sum_s D_{cs}$ der Chargen einer Kampagne, den vorgegebenen Fertigstellungsterminen und den Verkettungen zwischen mehreren Chargen können bereits Restriktionen der erlaubten Startzeitintervalle berechnet werden, indem vor Beginn des Branch&Bound-Prozesses die zulässigen Bereiche für die Variablen des Constraint-Netzes auf lokal konsistente Bereiche eingeschränkt und somit früheste und späteste Startzeiten für alle Chargen berechnet werden. Bei nicht verketteten Kampagnen berechnen sich der späteste Startzeitpunkt aus der Dauer der Charge und dem vorgegebenen Endtermin (Liefertermin). Neben dem Fertigstellungstermin bedeuten die vorgegebenen Fertigstellungstermine für Zwischenprodukte innerhalb der verketteten Produktionen bei fast allen Kampagnen zusätzliche Einschränkungen.

3 Gemischt-ganzzahlige Problemformulierung

Die gemischt-ganzzahlige Formulierung des in Abschnitt 2 beschriebenen Job-Shop-Problems mit limitierter Personalressource lehnt sich an das Projekt-Planungsbeispiel in [2] an und ist vollständig in [8] beschrieben. Entscheidungsvariablen δ_{tc} geben im Falle $\delta_{tc} = 1$ an, daß die Charge c zur Zeit t gestartet wird. Die Startzeiten s_c der Chargen werden mit den Entscheidungsvariablen über die Bedingung

$$s_c = \sum_{t=t_c}^{t^c} t \cdot \delta_{tc} \tag{1}$$

verknüpft, wobei die Grenzen t_c und t^c den Bereich möglicher Startzeiten für eine bestimmte Charge c eingrenzen. Diese Grenzen ergeben sich aus dem Rezepturgefüge, das den einzelnen Chargen unterliegt und werden mit Hilfe der Konsistenztests bzw. der Domain-Einschränkungen des Constraint-Netz Formalismus' bestimmt. Je enger die Grenzen, desto stärker reduziert sich die Menge der Entscheidungsvariablen. Die Binärvariablen δ_{tc} werden in N_c Mengen $\mathcal{S}_c$

$$\mathcal{S}_c := \{\delta_{tc} | t_c \leq t \leq t^c\}. \tag{2}$$

vom Typ SOS-1 zusammengefaßt, um das Branch&Bound-Verfahren effizienter zu gestalten. Eine weitere Entscheidungsvariable η steuert, ob auf Anlage 6 zuerst die Chargen des Verfahrens 6 oder die des Verfahrens 7 gefertigt werden. Das Rezepturgefüge, das den einzelnen Chargen unterliegt, wurde durch Ungleichungen der Form

$$s_{c_i} \geq e_{c_j} + 1, \tag{3}$$

dargestellt, wobei s_{c_i} den Startzeitpunkt einer Charge c_i aus einer Kampagne k_1 repräsentiert und e_{c_j} den Endzeitpunkt einer Charge c_j aus einer anderen Kampagne k_2 bedeutet. Der Endzeitpunkt e_{c_j} ergibt sich einfach aus Startzeit s_{c_j} und bekannter Chargendauer D_c gemäß

$$e_{c_j} = s_{c_j} + D_c. \tag{4}$$

Die Personalbeschränkung wurde ähnlich wie in [2] formuliert; siehe [8] für geringfügige Änderungen. Als Zielfunktion wurden wahlweise die Fertigungsdauer t_e aller Kampagnen

$$t_e := \min \max_k e_k \iff \min \{t_e | t_e \geq e_k\} \quad \forall k \tag{5}$$

oder die Summe Z aller Kampagnenendzeiten

$$Z := \min \sum_k e_k \tag{6}$$

minimiert. Aus dem Produktionsgefüge läßt sich für das vorliegende Beispiel $t_e \geq 362$ ableiten. Bezeichnet N_P die zur Verfügung stehende Anzahl von Mitarbeitern, so liefert ein numerisches Experiment [8], welches in oben skizziertem

MILP N_P als zusätzliche Variable aufnimmt und die Restriktionen um die Bedingung $t_e = 362$ ergänzt, beim Zielfunktional $\min N_P$ approximativ den Wert 2.04. Damit ist gezeigt, daß die LP-Relaxierung des MILPs für sämtliche Personalstände $N_P \geq 2.04$ den Wert 362 ergibt. Dieser Endzeitpunkt kann, wie verschiedene Optimierungsläufe (siehe [8]) mit dem Optimierungssystem XPRESS-MP (siehe [3]) und COME gezeigt haben, mindestens bei einem Personalstand von $4\frac{1}{2}$ Mitarbeitern eingehalten werden.

Mit Hilfe einer Homotopie, die beginnend bei $N_P = 10$ die Lösung der LP(N_P) bestimmt, die Basislösung speichert und als Startwert für LP($N_P - a$), $a \in [0,1]$, verwendet, läßt sich innerhalb weniger Minuten eine optimale Lösung bis zu $N_P = 6\frac{1}{2}$ gewinnen. Für kleinere Personalstände wächst der Rechenaufwand erheblich. Ursache dafür ist die Symmetrie des Problems. Die meisten LP-Relaxierung liefern den Wert 362 auf Kosten nicht-ganzzahliger δ_t, die jedoch sämtliche linearen Restriktionen erfüllen. Zur Zeit ist ein Branch & Cut Ansatz in Bearbeitung, um das Problem möglichst doch exakt zu lösen.

4 Propagierung in Constraint-Netzen

4.1 Definitionen

Betrachtet wird ein Optimierungsproblem der Form

$$\min_{(v_1,\ldots,v_n)\in S} Z(v_1, \ldots, v_n), \tag{7}$$

z.B. die quadratische Form

$$\min_{(v_1,v_2,v_3)\in S} \sum_{i=1}^{3} c_i \cdot v_i^2. \tag{8}$$

Jeder **Variablen** v_i muß ein **Domain** D_i zugewiesen werden, dies kann z.B. ein Integer-Intervall ($\{1,\ldots,10\}$) oder eine beliebige endliche Menge wie etwa {*rot, gelb, grün*} sein. Ein Domain sollte endlich sein. Dies garantiert, daß theoretisch alle Lösungen untersucht werden können. In der Praxis können auch unendliche Intervalle angegeben werden, wenn sichergestellt ist, daß durch die Constraints endliche Grenzen vorgegeben werden. Domains müssen darüberhinaus abzählbar sein (in den meisten Fällen ist diese Bedingung hinreichend, um mindestens eine Lösung bzw. die optimale Lösung zu finden). Die **zulässige Menge** S ist eine n-dimensionale Menge, $S \subseteq D_1 \times \ldots \times D_n$, die durch die (lokalen) Beziehungen (Constraints) zwischen den Variablen charakterisiert ist. Ein Werte$-n$-Tupel aus S heißt **Lösung** des Optimierungsproblems. Es heißt **optimale Lösung** des Optimierungsproblem, wenn es kein anderes Werte$-n$-Tupel mit kleinerem Wert der Zielfunktion (7) gibt. Die **Zielfunktion** $Z(v_1,\ldots,v_n)$ ist eine i.a. reellwertige Funktion auf einem n-dimensionalen Bereich zur Bewertung einzelner Lösungen. Ein **Constraint** $c_i(i_1,\ldots,i_l; R_i)$ stellt eine Beziehung zwischen den Werten von Variablen her. Erforderlich dazu ist neben der Angabe der Variablen die Spezifizierung einer **Relation** R_i, die für die zulässigen Werte der Variablen erfüllt sein muß:

$$c_i(i_1, ..., i_l; R_i)(D_{i_1}, ..., D_{i_l}) := (D_{i_1} \times ... \times D_{i_l}) \cap R_i. \qquad (9)$$

Im Sinne der Definition (9) handelt es sich bei einem Constraint c_i um eine Abbildung, die dem Mengen–l-Tupel $(D_{i_1}, ..., D_{i_l})$ die Menge $(D_{i_1}, ..., D_{i_l}) \cap R_i$ zuordnet. Auch die Relation R_i wird als eine Menge aufgefaßt. Die Indexmenge $\{i_1, ..., i_l\}$ kann mehrfach denselben Index enthalten, $l > n$ ist möglich. Für die Formulierung von Constraints ist nicht in jedem Fall Stetigkeit vorauszusetzen (z.B. Rechnen mit Integer-Intervallen), es ist keine vollständige Ordnungsrelation erforderlich (z.B. für Vergleiche), und die Variablen müssen nicht notwendig Zahlen sein z.B. $v_3 \in \{rot,\ gelb,\ grün\}$). Für jeden Constraint $c_i(i_1, ..., i_l; R_i)$ können für alle $j \in \{1, ..., l\}$ **Projektionen** pr_j definiert werden:

$$pr_j(c_i(i_1, ..., i_l; R_i)(D_{i_1}, ..., D_{i_l})) \rightarrow \tilde{D}_{i_j} \qquad (10)$$

Diese Projektionen identifizieren aus der durch den Constraint c_j definierten Menge durch Projektion der $j - ten$ Stelle Teilmengen des Domains D_j, so daß D_{i_j} ohne Informationsverlust durch $\tilde{D}_{i_j}$ ersetzt werden kann. Wenn für alle $j \in 1, ..., l$

$$pr_j(c_i(i_1, ..., i_l; R_i)(D_{i_1}, ..., D_{i_l})) = D_{i_j} \qquad (11)$$

gilt, dann heißt $c_i(i_1, ..., i_l; R_i)$ **lokal konsistent**. Für jeden beliebigen Wert $w_{\hat{j}} \in D_{\hat{j}}$ gibt es in diesem Fall Werte $w_k \in D_k$, $k = i_1, ..., \hat{j}, ..., i_l$, so daß $(w_{i_1}, ... w_{\hat{j}}, ... w_{i_l})$ den Constraint c_i erfüllt (greift man zwei oder mehr Werte heraus, ist dies nicht mehr gewährleistet). Durch die Verwendung der Projektionen pr_j wird die Berechnung erleichtert, da nicht weiter mit n- oder l-dimensionalen Mengen, sondern mit einfachen Mengen oder Werten gerechnet werden kann. Da das kartesische Produkt der Projektionen $pr_{i1} \times ... \times pr_{il}(c_i(i_1, ..., i_l; R_i))$ i.d.R. echte Obergrenze von $(D_{i1} \times ... \times D_{il}) \cap R_i$ ist, ergibt sich jedoch gleichzeitig ein Informationsverlust. Das **Constraint-Netz CN** definiert den zulässigen Bereich S eines Optimierungsproblems in Abhängigkeit von den Domains $D_1, ... D_n$ aller Variablen und der Menge C aller Constraints c_i, die durch die logische *Und-Bedingung* verknüpft sind:

$$CN(D_1, ..., D_n; C) = S = \wedge_i c_i \qquad (12)$$

Man spricht von **globaler Konsistenz** des Constraint Netzes, wenn für jedes n-Tupel $(s_1, ... s_n) \in S$ und für alle Constraints $c_1, ... c_m \in C$ gilt:

$$c_i(i_1, ..., i_l; R_i)(\{s_{i_1}\} \times ... \times \{s_{i_l}\}) = (s_{i_1}, ..., s_{i_l}), \qquad (13)$$

d.h. jede Lösung erfüllt alle Constraints. Entsprechend ergibt sich **Inkonsistenz** für jedes n-Tupel $(\bar{s}_1, ... \bar{s}_n) \notin S$:

$$\exists c_i \in C \text{ so daß } c_i(i_1, ..., i_l; R_i)(\{\bar{s}_{i_1}\} \times ... \times \{\bar{s}_{i_l}\}) = \{\} \qquad (14)$$

Globale Konsistenz ist eine stärkere Forderung als lokale Konsistenz für alle Constraints, wie am Beispiel von drei Ampeln ersichtlich: Jede Ampel v_1, v_2, v_3 zeigt rot oder grün; die Constraints $v_1 \neq v_2$, $v_1 \neq v_3$, $v_2 \neq v_3$ können jeweils jede für sich, d.h. lokal, erfüllt werden, eine Lösung, die allen Ungleichungen gleichzeitig genügt, d.h. global konsistent ist, gibt es aber offensichtlich nicht. **Ziel der Propagierung** von Constraint-Netzen ist das Erreichen globaler Konsistenz, d.h. die Bestimmung derjenigen Werte l-Tupel, die allen gegebenen Beschränkungen (Constraints) genügen ([12]). Dazu wird zunächst lokale Konsistenz für die einzelnen Constraints hergestellt. Die Domains der Variablen werden dann durch Berücksichtigung von immer mehr Constraints ständig weiter eingeschränkt. Für tiefergehende Details sei auf [5] verwiesen.

4.2 Algorithmische Aspekte

In COME steht einerseits ein **Branch&Bound**-Verfahren zur exakten Optimierung zur Verfügung, andererseits können aber auch **generierende Heuristiken** (Monte-Carlo-Methode, Simulated Annealing) oder unvollständiges Branch & Bound aufbauend auf Propagierung in Constraint-Netzen angewandt werden.

Vor Beginn des eigentlichen Branch&Bound-Verfahrens sowie nach jedem Verzweigungsschritt erfolgt eine Überprüfung auf lokale Konsistenz. Ist allen Variablen ein fester Wert zugewiesen, so wird anhand der Constraints überprüft, ob das n-Tupel $(v_1, ...v_n) \in S$ ist, d.h. ob globale Konsistenz gegeben ist. Ist dies der Fall, so wird $(v_1, ...v_n)$ als zulässige Lösung registriert. Die Konsistenzprüfung für Teillösungen verhindert, daß zu viele unzulässige Lösungen getestet werden müssen, Informationen werden möglichst umfassend ausgenutzt, die Laufzeit wird verkürzt. Beim **Branch&Bound** besteht die Möglichkeit, das Verfahren nach einer bestimmten Laufzeit bzw. nach einer festzulegenden Anzahl von Schritten, d.h. von Lösungen, zu stoppen (unvollständiges Branch&Bound). In diesem Fall ist nicht sicher, ob das bis zu diesem Zeitpunkt als beste Lösung festgestellte n-Tupel aus S das Optimum ist. In den meisten Fällen wird allerdings schon nach ca. 10% der Rechenzeit das exakte Optimum gefunden, die übrige Zeit ist notwendig, um zu prüfen, ob diese Wertekombination tatsächlich das Optimum bildet.

Die **generierenden Algorithmen** in COME arbeiten im Gegensatz zu anderen Verfahren nicht mit Penalisierung, um die Zulässigkeit der Lösungen zu gewährleisten, statt dessen wird direkt überprüft, ob alle Constraints erfüllt sind. Damit vermeidet man weitere durch die Penalisierung erzeugte lokale Nebenminima. Allerdings hat man so viele unzulässige Tupel zu prüfen. Für sämtliche Heuristiken kann dasselbe Constraint Netz zugrunde gelegt werden wie für die exakte Optimierung; dies erleichtert ein "Umschalten" zwischen exakten und heuristischen Verfahren. Für generierende Algorithmen müssen allerdings zusätzlich Startlösungen, Umgebungen und Entscheidungsfunktionen spezifiziert werden.

5 Constraint-Netz und Ergebnisse

5.1 Modellbildung mit COME

Als Zielfunktionale werden wieder die in Abschnitt 3 vorgestellten Ansätze (5) und (6) betrachtet, d.h. die Endzeit t_e der letzten Charge oder die Summe Z aller Kampagnen-Endzeiten e_k wird minimiert. Das Rezepturgefüge wird wieder gemäß (3) erfaßt. Die richtige Verknüpfung von Chargen innerhalb einer Kampagne wird durch

$$s_{c+1} - s_c \geq D_c \quad ; \quad \forall k = 1, ..., N_K, \quad \forall c = N_f(k), ..., N_l(k) - 1 \qquad (15)$$

gewährleistet, wobei $c = N_f(k)$ bzw. $c = N_l(k)$ die erste bzw. die letzte Charge der Kampagne k bezeichnet. Die Kampagnen 6 und 7 sollen hintereinander auf Anlage 6 laufen, d.h.

$$s_f(6) \geq s_l(7) + D_l(7) \quad \lor \quad s_f(7) \geq s_l(6) + D_l(6) \qquad (16)$$

Schließlich wird noch eine Bedingung benötigt, die sicherstellt, daß alle J_c Schritte s einer Charge c unmittelbar aufeinander folgen müssen:

$$s_{c(s+1)} - s_{cs} = D_{cs} \quad ; \quad s = 1, ..., J_c, \forall c \qquad (17)$$

Sämtliche auf Binärvariablen beruhende Personalrestriktionen sowie (1-3) entfallen, da in COME spezielle Objekte zur Modellierung von Ressourcen zur Verfügung stehen. Die Anlagen werden als Objekte definiert, die mit einem Zeitstrahl von 1 bis N_T versehen sind, auf dem Aktivitäten eingeplant werden können. Da die einzelnen Arbeitsschritte der Chargen (insgesamt 329) jeweils unterschiedlichen Personalbedarf haben, werden sie als eigenständige Aktivitäten behandelt. Für die Modellierung des Personalstandes ist ebenfalls eine mit einem Zeitstrahl versehene Klasse vorgesehen. Eine Aktivität wird gleichzeitig auf einer Maschine und auf dem Personalzeitstrahl eingeplant. Das Arbeiten mit Belegungsvariablen —wie bei XPRESS-MP notwendig— entfällt also bei COME, es müssen allerdings stattdessen die verschiedenen Zeitstrahlen verwaltet werden.

5.2 Ergebnisse

Mit COME können Lösungen gefunden werden, sofern mindestens $N_P = 3$ Mitarbeiter zur Verfügung stehen. Die Rechenzeit Δt auf einer IBM $RS/6000$ beträgt etwa eine Stunde; es handelt sich dabei jeweils nur um eine erste zulässige Lösung, nicht unbedingt um das Optimum — innerhalb der folgenden Stunden (bis zu 3 Tagen) konnte bisher allerdings in keinem Fall eine bessere Lösung gefunden werden. In den Fällen, in denen der Optimalitätsbeweis nicht möglich ist, kann mit Hilfe der LP-Relaxierung und einer mit CNP gefundenen Lösung die Qualiät der Lösung bewertet werden. Die LP-Relaxierung und ihr gefundener Lösungswert z_{LP} dient als untere Schranke z_u, die CNP-Lösung z_{CNP} als obere Schranke z_o. Dann gibt

$$G := \frac{z_o - z_u}{z_u} \qquad (18)$$

einen garantierten Maximalabstand der CNP-Lösung von der optimalen Lösung $z_*, z_u \leq z_* \leq z_o$ in dem Sinne an, daß $\frac{z_{CNP}-z_*}{z_*} \leq G$ ist. Ziel weiterer Untersuchungen ist es daher, möglichst realistische Schranken z_u und z_o zu gewinnen. Die Ergebnisse einer Untersuchung der Abhängigkeit der gesamten Fertigungsdauer von der Personalkapazität sind in Tabelle 2 auf Basis der besten gefundenen Lösungen zusammengefaßt. Die Art der Aufzählung — immer beginnend

Tabelle2. Diese Tabelle gibt die Rechenzeiten Δ_t (auf IBM RS-6000) und erzielten Fertigungsdauer t_e *bzw.* Z bei gegebener Personalzahl N_p und kurzdauernder Überauslastung U in Prozent an. G gibt die Qualitätsbewertung der Lösung in Prozent gemäß (18) an; 0 bedeutet bewiesene Optimalität.

N_p	U	$\Delta_t[h]$	t_e	$t_e[h]$	$G[\%]$	$Z[h]$
3	100.0%	1:00:48	22^d17^h	545 (100 %)	50.6	4186 (100 %)
$3\frac{1}{3}$	111.0%	0:30:07	19^d11^h	467 (85.7%)	29.0	3813 (91.1%)
4	100.0%	$4{:}45{:}48^1$	16^d01^h	385 (100.0%)	6.4	3242 (100 %)
$4\frac{1}{2}$	112.5%	0:43:32	15^d02^h	362 (94 %)	0.0	2988 (92.2%)

[1] mit 486er PC, 66 Hz

mit den kleinsten Werten im zulässigen Bereich — legt die Vermutung nahe, daß zumindest in einigen Fällen bereits das Optimum gefunden ist, ohne dies exakt bewiesen zu haben. Zur Abschätzung können aber einige Schranken angegeben werden. Für beliebige Personalzahlen N_P bildet 362 eine untere Schranke. Für Werte $N_P \leq 2.48$ läßt sich diese Schranke verbessern, indem man die Summe aller Mannstunden durch den Personalstand dividiert. Für $Np = 2$ ergibt sich dabei der Wert 450.1. Die Chargen der Kampagnen 1,2,3,4,8 und 9 beginnen alle mit Personalbedarf 2, diese Chargen können bei einem Personalstand von 2 Personen nicht gleichzeitig bearbeitet werden. Außerdem haben Chargen der Kampagne 10 in der 6. Betriebsstunde Personalbedarf 2, können sich also nur in der 1. bis 5. Betriebsstunden mit Chargen der Kampagnen 1,2,3,4,8,9,10 überschneiden. Dies ergibt insgesamt 1219 Stunden Bearbeitungszeit allein für Kampagnen 1,2,3,4,8,9 und 10. Mit $N_P = 2$ ist das Zeitlimit von 840 Std. also nicht mehr einzuhalten. Besonders hinzuweisen ist auf das Ergebnis für $N_P = 4\frac{1}{2}$ in Tabelle 2: Deutet man diese Zahl so, daß 4 Arbeitskräfte kurzfristig über 100% ausgelastet sein dürfen (nämlich in diesem Fall bis zu 112.5%), so kann man einen wesentlich früheren Endtermin erzielen. In 44 Stunden liegt die Auslastung dabei über 100%, in 12 Std. ist $N_P = 4\frac{1}{6}$, in 23 Std. ist $N_P = 4\frac{1}{3}$ und nur in 9 Std. ist $N_P = 4\frac{1}{2}$, d.h. die Auslastungsgrenze wird nur in seltenen Fällen erreicht. 360 Stunden entsprechen 30 Schichten à 12 Stunden, d.h. im Durchschnitt besteht in 3 Stunden im Laufe von zwei aufeinanderfolgenden Schichten eine Überauslastung - tatsächlich sind es bis zu 7 Stunden während 2 aufeinanderfolgenden Schichten. Ähnliches gilt für eine Personalzahl $Np = 3\frac{1}{3}$ statt $N_P = 3$. In diesem Fall ist in insgesamt 58 Stunden die Auslastung von 100% überschritten, d.h.

im Durchschnitt entfallen wieder auf jeweils 2 der 39 zur Bearbeitung notwendigen Schichten 3 Stunden mit Überauslastung des Personals. Weitere Ergebnisse im Hinblick auf die Auswirkung der Reihenfolgebedingung und den Einfluß der Zielfunktionale finden sich in [8].

6 Job-Scheduling in einem Cluster paralleler Workstations

In diesem Abschnitt sei noch ein Modell für optimales Job-Scheduling zur Berechnung von Molekülen in einem Cluster aus Workstations beschrieben. Dabei soll an dieser Stelle auf die spezielle Modellrealisierung nicht eingegangen werden, sondern eine generische, nur die logischen Verknüpfungen berücksichtigende Formulierung präsentiert werden.

6.1 Problembeschreibung

6.1.1 Moleküle, Arbeitspakete: Eine Gleichgewichtsreaktion ist beispielsweise eine Reaktion des Typs

$$A + B + C \rightleftharpoons D + E$$

d.h. die Moleküle A, B und C reagieren ohne Verluste zu Molekülen D und E. Die Anzahl der unterschiedlichen bzw. resultierenden Moleküle ist dabei variabel. Die quantenmechanischen Berechnungen für sämtliche an einer Reaktion beteiligten Moleküle werden als ein **Arbeitspaket** (Anzahl Arbeitspakete N_P, $N_P \approx 4 - 5$) bezeichnet; ein Arbeitspaket p umfaßt $N_M(p)$ (zwischen 4 und ca.30) **Moleküle**, die wiederum jeweils aus $N_A(p, m)$ **Atomen** ($N_A(p, m) \approx 5 - 50$) bestehen. Für die Bearbeitung jedes Arbeitspaketes p sollen eine **Priorität** P_p und eine **Zielzeit** T_p festgelegt werden können. Für jedes Molekül ($m = 1, ..., N_M(p)$) des Arbeitspaketes p werden in einem ersten Schritt die Geometrie und im zweiten Schritt bestimmte physikalische und chemische Eigenschaften berechnet, wobei sich dieser Schritt in drei Teilschritte untergliedert. Nach der Berechnung der Geometrie (S_1) ist eine manuelle Überprüfung des Ergebnisses (S_2) notwendig, bevor die Ableitung der Moleküleigenschaften (S_3-S_5) begonnen wird. Die manuelle Überprüfung soll nur während der Arbeitszeit, also von 8 bis 17 Uhr an Wochentagen, stattfinden und wird als eigener Bearbeitungsschritt geführt, der keine Maschinenressourcen benötigt; die Daten aus S_1 werden allerdings bis zu dieser Prüfung auf den Festplatten der beteiligten Rechner gespeichert. Die Reihenfolge von S_3 und S_4 ist beliebig, sie müssen aber beide vor Beginn von S_5 abgeschlossen sein. Werden die S_3 und S_5 eines Arbeitspaketes auf verschiedenen Rechnern durchgeführt, so entstehen **Umrüstverluste** bzw. **Transferzeiten** V_{pm}; diese Umrüstzeit wird im Modell als S_6 bezeichnet. Umrüstverluste zwischen den übrigen Schritten sind vernachlässigbar. Jeder der Schritte S_1, S_4 und S_5 kann parallel mehrere Rechner nutzen, wobei für S_1 die Aufteilung so vorgenommen wird, daß alle beteiligten Workstations gleichzeitig rechnen, während für S_4 und S_5 in Abhängigkeit von der Anzahl $N_A(p, m)$ der Atome eines Moleküls die Berechnungen verschiedene Dauern haben und zu unterschiedlichen Zeitpunkten beginnen können. Die **erforderlichen Rechenzeiten** (typischerweise 10^2 bis 10^6 CPU-Sekunden) werden für die weitere Bearbeitung in CPU-Zeit vorgegeben. Für S_2 wird grundsätzlich eine Viertelstunde veranschlagt.

6.1.2 Beschreibung des Workstation-Clusters: Zur Verfügung steht derzeit ein Cluster von $N_R = 16$ Maschinen. Die Bearbeitungszeit für S_1 wird bei paralleler Bearbeitung auf mehreren Rechnern nichtlinear verkürzt in Abhängigkeit davon, welche und wie viele Rechner eingesetzt werden. Der Zusammenhang zwischen der Anzahl u_{pms} der zur Berechnung des $s-ten$ Schrittes ($s = 1, 3, 4, 5$) für Molekül m des Arbeitspaketes p eingesetzten Rechnern und der **reduzierten Rechenleistung** wird durch die Funktion $F(u_{pms})$, $0 \leq F_{pms} \leq 1$, spezifiziert, die zunächst als unabhängig davon angesehen wird, welche Rechner für die Berechnung eingesetzt werden. Im Vektor $\rho_{pms} = [\delta_{pms}(1), ..., \delta_{pms}(N_R)]$, $\delta_{pms}(r) \in \{0, 1\}$ wird die Information, welche Rechner für einen bestimmten Rechenschritt im Einsatz sind, festgehalten, wobei noch die Belegungsvariable δ_{pmsr} und die detaillierte, die Zeit mit einbeziehende Belegungsvariable δ_{pmsrt} verwendet werden:

$$\delta_{pmsr} := \delta_{pms}(r) = \begin{cases} 1, & pms \text{ läuft im Planungszeitraum auf Rechner } r \\ 0, & \text{sonst} \end{cases} \tag{19}$$

$$\delta_{pmsrt} = \delta_{pms}(r, t) := \begin{cases} 1, & pms \text{ läuft auf } r \text{ im Zeitintervall } t \\ 0, & \text{sonst} \end{cases} \tag{20}$$

Die spezifische Rechenleistung des Rechners r bzgl. des langsamsten Rechners wird durch den **Performance-Faktor** L_r, $L_r \geq 1$, ausgedrückt. Zu berücksichtigen sind weiter die **Kapazität der Arbeitsspeicher** A_r und der **Festplatten** $F_r (r = 1, ..., N_R)$. Die Kapazität der Arbeitsspeicher wird vorerst nicht in die Optimierung miteinbezogen, da $z.Zt.$ die Festplattenkapazitäten für die betrachteten Rechenschritte jeweils eine stärkere Beschränkung darstellen, eine Restriktion bezüglich der Arbeitsspeicher also nicht aktiv wäre.

6.1.3 Optimierungsziele: Die Berechnung der Arbeitspakete soll entweder
1. hinsichtlich der gesamten Bearbeitungszeit oder
2. hinsichtlich der Prioritäten oder
3. bezüglich der Überschreitung festgelegter Endtermine

aller vorliegenden Arbeitspakete über einen Zeitraum von mehreren Wochen optimiert werden. Ein mit diesen konkreten Zielfunktionalen verbundener Aspekt ist es, die Auslastung der Rechner zu erhöhen und die planerische Arbeit des Cluster-Koordinators zu unterstützen bzw. erheblich zu reduzieren. Außerdem sollen diejenigen Moleküle und diejenigen Rechner (Plattenplatz, Arbeitsspeicher) identifiziert werden, die als kritische "bottle necks" anzusehen sind, sowie das gesamte Modell unter dem Blickwinkel einer Sensitivitätsanalyse untersucht werden. Langfristig angestrebt ist ein dynamisches Planungssystem, das den momentanen evtl. durch nicht vorhersehbare Störungen modifizierten Zustand des Clusters erfaßt und darauf aufbauend optimiert.

Mit den einfachen Annahmen $N_P \approx 5$, $N_M(p) \approx 10$ und $Ns = 5$ folgen formal 920 Unbekannte. Einige dieser Variablen sind jedoch eng und direkt gekoppelt, so folgt aus der Endzeit e_p des Arbeitspaketes p direkt aus der Kenntnis aller e_{pm5}, diese wiederum aus Startzeiten s_{pms} und Dauern d_{pms}. Dies führt zu erheblichen Einschränkungen von Freiheitsgraden und erhöht damit die Chance für die Rechenbarkeit des Problems, zumindest auf Basis der Constraint-Netze. Die Belegungsvariablen sind nicht in die genannte Zahl mit einbezogen. Die δ, ρ sind hier im Hinblick auf die Bildung eines gemischt-ganzzahligen Modells eingefügt. Formal ergeben sich in einem gemischt-ganzzahligen Modell $\approx 4000 \cdot (N_T + 1)$ binäre Variablen, wobei N_T die Anzahl der betrachteten Zeitintervalle ($N_T \approx 10^5$) repräsentiert. Zwar ist auch dies nur eine Obergrenze, aber die Größenordnung der Anzahl binärer Variablen zeigt die Schwierigkeit, das Problem in der vorliegenden Form als gemischt-ganzzahliges Modell zu behandeln.

6.2 Mathematisches Modell

6.2.1 Zielfunktionen: Die drei genannten Zielfunktionen (minimale Gesamtbearbeitungszeit, minimale Summe der gewichteten Endzeiten der Arbeitspakete, minimale Überschreitung der Zielzeiten) nehmen folgende mathematische Form an:

$$\min(\max_p e_p), \quad \min \sum_{p=1}^{N_A} \frac{1}{P_p} e_p, \quad \min \sum_{p=1}^{N_A} z_p \tag{21}$$

Die Prioritäten des zweiten Zielfunktionals sind hierbei so geordnet, daß dasjenige Arbeitspaket, das als erstes fertig sein soll, mit einer niedrigen Zahl, z.B. 1, belegt wird. Arbeitspakete niedrigerer Priorität erhalten höhere Zahlen, z.B. zwischen 1 und 100. Bei Zielfunktion 3 gibt z_p die Überschreitung der gewünschten Zielzeit T_p an; die Zielzeiten T_p sind so gut wie möglich einzuhalten. Die Überschreitung kann durch eine Obergrenze T_p^+ beschränkt werden. Hierfür sind folgende zusätzliche Nebenbedingungen erforderlich:

$$e_p \leq T_p + z_p \quad , \quad z_p \leq T_p^+ \quad ; \quad \forall p \tag{22}$$

6.2.2 Nebenbedingungen: Sie bilden ein System zehn gekoppelter Relationen. 01) Festlegung der Reihenfolge der Rechenschritte für ein Molekül.

$$s_{pm(s+1)r} \geq e_{pmsr} \quad ; \quad \forall p \forall m \forall r \ s = 1, 2, 4 \tag{23}$$

$$s_{pm4r} \geq e_{pm2r}, s_{pm5r} \geq e_{pm6r}, s_{pm6r} \geq e_{pm3r} \quad ; \quad \forall p \forall m \forall r \tag{24}$$

02) Endzeitpunkt der Berechnung eines Schrittes für ein Molekül m

$$e_{pmsr} = s_{pmsr} + d_{pmsr} \quad ; \quad \forall p \forall m \forall s \forall r \tag{25}$$

$$e_{pms} = \max_{r}\{e_{pmsr}\} \quad ; \quad \forall p \forall m \forall s \tag{26}$$

03) Endzeitpunkt der Berechnung eines Arbeitspaketes p

$$e_p = \max_{m}\{e_{pm5}\} \quad ; \quad \forall p \tag{27}$$

04) Beschränkung für die parallele Aufteilung eines Rechenschrittes für Molekül m aus Arbeitspaket p, auf mehrere Rechner; der Job pms darf auf höchstens U_{pms} Workstations bearbeitet werden.

$$\sum_{r=1}^{N_R} \delta_{pms}(r) = u_{pms} \quad , \quad u_{pms} \leq U_{pms}, \quad ; \quad \forall p \forall m \; s = 1, 4, 5 \tag{28}$$

05) Wenn S_1 auf mehrere Rechner aufgeteilt wird, dann muß ein besonders leistungsstarker Rechner — diese werden im folgenden mit Rechner 1 oder Rechner 2 bezeichnet — dabei sein.

$$u_{pms} > 1 \Rightarrow [\delta_{pms}(1) = 1 \vee \delta_{pms}(2) = 1] \quad ; \quad \forall p \forall m \quad s = 1 \tag{29}$$

06) Auf jeder Maschine höchstens 1 Job pro Zeiteinheit. Später soll auch zugelassen sein, daß ein Rechner gleichzeitig 2 oder 3 Jobs bearbeiten kann. Wartezeiten, d.h. Zeiten während derer Daten auf der Festplatte gespeichert bleiben, werden nicht als Jobs gerechnet, die reduzierte Festplattenkapazität wird allerdings berücksichtigt.

$$\sum_{s} \delta_{pms}(r,t) \leq 1 \quad ; \quad \forall r \forall t \forall p \tag{30}$$

$$\delta_{pms}(r) \leq 1 \iff [\forall t : s_{pms} \leq t \leq e_{pms} \, , \, \delta_{pms}(r,t) \leq 1] \tag{31}$$

07) Berechnung der Gesamtdauer d_{pmsr} eines Rechenschrittes pms aus der auf den langsamsten Rechner bezogenen Referenzdauer Δ_{pms} eines Schrittes bei gegebener *Datentransferzeit* V_{pm} und *Skalierungsfaktor* A.

$$\forall p \forall m \forall r \quad d_{pm1r} = A \cdot \frac{\Delta_{pm1}}{L_{1\,oder\,2}F(u_{pm1})} + \frac{(1-A) \cdot \frac{\Delta_{pm1}}{L_r F(u_{pm1})} \cdot \delta_{pm1}(r)}{\sum_{i=1}^{Nr}(\frac{\Delta_{pm1}}{L_i F(u_{pm1})} \cdot \delta_{pm1}(i))} \tag{32}$$

$$d_{pm2r} = \frac{1}{4}Stunde \quad ; \quad \forall p \forall m \forall r \tag{33}$$

$$d_{pm3r} = \frac{\Delta_{pm3}}{L_r F(\rho_{pm3})} \cdot \delta_{pm3}(r) \quad ; \quad \forall p \forall m \forall r \tag{34}$$

$$d_{pmsr} = \frac{\Delta_{pmsr}}{L_r F(\rho_{pms})}, \sum \Delta_{pmsr} = \Delta_{pms} \quad ; \quad \forall p \forall m \forall r \; s = 4, 5 \tag{35}$$

$$d_{pm6r} = V_{pm} \quad ; \quad \forall p \forall m \forall r \tag{36}$$

08) Beschränkung des Plattenbedarfs R_{pms} durch die jeweilige Festplattenkapazität F_r

$$R_{pms} > F_r \Rightarrow \delta_{pms}(r) = 0 \quad , \quad s = 3, 4, 5, 6 \tag{37}$$

$$R_{pm1} \cdot \frac{\Delta_{pm1}}{L_r F(u_{pm1})} \cdot \delta_{pm1}(r) / \sum_{i=1}^{N_r} \left(\frac{\Delta_{pm1}}{L_i F(u_{pm1})} \cdot \delta_{pm1}(i) \right) \leq F_r \quad ; \quad \forall p \forall m \forall r \quad (38)$$

Die Plattenplatzrestriktionen gehen von der Annahme aus, daß zu Beginn eines Arbeitsschrittes der gesamte durch R_{pms} angeforderte Plattenplatz unmittelbar und für die gesamte Zeitdauer belegt wird; es wird also nicht berücksichtigt, inwieweit der zeitlich aufgelöste benötigte Plattenplatz $R_{pms}(t')$ während der Arbeitsphase eines Schrittes variiert. Es muß also lediglich sichergestellt werden, daß $R_{pms} \geq \max_{t'}\{R_{pms}(t')\}$.

09) Ausführung von S_2 nur während der Arbeitszeit (8-17 Uhr wochentags)

10) Die Umrüstzeit (=Datentransferzeit) V_{pm} zwischen S_3 und S_5 berechnet sich aus der Anzahl der hinzukommenden Rechner multipliziert mit dem Plattenplatzbedarf und dividiert durch die Geschwindigkeit des Netzwerkes.

Für einen gemischt-ganzzahligen Ansatz wird eine *Zeitdiskretisierung* so vorgenommen, daß der Job kleinster Dauer bezogen auf eine Zeiteinheit etwa die Dauer 1 hat. Für die auf Constraint-Netzen basierte Formulierung kann als Zeiteinheit $\Delta t = 1$ Minute bis zu $\Delta t = 15$ Minuten gewählt werden.

6.3 Mathematischer Lösungsansatz mit Constraint-Netzen

Bei dem in Abschnitt 6.2 beschriebenen Modell handelt es sich um ein diskretes, nicht-lineares, beschränktes Optimierungsproblem. Grundsätzlich kann das Problem im Rahmen der in COME zur Verfügung gestellten *CNP* behandelt werden, jedoch läßt die Komplexität des Modells (Zahl der Freiheitsgrade, Zahl der Nebenbedingungen und Art der Verknüpfung) auch hier Schwierigkeiten erwarten. Aus diesem Grunde und auch, um zu einer recht schnellen Lösung des Problems zu gelangen, soll zunächst der folgende Dekompositionsansatz verfolgt werden; seine Realisierung und damit erzielte Ergebnisse sind bei [8] beschrieben.

6.3.1 Dekompositionsansatz: Für einen bestimmten Rechenschritt s eines Moleküls m im Paket p wird der in Abschnitt 6.1.2 definierte Vektor $\vec{p}_{pms}$ als Teilfreiheitsgrad einer generierenden Heuristik, z.B. Simulated Annealing (SA) ([10], [1]) verwendet; er spezifiert die Rechnerzuweisung bezüglich der Aufgabe "pms". Der Vektor $\mathbf{x}$ sei aus sämtlichen Aufgaben, d.h. aus allen *pms*-Kombinationen zusammengesetzt. Als Zielfunktional $f(\mathbf{x}, \mathbf{p}, s(\mathbf{x}))$ sei ein Kandidat aus (21) gewählt. Mit Hilfe des SA wird nun das Minimierungsproblem

$$\min_{\mathbf{x}} f(\mathbf{x}, \mathbf{p}; s) \qquad (39)$$

gelöst, wobei $\mathbf{p}$ verschiedene Parameter wie Festplattenkapazitäten, CPU Daten, benötigte Rechenzeiten etc., aber auch Rechendauern auf den beteiligten Rechnern beinhaltet. Zu beachten ist aber, daß sich $f(\mathbf{x}, \mathbf{p}; s(\mathbf{x}))$ als Lösung eines Minimierungsproblems, genauer eines Schedulingproblems bestimmt. Der Vektor $\mathbf{s}$ ergibt sich bei gegebenen $\mathbf{x}$ und $\mathbf{p}$ aus

$$\mathbf{s} = \mathbf{s}(\mathbf{x}, \mathbf{p}) = argmin\{f(\mathbf{x}, \mathbf{p}; s)\} \qquad (40)$$

als Lösung des inneren Minimierungsproblems und repräsentiert die Startzeiten s_{pms} der einzelnen Jobs "pms" auf den durch x vorgegebenen Workstations.

7 Diskussion

Die bisherigen Untersuchungen zeigen die grundsätzliche Eignung der Constraint-Netz-Propagierung zur Lösung von Scheduling-Problemen insbesondere auch von nicht-linearen Problemen. Der Nachweis der Optimalität erweist sich auch auf Basis der *CNP* als schwierig. Jedoch bietet es sich bei den vorgelegten Minimierungsproblemen an, mit Hilfe der LP-Relaxierung der gemischt-ganzzahligen Formulierung eine untere Schranke und mit Hilfe einer via *CNP* abgeleiteten zulässigen Lösung eine obere Schranke zu bestimmen. Damit ist in den Fällen, in denen die Optimalität nicht bewiesen ist, doch wenigstens eine garantierte Schranke berechnet und damit eine Bewertung der Lösungsqualität möglich.

References

1. Aarts E., Korst J. : Simulated Annealing and Boltzman Machines. Chichester, (1993), New York .
2. Ashford R.W. , Daniel R. : Some Lessons in Solving Practical Integer Problems. J. Opl. Res. Soc. 43(5) (1992), 425–433.
3. Ashford R.W. , Daniel R. : Mixed Integer Programming in Production Scheduling: A Case Study. in: Ciriani T.A. & Leachman R.C. (Eds.) Optimization in Industry, John Wiley & Sons, New York, 1993.
4. Blasewicz J., Ecker K., Schmidt G., Weglarz J. : Scheduling in Computer and Manufactoring Systems. (1993), Berlin, Heidelberg.
5. Bücker M. : Ein allgemeines Konzept zur Modellierung und Lösung diskreter Optimierungsprobleme. Habilitationsschrift, Fakultät für Wirtschaftswissenschaften der Universität Karlsruhe, Karlsruhe, 1995.
6. Grötschel M. , Lovász L. : Combinatorial Optimization. in: Graham R., Grötschel M. & Lovász L. (eds.) Handbook on Combinatorics, North Holland, 1994.
7. Güsgen H.-W. : Constraints. Eine Wissensrepräsentationsform. Arbeitspapiere der Gesellschaft für Mathematik und Datenverarbeitung mbH, (1985), St.Augustin.
8. Heipcke S. : Optimales Scheduling mit Contraint Netzen. Diplomarbeit, Katholische Universität Eichstätt, Eichstätt, 1994.
9. Kallrath J. : Diskrete Optimierung in der chemischen Industrie. in: Mathematik in der Praxis - Fallstudien aus Industrie, Wirtschaft, Naturwissenschaften und Medizin. Springer Verlag, Heidelberg, 1994.
10. Metropolis N., Rosenbluth A., Rosenbluth M., Teller A., Teller E. : Equation of state by fast computing machines. Journal of Chemical Physics 21 (1953), 1087–1092.
11. Nemhauser G.L. , Wolsey L.A. : Integer and Combinatorial Optimization. John Wiley & Sons, New York, 1988.
12. Winston P.H. : Künstliche Intelligenz. Bonn, MA Reading Mass., 1987.

Interpreting Clinical Questions –

Medical Text Analysis Supports Image Presentation

Martin Schröder

Philips Research Laboratories
Department Technical Systems, Hamburg

Abstract

Medicine is a domain where natural language documents play an important role. They contain a lot of useful information that is not directly accessable by formal procedures. Only with the help of a semantically oriented natural language analysis the contents of the documents can be made explicit in a structured way. In this paper we describe the linguistic and knowledge-based processing of german clinical questions by the text analysis system METEXA. The results are used to support the selection of images in the Cooperative Clinical Workstation, a reporting workstation for radiology. Depending on categories of clinical questions, the workstation can automatically present images that the radiologist needs for reporting. The METEXA system performs lexical, morphological, syntactic, and semantic processing. The semantics of an utterance is represented by a Conceptual Graph. In a further processing phase, the clinical questions are classified by a rule-based resolution procedure.

Introduction

Medicine is a domain where the processing of routine text documents plays an important role. In the past several projects have tried to address some issues in this area by linguistic and knowledge-based processing of medical documents. In the Linguistic String Project (Sager 87) a system has been developed over 10-15 years. The coverage is broad enough for practical applications (Borst et al. 91, Sager et al. 92). However, the system lacks a formal knowledge representation based on predicate logic. More recent approaches are

- a report analysis system developed at the University Hospital at Geneva (Baud et al. 92),
- a system to extract implicit information out of medical reports (Cavazza et al. 92),
- a system to generate natural language reports that have been specified with a graphical interface (Bernauer & Goldberg 93),
- the multilingual European AIM project MENELAS (Zweigenbaum et al. 94),
- the MediTAS system for the analysis of cytopathological reports (Pietrzyk 93).

A related topic is the definition of terminological knowledge for the semantic modelling of medical index systems like SNOMED (Campbell & Musen 92, Ingenerf 93). A more detailed overview of the field of medical language processing can be found in (Schröder 93b, 94).

It is striking that most of the projects in the area of medical language processing use the knowledge representation language *Conceptual Graphs* (Sowa 84, 91). Conceptual Graphs are a logic-based representation formalism that allows the representation of language related knowledge as well as domain oriented knowledge. An overview of applications in the medical domain can be found in (Ellis 93).

METEXA (MEdical TEXt Analysis) is a natural language processing system that covers all linguistic and knowledge processing levels, from morphogical analysis to domain-dependent inference. The METEXA system has initially been designed for the semantic analysis of radiological reports of the thorax (chest) (Schröder 92, 93a, 94). The core of the system, however, was designed to be application-independent. This could be proved with a new task, where METEXA was applied to the analysis of clinical questions ('klinische Fragestellungen'). A clinical question is formulated by the referring physician and contains information about observed symptoms and suspected diseases in a telegraphic style. It showed that only the application-dependent sources, mainly the lexicon and the domain-dependent interpretation, had to be changed, while the core of the system remained unchanged. Independent of this, however, some components have been further developed, like the reconstruction of abbreviations and the definition of selectional restrictions in semantic analysis. In this paper we describe the application of METEXA to the analysis and categorisation of clinical questions.

Cooperative Clinical Workstation

The text analysis system described here serves as one component of the Cooperative Clinical Workstation *CCW* (Wendler et al. 92a, 92b), a medical image workstation designed to act as a cooperative dialogue partner in diagnostic radiology. The CCW system can automatically select relevant information (e.g., from current and previous examinations) and generate a meaningful and appropriate image arrangement on the display screen. A snapshot of a working session with CCW is shown in the next picture:

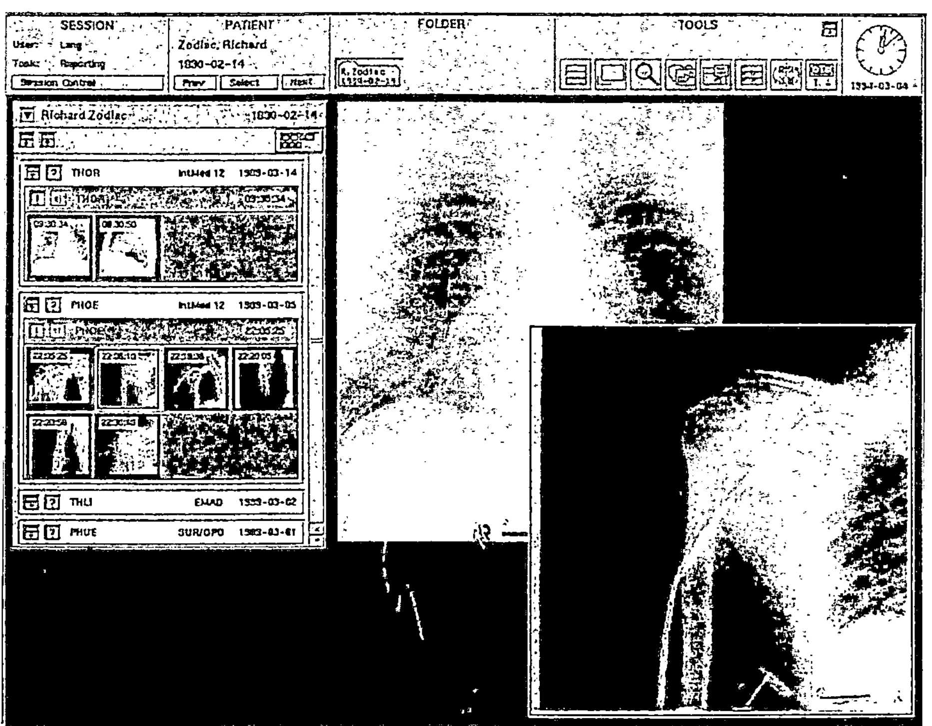

The cooperative system response is based on explicit (formalized and computer-accessable) models of diagnostic information requirements. These models are context dependent and take into account that diagnostic information needs vary with radiological work procedures, workstation users, and patient cases. From clinical knowledge acquisition it became clear that the proposed cooperative actions can be realized only if sufficient sources of evidence (knowledge, facts, data) for the decision process are available. Four principle information sources can be identified:

1. The general domain model of the medical diagnostic process including knowledge about general procedures and concepts found in radiological practice,
2. task and user models defining heuristics about information requirements for specific, predefined diagnostic tasks,
3. domain status data describing the properties of all currently available radiological objects, e.g., all available information on currently existing patients, examinations, images, clinical questions, or diagnostic reports,
4. interactive data obtained from the user's input during the working session.

For the representation of these models, rule-based and object-oriented techniques were applied. The formal description of context-dependent diagnostic requirements was achieved using a rule-based representation system, the expert system shell NEXPERT/OBJECT. The main task of this component is to determine sets of *mandatory images*, *useful images*, and *images of secondary interest*. *Mandatory images* will be displayed on the screen automatically, *useful images* are preloaded but shown only on the user's request, and *images of secondary interest* are not preloaded and shown only as miniature versions in pictorial indexes.

Semantic text analysis is needed to make domain status data (point 3) formally accessible: Important data is often contained in natural language documents, like clinical questions and diagnostic reports. The natural language documents, however, exhibit the whole variety of natural language, so that the relevant information cannot be accessed immediately by formal procedures. For example, in the object REQUEST_FORM the formal properties *clinical question*, *requested examination type*, *actual disease*, *supposed diagnosis*, and *basic disease* (among others) have to be filled with data of the current examination. Some of the values can be inferred from the clinical question that was written by the referring physician, at least the category of the *clinical question*. This is the central topic of this paper: How can a value of the formal category *clinical question* be inferred from a natural language utterance?

The Task

From studying a large number of clinical request forms, 15 different categories of *clinical questions* have been identified as a first starting point. An important subset of them is listed here, together with the concept type of the category's argument:

- Verdacht_auf   [PATHO]   (suspicion_of)
- Ausschluß_von   [PATHO]   (exclusion_of)
- Suche_nach   [PATHO]   (search_for)
- Pre_op_Kontrolle   [MEDMASSNAHME]   (pre_op_control)
- Post_op_Kontrolle   [MEDMASSNAHME]   (post_op_control)
- Zustand_nach   [PATHO] or [MEDMASSNAHME] (state_after)
- Verlaufskontrolle   [DATE]   (comparing_follow-up)

When a patient is sent to the radiology department for a radiological examination, the referring physician formulates a short request in natural language called "clinical question" (the utterance, however, in most cases contains more information than only the category listed above). Here are three examples of utterances that deal with the search for metastatic nodules:

1. meningeale Infiltrate NPL-Suche
2. Colon-Ca. 1978. Leberfiliae ?
3. Tu. Nachsorge, Z.n. OL-Res. li.

For each utterance one or more of the above categories have to be determined. If several categories for one utterance can be found, the subsequent NEXPERT/OBJECT based expert system will decide what the most relevant category is. One of the most important categories in the current application is 'Verlaufskontrolle' (comparing follow-up), because in this case the new image has to be compared with former images. In many utterances the date of the former examination is stated explicitly:

4. exacerb. Emphysembronchitis, Verlaufskontrolle. i. Vergl. z. 11/88 Besserung der Infiltrate re.basal
5. Aneurysma der thorakalen Aorta, Verlaufskontrolle im Vergl. zum 10.11.89
6. Z.n. AKE 1985, jetzt Dyspnoe, Vergl. Vorbefund 4/89

These examples show that the language processing system has to be very robust, because the sublanguage has a telegraphic style using a lot of abbreviations. As a consequence, the most important processing levels for the natural language system are (for a deeper discussion see Schröder 94):

- Recognizing abbreviations, dates, and numbers,
- syntactic analysis emphasizing complex noun phrases, but without relying on correct morpho-syntactic features,
- emphasis on the semantic structure of the utterances, taking into account the underlying domain knowledge.

In general the system has to be robust against minor variations of the input, e.g. missing punctuation, or a wrong use of capital/small letters at the beginning of a sentence. A sentence boundary should be detected by syntactic means, even if there is no comma or full stop in between.

The high variety of the utterances on the verbal surface shows that the construction of a surface-independent semantic representation is already a big step towards the automatic evaluation of natural language utterances. For the semantic representation of utterances, as well as for the representation of the domain knowledge, the logic-based representation formalism *Conceptual Graphs* is used (Sowa 84, 91). In the following we will show how a Conceptual Graph is constructed from the utterance, and how the categories of clinical categories can be inferred from the semantic representation.

The METEXA System

As a consequence of the above insight that the construction of a surface-independent semantic representation is the most important milestone in the processing of an utterance, the processing consists of two phases:

Phase 1: Linguistic and knowledge-based analysis, resulting in a semantic representation (Conceptual Graph). The same utterance can have several interpretations.

Phase 2: Domain-specific interpretation of the semantic representation, resulting in another Conceptual Graph. One of the solutions of phase 1 is chosen as the starting point of phase 2. The resulting Conceptual Graph contains values that can be written into a database.

The processing components of phase 1 are independent of the specific kind of text (e.g. reports, clinical questions), and they are the core of the METEXA system (the application-dependent knowledge sources like the lexicon, however, have to be adapted to the specific application). Phase 2 depends on the special domain of the texts and on the specific purpose of the text analysis system. This phase might look very different for the processing of radiological reports or clinical questions. However, there is a deep interdependence between the two phases, because they use not only the same knowledge representation formalism, but the same type lattice and the same set of semantic relations. The concept types are used, for example, in the lexical semantics as well as in the domain-dependent rule-based inference system.

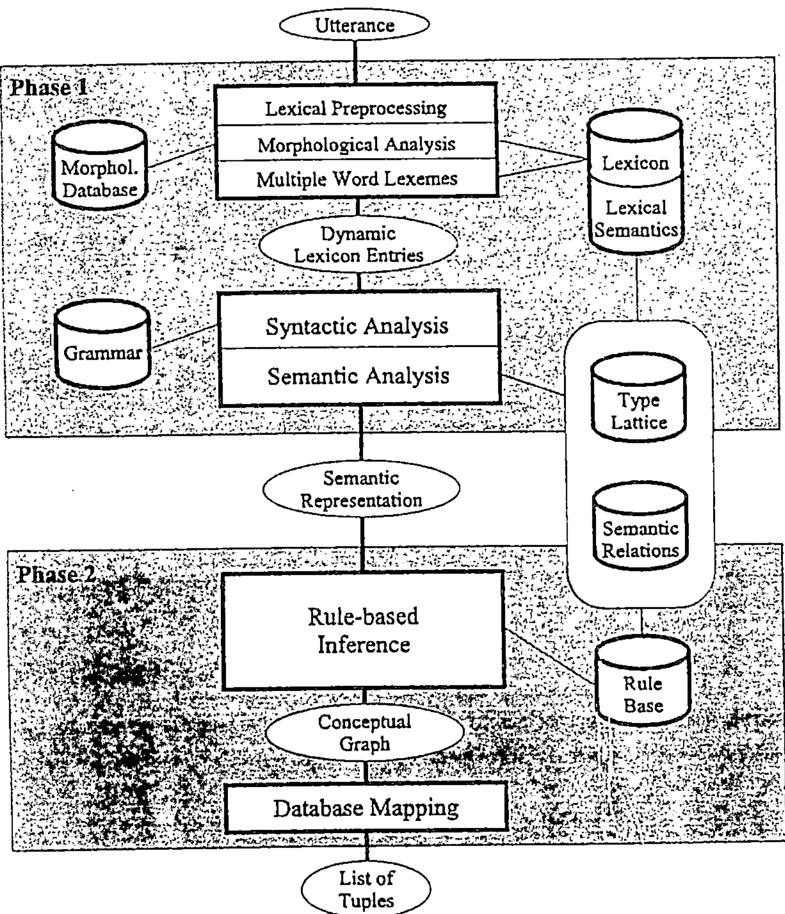

Phase 1: Analyzing natural language utterances

Natural language utterances are analyzed on several levels: on the lexical, morphological, syntactic and semantic level. A short overview of all processing components will be given, with an emphasis on the selectional restrictions in the lexical semantics.

Lexical and morphological processing

The *dynamic lexicon* is constructed, which contains the complete lexical information concerning the current input phrase. The parser works on the dynamic lexicon entries alone. This is efficient for backtracking over multiple interpretations of the input phrase.

Lexical preprocessing

Lexical preprocessing is a name for several different activities that are performed before morphological analysis and access to the lexicon.

- Detection of cardinals and ordinals.
- Detection of dates (e.g. 12.3.89, 3/89)
- Detection of uninflected multiple symbol abbreviations (e.g. i.v., V.a., Z.n.). The list of symbols is replaced by the expanded form (intravenös, Verdacht_auf, Zustand_nach).
- Detection of uninflected ambigious single symbol abbreviations (e.g. LE can stand for Laryngektomie, Lungenembolie, Lymphadenektomie, or Lupus erythematodes). Because abbreviations can be ambigious, they may not simply be replaced by an expanded form. A more sophisticated mechanism has been designed to handle ambiguity.

Morphological analysis

Inflected input words are reduced to their stem by splitting off the ending. For each ending that could be split off, the lexicon is accessed with the remaining stem. According to the syntactic category and the inflection class of the lexicon entry it can be checked whether the ending that was split off is a valid ending for that lexeme. Finally the lexical semantics is determined, and the lexical information for that input word is added to the *dynamic lexicon*. Two knowledge sources are used for morphological analysis:

- **Lexicon:** The lexicon is a stemform lexicon, i.e. each different stem can be accessed directly. For each lexeme there is a "main entry" that contains all lexical information for that lexeme (syntactic category, inflection class, morphological data, syntactic features, lexical semantics in a condensed format). The other stem entries are pointing to that main entry. The lexicon is implemented as a lexicon database on secondary storage with fast hashing access.
- **Morphological Database:** The morphological database contains the definitions of the inflection classes for nouns, verbs, and determiners. Roughly speaking, the inflection class specifies which morpho-syntactic features belong to which ending. The user doesn't have to know about the inflection classes, because the inflection class of new lexicon entries are determined "by example" during lexical acquisition. Moreover, the morphological database contains the endings tree. The endings tree specifies the possible endings in German morphology to allow efficient processing.

Multiple word lexemes

A multiple word lexeme is a sequence of words that has to be read as a semantic unit (e.g. 'große Gefäße', 'large vessels'). The single words can be inflected, so that the multiple word lexeme can be determined only after morphological analysis. Using the same technique idiomatic expressions (e.g. kein krankhafter Befund) and greco-latin expressions (e.g. Angina pectoris) can be treated. The lexical semantics of a multiple word lexeme can be an atomic concept (e.g. [ANAT: große_Gefäße]).

Syntactic analysis

The parser is a bottom-up parser embedded in Prolog (Matsumoto et al. 1983). It is similar to Definite Clause Grammars (DCGs) in Prolog, where the grammar rules are written as Prolog terms. The difference is that DCGs in Prolog have a top-down control structure, whereas BUP grammar rules are parsed bottom-up. Phrases that have been parsed successfully are recorded in a well-formed substring table. This corresponds to the chart in a chart parser. The syntactic structure of a phrase is represented by a feature structure, which is built up using unification. Up to now only the syntactic categories of the lexemes (N, V, ADJ, PREP, etc.) and the nonterminals of the grammar (NP, PP, etc.) are used as attribute names. The grammar has about 90 grammar rules and covers the syntax of complex noun phrases and adverbial phrases nearly completely. For a detailed description of the syntactic analysis see (Schröder 94).

Semantic analysis

The semantic representation of an utterance is a Conceptual Graph, where one concept is selected as the head concept. As an example, the Conceptual Graph of the utterance 'Z.n. AKE 1985' ('Zustand nach Aortenklappenersatz 1985') is shown. The concepts, consisting of a type label and an optional referent field, are drawn as boxes; the semantic relations are drawn as circles:

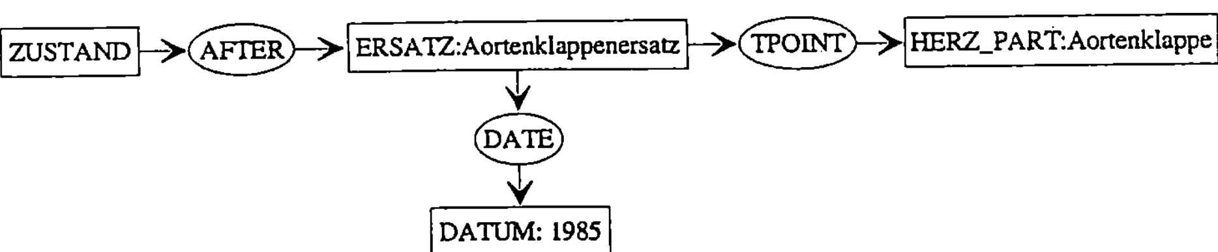

When the syntactic analysis has recognized the phrase "Zustand nach Aortenklappenersatz" as a noun phrase that is modified by a prepositional phrase, the head concepts of the two noun phrases ([ZUSTAND], [ERSATZ: Aortenklappenersatz]) are connected by a semantic relation. A list of selectional restrictions is defined with the head concept of each semantic representation. The semantic relation between the two head concepts must occur in the list of selectional restrictions of both head concepts, and the attached concepts must be compatible with one another. In this case, ERSATZ is a subtype of MEDMASSNAHME, and ZUSTAND is a subtype of EREIGNIS:

Zustand:

Head concept:	[ZUSTAND]
Selectional restriction:	[ZUSTAND]->(AFTER)->[MEDMASSNAHME]
Conceptual graph:	[ZUSTAND]

nach:
Selectional restriction: [EREIGNIS]->(AFTER)->[EREIGNIS]
Aortenklappenersatz:
Head concept: [ERSATZ:Aortenklappenersatz]
Selectional restriction: [ERSATZ]<-(AFTER)<-[EREIGNIS]
Conceptual graph: [ERSATZ:Aortenklappenersatz]->
(OBJ)->[HERZ_PART:Aortenklappe]
Zustand nach Aortenklappenersatz:
Head concept: [ZUSTAND]
Selectional restriction: [ZUSTAND]->(AFTER)->[EREIGNIS]
Conceptual graph: [ZUSTAND]->(AFTER)->
[ERSATZ:Aortenklappenersatz]->
(OBJ)->[HERZ_PART:Aortenklappe]

For the sake of clarity only one selectional restriction is listed here. There may be an arbitrary number of them (typically 10 to 30).

Lexical semantics and selectional restrictions

The semantic description of a lexeme is a conceptual graph. One concept of the graph is the head concept, which specifies the concept type of this lexeme (or phrase). At the current stage of the system, the following kinds of conceptual graphs are used for lexical semantics:

Hinweis   [HINWEIS]
Tumor   [PATHO: Tumor]
Frakturhinweis   [HINWEIS]->(THEME)->[PATHO: Fraktur]
Oberlappenresektion [OP_MASSNAHME: Resektion]->(OBJ)->
[LUNGE_PART: Oberlappen]
Leberfiliae   [PATHO: Filiae]<-(PATHO)<-[ORGAN: Leber]

The first concept is always the head concept. For compound words, it usually describes the concept type of the last subword. In general, an arbitrary complex conceptual graph can be used to describe the lexical semantics.

For the compositional construction of a semantic representation three kinds of information are needed: the syntactic structure, the lexical semantics of a subphrase, and the corresponding set of selectional restrictions. Selectional restrictions specify the possible contextual semantic relations of a lexeme. As an example,

[ANAT]->(PATHO)->[PATHO]

specifies that an anatomical entity can be connected to a pathological alteration via the relation PATHO ("has pathological alteration"). A list of these relations is attached to every iexeme. To state it precisely: The list of relations specifies which relations are *allowed* for this lexeme, and what the concept type of the connected concept is. (The mechanism of selectional restrictions has been inspired by Pazienza & Velardi 87).

The basic idea is that the list of selectional restrictions is attached to every single lexeme. Viewed this way, the selectional restrictions are a part of the lexicon. As this would be very inefficient (a lot of information had to be duplicated), selectional restrictions can be inherited from concept types higher up in the hierarchy:

- **Inherited selectional restrictions.** For each concept type an arbitrary number of selectional restrictions can be specified. They are inherited by all its subtypes. Examples:

   [ANAT]->(PATHO)->[PATHO]

   [EREIGNIS]->(AFTER)->[EREIGNIS]

   The inherited relations are evaluated when a lexicon entry is retrieved. The system selects those selectional restrictions whose first concept type is a supertype of the lexical head concept type.

- **Direct selectional restrictions.** Selectional restrictions can be defined directly at the lexicon entry. They are valid for this lexicon entry only. If a direct selectional restriction is defined, it overrides an inherited selectional restriction for the same semantic relation. This way exceptions can be described easily.

The direct selectional restrictions are defined together with the lexical semantics of a lexeme. For example, the following restrictions are listed with the lexeme "Hinweis":

   [HINWEIS]:

   [HINWEIS]->(THEME)->[PATHO]

   [HINWEIS]->(THEME)->[ANAT]

The left concept type of the selectional restriction must always be the same as the head concept type, or a subtype of it. The second possibility is used for words with a different semantics in different contexts, e.g. the attribute 'normal' is a report status with respect to anatomical entities, and it is a gradual specification with respect to spatial extensions. Both NORMALSTATUS and GRAD_SPEZ are subtypes of ATTRIBUTE (BFST stands for "Befundstatus", QSPEC for "quantitative specification"):

   [ATTRIBUTE: normal]:

   [NORMALSTATUS]->(BFST)->[ANAT]

   [GRAD_SPEZ]->(QSPEC)->[AUSDEHNUNG]

Words that correspond to semantic relations, like prepositions, have a different lexical semantics. This is illustrated with the preposition 'auf':

   auf: RELATION:

   [HINWEIS]->(THEME)->[PATHO]

   [HINWEIS]->(THEME)->[VORLIEGEN]

The marker 'RELATION' indicates that this word is mapped to a semantic relation and not to a head concept. The list of selectional restrictions specifies the possible relations.

Phase 2: Domain-dependent interpretation

The domain-dependent interpretation is the second phase of processing (see the architecture diagram). It starts with the semantic interpretation of an utterance and delivers a Conceptual Graph as the result. The kind of interpretation in phase 2 depends on the specific application and the specific task. At the current state of the system, the task is the classification of clinical questions. Every clinical question has to be mapped to one or several of 15 categories of clinical questions. Some of the clinical questions that occur most frequently have been listed above. A rule-based inference mechanism is used for the classification.

Rule-based inference

A Prolog-like resolution method for Conceptual Graphs has been implemented according to (Fargues et al. 1986). The basic idea of this inference engine is very similar to Prolog. There is a knowledge base, which consists of rules and facts (facts are special cases of rules, like in Prolog). The antecedents and the consequence of the rules can be arbitrary complex Conceptual Graphs:

IF <Conceptual Graph 1> AND
<Conceptual Graph 2> ...
<Conceptual Graph n> AND
THEN <Conceptual Graph> .

The Conceptual Graphs that describe the semantics of the utterance are the facts. The inference engine works goal-driven: An initial goal is given, and an inference path is constructed via backward chaining, until the goal can be proved from the facts (or not). Multiple solutions are found via backtracking. A solution is a specialization (instantiation or specialization of a type) of the initial goal. Example:

Query: [KLIN_FRAGESTELLUNG]->(THEME)->[UNIV].
Result: [KLIN_FRAGESTELLUNG: Suche_nach]->(THEME)->
[PATHO: Metastasen].

The relevant values are finally extracted from the Conceptual Graph. The list of tuples ([Suche_nach, Metastasen]) is written to the database of the Clinical Workstation.

Interpretation of clinical questions

The rule base consists of about 60 rules. The antecedents of the rules describe semantic patterns of the verbal surface. The consequence of a rule maps the pattern to a value of the concept type KLIN_FRAGESTELLUNG (clinical question) and an argument that further describes the clinical question (e.g. a value of PATHO). Here are three examples of rules that deal with the search for a pathological alteration:

Rule SEARCH1:
IF [SUCHE]->(THEME)->[PATHO:_x].
THEN [KLIN_FRAGESTELLUNG: Suche_nach]->(THEME)->[PATHO:_x].
Rule SEARCH3:
IF [INTERROGATIV: ?]->(MOD)->[PATHO:Filiae].
THEN [KLIN_FRAGESTELLUNG: Suche_nach]->(THEME)->
[PATHO:Metastasen].
Rule SEARCH4:
IF [MEDMASSNAHME: Tumornachsorge].
THEN [KLIN_FRAGESTELLUNG: Suche_nach]->(THEME)->
[PATHO:Metastasen].

In rule SEARCH1, the instance of the pathological alteration, denoted by the variable x, is passed through to the consequence. Rule SEARCH3 matches "Filiae" followed by a question mark, and rule SEARCH4 matches exactly the lexeme 'Tumornachsorge'. We will now show how the example utterances 1-3 (see above) are interpreted:

Example 1: meningeale Infiltrate NPL-Suche

  [PATHO: Infiltrat]->(PATTR)->[PATTRIBUT: meningeal].

  [SUCHE]->(THEME)->[PATHO: Neoplasma].

 Result of the rule application:

  [KLIN_FRAGESTELLUNG: Suche_nach]->(THEME)->[PATHO: Neoplasma].

The solution is found by rule SEARCH1 with the semantic pattern [SUCHE]->(THEME)->[PATHO:_x].

Example 2: Colon-Ca. 1978. Leberfiliae ?

  [PATHO: Karzinom]-

    (TPOINT)->[DATUM: 1978]

    (PATHO)<-[ANAT: Colon],.

  [PATHO: Filiae]-

    (MOD)<-[INTERROGATIV: ?]

    (PATHO)<-[ORGAN: Leber],.

 Results of the rule application:

  [KLIN_FRAGESTELLUNG: Suche_nach]->(THEME)->[PATHO: Metastasen].

  [KLIN_FRAGESTELLUNG: Abklaerung_von]->(THEME)->[PATHO: Filiae].

The pattern [INTERROGATIV: ?]->(MOD)->[PATHO:Filiae] matches the antecedent of rule SEARCH3, the second solution is found by another rule matching the same pattern.

Example 3: Tu. Nachsorge, Z.n. OL-Res. li.

  [MEDMASSNAHME: Tumornachsorge].

  [ZUSTAND]->(AFTER)->[OP_MASSNAHME: Resektion]-

    (LOC)->[SEITE: links]

    (OBJ)->[LUNGE_PART: Oberlappen],.

 Results of the rule application:

  [KLIN_FRAGESTELLUNG: Suche_nach]->(THEME)->[PATHO: Metastasen].

  [KLIN_FRAGESTELLUNG: Post_op_Kontrolle]->(THEME)->

            [OP_MASSNAHME: Resektion].

  [KLIN_FRAGESTELLUNG: Zustand_nach]->(THEME)->

            [OP_MASSNAHME: Resektion].

Three categories can be found for the whole utterance. The first solution is found by the application of rule SEARCH4. The categories 'Post_op_Kontrolle' and 'Zustand_nach' are found by other rules that match the pattern

 [ZUSTAND]->(AFTER)->[OP_MASSNAHME: Resektion].

For each category of a clinical question there exists a set of rules (typically 1 to 10 at the moment) that extracts the relevant values from the semantic representation of the utterance. Here is another example of the very important category 'Verlaufskontrolle' (comparing follow-up):

Example 4: exacerb. Emphysembronchitis, Verlaufskontrolle. i. Vergl. z. 11/88 Besserung
     der Infiltrate re.basal

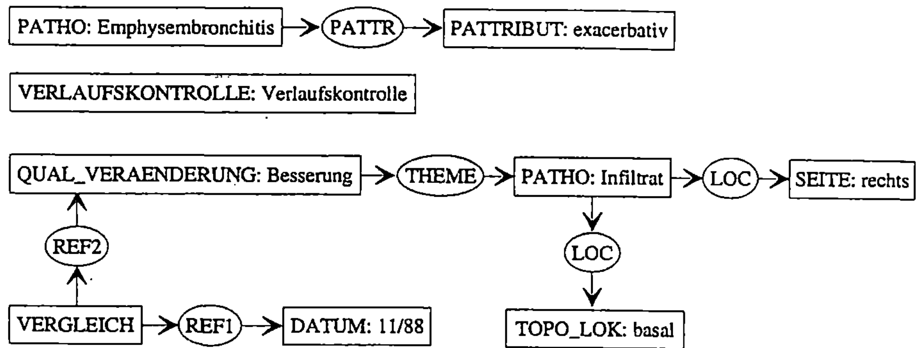

Result of the rule application:

[KLIN_FRAGESTELLUNG: Verlaufskontrolle]->(THEME)->[DATUM: 11/88].

The result is delivered by rule COMPARE1:

IF   [QUAL_VERAENDERUNG]<-(REF2)<-[VERGLEICH]->(REF1)-> [DATUM:_x].

THEN [KLIN_FRAGESTELLUNG: Verlaufskontrolle]->(THEME)->[DATUM:_x].

Filling the Schema

The information contained in the clinical question must be mapped to a knowledge structure to be directly accessable by further decision procedures. A *schema* (or *frame*) has been designed to capture the basic facts about an examination. The schema has the syntactic form of a Conceptual Graph (see Sowa 84):

[RAD_UNTERSUCHUNG]-	(radiological examination)
(FGS)->[FRAGESTELLUNGSTYP]	(category of the clinical question)
(ANT)->[ANAT]	(anatomical entity)
(PAT)->[PATHO]	(pathological alteration)
(MSN)->[MEDMASSNAHME]	(medical treatment)
(LAT)->[SEITE]	(laterality)
(TMP)->[ZEITANGABE]	(event with time information)
(VGL)->[VERGLEICH],.	(comparison)

The slots in the schema are filled with information from the utterance. The information is obtained by a query to the rule-based interpreter. In the case that there are no rules defined the operation is a simple projection. Example:

215207 Z.n. Nephrektomie li. 4/87. Staging

The leading number is a unique identification number for the examination. It is used as the referent in the instance of a schema.

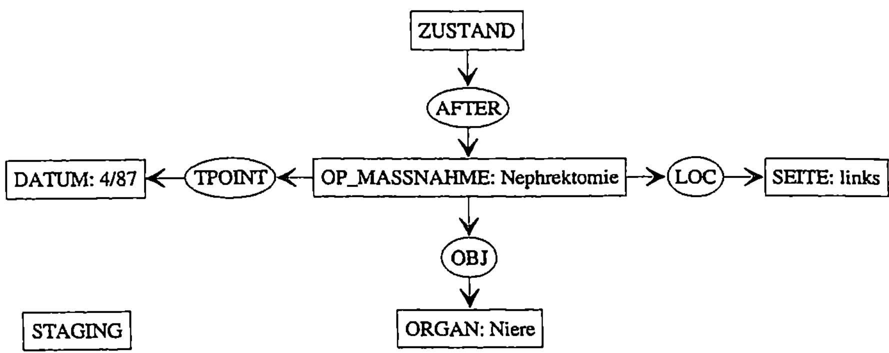

Which anatomical entity is mentioned?

    Query: [ANAT].

    Result: [ORGAN: Niere].

Is there a timepoint of an event mentioned?

    Query: [ZEITANGABE]<-(TPOINT)<-[EREIGNIS].

    Result: [DATUM: 4/87]<-(TPOINT)<-[OP_MASSNAHME: Nephrektomie]

The results can be joined to the schema via predefined concept types (e.g. ANAT, ZEITANGABE):

    [RAD_UNTERSUCHUNG: 215207]-

        (FGS)->[FRAGESTELLUNGSTYP: Staging]

        (ANT)->[ORGAN: Niere]

        (PAT)->[PATHO]

        (MSN)->[OP_MASSNAHME: Nephrektomie]

        (LAT)->[SEITE: links]

        (TMP)->[DATUM: 4/87]<-(TPOINT)<-[OP_MASSNAHME: Nephrektomie]

        (VGL)->[VERGLEICH],.

This schema contains information that is useful for automatic image selection and the order of image presentation. It is planned that the information can be accessed by the expert system that determines the currently focussed images.

Coupling METEXA and the Clinical Workstation

The text analysis system METEXA and the Cooperative Clinical Workstation CCW are two separate processes, which run on a cluster of UNIX workstations (SUN SparcStation):

- METEXA is implemented in *Prolog by BIM*. The system can be run interactively or in batch mode. In the current application the system is a background process that takes a string as its input and delivers a list of attribute values as its output.
- CCW is implemented in *Objective C* and *NEXPERT/OBJECT*. It is a graphical user interface that gets its input from an underlying information system (image and document database).

The two processes are coupled via a remote procedure call (rpc): As soon as the database attribute 'clinical question' is filled with the string of the natural language utterance, a remote procedure call is sent to the text analysis system. After a few seconds (usually 3-5) the attribute values are sent back to the database, where they are written into another database attribute. They can then be accessed by the subsequent image selection component.

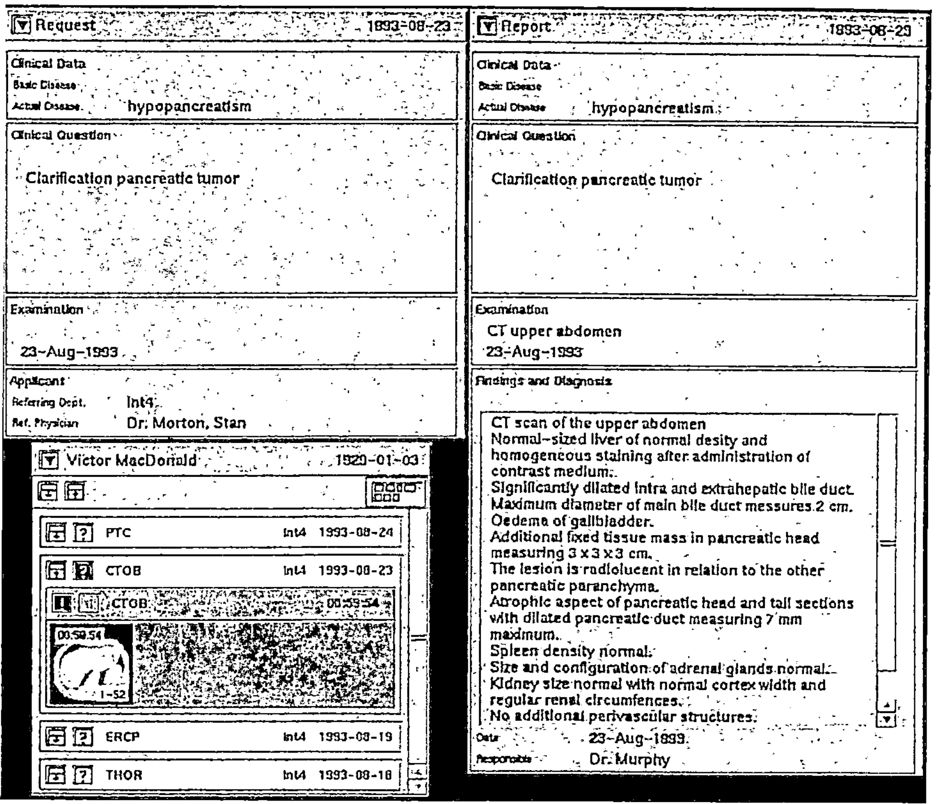

The picture shows a snapshot of the CCW graphical interface. On the left is a window with the request containing the clinical question, the referring physician and some other information. On the right is window that shows the complete radiological report after it has been dictated by the radiologist.

Conclusion

METEXA is a natural language processing system that performs a useful task in a practical application: It extracts relevant information from natural language documents. Without the semantic processing of the text the information would not be directly accessible. Although the quality and detail of the semantic representation may in some respects not yet meet the requirement of a theory of language, the results are good enough to deliver useful information in the current application.

There is an important difference between many research-oriented systems and this application-oriented system: Many research-oriented systems focus on the treatment of difficult phenomena of language that can be illustrated by a few example sentences. In the current application most single utterances are relatively easy to interprete, but there are thousands of utterances that have to be treated. The breadth of variations on all linguistic levels is enormous. The challenge is to find knowledge structures and processing methods that can handle a wide variety of utterance variations. The techniques we have designed have proved to be a good starting point in that direction, although a lot needs to be done.

In the future the coverage of the system will be broadened, especially the lexicon has to be enhanced. A very important feature is the robustness of the system: At the current state, the processing of an utterance stops when the system encounters an unknown word. This is not acceptable for everyday-use: In most cases the utterance contains enough information so that the result is already useful. Other strategies concerning unknown words are context-sensitive expectations ('Verdacht auf ...' expects a pathological alteration), or the morpho-semantic analysis of compound words ('...-itis' is a pathological alteration, independent of what the beginning of the word is). Other work will focus on the improvement of the classification of clinical questions. This demands a close cooperation with the clinical expert.

References

Bernauer, J., and Goldberg, H.: Compositional classification based on Conceptual Graphs. In: Andreassen, S. et al. (eds.): *Artificial Intelligence in Medicine*. IOS Press, 1993, pp. 348-359.

Baud, R. H., Rassinoux, A.-M., and Scherrer, J.-R.: Natural Language Processing and Semantical Representation of Medical Texts. *Methods of Information in Medicine* 31, pp. 117-125, 1992.

Borst, F., Lyman, M., Nhan, N.T., Tick, L.J., Sager, N., and Scherrer, J.-R.: TEXTINFO: A tool for automatic determination of patient clinical profiles using text analysis. In: Clayton, P.D. (ed.): *Assessing the Value of Medical Informatics. Fifteenth Annual Symposium on Computer Applications in Medical Care*. McGraw-Hill, New York, 1991, pp. 63-67.

Cavazza, M., Dore, L., and Zweigenbaum, P.: Model-based natural language understanding in medicine. In: Lun, K.C. et al. (eds.): *Proceedings of MEDINFO 92*, Elsevier Science Publ. (North Holland), pp. 1356-1361.

Campbell, K.E., and Musen, M.A.: Representation of clinical data using SNOMED III and Conceptual Graphs. In: *The 16th Annual Symposium on Computer Application in Medical Care*. Washington D.C., 1992.

Ellis, G.: Managing large databases of complex medical knowledge using Conceptual Graphs. In: Hovenga, J.S., and Whymark, G.K. (eds.): *Proceedings of the National Health Conference. Health Informatics Society of Australia*. Brisbane, Queensland, Australia, ISBN 0-646-14746-3. August 1993.

Ingenerf, J.: *Benutzeranpaßbare semantische Sprachanalyse und Begriffsrepräsentation für die medizinische Dokumentation*. Sankt Augustin: Infix, 1993 (DISKI 43), ISBN 3-929037-43-2.

Matsumoto, Yuji; Tanaka, Hozumi; Hirakawa, Hideki; Miyoshi, Hideo; and Yasukawa, Hideki: BUP: A bottom-up parser embedded in Prolog. *New Generation Computing*, 1, pp. 145–158, 1983.

Pazienza, M. T., and Velardi, P.: A structured representation of word-senses for semantic analysis. *Proceedings of the European ACL* 1987, pp. 249-257.

Pietrzyk, P. M.: Literal meaning of sentences from medical free text. In: Reichert, A., et al. (eds.): *Proceedings of MIE 93, Eleventh International Congress of the European Federation for Medical Informatics*. Freund Publishing House Ltd., London, 1993, pp. 64-67.

Sager, N., Friedman, C., and Lyman, M. S.: *Medical Language Processing: Computer Management of Narrative Data*. Addison-Wesley, Reading (MA), 1987.

Sager, N., Lyman, N., Nhan, N.T., Tick, L.J., Borst, F., and Scherrer, J.-R.: Clinical knowledge bases from natural language patient documents. In: Lun, K.C. et al. (eds.): *Proceedings of MEDINFO 92*, Elsevier Science Publ. (North Holland), pp. 1375-1381.

Schröder, M.: Knowledge-based Processing of Medical Language: A Language Engineering Approach. In: *Proceedings of the 16th German AI-Conference (GWAI-92)*, Springer Lecture Notes on AI, Vol. 671, Springer-Verlag, 1992, pp. 221-234.

Schröder, M.: Knowledge-based analysis of radiological reports using Conceptual Graphs. In: Pfeiffer, H.D., and Nagle, T.E. (eds.): *Conceptual Structures: Theory and Implementation*. Lecture Notes in Artificial Intelligence 754. Springer-Verlag, Berlin, 1993a (Proceedings of the 7th Annual Workshop on Conceptual Graphs, Las Cruces, New Mexico (USA), July 1992, pp. 213-222).

Schröder, M.: Sprachverarbeitung in der Medizin – Anwendungen und Methoden. *Künstliche Intelligenz KI* 3/1993b (September), pp. 50-56.

Schröder, M.: *Erwartungsgestützte Analyse medizinischer Befundungstexte – Ein wissensbasiertes Modell zur Sprachverarbeitung*. „infix"-Verlag, Sankt Augustin, DISKI 54, ISBN 3-929037-54-8, 1994. (Dissertation, Universität Hamburg, Fachbereich Informatik, 1993.)

Sowa, J.F.: *Conceptual Structures: Information Processing in Mind and Machine*. Addison-Wesley, Reading (MA), 1984.

Sowa, J.F.: Towards the expressive power of natural language. In: Sowa, J.F. (ed.): *Principles of Semantic Networks: Explorations in the Representation of Knowledge*. Morgan Kaufmann Publishers, San Mateo (CA), 1991, pp. 157-189.

Wendler, Th., Mönnich, K.J., and Schmidt, J.: Digital Image Workstations. In: Osteaux, M. (ed.): *Hospital Integrated Picture Archiving and Communication Systems – A Second Generation PACS Concept*. Springer-Verlag, Berlin, 1992a, pp. 173-210.

Wendler, Th., Grewer, R., Mönnich, K.J., Schmidt, J., and Svensson, H.: Cooperative Image Workstation Based on Explicit Models of Diagnostic Information Requirements. *Journal of Digital Imaging*, Vol 5, No 4, November 1992b, pp. 230-241.

Zweigenbaum, P., and Consortium MENELAS: MENELAS: an access system for medical records using natural language. *Computer Methods and Programs in Biomedicine*, 1994 (to appear).

Komplexitätsbeherrschung durch den Einsatz wissensbasierter Systeme
Beispiele erfolgreicher Expertensystem-Projekte in der Mercedes-Benz AG

Peter Mertens, Mercedes-Benz AG, 70322 Stuttgart

Die Qualität von Produktion und Produkt und die Geschwindigkeit der Produktentwicklung sind zunehmend entscheidende Erfolgsfaktoren im internationalen Wettbewerb. Nicht mehr die Großen fressen die Kleinen, vielmehr werden die Langsamen von den Schnellen gefressen. Vor diesem Hintergrund kommt dem Produktionsfaktor Wissen eine entsprechend große Bedeutung zu. Expertensysteme gewinnen somit in der industriellen Fertigung und hier besonders durch die zunehmende Automatisierung und Vernetzung von Fertigungsanlagen an Bedeutung, wenn es darum geht, die ohnehin oft überproportional belasteten Fachkräfte von Routinearbeiten zu entlasten.

Auswahl von Expertensystem-Projekten

Trotz der zunehmenden Bedeutung wissensbasierter Systeme bedarf die Auswahl von geeigneten Anwendungsfeldern und leistungsfähigen Software-Werkzeugen einer systematischen Analyse der Problemstrukturen. Entscheidungen für den Einsatz von Expertensystemen müssen aufgrund objektiver Erfolgsfaktoren getroffen werden und erfordern eine sehr detaillierte Projektplanung sowie eine ganzheitliche, objektive Wirtschaftlichkeitsbetrachtung.

Im folgenden werden vier Expertensystem-Projekte beschrieben, die sich derzeit im serien- oder pilothaften Einsatz befinden. Alle vier Systeme tragen dazu bei, in anspruchsvollen Planungs- und/oder Fertigungsprozessen die Komplexität zu beherrschen und Abläufe und Prozesse zu optimieren.

Ziehteil-Auslegungs-System (ZAS)

Hohe Anforderungen an Form und Qualität von Fahrzeugaußenhautteilen erfordern eine frühzeitige Integration von Ziehbarkeitsinformationen bereits in der Gestaltungsphase. Entsprechende Iterationsschleifen zur Korrektur und Anpassung der Bauteilegeometrie aufgrund von in der Erprobung auftretenden Qualitätsmängeln sollten weitestgehend vermieden werden (Bild 1)

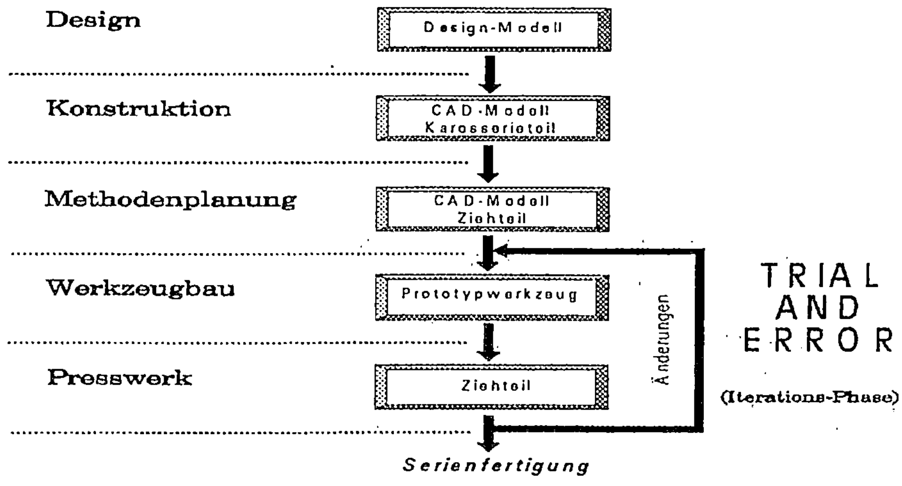

Bild 1: Ziehteilauslegung mit "späten Änderungsschleifen" [Fickenscher '93] [1]

Der Einsatz von spezifischen Simulationsprogrammen in der Iterationsphase hat bereits eine erhebliche Reduktion von Kosten und Zeit bewirkt, doch erfordern diese Programme noch ein erhebliches Sachwissen und entsprechende EDV-Erfahrung, so daß der Wunsch nach einer wissensbasierten Unterstützung in dem Projekt ZAS (Ziehteil-Auslegungs-System) realisiert wurde. Grundlage bildet dabei einerseits ein Expertensystem, das über das Erfahrungswissen der Methodenplaner und Werkzeugmacher verfügt und andererseits eine Datenbank, in der die Geometrieinformationen schon hergestellter Ziehteile abgelegt sind. Auf diese Datenbank greift das Expertensystem bei Bedarf zu.

Das Expertensystem unterstützt den Methodenplaner dabei nun in allen Phasen des Prozesses der Ziehteilauslegung durch geeignete Funktionen. Dazu muß es in der Lage sein, die Ausgangsgeometrie des Ziehteils, insbesondere in kritischen Bereichen (z. B. Einprägungen), anhand von geometrischen Kennwerten zu untersuchen. Auf dieser Untersuchung aufbauend sollen dann vom Expertensystem Aussagen zur Herstellbarkeit der Geometrie gemacht werden. Nach einer entsprechenden Anpassung der Geometrie durch den Methodenplaner kann dann das System erneut angewendet werden, bis schließlich keine Änderungen mehr notwendig sind. Ziel der Systemanwendung ist es, daß der Werkzeugbau eine schon nahezu optimale Ziehteilgeometrie zur Erstellung des Ziehwerkzeuges erhält (Bild 2).

1) *Fickenscher, O.: Beitrag zur Entwicklung eines Expertensystems zur Analyse von Karosserieziehteilen .*
1993 Diplomarbeit Verfahrensentwicklung Sindelfingen, Abteilung VCU

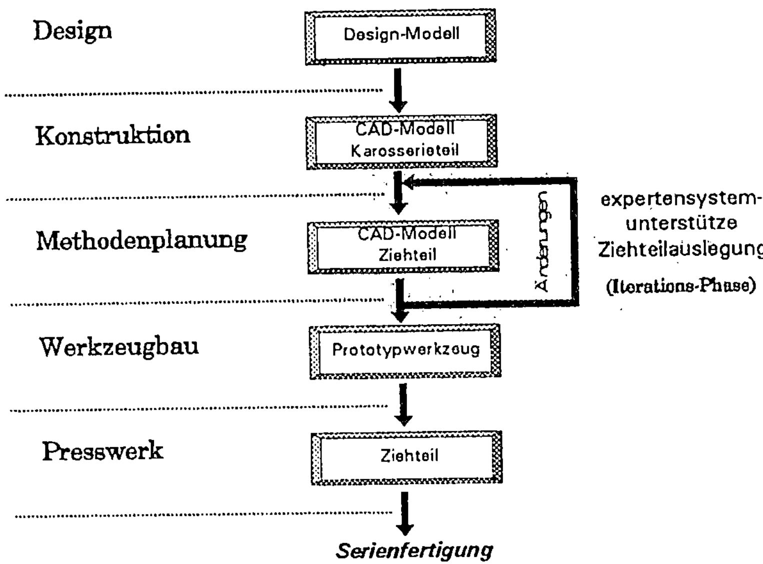

Bild 2: Ziehteilauslegung mit "frühen" Änderungsschleifen [Fickenscher '93]

Abgesehen von der Optimierung von Kosten und Durchlaufzeiten für die Ziehteilauslegung kann durch die dauerhafte Speicherung und Verfügbarkeit des sensiblen know how auch eine Erleichterung der Einarbeitung neuer Mitarbeiter erfolgen. Die Gesamtzielsetzung des ZAS-Systems integriert zusätzlich die in Bild 3 dargestellten Funktionalitäten.

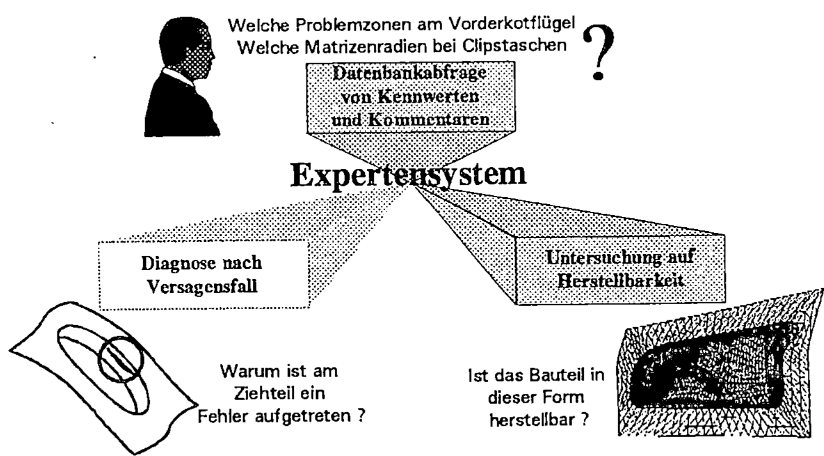

Bild 3: Problemzonen und Bauteilversagensanalyse mit ZAS [Fickenscher '93]

Der prinzipielle Aufbau des Systems und die Integration der verschiedenen Kommunikationsmodule wird in Bild 4 dargestellt. Das System wurde auf einem Großrechner unter MVS entwickelt und auf Workstationebene unter UNIX portiert, als Expertensystem-Entwicklungswerkzeug wurde Aion DS verwendet.

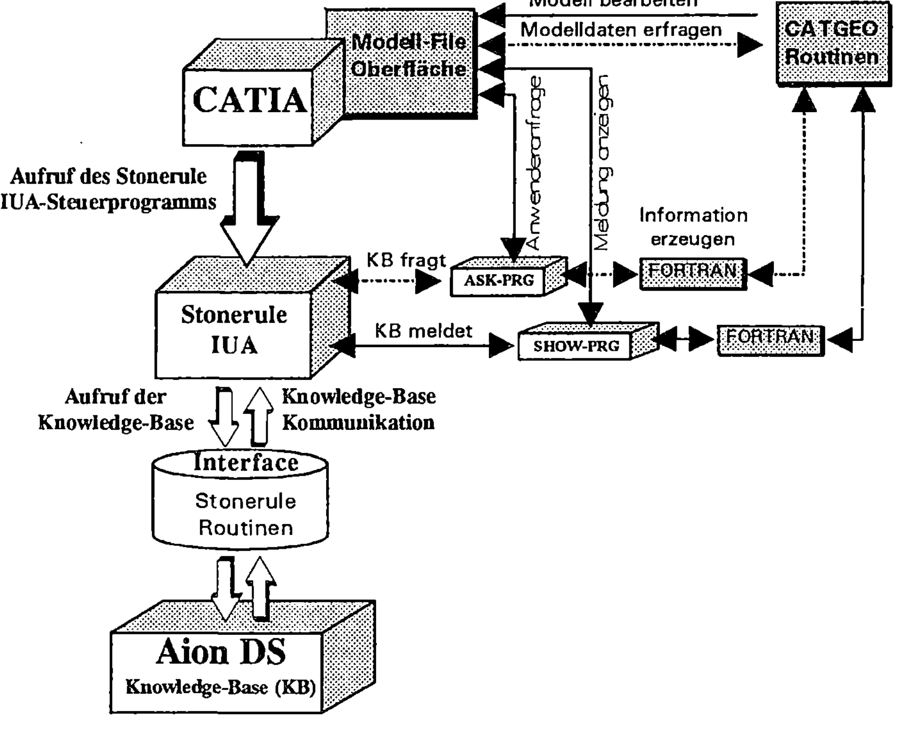

Bild 4: Systemtechnischer Aufbau von ZAS [Fickenscher '93]

Im Zusammenhang mit dem Ziehteilauslegungssystem wird CATIA derart eingesetzt, daß es quasi die Basisplattform für das gesamte System bildet. So erfolgt sowohl der Aufruf des Expertensystems, als auch die nachfolgende Kommunikation mit dem Benutzer ausschließlich aus der CATIA-Umgebung und zwar unter Verwendung der dafür intern vorhandenen Schnittstelle sowie zusätzlicher Schnittstellensoftware (Bild 4).

Während der Systemausführung wird dabei die Kontrolle über den Programmablauf an das Expertensystem abgegeben und von diesem das weitere Geschehen bestimmt. Die bestehende CATIA-Sitzung bleibt jedoch im Hintergrund ebenfalls erhalten und wird bei allen Ein-/Ausgabevorgängen des Benutzers aktiviert, d. h. sie wird zur Anwenderkommunikation herangezogen. Für den Benutzer erscheint es daher nach dem Aufruf des Expertensystems, als ob nach wie vor CATIA für die Programmsteuerung verantwortlich wäre.

Ferner erfolgt über CATIA aber auch die für das Ziehteilauslegungssystem notwendige Darstellung des zu untersuchenden Bauteils. Hierdurch können die in Verbindung mit dem Bauteil notwendigen Benutzereingaben (z. B. die Wahl der Problemzone) unter direkter Bezugnahme auf das Bauteil selbst vorgenommen werden. Das Expertensystem greift dabei auch für diese Eingaben auf CATIA zurück, indem es die von CATIA dazu bereitgestellten Funktionalitäten über Unterprogramme aufruft und mittels diesen das CATIA-Modell anspricht.

Das Ziehteilauslegungssystem befindet sich derzeit in der pilothaften Erprobung. Ziel dabei ist es, dieses System bei der Pkw-Konstruktion, der Methoden-Planung, der Umform-Simulation, der Werkzeuginbetriebnahme sowie der Blechteil-abpressung im Sinne einer Erfahrungsverbesserung einzusetzen.

DAX - Diagnose von Automatikgetriebeschaltplatten mit einem Expertensystem

Das Automatikgetriebe bei Mercedes-Benz zeichnet sich u. a. durch einen besonders hohen Schaltkomfort aus. Die erforderlichen Schaltvorgänge werden von sogenannten Schaltplatten gesteuert. Die Schaltplatten arbeiten hydraulisch und steuern aufgrund von Eingangsgrößen wie Fahrgeschwindigkeit, Gangstufe etc. die Bremsbänder und Kupplungen des automatischen Getriebes. Um die hohen Qualitätsanforderungen zu erreichen, wird jede Schaltplatte vor ihrem Einbau ins Getriebe an einem speziellen Prüfstand getestet. Bei diesem Test werden alle Fahrsituationen simuliert und die Ausgangsgrößen (hydraulische Drücke) der Schaltplatte mit Sollgrößen verglichen. Bei signifikanten Abweichungen wird ein Prüfprotokoll ausgedruckt, anhand dessen der Prüfer entscheidet, ob die Platte in die Nacharbeit muß (Bild 5).

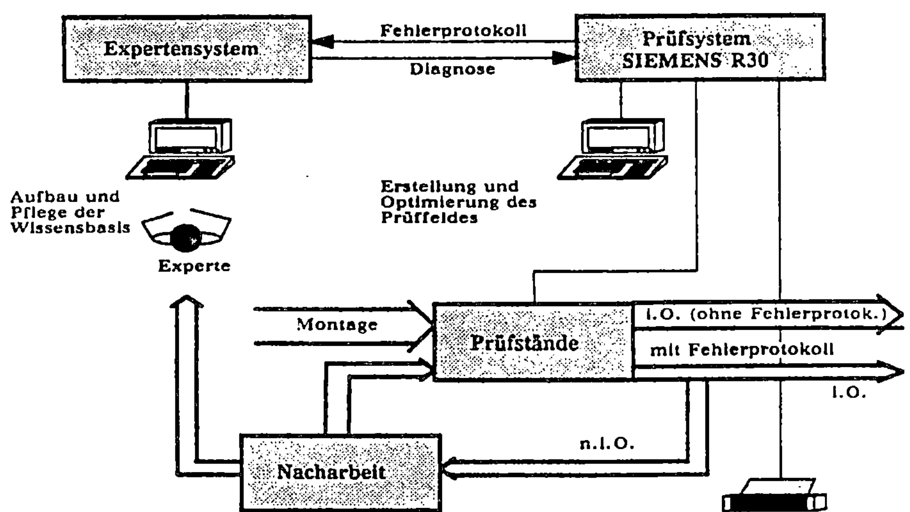

Bild 5: Regelkreis zur Einbindung von Dax ins Prüffeld

Die Diagnose der Schaltplatte ist aus folgenden Gründen schwierig:
- oftmals lange Prüfprotokolle
- sehr viele Kombinationsmöglichkeiten bei Druckabweichungen
- steigende Variantenvielfalt.

Ziel des Expertensystems DAX war es, die Diagnose von Fehlern aufgrund der Druckabweichungen beim Prüflauf durchzuführen. Dadurch sollen der Prüfer am Prüfstand und der Nacharbeiter unterstützt werden. Durch die maschinell erfaßten Diagnosen können Schwachstellenanalysen durchgeführt werden. Als Projektziele wurden definiert:
- Unterstützung der Prüfer und Nacharbeiter bei der Fehlerdiagnose
- Schwachstellenanalyse von Schaltplattenfehlern
- Erfahrungsaufbau für neue Schaltplattengeneration.

Der Ansatz eines wissensbasierten Systems wurde gewählt, da klassische Ansätze bei der Vielzahl von Prüfschritten, Diagnosen und deren kombinatorischen Abhängigkeiten nicht verwaltbar gewesen wären.

Unter den wissensbasierten Ansätzen gibt es die Alternativen modellbasierte oder regelbasierte Diagnose. Der modellbasierte Ansatz ist aus heutiger Sicht durch die hohe Komplexität der Schaltplatte, die bis zu 200 Einzelteile enthält, nicht effizient einsetzbar. Ein Ansatz mit Regeln, die Druckabweichungen als Symptome und Schaltplattenfehler als Diagnosen miteinander verbinden, ist wesentlich schneller und effizienter zu realisieren. Regeln haben beispielsweise die Form: "Wenn Abweichung in Schritt 93 B2, dann verdächtige Kommandoschieber K2".

Die Integration erfolgte durch eine Online-Kopplung (über DUST 3964R) des Expertensystem-PC's mit dem Prozeßrechner R30, der den Prüflauf am Prüfstand steuert (Bild 6):

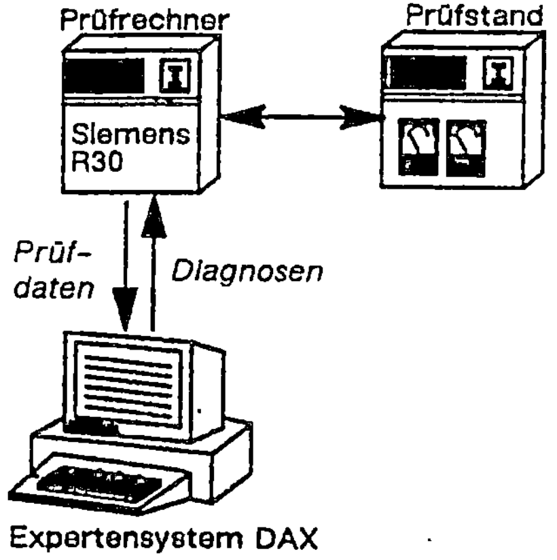

Bild 6: Vernetzung von Prüfstand und DAX

Das Expertensystem wurde mit dem Expertensystem-Tool MED2 entwickelt, das speziell für heuristische Diagnoseprobleme geeignet ist. Der Anwender in der Produktion ist in der Lage, mit diesem Tool selbständig die Wissensbasis zu pflegen.

Mit dem Ziel einer schnelleren Diagnose und einem kostengünstigen Einsatz an den anderen Prüfständen wurde ein Regelcompiler zur Transformation der Wissensbasis in ein C-Programm entwickelt. Das so erzeugbare C-Programm benötigt noch Diagnosezeiten von unter 3 Sekunden. Damit ist es möglich, mit zwei PC-386SX alle drei Prüfstände online zu bedienen. Das Tool MED2 wird nur noch für die Wissensbasispflege eingesetzt. Mit dieser Konfiguration ist das System seit 7/91 erfolgreich im Einsatz.

ESPANDA - Expertensystem zur Zerspandatenberatung [2]

Das Expertensystem ESPANDA wurde von der inpro Berlin in Zusammenarbeit mit Mercedes-Benz, Volkswagen, Siemens, Krupp und Gühring entwickelt und von dem Softwarehaus Sidata kommerziell umgesetzt. Die zerspanende Bearbeitung nimmt in der Fertigung eine Schlüsselposition ein. Hohe Werkzeugkosten und teure Maschinen zwingen zur Ermittlung optimaler Zerspanbedingungen. Die Bewältigung dieser Aufgabe erfordert einen hohen Personal- und Zeitaufwand. Der für den Erwerb des "Zerspanungswissens" benötigte Zeitaufwand ist erfahrungsgemäß sehr hoch und macht die Konservierung dieses Wissens besonders wünschenswert.

Durch die Weiterentwicklung der Werkstoffe, Werkzeuge und Maschinen steigen zunehmend die Anforderungen an die zuständigen Betriebsmittel- und Fertigungsplaner. Zielsetzung von ESPANDA ist die Unterstützung der Fertigungsplaner bei der Festlegung der Betriebsmittel und Bearbeitungswerte, wobei sich das derzeitige Einsatzgebiet bei der Mercedes-Benz AG auf Bohroperationen beschränkt (Bild 7 und 8) [inpro].

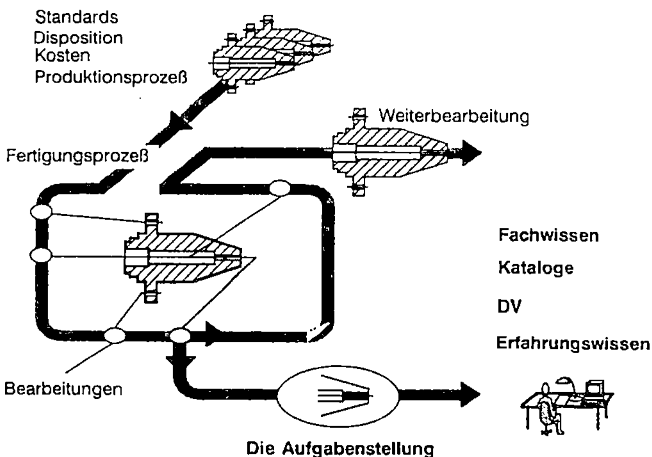

Bild 7: Problemkontext und Aufgabenstellung [inpro]

2) Die Beschreibung der Systeme Espanda und Sigma basiert im wesentlichen auf internen Berichten der inpro Berlin

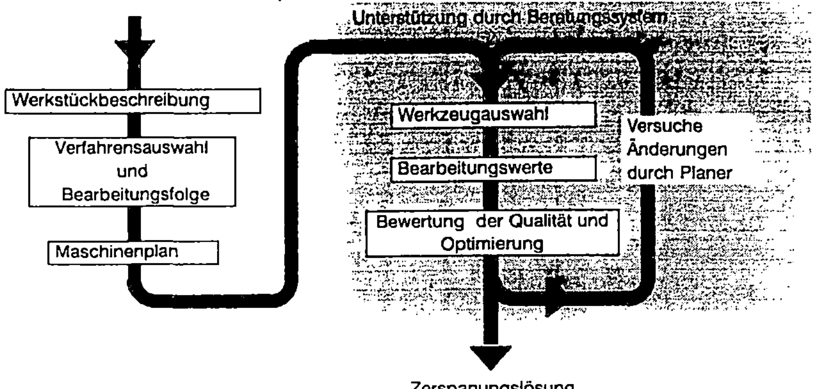

Bild 8: Einbettung und Aufgabenstellung [inpro]

In einer Orakel-Falldatenbank werden aktuelle Bearbeitungsfälle mit allen technologischen Kennwerten nach Analogien in Problemklassen gespeichert. Für alle Fälle einer Problemklasse gelten die technologisch gleichen Lösungen mit spezifischen Ausprägungen. Bei einer nicht wissensbasierten reinen Datenbanklösung muß der Benutzer in der Lage sein, aufgrund der Datenbankeinträge Analogien zu erkennen und auf seinen konkreten Fall hin uminterpretieren. Genau diese Aufgabe übernimmt die wissensbasierte Komponente von ESPANDA. Vom System wird automatisch nach ähnlichen Bearbeitungsfällen aufgrund der Beschreibung des aktuellen Zerspanungsproblems gesucht und eine Anpassung der gefundenen Analogiefälle an die aktuelle Zerspanungsaufgabe vorgenommen (Bild 9). Der hier gewählte induktive Lösungsansatz (Bild 10) hat den entscheidenden Vorteil gegenüber einer vollständigen Modellierung des Lösungsraums, daß die Wissensakquisition anhand verfügbarer Beispiele und Datenbestände erheblich erleichtert wird und die Erweiterung des Systems kontinuierlich erfolgen kann. Komplizierte und vollständig abgebildete Ausschlußregeln für z. B. bestimmte Werkstoff/Schneidstoffkombinationen sind nicht erforderlich, da sich das System grundsätzlich auf bereits durchgeführte Vergleichsoperationen abstützt. ESPANDA wurde auf Workstationbasis mit dem LISP-basierten Expertensystem-Tool KOBRA von inpro entwickelt.

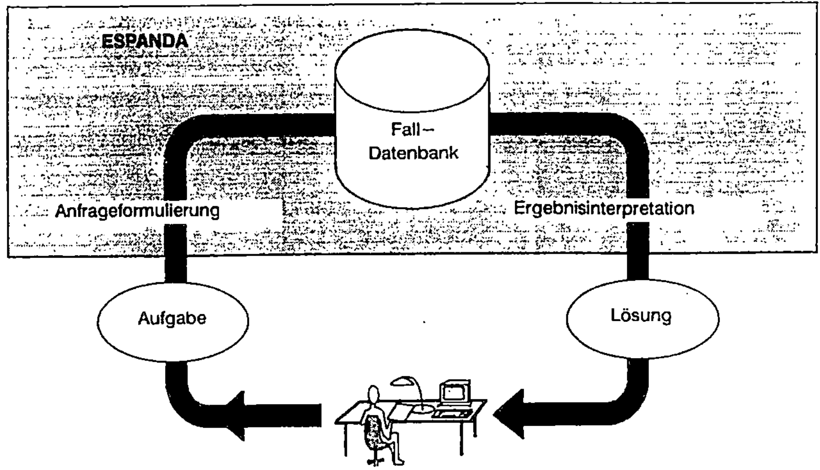

Bild 9: Nutzung von ESPANDA zur Problemlösung [inpro]

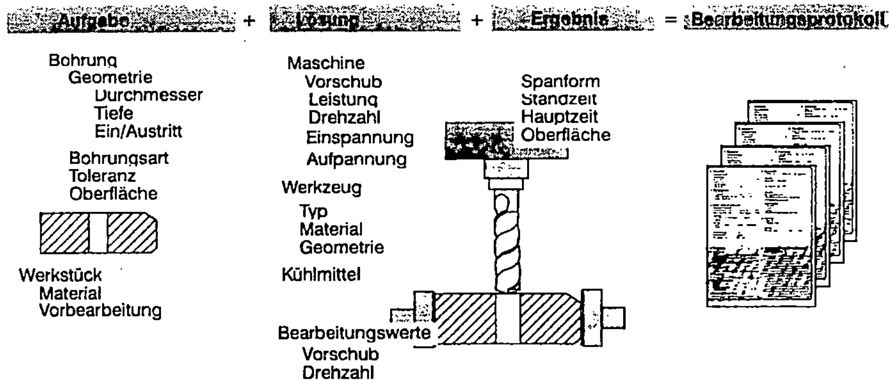

Bild 10: Aufbau des Bearbeitungsprotokolls [inpro]

SIGMA - System zur Unterstützung der Maschineninstandhaltung und -bedienung [2]

Neue Produktionsanlagen erreichen erst geraume Zeit nach ihrer Installation eine zufriedenstellende Verfügbarkeit, da das für den störungsfreien Betrieb und die Instandhaltung erforderliche anlagenspezifische Wissen erst während der Anlaufphase erworben werden kann.

Informationen zu Anlagenstruktur und -funktion sowie zur Störungsdiagnose sind zu Beginn der Anlaufphase nur dem Anlagenhersteller in vollem Umfang bekannt. Auch das mit der Anlage gelieferte Steuerungsprogramm stellt neue Anforderungen an das Bedien- und Instandhaltungspersonal. In der Anlaufphase werden die Programme geändert und optimiert. Im weiteren Betrieb ziehen Änderungen an der Anlage auch Änderungen im Steuerungsprogramm nach sich. Das Erfahrungswissen der Anlagenbetreiber wird erst mit Beginn der Anlaufphase schrittweise aufgebaut, die gewonnenen Erfahrungen liegen dann aber verteilt vor und sind in ihrer Gesamtheit nur schwer zugänglich.

Diese Problematik gab den Anstoß, ein System zu entwickeln, welches eine gesamtheitliche Sicht der Anlage ermöglicht. Als Pilotanlage dient dabei eine Transferstraße zur Bearbeitung von Wasserpumpengehäusen bei Mercedes-Benz im Werk Berlin-Marienfelde.

Ziel ist die Unterstützung des Bedien- und Instandhaltungspersonals von komplexen SPS-gesteuerten Anlagen sowie der Integration von Instandhaltungsaufgaben in die Produktion durch den Einsatz eines wissensbasierten Systems. Das System soll einerseits die Anlaufphase verkürzen, andererseits in der Produktionsphase die Verfügbarkeit der Anlage erhöhen.

Den Anwendern steht dazu bereits .mit Beginn der Anlaufphase eine Kernwissensbasis zur Verfügung, die in enger Kooperation mit dem Anlagenhersteller (hier Ex-Cell-O) aufgebaut wurde. Diese Kernwissensbasis beinhaltet in einem objektorientierten Ansatz das strukturell/funktionale Anlagenwissen über Hydraulik, Mechanik und Elektrik sowie die Funktionen zur Interpretation von Steuerungsprogrammdaten. Das System ist mit der Steuerung der Anlage (SPS) verbunden, so daß eine Online-Datenaufnahme möglich ist. Hierzu wurde die Workstation, auf der das wissensbasierte System abläuft, über eine Kommunikations-Interface des Steuerungsherstellers SIEMENS auf Basis des MMS-Kommunikationsstandards (Manufacturing Message Specification, ISO/IEC 9505) mit der SPS-Kopfsteuerung verbunden Es können dabei gezielt diagnoserelevante Daten aus der SPS sowie aus den Steuerungen der einzelnen Bearbeitungsstationen abgerufen werden (Bild 11) [inpro].

2) Die Beschreibung der Systeme Espanda und Sigma basiert im wesentlichen auf internen Berichten der inpro Berlin

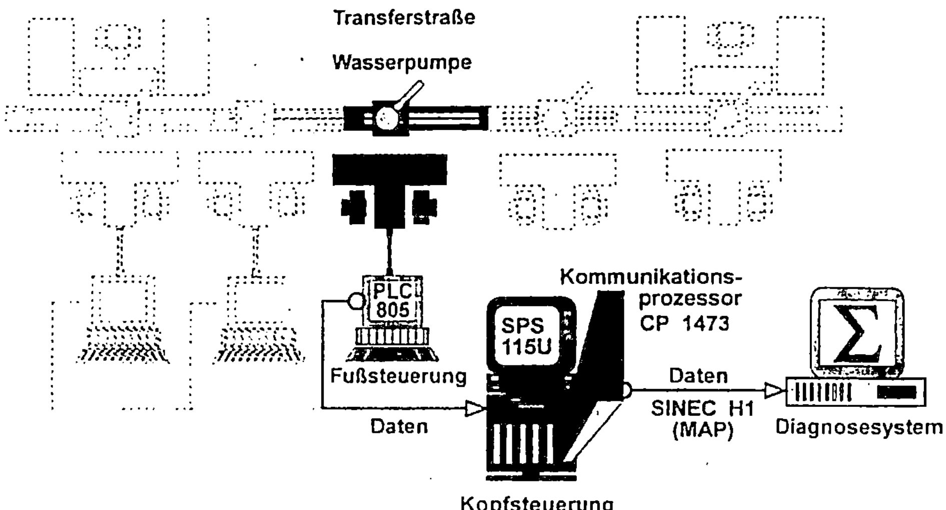

Bild 11:   Gesamtsystem Konfiguration [inpro]

Sigma wurde mit dem von der inpro entwickelten Lisp-System "Primus" auf PC-Basis programmiert und anschließend in C auf Workstationbasis unter UNIX- und OSF-Motiv implementiert. Die im Juli 1993 durchgeführte Pilotinstallation im Mercedes-Werk Berlin-Marienfelde wurde im Herbst '93 einem Leistungstest unterzogen, der den Nachweis der Wirtschaftlichkeit dieses Expertensystems mit einem Return on Investment von 2 Jahren erbrachte.

In der aktuellen Systemversion sind folgende Komponenten enthalten:
- Akquisitionskomponente (Wissensverarbeitung)
- Online-Kopplung von Workstation und SPS auf MAP-Basis (MMS, ISO Level 7)
- Grafikeinbindung als Lokalisierungshilfe (ca. 100 Videobilder der Anlage, ca. 600 Stromlaufpläne)
- Einbau-, Ausbau-, Reparatur- und Sicherheitshinweise in Form von Hilfstexten
- Beschreibung von Bauteilfunktionen und -eigenschaften (z. Zt. ca. 12 000 Objekte, 5 000 Regeln, 3 900 Funktionen)
- kompletter Bauteilbaum der Anlage

Einsatz von Projektmanagement in großen IV-Projekten der Mercedes-Benz AG

Experten-Systeme sind als Investitionen zu betrachten, die der nachhaltigen Steigerung der Wettbewerbsfähigkeit des Unternehmers dienen sollen, entsprechend ist bei der Abwicklung der Projekte darauf zu achten, daß wertvolle Kapital- und Personalressourcen nutzenorientiert eingesetzt werden: der Mitteleinsatz muß sich nach dem Rückfluß einer IV-Investition richten; ist der Rückfluß nicht berechenbar, sind andere quantitative (z. B. Zeit) und qualitative Nutzenapekte nachzuweisen.

Im Sinne einer möglichst effizienten Abwicklung eines Expertensystem-Projektes müssen vor Projektbeginn. die wesentlichen Ziele des Projektes sowie die notwendigen Rahmenbedingungen - wie Mitarbeiterkapazitäten und Finanzierung - geklärt werden. Zu diesem Zweck führen die anfordernden Bereiche ein gesondertes IV-Vorprojekt durch, dessen Gesamtdauer sechs Kalendermonate nicht überschreiten sollte. Die Vorteile einer eindeutigen organisatorischen Trennung zwischen "IV-Vorprojekt" und IV-Projekt ergeben sich wie folgt:
- klarer Übergang zwischen Linien- und Projektarbeit
- frühzeitige Priorisierung von Projekten
- hohe Planungsqualität durch klar definierten Projektantrag
- schneller Projektanlauf durch Vorabbereitstellung aller notwendigen Ressourcen
- Entzerrung des Portfolios
- Vermeidung von "Platzhalter-Projekten"
- Vereinbarkeit mit der verabschiedeten IV-Strategie

Endprodukt des Vorprojektes ist der Projektantrag (Bild 12). Er bildet die Basis für die Freigabe der IV-Investition und schafft damit die Voraussetzungen für den Start des eingeleiteten IV-Projektes.

Hauptthemen	Im Antrag erforderliche Informationen
Projektaufgabe	- Beschreibung der geschäftlichen Problemstellung - Beschreibung möglicher organisatorischer/geschäftlicher Lösungsoptionen - Realisierungsbedingungen (Rahmenbedingungen) - Strategische Relevanz
Projektziele	- Darstellung Projektziel - Darstellung der unterstützten Geschäftsprozesse - Meßbare und bestimmbare Einzelziele
Wirtschaftlichkeit	- Grobschätzung Kosten/Nutzen der vorgeschlagenen Lösungen je Einsatzort
Untersuchungs-rahmen	- Abgrenzung des Untersuchungsrahmens - Einsatzorte - Systemzuordnung, Systemeigner, Dateneigner
Besetzungsplan	- Projektleiter (Namen und vereinbarte Kapazitäten) - Projektgruppe (Namen und vereinbarte Kapazitäten) - Experten und Berater (Namen und vereinbarte Kapazitäten) - Mitwirkende Fachbereiche - Hauptverantwortlicher (Name), ggf. Lenkungsausschuß (Namen)
Berichtswesen	- Zyklus des Projektstatusberichts
Projektgesamt-planung	- Inhaltliche Gliederung (Modularisierung) - Meilensteine mit Terminplanung - Gesamtaufwand und Aufwand aller Phasen in MM (Projektleiter, Projektgruppe; Experten, externe Mitarbeiter) - Gesamtbudget (Sachkosten, Personalkosten, SG-Kosten) und Budget der ersten Phase - Kostenaufteilung
Feinplanung für erste Phase	- Arbeitspakete mit Start- und Endterminen und Abhängigkeiten - Aufwand pro Arbeitspaket - Benötigte Betriebsmittel - Budgetplanung (Sachkosten, Personalkosten, SG-Kosten)
Risikoanalyse	- Darstellung der Risiken des Projektes - Konsequenzen bei Nicht-Realisierung
Unterschriften	- Anfordernde Bereiche (einschließlich Kostenübernahmeerklärung)

Bild 12: Inhalt des Projektantrages für IV-Projekte

IV-Projekte insbesondere aber Expertensystemprojekte werden in der Regel von interdisziplinär besetzten Teams durchgeführt, die in kurzer Zeit sehr komplexe bereichsübergreifende Probleme zu bewältigen haben. Hierzu wird eine temporäre Projektorganisation geschaffen, die eine effiziente und schnelle Durchführung der einmaligen Aufgaben gewährleistet. Gegenüber den anfordernden Bereichen hat die

Projektorganisation die Funktion eines "Dienstleitungscenters", das in ihrem Auftrag die Erstellung eines Expertensystems übernimmt.

Für den Projekterfolg ist die Aufteilung in Teilaufgaben genauso wichtig wie eine ständige intensive Interaktion der Teammitglieder und eine gemeinschaftlich getragene Lösung. Die Projektorganisation ist so auszugestalten, daß innerhalb des Projektauftrags uneingeschränkte Handlungs- und Entscheidungsfähigkeit gewährleistet ist; schon bei Projektbeginn sind die entsprechenden Voraussetzungen zu schaffen. Den Kern der Projektorganisation bilden der Hauptverantwortliche, der Projektleiter und das Kernteam. Der Hauptverantwortliche repräsentiert als Linienvorgesetzter des anfordernden Bereiches den "Hauptinvestor" und vertritt dessen Interessen. Der Hauptverantwortliche trägt die Gesamtverantwortung für die IV-Investition (Bild 13), der Projektleiter ist für den planungsmäßigen Projektablauf, d. h. Termine, Kosten und Inhalt verantwortlich.

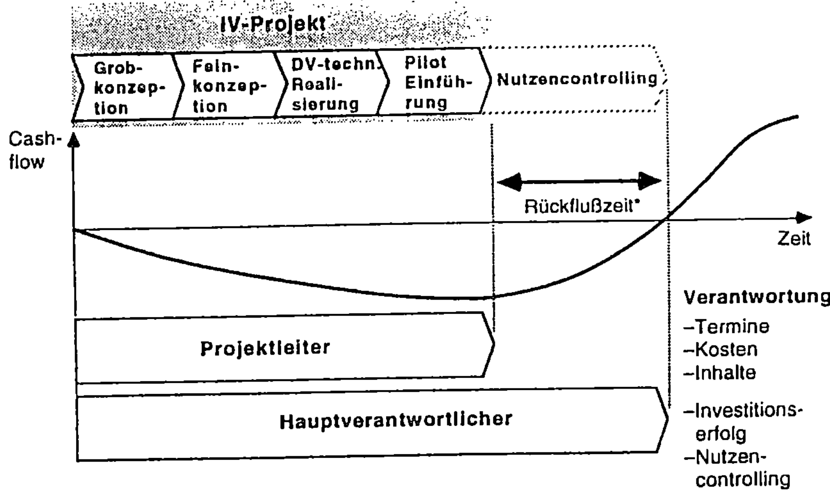

Bild 13: Verantwortungsteilung zwischen Projektleiter und
Hauptverantwortlichem

Die Hauptphasen von IV-Projekten sind wie folgt gegliedert:
- Vorprojekt
- Grobkonzeption
- Feinkonzeption
- DV-technische Realisierung
- Einführung
- Nutzencontrolling

Während der Grobkonzeption können durch systematische Hinterfragung der relevanten Arbeitsabläufe, Zero-Base-Untersuchungen und durch die Erarbeitung kreativer Lösungsansätze erhebliche Kosteneinsparungen realisiert werden. Erst daran anschließend wird der Anpassungsbedarf in Form einer

Systemkurzbeschreibung und einer funktionellen Grobspezifikation erarbeitet. An dieser Stelle ist zu entscheiden, ob und in welchem Umfang die Systementwicklung selbst betrieben oder an externe Dienstleister vergeben wird (Make-or-buy-Konzept).

In der Phase der Feinkonzeption geht es um die Erarbeitung und endgültige Festlegung des Pflichtenheftes. Das Pflichtenheft sollte neben der funktionellen Feinspezifikation die Beschreibung des Einsatz- und Wartungskonzepts, des DV-technischen Umfelds, der Qualitätssicherung sowie des Lieferumfangs mit Abnahmeregelungen umfassen.

Durch das verbindliche Festschreiben des Pflichtenheftes (Unterschrift der anfordernden Bereiche), das als Grundlage für die Beauftragung externer aber auch interner Softwarehersteller dient, werden spätere, häufig sehr kostenintensive Änderungen ausgeschlossen. In einer Projektwertanalyse werden Kosten und Nutzen einzelner Systemfunktionen in Abstimmung mit den späteren Nutzern systematisch hinterfragt. Darüber hinaus ist es häufig zweckmäßig, einen Prototyp als Systemnukleus keinesfalls aber ein reines Demo- oder Showsystem zu entwickeln. Hier bieten besonders Expertensystemshells gute Vorraussetzungen für Rapid Prototyping und eine damit einhergehende iterative Systementwicklung.

In der Phase der DV-technischen Realisierung stellen Projektleiter und Kernteam in Zusammenarbeit mit dem Systemrealisierer sicher, daß die fachlichen und technischen Anforderungen erfüllt werden. Dazu werden in regelmäßigen Review-Sitzungen Fertigstellungsstatus und ggf. Realisierungsprobleme diskutiert. In enger Abstimmung mit dem Systemrealisierer werden Abnahmetests (System-, Funktions- und Integrationstests) durchgeführt und dokumentiert. Darüber hinaus ist die frühzeitige Schaffung der notwendigen Rahmenbedingungen für die Pilotinstallation von entscheidnder Bedeutung. Parallel zur DV-technischen Realisierung sind die Systemdokumentation (für IV-Bereiche bzw. Fachbereiche) und geeignete Schulungsunterlagen für die Einführung des Systems beim Nutzer zu erstellen. Die frühzeitige Einbindung des örtlichen Betriebsrates ist in aller Regel ebenso erfolgsfördernd wie die Einbindung der späteren Nutzer des Systems.

In der Phase der Einführung stellen der Projektleiter und das Kernteam sicher, daß das System installiert und in funktionsfähigem Zustand übergeben wird. Mit den Nutzern werden fachlich-organisatorische Abnahmeprotokolle erstellt. Zudem ist als wichtige Voraussetzung für den späteren Nachweis über die Amortisierung der Systeminvestition ein Nutzencontrolling-Konzept zu erstellen, auf dessen Basis der Systemnutzer die durch das System ermöglichten Einsparungen nachweisen kann. Mit erfolgreichem Abschluß der Einführungsphase wird der Projektleiter entlastet.

Resümee

Kurzfristig erscheint gerade der Bereich kleinerer Anwendungen für Expertensystem-Projekte auf einen sehr fruchtbaren Nährboden zu fallen. Überall dort, wo sogenanntes Katalogwissen vorhanden ist, also Wissen, das bereits logisch strukturiert in Form von Beschreibungen und Beispielen vorliegt, lassen sich wissensbasierte Systeme mit relativ geringem Aufwand entwicklen. Der Vorteil gegenüber einfachen Datanbankimplementierungen liegt z. B. bei der guten Entwicklungsunterstützung durch Expertensystem-Entwicklungswerkzeuge sowie in der Möglichkeit, das Verarbeitungs- und Kontextwissen, das zur automatischen Ableitung von Lösungen notwendig ist, gut repräsentieren zu können.

Betrachtet man die Softwareinnovationszyklen der Vergangenheit, so befinden wir uns wahrscheinlich noch am Anfang einer Entwicklung, deren zukünftige Richtung nicht zuverlässig abgeschätzt werden kann. Aus diesem Grunde aber die weitere Entwicklung zurückhaltend zu beobachten und erst dann eigene Aktivitäten zu entwicklen, wenn eine vermeintliche Stabilität zu erkennen ist, wäre sicherlich genauso falsch, wie ein zu euphorisches Engagement. Durch die Anwendung wissensbasierter Technologie kann die Entwicklungsdauer einer Problemlösung teilweise drastisch reduziert werden, dies gilt im wesentlichen aber für kleinere und mittlere Anwendungen, bei denen das Sachwissen bereits gut strukturiert und teilweise logisch aufbereitet zur Verfügung stehen.

Überwachung und Diagnose -
gemeinsam geht es besser

Heinz Marburger
Mikroelektronik Anwendungszentrum Hamburg GmbH
Karnapp 20
21079 Hamburg
hm@maz-hh.dpe.de

Zusammenfassung

Die Verringerung der Instandhaltungskosten und die Erhöhung der Maschinenverfügbarkeit sind wesentliche Faktoren für den wirtschaftlichen Betrieb von Maschinen und Anlagen. Die Beeinflussung dieser Faktoren wird mehr und mehr bestimmt durch den Einsatz von rechnerbasierten Lösungen, z.B. Maschinendatenerfassungssysteme mit hochwertiger Sensorik, Schwingungsanalyseverfahren oder wissensbasierte Überwachungs- und Diagnosesysteme. Die verfügbaren Systeme sind aber bislang in der Regel auf eine bestimmte Interpretationsebene beschränkt gewesen. In diesem Papier wird ein integrierendes System bestehend aus Hard- und Softwarekomponenten vorgestellt, die eine durchgehende Verarbeitung von der Überwachung über Prognose und Diagnose bis zur Reparatur realisiert.

1. Überwachung und Diagnose zur Optimierung von Produktionszielgrößen

1.1. Zielgößen: Maschinenverfügbarkeit und Instandhaltungskosten

Beim Betrieb von Maschinen und Anlagen gewinnt die Optimierung der Produktionszielgrößen

- Erhöhung der Maschinenverfügbarkeit

- Verringerung der Instandhaltungskosten

immer stärkere Bedeutung. Diese beiden Zielgrößen sind nicht scharf voneinander zu trennen. So kann einerseits die Maschinenverfügbarkeit z.B. dadurch erhöht werden, daß unvorhergesehene Ausfälle vermieden werden. Dieses kann durch eine stetige Überwachung der Maschinen und darauf basierenden Fehlervorhersagen erreicht werden. Überwachung und Fehlerprognose verringern aber auch die Instandhaltungskosten und zwar in der Weise, daß von einer zyklischen Wartung zu einer zustandsorientierten Wartung übergegangen werden kann. Durch die Ausnutzung des Verschleißvorrates von Maschinenkomponenten können beachtliche Kosten in der Instandhaltung eingespart werden.

Andererseits kann mit einer Senkung der Instandhaltungskosten, z.B. durch eine gezieltere Fehlerbehebung auf der Basis einer aussagekräftigen Prognose, eine Verringerung der Instandhaltungszeiten einhergehen, die sich wiederum positiv auf die Maschinenverfügbarkeit auswirken.

Hiermit haben wir bereits zwei wesentliche Ansatzpunkte zur Beeinflussung der Produktionszielgrößen dargestellt: stetige Überwachung der Maschinen und Fehlervorhersage.

Zusätzlich zur Fehlerprognose wirkt eine exakte Fehlerdiagnose positiv auf die Zielgrößen. Die genaue Lokalisierung der Ursache eines Fehlers ermöglicht eine gezielte Fehlerbehebung. Dies bedeutet nicht nur, daß die richtige Teilkomponente der Maschine und das zu reparariende Teil identifiziert wird, sondern auch eine Verbesserung des Ressourceneinsatzes des Instandhaltungspersonals. Schließlich können die Instandhaltungskosten noch dadurch beeinflußt werden, daß das Instandhaltungspersonal bei der Ursachensuche und der Reparatur durch geeignete rechnerbasierte Handlungsanweisungen und entsprechende Graphiken unterstützt wird.

1.2. Lösungen zur Beeinflussung der Zielgrößen

Diese kurze Darstellung verdeutlicht, daß Lösungen zur Beeinflussung der beiden Produktionszielgrößen alle Teilaufgaben aus Abbildung 1 abdecken müssen. Sie müssen Lösungen für die Überwachung, die Vorhersage, die Diagnose und die Reparatur bereitstellen.

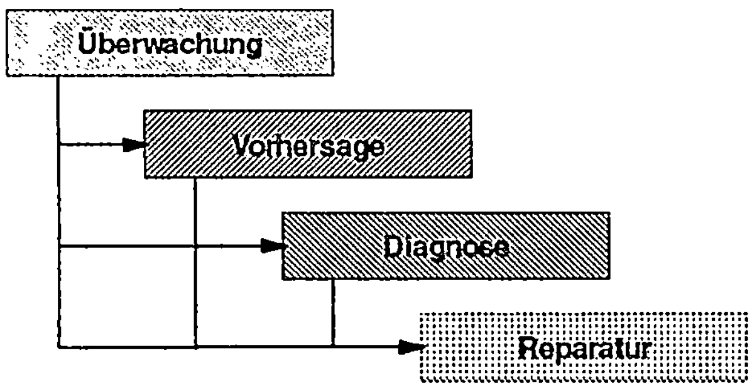

Abbildung 1: Teilaufgaben zur Beeinflussung der Produktionszielgrößen

Auf der Seite von Methoden und Verfahren existieren heute eine Vielzahl von Lösungsansätzen, um die Teilaufgaben zu bewältigen. Dazu gehören u.a. (siehe auch Frank 1994, Isermann 1994)

- signalgestützte Verfahren

- analytisch modellgestützte Verfahren

- wissensgestützte Verfahren.

Die Menge der speziellen Verfahren ist sehr groß und es muß jeweils problemspezifisch geprüft werden, welches das geeignetste ist.

Auf der DV-technischen Seite ist die Zahl der Systeme, die zur Lösung der Aufgaben angeboten werden ebenfalls sehr umfangreich. Dazu gehören z.B.

- Maschinendatenerfassungssysteme

- dezentrale Datensammler mit off-line Auswertesystemen

- Visualisierungswerkzeuge für Prozeßparameter

- Grenzwertüberwachung in speicherprogrammierbaren Steuerungen

- spezielle Schwingungsanalysegeräte

- wissensbasierte Diagnosesystemshells

- multimedia Reparaturunterstützungssysteme.

Zur Zeit gibt es aber nur wenige Ansätze, die eine umfassende Gesamtlösung für den Problemkreis anbieten. Durch die Heterogenität der Teilsysteme werden Systementwicklungen mit erheblichen Integrationskosten belastet. Erschwerend wirkt sich dabei aus, daß die Teilsysteme in der Regel nicht offen sind. Im folgenden wird eine Lösung dargestellt, die sowohl eine homogene Systementwicklung als auch den Anschluß an andere Systeme ermöglicht.

2. Überwachung und Diagnose mit DiaMon

Das System DiaMon wurde auf der Basis der Erkenntnis entwickelt, daß heute existierende Systeme zur Überwachung, Prognose, Diagnose und Repraturunterstützung nur suboptimale Lösungen anbieten. Insbesondere existieren kaum Lösungen, die eine Abdeckung des in Abbildung 2 dargestellten Umfangs ermöglichen.

Auf der Basis von Sensorwerten und Maschinendaten sollen in einem ersten Schritt der Vorverarbeitung Signalanalysen durchgeführt und Prozeßvariablen abgeleitet werden. Die so erzielten Werte dienen im zweiten Schritt der Bestimmung kritischer

Fehler und Symtomatiken. Bei kritischen Fehlern können in diesem Schritt Alarme erzeugt werden. Im dritten Schritt werden in einer Online-Diagnose Auswirkungen und mögliche Ursachen bestimmt, die wiederum in Alarme umgesetzt werden können. Während dieses Schrittes werden auch Vorhersageberechnungen durchgeführt, die Aussagen über die Reststandzeiten von Komponenten liefern. Sollte eine Störung oder ein Fehler aufgetreten sein, wird in der interaktiven Diagnose ggf. unter Einbeziehung von weiteren Beoabachtungen und Messungen eine Ursachenbestimmung und die Reparatur durchgeführt.

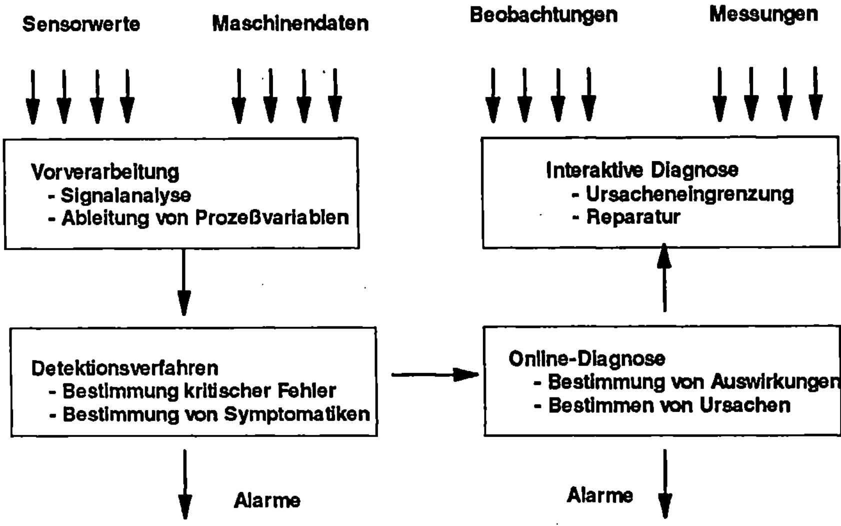

Abbildung 2: Von der Vorverarbeitung zur Reparatur

Natürlich können all diese Aufgaben auch durch einzelne Systeme abgedeckt werden. Dabei treten aber in der Regel die bekannten Phänomene auf wie

- Mehrfachhaltung von Daten und die damit verbundenen Konsistenzprobleme

- Mehrfacherfassung von Daten mit ihrem Fehlerpotential bei der Eingabe

- Informationslücken zwischen den einzelnen Schritten.

2.1. Die Architektur

DiaMon besteht aus speziellen aufeinander abgestimmten Hard- und Software-komponenten, wobei soweit wie möglich Hardwarestandards eingesetzt werden. Für die Meßwerterfassung und -verarbeitung wurde eine spezielle Hardware entwickelt, um den stetig wachsenden Anforderungen gerecht zu werden, die sich aus der Schwingungsanalyse, z.B. zur Lagerüberwachung, ergeben. Abbildung 3 gibt einen Überblick über das System.

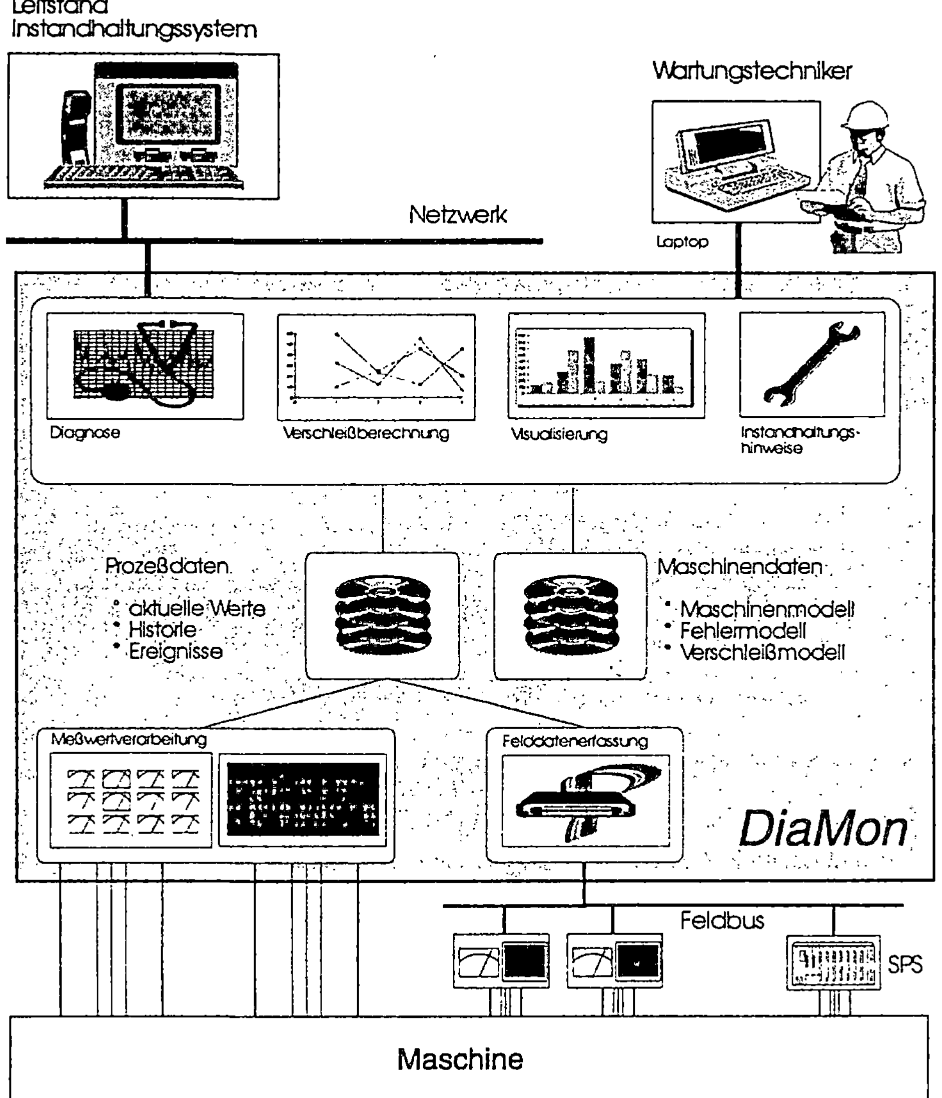

Abbildung 3: Architektur von DiaMon

Auf der Feldebene bietet DiaMon verschiedene Schnittstellen an. Die Spezialhardware sorgt für die schnelle Verarbeitung der Daten, die von der Maschine geliefert werden können. Die Hardware bietet analoge und digitale Eingangskanäle, deren Daten von einem Signalprozessor verarbeitet werden. Neben diesen Eingängen können über einen Feldbus Informationen von anderen Systemen und auch von im Feld stationierten Instanzen der Spezialhardware aufgenommen werden. Zusätzlich zum Feldbus steht auch noch eine serielle Schnittstelle zur Verfügung.

Die Kommunikation zu einem übergeordneten Leitsystem findet über Standardnetzwerke mit Standardprotokollen statt. Für den Servicetechniker steht eine Schnittstelle zu einem Standard-Laptop zur Verfügung.

2.2. Die Funktionen

Das System bietet Benutzer- und Systemschnittstellen für die folgenden Einsatzszenarien:

- Online-Überwachung und Diagnose

- Interaktive Diagnose und Instandhaltung

- Projektierung des Systems.

2.1. Online-Überwachung und Diagnose

In der Online-Überwachung und Diagnose werden alle die Maschine betreffenden Ereignisse aufgezeichnet, ausgewertet und protokolliert. Aufzeichnung bedeutet Erfassung von analogen und digitalen Meßwerten, die Vorverarbeitung der Meßwerte sowie die Abspeicherung der Daten in der dynamischen Datenbank. Neben Standardmeßgrößen wie z.B. Temperatur, Drehzahlen, Maschinenzuständen werden auch Schwingungssignale erfaßt und entsprechend algorithmisch aufbereitet, so daß sie für die weiteren Funktionen verwendbar werden.

Aufsetzend auf den aufbereiteten Meßdaten, Informationen über die Maschinen sowie Zustand und Leistungsgrad von Komponenten werden folgende Funktionen ausgeführt:

- Grenzwertüberwachung von Prozeßparametern

- Ableitung von möglichen Auswirkungen auf der Basis eines wissensbasierten Fehlermodells (siehe Unbehend 1994)

- Verschleißberechnungen für Maschinenteile (siehe Kahl 1994)

- Trendberechnungen für die Restlebensdauer von Komponenten

Die einzelnen Funktionen werden ereignisgesteuert aktiviert. Alle relevanten Ergebnisse von Berechnungen und Diagnosen werden protokolliert. Auszüge aus den Protokollen werden an ein übergeordnetes Leitsystem abgeschickt, so daß der Leitstand jederzeit über den aktuellen Zustand informiert ist und bei einer Gefahr für die Maschine oder ein Werkstück sofort eingreifen kann. Die Protokolle stehen auch dem Servicetechniker vor Ort zur Fehlersuche zur Verfügung.

2.2. Unterstützung des Service

Für Routineüberprüfungen, Fehlersuche und Reparatur bietet DiaMon eine interaktive Schnittstelle über den Service-Laptop. Dem Wartungstechniker vor Ort stehen die folgenden Funktionen zur Verfügung:

- Unterstützung bei der Ursachensuche im Fehlerfall

- Unterstützung bei Reparatur und Instandhaltung

- Visualisierung von Prozeßparametern

- Trenddarstellungen von Verschleißberechnungen

- Aktualisierung der Maschinendatenbank.

2.3. Projektierung des Systems

Für die Entwicklung und Anpassung des Systems auf die speziellen Anforderungen der zu überwachenden Maschinen stehen dem Projekteur komfortable Editoren zur Verfügung. Mit ihnen ist es möglich, die Funktionen des Systems zu definieren und zu parametrieren. Über Editoren können die relevanten Daten eingegeben werden. Für die Formulierung des Fehlermodells steht ein graphischer Editor zur Verfügung. Die Definition und Formulierung von Berechnungsvorschriften von Prozeßvariablen wird über Funktionseditoren durchgeführt. Der Projekteur wird vom System bei seinen Arbeiten durch syntaktische und semantische Prüfungen unterstützt.

Die Projektierung eines Systems erfolgt in der Regel in zwei Stufen: Auf der ersten Stufe werden die relevanten Daten durch den Hersteller eingegeben. Auf der zweiten Stufe kann der Betreiber seine spezifischen Daten eingeben. Diese umfassen sowohl seine spezifischen Teiledaten als auch die besonderen Umgebungs- und Einsatzbedingungen, die für eine Überwachung und Diagnose relevant sind. Im Projektierungssystem sind Schutzmechanismen vorgesehen, die sicherstellen, daß die Daten, die der Hersteller einer Maschine eingegeben hat, nicht von einem Betreiber geändert werden können.

2.3. Ein Beispiel

An Hand eines Beispiels zur Überwachung und Diagnose einer Pumpe soll im folgenden die Wirkungsweise von DiaMon im Einsatz kurz gezeigt werden.

Die Überwachungsfunktion stellt eine Grenzwertverletzung eines Prozeßparameters fest. Aufgrund dieser Verletzung wird das Online-Diagnosemodul aktiviert. Dieses Modul erstellt eine Grobdiagnose, z.B.

Fehler: Kavitation ist zur befürchten
Einschätzung: Gefährdung für die Pumpe
Abhilfe: Stand-by-Pumpe schalten; Service vor Ort schicken

und meldet dieses an das Leitsystem.

Der Leitsystem-Operator schickt nach Schaltung der Stand-by-Pumpe einen Techniker vor Ort. Dieser meldet sich als Service an und aktiviert das Service-Modul. Die Fehlermeldung wird aufgeschaltet und dem Techniker werden mögliche Ursachen für den Fehler aufgezeigt. Durch Einstieg in die interaktive Diagnose kann der Techniker selbst- oder systemgesteuert die relevanten Prüfungen durchführen, um die tatsächliche Ursache zu lokalisieren. Wenn er die Ursache identifiziert hat, wird er durch Handlungsanweisungen, Bilder und Prüfungen bei der Reparatur unterstützt. Nach Ausführung der Reparatur aktualisiert der Techniker die Datenbank, z.B. Eingabe der neuen Teilenummer bei Tausch, Zurücksetzen der Meßwerthistorie etc.

Nach Abschluß seiner Arbeiten kann er eine Meldung an das Leitsystem absetzen, daß die Komponente wieder einsatzbereit ist.

3. Einsatzfelder und Nutzeffekte

DiaMon ist ein Überwachungs- und Diagnosesystem für optimalen Betrieb und zu-standsorientierte Wartung. Die maßgeschneiderte Anpassung der Konfiguration und Funktion erlaubt die Aufzeichnung des Maschineneinsatzes und bietet Schnittstellen zum Service und zu übergeordneten Systemen. Das Konzept von DiaMon wurde an verschiedenen Applikationen getestet, z.B. Pumpen, Werkzeugmaschinen oder Flurförderzeuge.

Durch das integrierte Zusammenspiel von verschiedenen Aufgabenbereichen können mit dem System unterschiedliche Nutzeffekte erzielt werden. Für den Maschinenbetreiber ergeben sich durch den Einsatz von DiaMon die Vorteile

- Erhöhung der Maschinenverfügbarkeit und

- Verringerung der Instandhaltungszeiten.

Aber nicht nur für den Maschinenbetreiber sind Systeme dieser Art nutzbringend. Auch der Maschinenhersteller profitiert von ihnen: Die Dokumentation der Maschinenzustände durch die Prozeßparameter in der Datenbank des Systems liefert eine Basis für

- die Klärung von Gewährleistungsansprüchen sowie

- die Weiterentwicklung des Produktes.

Wenn der Maschinenhersteller selbst die Wartung seiner Maschinen übernimmt, dann wirken für ihn natürlich auch die Vorteile des Systems bei der Instandhaltung. Er kann

- die Fehlersuchzeiten und Reparaturzeiten verkürzen,

- die Qualität seines Service erhöhen und

- seine Servicelogistik verbessern.

Literatur

Frank 1994
Frank, P.M.: Diagnoseverfahren in der Automatisierungstechnik. In: at - Automatisierungstechnik, Vol. 42, Nr. 2. R. Oldenbourg Verlag 1994

Isermann 1994
Isermann, R. (Hrsg.): Überwachung und Diagnose. Moderne Methoden und ihre Anwendungen bei technischen Systemen. Düsseldorf: VDI-Verlag 1994

Kahl 1994
Kahl, B.: Beitrag zur modellgestützten Verschleißdiagnose von Maschinen. Diplomarbeit Universität Rostock, 1994

Unbehend 1994
Unbehend, Ch.: Knowledge based monitoring and diagnosis in machine maintenance. To appear in: Proceedings of Intelligent Systems Engineering, Hamburg, 1994

Planbasierte Hilfeverfahren für direkt-manipulative Systeme

Markus A. Thies

DFKI
Stuhlsatzenhausweg 3
66123 Saarbrücken
thies@dfki.uni-sb.de

Zusammenfassung. In den letzten Jahren wurden planbasierte Hilfesysteme entworfen, deren Einsatzgebiet auf Applikationen mit kommandoorientierten Schnittstellen beschränkt ist. Die Bedeutung dieser kommandoorientierten Applikationen rückt aber durch die weite Verbreitung graphischer Fenstersysteme in den Hintergrund. Die neuen Interaktionsformen graphischer Benutzungsoberflächen, wie z.B. die *direkte Manipulation*, bieten dem Benutzer eine leichtere Bedienung und eine größere Flexibilität. Erleichtert diese Flexibilität einerseits dem erfahrenen Benutzer die Arbeit mit einem solchen System, so kann ein ungeübter Benutzer aufgrund der entstehenden Komplexität leicht auf Probleme stoßen. Die Einbeziehung graphischer Benutzungsoberflächen in das Anwendungsgebiet *planbasierter Hilfesysteme* wird notwendig. Die sich hieraus ergebenden Anforderungen verhindern allerdings eine schnelle Adaption bisheriger planbasierter Hilfesysteme: es sind hierfür neue Ansätze zur Modellierung von Plänen und Verfahren zu entwickeln.

1 Einführung und Motivation

„Intelligente" Hilfesysteme stellen eine wesentliche Weiterentwicklung bisheriger Hilfesysteme dar. Zwar sind heutzutage Hilfesysteme bereits Standard in vielen kommerziellen Applikationen – neuerdings wird hierfür der Begriff *Help Desk Application* verwendet[1] –, jedoch besitzen sie bisher nicht die Fähigkeit, auf die Individualität des Benutzers einzugehen [26]. Diese Einschränkung versuchen „intelligente" Hilfesysteme zu umgehen, indem sie den Benutzer bei seiner Arbeit mit einer Applikation „beobachten". Sie versuchen Rückschlüsse auf mögliche Ziele des Benutzers zu gewinnen, um ihm in konkreten Fehlersituationen Hilfe geben zu können. Diese Schlußfolgerungen werden auf der Basis von gespeicherten Plänen gezogen. Diese Pläne modellieren typische Vorgehensweisen eines Benutzers beim Durchführen von Aufgaben.

In den letzten Jahren wurden solche planbasierten Hilfesysteme entworfen, deren Einsatzgebiet auf Applikationen mit kommandoorientierten Schnittstellen beschränkt ist [10, 11, 30, 15, 7, 5]. Die Bedeutung dieser kommandoorientierten

---

[1] Der Name *Help Ware* wurde als eingetragenes Warenzeichen registriert.

Applikationen rückt aber durch die weite Verbreitung graphischer Fenstersysteme in den Hintergrund. Die neuen Interaktionsformen graphischer Benutzungsoberflächen, wie z.B. die *direkte Manipulation*, bieten dem Benutzer eine leichtere Bedienung und eine größere Flexibilität. Erleichtert diese Flexibilität einerseits dem erfahrenen Benutzer die Arbeit mit einem solchen System, so kann ein ungeübter Benutzer aufgrund der entstehenden Komplexität leicht auf Probleme stoßen. Die Einbeziehung graphischer Benutzungsoberflächen in das Einsatzgebiet *planbasierter Hilfesysteme* wird notwendig. Die sich hieraus ergebenden Anforderungen verhindern allerdings eine schnelle Adaption bisheriger planbasierter Hilfesysteme: es sind hierfür neue Ansätze zur Modellierung von Plänen und Verfahren zu entwickeln.

Es werden im folgenden zwei Systeme vorgestellt, deren Anwendungsgebiet bereits auf Applikationen mit graphischer Benutzungsoberfläche ausgedehnt wurde.

Innerhalb des Hilfe- und Tutorsystems *Hytask* zur Unterstützung des Benutzers im Umgang mit dem Spreadsheet-Programm *Excel*, übernimmt die Komponente *Planet* die Erkennung von Plänen [19]. Mit dem Bezug zur aktuellen Handlungsweise des Benutzers ermöglicht der Planerkenner *Planet* einen passiven, kontextsensitiven Einstieg in das hypermediale Hilfesystem *Hytask*, welches statische Hilfetexte, Illustrationen und statische Tutorien anbietet. Durch die Fokussierung auf eine Hilfestrategie (kontextsensitiver Einstieg in *Hytask*) war eine Berücksichtigung der Möglichkeiten und Besonderheiten graphischer Benutzungsoberflächen nicht erforderlich.

Das Hilfesystem *Mathilde* [16] unterstützt den Benutzer im Umgang mit dem Text-Editor *ComfoTex*, der unter der graphischen Benutzungsoberfläche *MS-Windows* läuft. Sobald *Mathilde* anhand von Plänen eine suboptimale Vorgehensweise erkennt, präsentiert es dem Benutzer textuelle Ratschläge in einer Dialogbox. Der Planerkenner in *Mathilde* greift als Eingabe *Events* direkt aus der Nachrichtenschleife von *MS-Windows* ab. Dadurch fehlt der Bezug zu applikationsspezifischen Daten wie beispielsweise selektierte Objekte und ihre Attribute. Dies ist ein Grund für die eingeschränkte Ausdrucksfähigkeit der Plansprache, die in *Mathilde* entwickelt wurde.

Um neue Ansätze planbasierter Hilfesysteme für graphische Benutzungsoberflächen entwickeln zu können, müssen die Eigenschaften und Unterschiede zu kommandoorientierten Oberflächen beschrieben werden.

1.1 Graphische Benutzungsoberflächen

Eine oberflächliche Betrachtung der Applikationen, welche die Interaktionsform der direkten Manipulation unterstützen, kann zu der These führen, daß diese Applikationen prinzipiell einfacher zu bedienen sind und ein Hilfesystem daher nicht notwendig ist. Im Vergleich zu kommandoorientierten Applikationen ist die Bedienbarkeit zwar intuitiver, graphische Benutzungsoberflächen führen jedoch zu neuen Fehlerquellen, deren Ursachen weniger in der Syntax der Aktionen als im Applikationskontext und Aufgabenkontext zu finden sind:

– Parallele Bearbeitung von mehreren Aufgaben
  Der Benutzer kann parallel an mehreren Aufgaben arbeiten. Dies bringt
  Vorteile für erfahrene Benutzer, kann jedoch bei unerfahrenen Benutzern
  oder Gelegenheitsbenutzern zu „Orientierungslosigkeit" führen. Damit wird
  eine Situation bezeichnet, in welcher der Benutzer nicht ohne weitere Hilfe
  Aufgaben weiterführen oder beenden kann.
– Verwendung unterschiedlicher Views
  Die Menge der anwendbaren Aktionen kann in bestimmten Views einge-
  schränkt oder verändert sein; ebenso kann die Menge der darstellbaren Ob-
  jekte in bestimmten Views restringiert sein.
– Komplexität der Aktionen
  • Eine Reihenfolgenabhängigkeit bei der Durchführung von Aufgaben ist
    nicht vorhanden. Die Dialoginitiative geht vom Benutzer aus, was wie-
    derum bei unerfahrenen bzw. Gelegenheitsbenutzern zu Unsicherheiten
    bei der Durchführung von Aufgaben führen kann.
  • Relationen zwischen Aktionen, Objekten und Views müssen während der
    Bearbeitung von Aufgaben vom Benutzer berücksichtigt werden.
– Komplexität der dargestellten Objekte
  • Hierarchierelationen zwischen Objekten sind bei der Bearbeitung von
    Aufgaben durch den Benutzer mit einzubeziehen.
  • Abhängigkeitsbeziehungen zwischen Objekten sind ebenfalls vom Benut-
    zer zu berücksichtigen.
  • Komplexe Strukturen werden vereinfacht visualisiert.

Abb. 1. Intuitive Bedienung?!

Aktionen, die in Applikationen mit graphischen Benutzungsoberflächen verfügbar sind, können in zwei Gruppen aufgeteilt werden [27]: *navigatorische* und *nicht-navigatorische* Aktionen.

Navigatorische Aktionen dienen in erster Linie der „Verwaltung" der Benutzungsoberfläche durch den Benutzer (vgl. *window housekeeping* [21, S.337]). Hierunter fallen Aktionen zum Verschieben, Verändern der Größe, Minimieren von Views oder zum Öffnen und Schließen von Views. Daneben dienen navigatorische Aktionen auch der Organisation der Darstellung von Objekten innerhalb von Views. So können durch navigatorische Aktionen einzelne Objekte zu der Menge der dargestellten Objekte hinzugefügt oder aus ihr gelöscht werden. Auch der sichtbare Bereich von Views wird durch navigatorische Aktionen, wie beispielsweise dem *scrolling*, verändert. Das Gleiche gilt für das Auswählen bestimmter Objekte auf der Benutzungsoberfläche mit Hilfe des Eingabemediums.

Nicht-navigatorische Aktionen sind applikationsspezifisch und dienen zur Manipulation von Applikationsobjekten.

2 Das System Iust$^+$

Das System *Iust*$^+$ ist ein planbasiertes Hilfesystem für Applikationen mit graphischer Benutzungsoberfläche, das neue Ansätze zur Berücksichtigung der Eigenschaften dieser Oberächen aufzeigt.

2.1 Architektur

Die Architektur und der Datenfluß innerhalb des Systems ist in Abbildung 2 dargestellt: Vom Benutzer erfolgreich ausgeführte Aktionen werden in einer Dialoghistorie protokolliert und an den Planerkenner übergeben. Der Planerkenner erstellt den Aufgabenkontext, indem er diese Aktionen gemäß den Plandefinitionen, die in der statischen Planbasis repräsentiert sind, auf Planhypothesen aus der dynamischen Planbasis abbildet. Der Aufgabenkontext wird durch die Menge der Planhypothesen, die in der dynamischen Wissensbasis enthalten sind, definiert.

Eine zweite wichtige Komponente zur Planverarbeitung bildet diejenige zur Planvervollständigung. Sie generiert Aktionssequenzen, die notwendig sind, um das Ziel von Planhypothesen, welche noch nicht erkannt sind, zu erreichen. Der Planvervollständiger baut hierbei auf den aktivierenden Sequenzen der Planhypothesen auf und komplettiert diese durch die Generierung von Sequenzen fehlender Elemente.

Navigatorische Aktionen – sie werden während des Planerkennungsvorganges nicht weiter verarbeitet – werden von der Plangenerierungskomponente bei der Erzeugung von Interaktionsschritten berücksichtigt. Sie greift dazu auf das Applikationsmodell zurück, um Vor- und Nachbedingungen von Aktionen zu erfassen. Die generierten Interaktionsschritte werden direkt an die Hilfekomponenten weitergereicht.

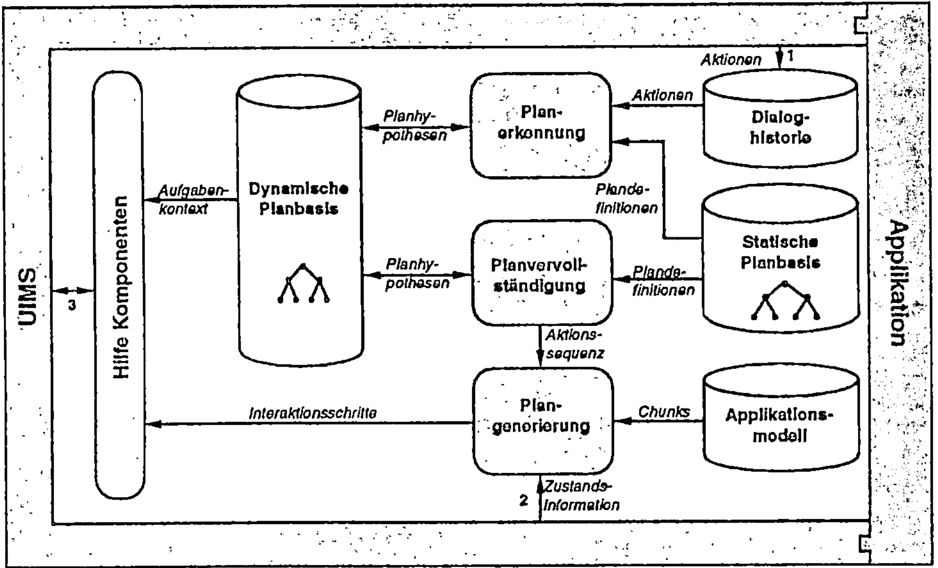

Abb. 2. Systemarchitektur und Datenfluß

2.2 Aufbau der Wissensbasis

Eine wesentliche Grundlage für die Erzeugung von Hilfestellungen ist die Modellierung des hierfür benötigten Wissens. So müssen Pläne für typische Aufgaben modelliert werden, die mit der Applikation durchgeführt werden können, um auf Benutzerziele schließen zu können. Die Definitionen von Vor- und Nachbedingungen von Applikationsaktionen werden in einem Applikationsmodell repräsentiert.

Statische Planbasis. Die *statische Planbasis* enthält vordefinierte Pläne. Während des Erkennungsvorganges dient sie als *Abbildungsvorschrift* für die Zuordnung von beobachteten Aktionen zu Plänen. Sie verändert sich während der Laufzeit des Planerkenners nicht. Pläne und ihre Ziele sind parametrisierbar und können hierarchisch angeordnet werden.

Die Definition der statischen Planbasis erfolgt mit der speziell entwickelten Plansprache GPL^+ (Goal Plan Language). Sie bietet erweiterte Definitionskonstrukte, um auch Eigenschaften, die graphischen Benutzungsoberflächen inhärent sind, modellieren zu können.

In Abbildung 3 ist der strukturelle Aufbau der statischen Planbasis dargestellt. Die beiden Hierarchiestufen *Zielebene/Aktionsebene* und die darüberliegende *Planebene* können 0 oder $n - mal$ in der statischen Planbasis definiert werden. Dies wird durch die an die *Kleene'sche Hülle* angelehnte Notation (*) dargestellt. Daraus folgt, daß mit der Sprache GPL^+ Planbasen formuliert werden können, die wenigstens *eine* und maximal $n + 1$ Planhierachiestufen besitzen.

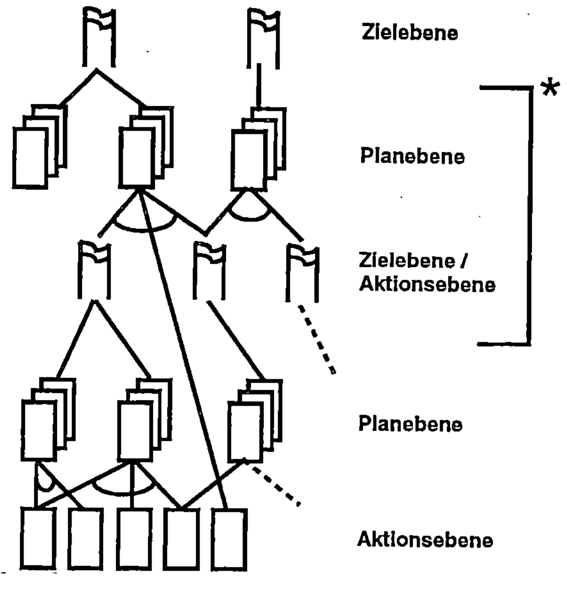

Abb. 3. Struktureller Aufbau der statischen Planbasis

Aktionen. Die mit *GPL*[+] formulierbaren *Aktionen* entsprechen *nicht-navigatorischen Aktionen. Navigatorische Aktionen* werden allein während des Plangenerierungsprozesses berücksichtigt und kommen nur im Applikationsmodell zur Anwendung (s. Abschnitt 2.3).

Definition 1 Aktion in GPL[+]. Eine *Aktion* ist ein terminales Element eines Planes, das nicht weiter zerlegbar ist und nicht von navigatorischer Art ist.

Pläne. Pläne sind Handlungsbeschreibungen zum Erreichen bestimmter Ziele. In *GPL*[+] wird ein Plan als eine Menge von Aktionen und Subzielen aufgefaßt. Durch temporale Constraints kann eine Halbordnung über diese Menge definiert werden.

Definition 2 Plan. Ein *Plan* besteht aus einer endlichen Multimenge von Elementen (Aktionen und Subziele), für die eine partielle Ordnung bezüglich der Ausführungszeitpunkte ihrer Elemente definiert ist. Desweiteren können weitere einschränkende Bedingungen für Parameterbelegungen der Elemente sowie zur Hypothesenverstärkung und -abschwächung spezifiziert sein. Eine hinsichtlich der partiellen Ordnung korrekten Ausführung der Elemente unter Einhaltung der einschränkenden Bedingungen führt zu dem Zielzustand des Planes.

Mit Hilfe von Constraints können Abhängigkeiten und Beziehungen zwischen einzelnen Elementen eines Planes definiert werden:

1. Zeitliche Abhängigkeiten zwischen Elementen des Planes werden durch *temporale Constraints* definiert.

(a) *Relative temporale Constraints* drücken Vorgänger- und Nachfolgerbeziehungen aus.

(b) *Absolute temporale Constraints* werden zur Einhaltung von exakten Zeitpunkten des Auftretens bestimmter Element eines Planes verwendet.

2. *Notwendige und optionale Elemente* eines Planes werden durch Constraints definiert, die eine minimale oder maximale Anzahl an Wiederholungen eines Elementes innerhalb eines Planes spezifizieren. Dabei wird *Optionalität* durch die Angabe von 0 und *Notwendigkeit* durch die Angabe von 1 ausgedrückt.

3. *Relationen zwischen Parametern* werden ebenfalls zur weiteren Überwachung der Zuordnung von beobachteten Aktionen bzw. erreichten Subzielen zu Plänen eingesetzt. Folgende Constraints sind zwischen Parametern von Elementen eines Planes definierbar: *Gleichheit/Ungleichheit, Typgleichheit/-ungleichheit, explizite Typangche, expliziter Wert* und *Objekthierarchiebeziehung.*

4. *View-Constraints* restringieren ebenfalls die Möglichkeit der Zuordnung von Aktionen und Zielen zu Plänen.
Jede Aktion führt einen impliziten Parameter mit, der das View enthält, indem die Aktion aktiviert wurde. Folgende Relationen sind zwischen Elementen eines Planes definierbar: *Viewgleichheit/-ungleichheit* und *explizites View.*

5. *Cancel-Constraints* ermöglichen die Erkennung von Abbruchsituationen eines Planes. Gründe für den Abbruch können bestimmte beobachtete Aktionen oder auch erreichte Ziele sein. Es werden Constraints auf der Ebene der Parameterbelegung zur Verfügung gestellt, um den Bezug zum konkreten Plan herstellen zu können.

Ziele. In *GPL*⁺ werden sämtliche Ziele, die mit der Durchführung von Plänen erreicht werden, explizit repräsentiert. Dies führt zu einer klaren Darstellung von alternativen Plänen für ein Ziel. Ziele sind parametrisierbar.

Definition 3 Ziel. Ein Ziel ist der Zustand, der nach der Ausführung eines Planes Gültigkeit besitzt. Das Ziel eines Planes kann wiederum ein notwendiges Teilziel bei der Durchführung eines anderen Planes sein. Für solche Ziele wird der Begriff Subziel verwendet.

Dynamische Planbasis. Vom Planerkenner aufgestellte Hypothesen über Pläne, die der Benutzer momentan verfolgt, werden in der *dynamischen Planbasis* abgelegt. Diese spiegelt dadurch zu jedem Zeitpunkt den aktuellen Aufgabenkontext und somit den Dialogkontext wider.

Definition 4 Planhypothese. Unter einer Planhypothese wird eine konkrete und (partiell) instantiierte Realisierung eines Planes der statischen Planbasis verstanden.

Die dynamische Planbasis entspricht strukturell der statischen Planbasis. Aktionen in der dynamischen Planbasis sind mit konkret beobachteten Aktionen und ihren Parameterbelegungen identisch.

Erlaubt die Plansprache GPL^+ bereits die Modellierung unterschiedlicher Planinteraktionen (Einbettung von Plänen, Planüberlappung, Alternativen sowie Planabbruch), so ermöglicht die konzeptuelle Trennung der Abbildungsvorschrift von Aktionen und Zielen zu Plänen (statische Planbasis) von der Menge der Planhypothesen (dynamische Planbasis) die Modellierung *multipler Planhypothesen*, also der zeitgleichen Verfolgung mehrerer Planhypothesen zu einem bestimmten Plan (tritt bei multipler Selektion auf).

Applikationsmodell. Eine Applikation wird durch ihre Funktionalität definiert. Als Funktionalität wird dabei die gesamte Menge der von der Applikation angebotenen Aktionen bezeichnet. Das Applikationsmodell beinhaltet die Modellierung dieser Aktionen, wobei zwischen *applikationsspezifischem* und *generischen* Teil (Aktionen, die allen Applikationen gemein sind) unterschieden wird. Die Modellierung umfaßt Vor- und Nachbedingungen der Aktionen. Das Applikationsmodell wird für die Generierung von Interaktionsschritten herangezogen. Interaktionsschritte können navigatorische und nicht-navigatorische Aktionen sein.

2.3 Verfahren zur Wissensverarbeitung

Das Planerkennungsverfahren. Der Planerkenner stellt das Kernstück des planbasierten Hilfesystems $Iust^+$ dar. Er schließt von einer Folge ausgeführter Aktionen auf zugrundeliegende Pläne. Dabei können beliebig viele Pläne aus der statischen und dynamischen Planbasis überwacht werden. Die Planerkennung beschränkt sich während des Prozesses auf die Verarbeitung von nicht-navigatorischen Aktionen, um eine sinnvolle Zuordnung von Aktionen zu Plänen zu gewährleisten. Würden *navigatorische Aktionen* bereits bei der Planerkennung berücksichtigt, so könnte beim Beobachten einer solchen Aktion theoretisch auf sämtliche modellierten Benutzerziele geschlossen werden, da navigatorische Aktionen prinzipiell Bestandteil eines jeden Planes sein können.

Der verwendete *Spreading-Activation-Algorithmus* kann informell als die Steuerung der Ausbreitung von Aktivierungen beschrieben werden. Aktionen geben Aktivierungen an Pläne weiter, die dann diese Aktivierung an ihre Ziele weiterleiten. Ziele geben ihre Aktivierungen analog zu Aktionen an Pläne weiter [28].

Die Ausbreitung von Aktivierungen endet, wenn ein Ziel nicht Subziel ist, also nicht in anderen Plänen enthalten ist. Sie endet ebenfalls, wenn die Aktivierung aufgrund von unerfüllten Constraints nicht weitergeleitet werden kann.

Dies verdeutlicht ein Beispiel (Abbildung 4): Nach Ausführung der durch den Benutzer ausgelösten Aktion a wird in der dynamischen Planbasis eine Instanz für diese erzeugt. Nach der Verifikation von Constraints gibt die Aktion ihre Aktivierung an die Pläne weiter, für die alle Constraints erfüllt waren. Hier sind dies die beiden Planhypothesen P und Q.

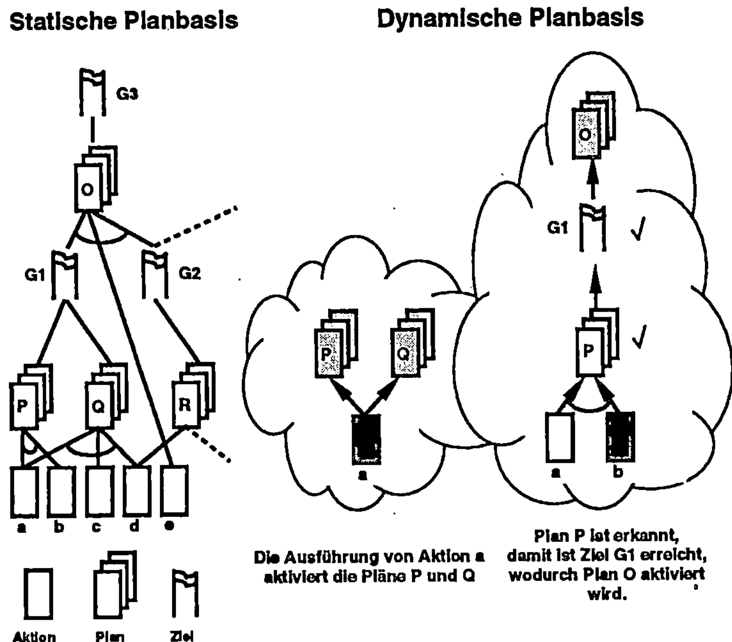

Abb. 4. Das Planerkennungsverfahren

Als nächstes aktiviert der Benutzer die Aktion *b*. Sie kann nur der Planhypothese *P* zugeordnet werden. Aktion *b* gibt deshalb ihre Aktivierung an diese Planhypothese weiter. Da keine weiteren Aktionen oder Subziele für die Durchführung von Planhypothese *P* notwendig sind, gilt diese als erkannt. Sie gibt nun ihre Aktivierung an ihr Ziel weiter, das daraufhin versucht, die Aktivierung an andere Planhypothesen weiterzureichen.

Das Plangenerierungsverfahren. Die eingesetzten Verfahren zur Planerkennung und Planvervollständigung verarbeiten nur nicht-navigatorische Aktionen, basierend auf vordefinierten Plänen. Navigatorische Aktionen sind jedoch wichtig, um Aktionen auf der Benutzungsoberfläche aktivieren zu können.

Solche Sequenzen von Interaktionsschritten werden von der Plangenerierungskomponente erzeugt, die das Wissen des Applikationsmodells verarbeitet. Der hierzu verwendete Algorithmus arbeitet nach einem *backward-chaining* Verfahren.

Die durch die drei Planverfahren erzeugte Kontextinformation bildet die Grundlage für die Hilfestrategien, die von *Iust*[+] verwendet werden.

2.4 Aufgabenorientierte, dynamisch generierte Animation

Die von *Iust*[+] generierten Hilfestellungen umfassen passive und aktive Hilfestrategien, wie graphische Orientierungshilfe [8], tutorieller Modus, selektiver Zugang zu einem hypertextbasierten Hilfesystem, analysierende und kooperative

Hilfe [27]. Schwerpunktmäßig wird in diesem Papier die neue Hilfestrategie der *aufgabenorientierten, dynamisch generierten Animation* behandelt [25].

Durch die Einführung graphischer Benutzungsoberflächen wird eine rein textuelle Darstellung von Hilfe ungeeignet: Relationen zwischen Objekten, z.B. räumliche Bezüge, sind textuell nur schwierig darzustellen. Ein Anwendungsexperte antwortet häufig einem ungeübten Benutzer auf die Frage, wie eine Aufgabe am Bildschirm auszuführen sei, mit „Ich zeige es Dir einmal." [21, S.205,S.461f].

Ein Schwerpunkt der neueren Animationspräsentation ist in der Visualisierung von Interaktionstechniken zu sehen. Eine animierte Präsentation der Interaktionstechniken *Selektieren* oder *Kopieren* mit einer Maus kann zeitliche Abläufe besser visualisieren als textuelle Darstellungen (s. Beispiel 1).

Beispiel 1.
Benutzer: „*Wie kopiere ich Datei* Anschreiben.txt *in das Verzeichnis* Briefe *?"*
System: „*Bewege die Maus an die Position von Datei* Anschreiben.txt. *Drücke nun gleichzeitig die SHIFT-Taste und die linke Maustaste nieder. Halte beide Tasten gedrückt und bewege die Maus zum Verzeichnis* Briefe. *Lasse nun beide Tasten wieder los. "*

Die verbale Beschreibung des Beispiels 1 wird noch umfangreicher und unübersichtlicher, wenn berücksichtigt werden muß, daß das Verzeichnis *Briefe* momentan nicht sichtbar ist. Bevor kopiert werden kann, müssen zuvor Fenster geöffnet werden, um beide Objekte (Datei *Anschreiben.txt* und Verzeichnis *Briefe*) gleichzeitig am Bildschirm sichtbar zu machen.

Eines der ersten Systeme, das Animation als Hilfemedium einsetzt, ist das System *GAK* (*Graphical Animation from Knowledge* [17]). Es setzt eine animierte 2D-Darstellung des Eingabemediums (z.B. Maus oder Stylus) als Erklärung für die Kausalität der Bewegung des Cursors in einer CAD-Anwendung ein. Ein Bezug zum aktuellen Bildschirminhalt bzw. zur Dialoghistorie wird nicht hergestellt, da das System nur vordefinierte Präsentationssequenzen einsetzt.

Im Gegensatz dazu geht das System *UIDE* [12, 24] bei der Generierung der Animationssequenz auf den momentanen Bildschirminhalt ein. Anhand eines Programms zum Entwurf von digitalen Schaltkreisen wird das Potential der Animation, wie sie innerhalb von *UIDE* realisiert ist, demonstriert [23].

Die bisherigen Hilfesysteme mit animierter Informationspräsentation lassen die Dialoghistorie außer acht und zeigen nur exemplarisch, wie eine Sequenz von Interaktionsschritten mit einem Eingabemedium auszuführen ist, um eine einzelne Aktion zu aktivieren. Sinnvoller wäre es jedoch, den bisherigen Kontext zu berücksichtigen: Parameterwerte können z.B. aus dem Aufgabenkontext ermittelt werden, um dadurch einen Bezug zur Aufgabe herzustellen, die ein Benutzer momentan verfolgt.

Beispiel 2. Das Problem des Benutzers liegt diesmal nicht primär in der Aktion des Kopierens, sondern darin, daß die Datei *Anschreiben.txt* aufgrund der großen Anzahl an Dateien im Verzeichnis im momentanen Ausschnitt nicht dargestellt wird, und der Benutzer nicht weiß, wie die Aktion zum Verschieben des sichtbaren Ausschnittes auszulösen ist².

Ein aufgabenbezogenes Animationssystem generiert etwa für das Beispiel 2 eine Sequenz von Interaktionsschritten, um die Datei *Anschreiben.txt* sichtbar zu machen und anschließend in das Verzeichnis *Briefe* zu kopieren. Anstelle der Präsentation einer exemplarischen animierten Darstellung der Ausführung der Aktion *kopiereDatei*, wird eine Animationssequenz generiert, die durch die Verwendung der konkreten Objekten (*Anschreiben.txt* und *Briefe*) sich auf die momentane Aufgabe und das Problem des Benutzers bezieht.

Analog zu diesem Beispiel kann das Problem des Benutzers auch in der dem Anwendungssystem zugrundeliegenden Objekthierarchie oder in der Verwendung unterschiedlicher Fenstertypen liegen. Für diese Fälle muß die Animation entsprechende Interaktionsschritte zum Hinzufügen existierender Objekte oder das Auswählen bzw. Erzeugen von Fenstern mit geeigneten Fensterattributen generieren.

Eine Ausdehnung der Kontextsensitivität der Animationsgenerierung auf die aktuelle Aufgabe des Benutzers ist erforderlich, da Probleme meist im Zusammenhang mit einer Aufgabe auftreten, die der Benutzer mit Hilfe der Anwendung erledigen möchte. Das Animationssystem kann, anhand der von einem planbasierten System ermittelten Aufgabe, Parameterwerte ableiten (Beispiel 2).

Mehrere Arbeiten über planbasierte Hilfesysteme haben gezeigt, daß es schwierig ist, allein aufgrund der beobachteten Aktionen eindeutig auf das Ziel des Benutzers zu schließen. Daraus kann abgeleitet werden, daß die alleinige Präsentation animierter Darstellungen oftmals nicht ausreicht, um dem Benutzer eindeutig das Ziel der Animation zu vermitteln. Hier wird Text gefordert, der die Animation erklärend begleitet (vgl. *narrated animation* [4]). Als Medium ist dafür die gesprochene Sprache vorzuziehen; sie ermöglicht dem Benutzer der Präsentation der animierten Darstellungen zu folgen, ohne mit den Augen laufend zwischen Animation und dargestelltem Text wechseln zu müssen.

Untersuchungen haben gezeigt, daß animierte Hilfe – im Vergleich zu rein textuellen Instruktionen – direkt nach dem Erlernen zu einer besseren Performanz der Benutzer führte. Eine Woche später wiesen diese Benutzer jedoch eine schlechtere und unsicherere Arbeitsweise auf, als diejenigen, die rein textuelle Instruktionen erhalten hatten [18].

In einer anderen Studie wird jedoch gezeigt, daß die Kombination von Animation und gesprochener Sprache den größten Lerneffekt und somit zur größten Arbeitseffizienz bei Benutzern führt [29].

Animation kann auch als Hilfemedium zur Erklärung der Bedienung und Wartung von realen Objekten eingesetzt werden [9, 2]. Der Einsatz realistischer 3D-Animation zur Erklärung der Bedienung von 3D-Eingabemedien (wie 3D-Mäuse, *Data-Gloves*, *Eye-Phone* oder *Data-Suits* [13, 9]) im Umgang mit Anwendungssoftware, wird in [14] vorgeschlagen.

---

² Unter dem Betriebssystem *OS/2* ist Verschieben durch das direkte Manipulieren des Verschiebebalkens möglich; unter dem graphischen Fenstersystem *X-Windows* hingegen muß hierzu die mittlere Maustaste betätigt werden, um den Ausschnitt direkt zu positionieren. Besitzt die angeschlossene Maus weniger als 3 Tasten muß eine zusätzliche Taste auf der Tastatur gedrückt werden.

Um das Ziel der aufgabenorientierten Präsentation animierter Darstellungen zu erreichen, muß die Animationskomponente mit einer Planerkennungs- und Planvervollständigungskomponente gekoppelt sein. Erst durch diese Komponenten kann neben dem aktuellen Kontext der Benutzungsoberfläche (Oberflächenkontext) auch der Bezug zu den Zielen des Benutzers (Aufgabenkontext) hergestellt werden.

Die im Prototyp *Iust*[+] realisierte animierte Hilfe unterscheidet drei Formen der Animation in ihrem Umfang und Ziel:

1. Animierte Darstellung der Aktivierung *einer* zukünftigen Aktion.
   Die Animation beschränkt sich darauf, die Aktivierung *einer* einzelnen Aktion unter Einbeziehung des aktuellen Oberflächen- sowie des Aufgabenkontextes zu präsentieren.
2. Beenden eines begonnenen Planes.
   Die Animation präsentiert sukzessiv die Aktivierung aller zukünftigen Aktionen, die zum Erreichen eines bestimmten Zieles (Aufgabe) notwendig sind. Dabei werden der Oberflächen- sowie der Aufgabenkontext berücksichtigt.
3. Exemplarische animierte Darstellung der Durchführung einer Aufgabe.
   Die Animation führt unter Berücksichtigung des aktuellen Oberflächenkontextes, jedoch ohne auf den Aufgabenkontext einzugehen, eine Aufgabe vollständig durch (*Animation from scratch*).

Zur Generierung animierter Interaktionsschritte wird ein Planungsprozeß eingesetzt, der sich aus zwei Schleifen zusammensetzt (Abbildung 5). Hierdurch kann sowohl auf Veränderungen des Aufgabenkontextes als auch auf Veränderungen der Benutzungsoberfläche eingegangen werden.

Die *innere Schleife* umfaßt die Plangenerierungskomponente und die Komponente zur Animationspräsentation. Diese Schleife dient als Rückkoppelungsschleife für Veränderungen an der Benutzungsoberfläche, wie sie beispielsweise durch die Ausführung von navigatorischen Aktionen entstehen können.

Die *äußere Schleife* umfaßt die Planerkennungs- und Planvervollständigungskomponente. Diese Schleife fungiert als Rückkoppelungsschleife, die Veränderungen des Aufgabenkontextes der Animationskomponente zur Verfügung stellt.

3   Zusammenfassung

Im vorliegenden Papier wird anhand des planbasierten Hilfesystems *Iust*[+] demonstriert, wie neue planbasierte Verfahren Anfängern und Gelegenheitsbenutzern von komplexen Applikationen auch bei graphischen Benutzungsoberflächen individuelle, aufgabenbezogene und in ihrem Detaillierungsgrad variierende Hilfeleistungen anbieten können. Die in *Iust*[+] angebotenen Hilfestrategien setzen Präsentationsmedien wie Graphik, Text und Animation ein, um dem Benutzer den sich hierdurch ergebenden Synergieeffekt zugänglich zu machen.

Ein Schwerpunkt dabei ist die *aufgabenbezogene Präsentation von animierten Darstellungen* der Durchführung von Interaktionsschritten. Anders als bisherige Hilfesysteme mit einer animierten Darstellung geht die *aufgabenbezogene*

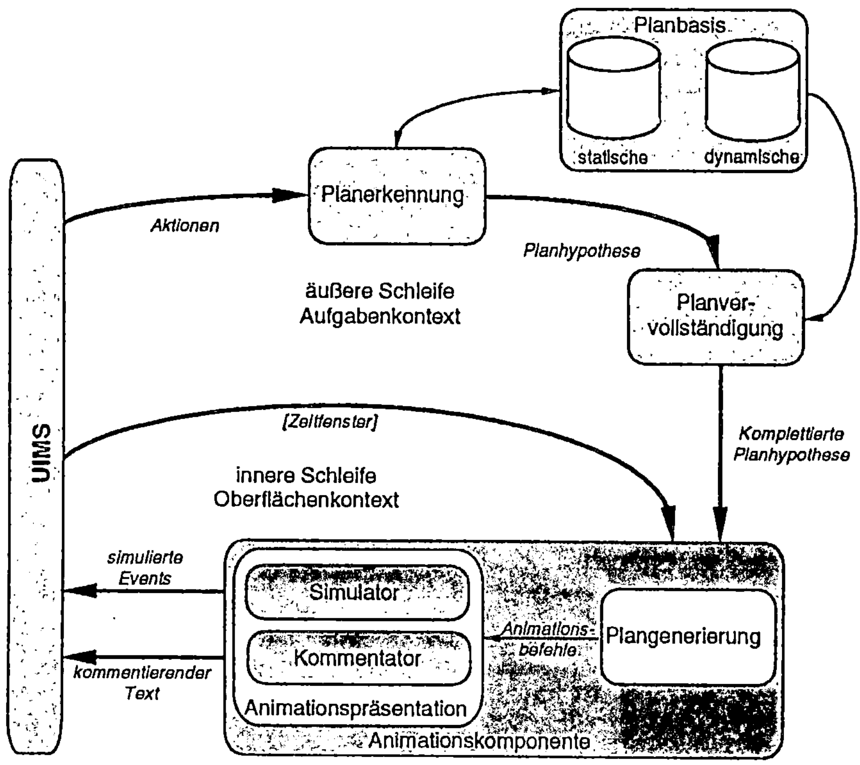

Abb. 5. Animationsgenerierung in 2 Phasen

animierte Hilfe nicht einzig auf den aktuellen Oberflächenkontext ein, sondern auch auf den aktuellen Aufgabenkontext.

Für *Iust*[+] wurde eine Plansprache mit neuen Konstrukten zur Modellierung von multipler Selektion, verschiedenen Fenster und Fenstertypen (View) und der parallelen Bearbeitung mehrerer Aufgaben durch den Benutzer entwickelt. Das verwendete Planerkennungsverfahren ist eine Weiterentwicklung des Spreading-Activation-Algorithmus. Die Weiterentwicklung erfolgte anhand der Anforderungen graphischer Benutzungsoberflächen.

Die Bedeutung der multiplen Selektion für die Planerkennung ist noch nicht vollständig bekannt. Sie kann, anders als in *Iust*[+], auch dahingehend interpretiert werden, daß ein einziger Plan verfolgt wird, der auf der möglicherweise heterogenen Menge von Objekten operiert. Hierzu müßten Konstrukte in der Plansprache enthalten sein, die eine *Quantifizierung von Parametermengen* erlauben. Offen bleibt jedoch weiterhin die Frage inwieweit verschiedene Pläne aufgrund einer multiplen Selektion automatisch zu einem Plan zusammengefaßt werden könnten. Hierbei treten Aspekte wie Planoptimierung und Planmodifikation in den Vordergrund.

Der kommentierende Text zu einer Animation wird anhand adaptierter vorgegebener Texte erzeugt. Dies führt dazu, daß nicht verbalisiert werden kann, warum ein bestimmter Interaktionsschritt in diesem Kontext, jedoch nicht in einem anderen auszuführen ist. Die Ergänzung der Animationsgenerierung durch eine *Erklärungskomponente* zur Generierung von erklärenden, kommentierenden Texten ist notwendig. Eine solche Komponente greift dazu auf die Ableitungsstruktur des Backward-chainers zu, um eine Begründung des Verhaltens der Animationskomponente zu generieren.

Literatur

1. ACM. *Proceedings of the International Workshop on Intelligent User Interfaces '93*, Orlando, FL, January 1993. acm Press.
2. E. André, W. Graf, J. Heinsohn, B. Nebel, H.-J. Profitlich, T. Rist, und W. Wahlster. *PPP-Personalized Plan-Based Presenter.* Document D-93-05, DFKI, 1992.
3. N. I. Badler, B. A. Barsky, und D. Zeltzer. *Making Them Move: Mechanics, Control, and Animation of articulated Figures.* San Mateo, California: Morgan Kaufmann Publishers, Inc, 1991.
4. N. I. Badler, B. L. Webber, J. Kalita, und J. Esakov. *Animation from Instructions.* In: Making Them Move: Mechanics, Control, and Animation of articulated Figures [3], Kapitel 3.
5. M. Bauer, S. Biundo, D. Dengler, J. Koehler, und G. Paul. *PHI – A Logic-Based Tool for Intelligent Help Systems.* In: Proceedings of the 13th International Joint Conference on Artificial Intelligence, Chambery, France, 1993. Auch als DFKI Research Report RR-92-52.
6. T. Catarci, M. F. Costabile, und S. Levialdi (Hrsg.). *Proceedings of the International Workshop AVI'92, Advanced Visual Interfaces,* Band 36: World Scientific Series in Computer Science, Rome, Italy, May 1992. World Scientific.
7. D. Dengler, M. Gutmann, und G. Hector. *Der Planerkenner REPLIX.* Memo 16, Institut für Informatik, Universität des Saarlandes, September 1987.
8. T. Fehrle und M. A. Thies. *InCome: A System to Navigate through Interactions and Plans.* In: H.-J. Bullinger (Hrsg.), Human Aspects in Computing: Design and Use of Interactive Systems and Information Management, Amsterdam, London, New York, Tokyo, 1991. Elsevier Science Publishers B.V.
9. S. Feiner. *Virtual Worlds for Visualizing Information.* In: Catarci et al. [6].
10. T. W. Finin. *Providing Help and Advice in Task Oriented Systems.* In: Proceedings of the 8th International Joint Conference on Artificial Intelligence, S. 176–178, Karlsruhe, Germany, 1983.
11. G. Fischer, A. Lemke, und T. Schwab. *Knowledge-based Help Systems.* In: Proceedings of the CHI'85 Conference on Human Factors in Computing Systems. acm Press, 1985.
12. J. D. Foley, C. Gibbs, W. C. Kim, und S. Kovacevic. *A Knowledge-based User Interface Management System.* In: Soloway et al. [22].
13. J. D. Foley, A. van Dam, S. Feiner, und J. Hughes. *Computer Graphics. Principles and Pratice.* The Systems Programming Series. Menlo Park, California: Addison-Wesley Publishing Company, 2. Auflage, 1990.
14. W. Graf und M. A. Thies. *Perspektiven zur Kombination von automatischem Animationsdesign und planbasierter Hilfe.* KI, 6(4), 1992. Auch als DFKI Research Report RR-92-09.

15. M. Hecking, C. Kemke, E. Nessen, D. Dengler, M. Gutmann, und G. Hector. *The SINIX Consultant: A Progress Report.* Memo Nr. 28, Projekt SC, Fachbereich Informatik, Universität Saarbrücken, Deutschland, 1988.

16. A. Hirschmann. *Das Hilfesystem MATHILDE.* Dissertation, Universität Regensburg, 1990.

17. D. Neiman. *Graphical Animation from Knowledge.* In: Proceedings of the 2nd National Conference of the American Association for Artificial Intelligence, Pittsburgh, PA, 1982. AAAI Press.

18. S. Palmiter und J. Elkerton. *An Evaluation of Animated Demonstrations for Learning Computer-based Tasks.* In: S. P. Robertson, G. M. Olson, und J. S. Olson (Hrsg.), CHI'91 Conference Proceedings : Reaching Through Technology, New Orleans,LA, 1991. acm Press.

19. K.-J. Quast. *PLANET, Planerkennung mit aktivierten Handlungsnetzen.* Sankt Augustin: GMD, 1991.

20. G. Salvendy und M. J. Smith (Hrsg.). *Human-Computer Interaction: Software and Hardware Interfaces. Proceedings of the 5th International Conference on Human-Computer Interaction, HCI International '93,* Adcances in Human Factors/Ergonomics, Orlando, FL, August 1993. Elsevier Science Publishers B.V.

21. B. Shneiderman. *Designing the User Interface. Strategies for Effective Human-Computer Interaction.* Reading, Massachusetts - Menlo Park, California - New York: Addison-Wesley, 2nd Auflage, 1992.

22. E. Soloway, D. Frye, und S. B. Sheppard (Hrsg.). *CHI'88 Conference Proceedings: Human Factors in Computing Systems,* Washington, D.C., 1988.

23. P. Sukaviriya und J. D. Foley. *Coupling a UI Framework with Automatic Generation of Context-Sensitive Animated Help.* In: Proceedings of the ACM SIGGRAPH Symp. on User Interfaces Software and Technology (UIST'90), Snowbird, UT, 1990. ACM SIGGRAPH, acm Press.

24. P. Sukaviriya und J. D. Foley. *Supporting Adaptive Interfaces in a Knowledge-Based User Interface Environment.* In: Proceedings of the International Workshop on Intelligent User Interfaces '93 [1].

25. M. A. Thies. *Animated Help as a Sensible Extension of a Plan-Based Help System.* In: Salvendy und Smith [20].

26. M. A. Thies. *Adpative User Interfaces.* In: Proceedings 13th World Computer Congress, IFIP Congress'94: Computer and Communications Evolution – The Driving Forces –, 1994. In Kürze erscheinend.

27. M. A. Thies. *Planbasierte Hilfeverfahren für direkt-manipulative Systeme: Erkennung, Vervollständigung und Visualisierung von Interaktionsplänen.* Nr. 67, infix, Sankt Augustin, Germany, 1994. Auch als Dissertation, Fakultät Informatik, Universität Stuttgart.

28. M. A. Thies und F. Berger. *Plan-Based Graphical Help in Object-Oriented User Interfaces.* In: Catarci et al. [6].

29. P. E. Waterson und C. E. O'Malley. *Using animated demonstrations in multimedia applications: Some suggestions based upon experimental evidence.* In: Salvendy und Smith [20].

30. R. Wilensky, D. N. Chin, M. Luria, J. Martin, J. Mayfield, und D. Wu. *The Berkeley UNIX Consultant Project.* Computational Linguistics, 14:35–84, 1988.

Fehlermanagement in Verkehrsinformationsnetzen

Dagmar Schüth[+], Wolfgang Nejdl[*], Rolf Hager[+]
Lehrstuhl für Informatik 4 ([+]) und 5 ([*])
RWTH Aachen
Ahornstr. 55, D-52056 Aachen
email: [schueth,nejdl,rolf]@informatik.rwth-aachen.de

Abstract

In this paper, an approach to fault management in traffic information networks to isolate network faults in infrastructure networks will be introduced. We will show, that model-based diagnosis is an efficient method for finding explanations consisting of the underlying fault events of system failures. A fault management system based on these concepts will be discussed and evaluated.

1. Einleitung

Die ständige Zunahme der Verkehrsbelastung auf den Autobahnen führt zu der Entwicklung von leistungsfähigen Verkehrsinformationsnetzen (VIN). Der Einsatz von festen und mobilen Kommunikationssystemen ermöglicht eine Beeinflussung des Verkehrsverhaltens, so daß die Verkehrssicherheit, die Auslastung der Autobahnen und der Fahrkomfort gesteigert und die Umweltverschmutzung verringert werden kann.

In Bild 1.1 ist ein Ausschnitt eines Verkehrsinformationsnetzes dargestellt. Die Spitze der Netzwerkhierarchie bildet eine Gruppe von Verkehrsrechnerzentralen (VRZ). Sie sind untereinander verbunden und jeweils für den Betrieb eines gesamten

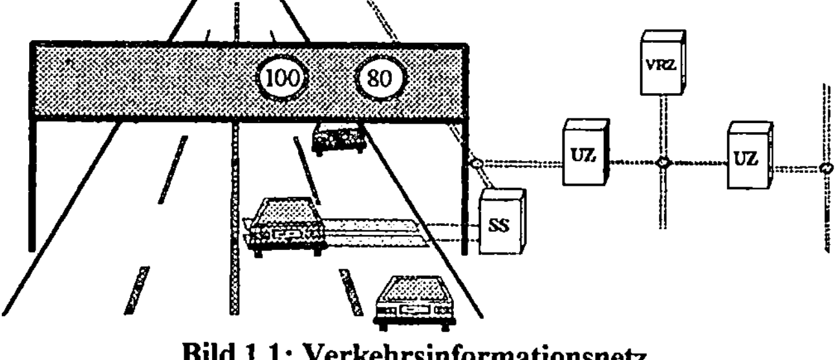
Bild 1.1: Verkehrsinformationsnetz

Bundeslandes verantwortlich. Sie verteilen ihre Aufgaben auf ihnen zugeordnete Unterzentralen (UZ). Diese wiederum überwachen mehrere Streckenstationen (SS), die direkt mit speziellen E/A-Kanälen verbunden sind. Letzere bilden die unterste Stufe des Verkehrsinformationsnetzes. Typische Beispiele sind Induktionschleifen zur Ermittlung von Verkehrsdaten, Wechselverkehrszeichen (WVZ), Sensoren für Wetterzustandserfassung, Radargeräte und elektronische Baken, die die Verbindung zwischen mobilen und festen Verkehrsinformationsnetzen herstellen ([2]).

Durch ständige Verbesserung und Neuentwicklung weiterer elektronischer Systeme und deren Integration in vorhandene Verkehrsinformationsnetze existiert heute eine heterogene Netzwerkstruktur, deren Reichweite die Ländergrenzen innerhalb Europas und der USA überschreitet ([6]). Die ISO (International Organization for Standardization) hat für das Betreiben eines solchen offenen Kommunikationsnetzes mit ihrem OSI-Referenzmodell ein Rahmenwerk geschaffen. Mit zahlreichen Standardisierungen hat sie zu der Definition eines Netzmanagements beigetragen und Vorgaben über seine Aufgaben und Struktur, die Definition von Managementinformation und die Spezifizierung von speziellen Managementfunktionen geliefert ([5]). Mit wachsender Größe der VIN nimmt insbesondere die Bedeutung des Fehlermanagements zu, zu dessen Aufgabe die Aufdeckung, Diagnose, Behebung und Prävention von Störungen gehören.

Die Funktionen der einzelnen Netzkomponenten werden durch autonome *Prozesse* realisiert, die dazu miteinander über Kommunikationsverbindungen Daten austauschen. Dieses System bildet den Rahmen für das zu entwickelnde Diagnose-Verfahren.

Bild 1.2 zeigt eine Menge von Prozessen und ihre Interaktionen. Der Prozeß *verkehr_rec* empfängt Verkehrsdaten vom zentralen Datenverteiler *vert_snd* über den Circuit[1] 7. Er schreibt sie direkt in einen Puffer und kann dann sofort für weitere Empfangsaufgaben zur Verfügung stehen. Sein

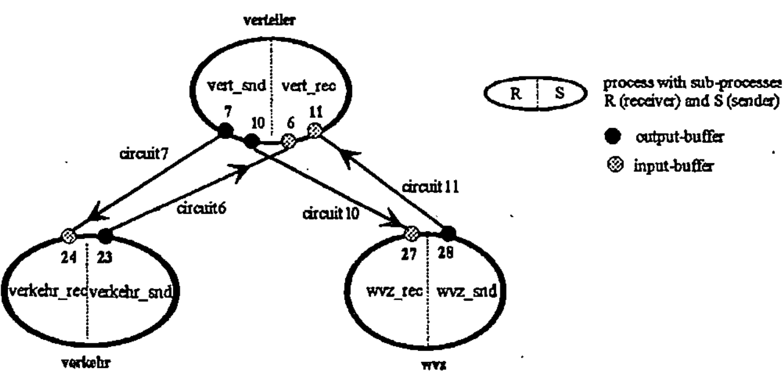

Partner *verkehr_snd* ermittelt daraus den aktuellen Verkehrszustand und sendet diesen zwecks weiterer Verteilung an *vert_rec*. Der Prozeß *wvz_rec* kann ihn dann von *vert_snd* empfangen und daraus die entsprechenden Maßnahmen für die Steuerung der Wechselverkehrszeichen ermitteln. Bei der Datenverteilung durch einen zentralen Prozeß werden viele Punkt-zu-Punkt-Verbindungen zusammengefaßt: alle Teilnehmer, die die Verkehrsdaten für die Realisierung ihrer Aufgaben benötigen, müssen keine eigenen Circuits zu *verkehr_snd* unterhalten, sondern nur zu *vert_snd*, was aus Sicht von *verkehr_snd* nur eine einzige Sende-Verbindung zu *vert_snd* ausmacht. Dadurch wird die Anzahl der möglichen Verbindungspartner stark eingeschränkt[2], was sich z.B. auf die Diagnose von Empfangsproblemen auswirkt (Bsp. 3.2).

In Verkehrsinformationsnetzen wird für die Zwecke des Fehlermanagements das Manager-Agent-Paradigma angewendet ([5]). Darin ist vorgesehen, daß alle autonomen Prozesse entdeckte Störungen in Form von Notifikationen an ihren zuständigen Manager senden. Das kann zu einer Flut von Folgefehlermeldungen und damit zur Erhöhung der Netzlast führen, unter der die Qualität des gesamten Systems leidet.

Im folgenden wird ein Diagnoseverfahren vorgestellt, welches die Ursache einer Störung unter Berücksichtigung der Notifikationsabhängigkeiten und zusätzlichem Kontextwissen ermittelt. Es ist zudem in der Lage, fehlende Meldungen durch den Ein-

---

[1]Circuit hier: gerichtete Punkt-zu-Punkt-Verbindung
[2]In dem untersuchten Modell gibt es Prozesse mit 1, 2 oder 4 direkten Verbindungspartnern.

satz von Hypothesen zu überbrücken und kann daher sowohl für die Diagnose wie auch zur Vermeidung redundanter Folgenotifikationen eingesetzt werden.

Das nächste Kapitel (2.1) rechtfertigt den hier gewählten Ansatz der modellbasierten Diagnose durch den Vergleich mit anderen bekannten Verfahren. Daran anschließend wird in Kapitel 2.2 ein Vorschlag zur Modellierung eines Verkehrsinformationsnetzes gemacht, der der Implementierung in einem Expertensystem zugrundeliegt, dessen Beschreibung in Kapitel 3 erfolgt. In Kapitel 4 wird auf die Beziehung zwischen den Notifikationsabhängigkeiten und dem modellierten System eingegangen.

2. Modellbasierte Diagnose

Der Algorithmus für die Fehlerdiagnose soll in der Lage sein, die tatsächliche Ursache einer Störung aufzudecken. Diese entspricht in einem Verkehrsinformationsnetz, wie es in Kapitel 1 dargestellt ist, einem fehlerhaften Ereignis, welches unabhängig von anderen Störungen auftritt.

2.1 Bekannte Fehlerdiagnoseverfahren

Methoden zur Diagnose sind im Bereich der Künstlichen Intelligenz zu finden, wozu bspw. die Einsetzung von Testsystemen (*diagnostics*), Entscheidungsbäumen und *Fault -Dictionary*'s gehören ([4]). Einen weit verbreiteten Ansatz stellen auch die regelbasierten Systeme (RBR: *rule based reasoning*) dar, bei denen empirisches Wissen der Form "wenn dieses Symptom auftritt, dann war zu 90% jene Komponente die Ursache" verarbeitet wird ([9], [1], [3]). Es werden Regeln für die Erklärung der Symptome definiert, ohne oder nur mit geringer Berücksichtigung des Systemverhaltens oder seiner Struktur. In einem Rechnernetz, dessen Konfiguration dynamisch und hierarchisch aufgebaut sein kann, ist dieser Ansatz ungeeignet, weil er nur wenig die Ersetzung von Komponenten oder die Erweiterung des Netzes durch Hinzunahme von neuen Teilnehmern unterstützt.

Der *modellbasierten* Diagnose liegt eine Verhaltensbeschreibung des zu diagnostizierenden Systems zugrunde. Sie wird nach dem Aufdecken einer Störung (*observation*) gestartet, die im Konflikt zu dem erwarteten Verhalten des Systems steht. Sie erfolgt somit symptom-gerichtet, wodurch automatisch eine Vorauswahl von Untersuchungen getroffen wird. Zudem kommt sie dadurch den ISO-Empfehlungen entgegen, weil sie im Gegensatz zu Testsystemen keine Polling-Mechanismen erforderlich macht, sondern die Notifikationen der Netzteilnehmer als Beobachtungen zum Starten des Diagnosevorganges einsetzt. Dieser liefert dann die Ursachen (*explanations*) für die Störungen. Die Verwendung von *Kontextdaten* (z.B. Beschreibung der Netztopologie) ist für die Diagnose nicht notwendig, dient aber dazu, die Lösungssuche zu beeinflussen und bestimmte Erklärungen vorab auszuschließen. Dadurch kann man die Lösungsfindung beschleunigen bzw. genauere Lösungen erzielen.

Für die Modellierung können Zwischenergebnisse aus der Entwurfsphase von Komponenten verwendet werden. Hierarchische Strukturen lassen sich ebenfalls integrieren, was z.B. in einem Rechnernetz von großer Bedeutung ist. Das ist ein wesentlicher Aspekt für hierarchische Diagnoseverfahren, bei denen eine iterative Verfeinerung der Ergebnisse erfolgt. Dieses kann für eine Vorabdiagnose in Komponenten (z.B. in den Agents) ausgenutzt werden, wodurch eine Datenreduzierung im Rechnernetz zu erwarten ist.

Im Vergleich zu den Fault-Dictionaries kann bei der modellbasierten Diagnose ein breiteres Fehlerspektrum überdeckt werden. Bei den Fault-Dictionaries wird vom Verfasser eine Vorauswahl von (einfachen) Simulationen getroffen, deren Auswirkungen analysiert werden müssen. Je komplexer das System ist, desto schwieriger ist die Erfassung aller Sonderfälle. Bei regelbasierten Systemen ist im Gegensatz zum modellbasierten Ansatz ein umfangreiches Erfahrungswissen zur Erstellung aller Regeln (*Regelbasis*) erforderlich. Zudem reicht dieses oft nicht aus, so daß auch Informationen über die Struktur und das Verhalten des Systems integriert werden müssen.

Im Bereich der modellbasierten Diagnose gibt es auch Ansätze zur Fehlerisolation in Protokollen ([10]). Die Modellierung erfolgt durch die Generierung von endlichen Automaten aus den Protokollbeschreibungen. In Rechnernetzen stellen die Protokollfehler eine Untermenge aller möglichen Fehler dar. Das Behandeln von Anwendungsfehlern muß prozeßspezifisch erfolgen, weil sie nicht durch das Protokoll erkannt werden können. In ([12]) wird der Schwerpunkt auf eine schnelle Fehlerdiagnose gelegt, zu deren Realisierung *Observers* verwendet werden, die parallel für die Aufdeckung von Störungen eingesetzt und nach und nach verfeinert werden können.

2.2 Modellierung

Zur Modellierung eines Rechnernetzes gehört sowohl die Spezifikation des Verhaltens der beteiligten Prozesse wie auch ihre Interaktionen untereinander. Zudem ist Kontextwissen erforderlich, aus dem die aktuelle Netztopologie mit den Verbindungskonstellationen und die Enthaltensrelationen hervorgeht.

Für die Verhaltensbeschreibung der Prozesse wurden endliche Automaten verwendet (Bild 2.1). Die Kreise bezeichnen die (für die Diagnose relevanten) Zustände, die Pfeile den Wechsel von einem Status in den anderen. Bei fehlerhaften Übergängen werden Notifikationen ausgesendet ("...!"). Die Kanten erhalten Gewichte, die ausdrücken, wie wahrscheinlich dieser Zustandswechsel ist. Er kann zudem an Bedingungen geknüpft sein (z.B. das Eintreffen einer Antwort des gewünsch

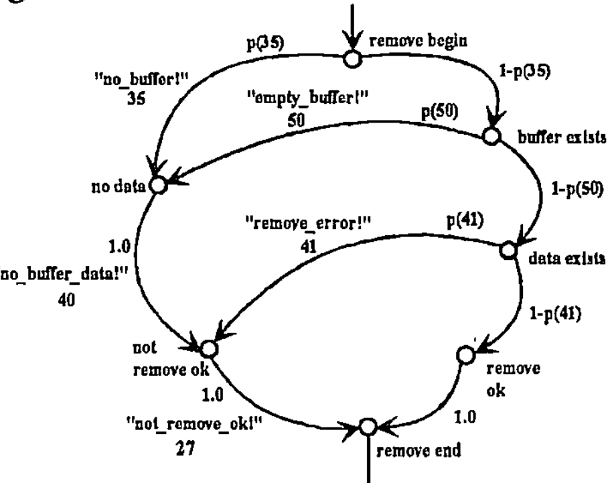

Bild 2.1: *remove*-**Baustein**

ten Partners bei einem Verbindungsaufbau) oder Aktionen initiieren (z.B. einen Anmeldewunsch an einen Partner). Diese sind in den Sendeprozess aus Beispiel 2.2 integriert worden. Das Zusammensetzen und die Einführung von neuen Teil-Automaten (*Bausteinen*) ermöglicht die Definition von vielen individuellen Prozessen. Im folgenden wird davon ausgegangen, daß die Prozeßbeschreibungen vollständig sind, so daß eine Diagnose immer alle möglichen Erklärungen finden kann. Damit wird der Fall ausgeschlossen, daß ein Prozeß einen nicht definierten Zustand annimmt oder unerlaubte Signale sendet.

Der in Bild 2.1 dargestellte *remove*-Baustein beschreibt das Verhalten eines Prozesses, der Daten aus einem Puffer lesen soll. Wenn er dort keine Einträge vorfindet, sendet er die Meldung *"empty_buffer!"*. Um diesen Fehler überhaupt entdecken zu können, muß er zuvor die Übergänge *remove_begin → buffer_exists* durchlaufen haben. Aus der Modellbeschreibung sind die Fehlerursachen durch Rückverfolgung aller möglichen Kantenfolgen bis hin zum *remove_begin* direkt ablesbar. Dieser Vorgang entspricht der Durchführung einer Abduktion [4].

Ein *Weg* ist eine Sequenz aufeinanderfolgender Zustände in einem Prozeß. Seine *(Weg)-Bewertung*, die ausdrücken soll, wie wahrscheinlich ihn der Prozeß durchlaufen hat, erfolgt unter Berücksichtigung entsprechender Gesetzmäßigkeiten aus der Stochastik. Unter den in ([8]) aufgeführten Voraussetzungen gilt für eine Störung g und die Menge aller ihrer Erklärungen expl(g):

$$P(g) = P\left(\bigvee_{e_i \in \exp\, l(g)} e_i \right) = \sum_{e_i \in \exp\, l(g)} P(e_i)$$

d.h. die Wahrscheinlichkeit für die Störung g ist die Summe der Gewichtungen aller Wege, die von g aus zurückverfolgt werden können und die ihre Ziele in expl(g) haben, d.h. deren Ziele Ur-Fehler aus expl(g) sind

Weiter gilt für einen Weg w ={$h_1,h_2,h_3,...h_n$}:

$$P(w) = P(h_1 \wedge h_2 \wedge ...h_n) = \prod_{i=1}^{n} P(h_i)$$

d.h. seine Bewertung setzt sich aus dem Produkt seiner Kantengewichte zusammen.

Beispiel 2.1: Für den *remove*-Baustein gilt dann: wenn ein Prozeß, der diesen Baustein besitzt, unbedingt in den Zustand *remove_begin* gelangt, kann der den Zustand *no_data* mit einer Wahrscheinlichkeit von (1-p(35))p(50) erreichen.

Die bisher vorgestellten Automaten reichen für die Modellierung eines Verkehrsinformationsnetzes noch nicht aus. Damit ist lediglich eine prozeßinterne Diagnose möglich. Für Folgefehlerbeziehungen, die sich auf andere asynchrone Prozesse ausweiten können, müssen zusätzlich externe Kanten integriert werden, die die Zustandsknoten von verschiedenen Prozessen verbinden. In Kapitel 3 wird dieses am Beispiel einer Empfangsstörung vorgeführt.

Beispiel 2.2: In Bild 2.2 ist ein typischer Sendeprozeß dargestellt. Hierbei kann es sich bspw. um den Prozeß *wvz_snd* einer Unterzentrale handeln, der die Stellbefehle für die Wechselverkehrszeichen zur Weiterleitung an den Datenserver *vert_rec* schickt.

Beim Starten der Applikation ist der Prozeß noch nicht vorhanden, weswegen er den Zustand *undefined* erhält. Er wird erst durch seinen zuständigen Mutterprozeß kreiert (>*create_req*<), der zudem auch für seine Abbruch-Überwachung verantwortlich ist. Falls das Kreieren beispielsweise aus Speicherplatzmangel mißglückt (<*create_rej*>), bleibt der Prozeß in dem Zustand *undefined*, ansonsten kann er zu *created* übergehen. Von dort aus durchläuft er seine Initialisierungsphase, in der er z.B. Datenbereiche anlegen oder Files mit Initialisierungsinformationen öffnen und lesen kann. Wenn dabei Fehler auftreten, kann der Prozeß nicht ordnungsgemäß arbeiten, weswegen er zum Zustand *exited* überwechselt und für erneute Kreierungs-Versuche anschließend wieder zu *undefined* wechselt.

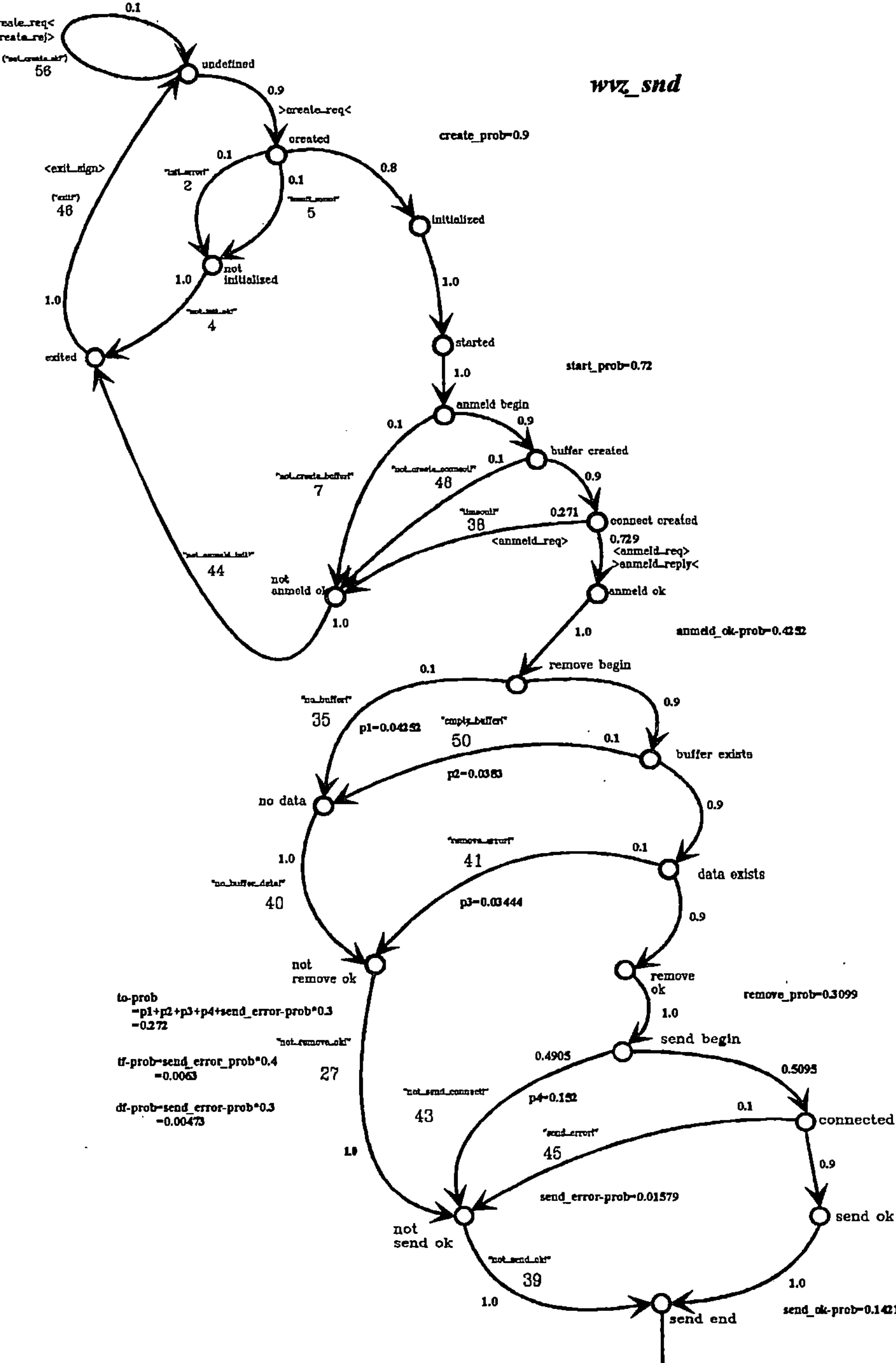

Bild 2.2: Der Sendeprozeß *wvz_snd* für Wechselverkehrszeichengeber

Wenn die Initialisierungsphase erfolgreich abgeschlossen wurde (*initialized*), kann der Prozeß gestartet werden. Da in diesem Fall keine Synchronisationen erforderlich sind, kann er direkt mit seiner Anmeldephase beginnen (*anmeld_begin*). Er durchläuft dazu einen *anmeld_init*-Baustein und ist demnach der Initiator für einen Verbindungsaufbau. In diesem Beispiel soll der Datenaustausch gepuffert werden, weswegen der Prozeß zunächst den erforderlichen Puffer kreieren muß. Da seine angestrebte Verbindungsart ein Circuit sein soll, muß er anschließend seinen Teil der Verbindung aufbauen. Danach sendet er seinen Anmeldewunsch (<*anmeld_req*>) an seinen zukünftigen Empfangspartner (z.B. den *vert_rec*) und wartet auf dessen Antwort. Wenn diese nach einem festgelegten Zeitraum nicht eingetroffen ist, bricht er mit seiner Anmeldephase erfolglos ab und läuft auf *exited*. Genauso verhält er sich, wenn zuvor schon Störungen aufgetreten sind. Nach geglückter Anmeldephase kann er direkt mit dem Sendevorgang beginnen (*anmeld_ok, remove_begin*). Dazu holt er sich zunächst die entsprechenden Daten aus seinem Sendepuffer. Wenn dabei Fehler auftreten, weil beispielsweise keine Daten im Puffer sind (*"empty_buffer!"*), kann der Prozeß auch das Senden nicht erfolgreich abschließen. Dann hat möglicherweise sein Empfangspartner ein Timeout, weil er innerhalb einer bestimmten Zeit die Daten erwartet.

An dieser Stelle wird ein Vorteil des modellbasierten Ansatzes deutlich: ein Sendepartner ohne den *remove*-Komplex kann keinen Pufferfehler als Erklärung für ein Timeout in seinem Empfangspartner liefern. Ein heuristischer Ansatz, der beispielsweise auf den Notifikationsabhängigkeiten aufbaut, kann diesem Sachverhalt nicht gerecht werden. Wenn der Prozeß die Daten fehlerfrei aus dem Puffer gelesen hat, startet er seinen Sendezugriff. Dabei können wiederum Störungen auftreten, weil z.B. die Kommunikationsverbindung unterbrochen ist (*"not_send_connect!"*) oder Protokollfehler aufgetreten sind (*"send_error!"*) (Parity-/ oder Check-Sum-Error, fehlende Synchronisationsbits, ...). Der Abbruch eines Partnerprozesses oder ein Defekt des Übertragungsmediums aufgrund eines Hardwarefehlers, stellen weitere externe Einflüsse dar, die bei der Diagnose berücksichtigt werden müssen.

Dieser Sendeprozeß besteht aus Bausteinen für die Initialisierung, den Verbindungsaufbau, das Lesen aus einem Puffer und seiner eigentlichen Sendephase. Zwischen den einzelnen Zustandsübergängen ist die Ersetzung und die Einfügung von Bausteine möglich, in denen der Prozeß seine speziellen Aufgaben erledigen kann. So gibt es bspw. in dem betrachteten VIN Prozesse, die auf Verbindungswünsche ihrer Partner reagieren und deswegen andere Anmeldephase durchlaufen (*anmeld_reply*). Außerdem sind Bausteine mit Startsynchronisationen integriert worden, sowie Prozesse mit speziellen Aufgaben, wie bspw. ein Uhrzeitserver und ein entsprechender Client ([11]). Empfangsprozesse kann man durch die Ersetzung des Remove-Send-Komplexes durch Receive-Insert-Bausteine erhalten. Typisch für das betrachtete VIN ist die Ähnlichkeit der beteiligten Komponenten bzgl. ihrer Prozeßaufteilung, in der sich ihre komplette Funktion widerspiegelt. Die modellierten Unterzentralen enthalten bspw. je zehn verwandte Prozeßpaare, deren Grundstrukturen den modellierten Sender- und Empfangstypen entsprechen.

3. Diagnose in DRUM

In den vorangegangenen Kapiteln wurde deutlich gemacht, weshalb ein Diagnose-Algorithmus erforderlich ist und wieso dafür ein modellbasierter Ansatz gewählt wurde. Nun soll zunächst gezeigt werden, wie man diesen Ansatz in einem Belief-Revision-System realisieren kann

Belief Revision ist ein Forschungsbereich der AI (Aritificial Intelligence), der sich mit der Erweiterung eines vorhandenen Wissensstandes beschäftigt. Dabei ist es möglich, bestehende Annahmen wieder zurückzunehmen, falls die neuen Informationen nicht mehr konsistent zu der alten Wissensbasis sind. Der vorhandene Wissensstand wird durch eine Menge von Regeln und Fakten definiert. Wenn eine neue Regel hinzugefügt werden soll, wird zunächst untersucht, ob sie konsistent zu der alten Wissensbasis ist. Falls ja, kann sie einfach darin aufgenommen werden; falls nein, können die Widersprüche, die durch sie entstanden sind, durch die Änderung der Wissensbasis aufgelöst werden (Revision), weil die neue Regel grundsätzlich glaubwürdiger ist.

Belief-Revision-Systeme können auch für die *modellbasierte Diagnose* verwendet werden. Die Wissensbasis besteht dann aus der Verhaltensbeschreibung des modellierten Systems, das in unserem Fall ein Verkehrsinformationsnetz mit vielen autonomen Prozessen ist. Die Diagnose wird aufgrund einer Beobachtung gestartet, die im Konflikt zu dem erwarteten Verhalten des Systems steht. Sie wird in diesem Netz durch die Notifikation eines Prozesses realisiert, der damit eine entdeckte Störung an seinen zuständigen Fehlermanager meldet. Im Belief-Revision-System entspricht sie den Informationen, um die die Wissensbasis erweitert werden soll.

Das erwartete Prozeßverhalten entspricht den revidierbaren Annahmen im Belief-Revision-System. Es wird zunächst angenommen, daß das System ordnungsgemäß funktioniert, d.h. die Zustandsübergänge aller Netz-Teilnehmer sind fehlerfrei. Dabei kann jeder von ihnen nur auf eine festgelegte Teilmenge aller seiner Zustände in einer bestimmten Reihenfolge treffen, wodurch sein *ok-Pfad*[3] festgelegt wird. In Bild 2.1 ist das der Pfad {*remove_begin→buffer_exists→data_exists→remove_ok→remove_end*}.

Bei der Revision von Annahmen können *Prioritäten* vergeben werden, wodurch die Rücknahme von weniger sicherem Wissen bevorzugt wird. Zudem kann man *fixes Wissen* definieren, dessen Wahrheitswert nicht verändert werden darf. Es kann für die Beschreibung der vorliegenden Netztopologie und der Prozesse mit ihren integrierten Bausteinen und Zuständen verwendet werden.

Für die eigentlichen Diagnoseschritte sind zusätzliche Regeln und Fakten notwendig, die vorgeben, wie man aus den Beobachtungen (Fehlermeldungen) einen Widerspruch zu den Annahmen ("System funktioniert einwandfrei") ableiten kann. Da für die Diagnose in unserem Fall nur das *Fehl*verhalten eines Prozesses von Bedeutung ist, reicht für die Beschreibung des Systems ein *Fehler*modell aus.

Im folgenden soll die Vorgehensweise des Diagnosealgorithmus am Beispiel des Sende-Prozesses *verkehr_snd* in einer DRUM-Implementation erläutert werden.

---

[3]Verzweigungen des *ok-Pfades* in mehrere alternative *ok-Pfade* sind durchaus möglich, auch wenn sie in den folgenden Beispielen aus Gründen der Übersichtlichkeit nicht auftreten

DRUM (dynamic revision and update machine) ([7]) ist die Implementierung eines Belief-Revision-Systems mit der Zielsetzung, nur die minimalen Annahmen zu revidieren. Unter "minimal" sollen sowohl die, mit der geringstmöglichen Priorität als auch sowenige Annahmen wie möglich verstanden werden.

Der Prozeß *verkehr_snd* gehört zu einer Unterzentrale. Er soll die von seinem Partner *verkehr_rec* aufbereiteten Verkehrsdaten an *vert_rec* leiten. Dazu muß er sie zunächst aus seinem Sendepuffer lesen, wobei er den *remove*-Baustein in Bild 2.1 durchläuft. Für seine Implementierung wurden die folgenden Prädikate eingeführt:

I. Verwendete Prädikate

proc_zust(P,B,Q) : der Prozeß P hat den Baustein B und darf darin den Zustand Q annehmen;

in(P,B,Q) : der Prozeß P befindet sich in dem Zustand Q des Bausteines B;

ok(P,B,Q) : der Prozeß P befindet sich in dem Zustand Q des Bausteines P und dieser Zustand liegt auf dem *ok-Pfad* des Prozesses und ist damit Bestandteil des Ausgangsmodells;

signal(P,S) : Prozeß P sendet das Signal "S!", welches auf sein Fehlverhalten hinweist und bei den Zustandsübergängen "*in* → *in*" oder "*ok* → *in*" ausgesendet wird;

test (all (P, v(P))) : für alle P für die v(P) gilt, ...(DRUM-spezifisch)

imp : logische Implikation (DRUM-spezifisch)

or : logisches "oder" (DRUM-spezifisch)

and : logisches "und" (DRUM-spezifisch)

Mit diesen Prädikaten kann nun das Verhalten des Prozesses modelliert werden:

II. Vorgehensweise

Die Revision wird nach Empfang eines Signals gestartet. Nachdem der Prozeßzustand ermittelt wurde, von dem das Senden der Notifikation ausging, erfolgt eine Rückverfolgung von "*in* → *in*"-Übergängen bis man beim *ok-Pfad* angekommen ist. Dieser wird explizit zerstört durch die Revision des entsprechenden *ok*-Zustandes, wodurch der Widerspruch zum Ausgangsmodell herbeigeführt ist.

Demnach wird eine *Abduktion* durchgeführt: ausgehend von einer Beobachtung *obs* (hier: das Signal) werden alle Erklärungen e_i (hier: die revidierten *ok*-Zustände) dafür gesucht, aus denen *obs* gefolgert werden kann.

Diese Vorgehensweise schreibt das Ausgangsmodell wie folgt vor:

III. Ausgangsmodell

Im Ausgangsmodell werden die Annahmen für das korrekte-Verhalten des Prozesses festgelegt, was die Definition seines *ok-Pfades* bedeutet. Für den Sendeprozess *verkehr_snd* sieht das dann so aus (vgl. Bild 2.2):

I= [..., ok (verkehr_snd, start, undefined), ok (verkehr_snd, start, created),

     ok (verkehr_snd, start, initialized), ok (verkehr_snd, start, started),

     ok (verkehr_snd, anmeld_init, anmeld_begin), ok (verkehr_snd, anmeld_init, buffer_created), ...]

Strukturelle Informationen, wie die Zusammensetzung von Komponenten oder die Netztopologie sollen bei der Revision nicht verändert werden. Die Struktur der Prozesse wird durch ihre Zustände und enthaltenen Bausteine definiert:

IV. Unveränderbare Fakten

Das fixe Wissen umfaßt die Definition des Prozesses durch seine erlaubten Bausteine und die Festlegung der Netztopologie. Beim Sendeprozess *verkehr_snd* sind bspw. die folgenden Fakten unveränderbar (vgl. Bild 2.2):

Fixed = [..., proc_zust(verkehr_snd, start, undefined), proc_zust(verkehr_snd, start, created),

proc_zust(verkehr_snd, start, initialized), proc_zust(verkehr_snd, start, not_initialized),

proc_zust(verkehr_snd, start, started), proc_zust(verkehr_snd, anmeld_init, anmeld_begin), ...]

Da der Diagnose ein Fehlermodell zugrundeliegt, sind zur Beschreibung des Prozeß-verhaltens nur die fehlerhaften Übergänge relevant:

V. Fehlerhafte Übergänge (*in→in*) (Regeltyp 1)

Es wird vorausgesetzt, daß jeder "*in →in*"-Übergang durch das Aussenden eines Signals angezeigt wird; z.B.

test(all(P, (proc_zust(P,remove,not_remove_ok) and in(P,remove,not_remove_ok) and

proc_zust(P,remove,no_data) and proc_zust(P,remove,data_exists))

imp (in(P,remove,no_data) or in(P,remove,data_exists)))):

Wenn für den Prozeß *P* der Zustand *not_remove_ok* im Baustein *remove* erlaubt ist und er sich in diesem Zustand befindet, muß er zuvor entweder im Zustand *no_data* oder *data_exists* desselben Bausteines gewesen sein (falls diese für ihn zulässige Zustände sind). Die anderen Übergänge werden analog beschrieben.

Mit den bisherigen Regeln ist es möglich, im Fehlerpfad durch sukzessiven Status-wechsel nach oben zu gelangen. Die Abbruchbedingung wird in VI. definiert:

VI. Herbeiführung der Widersprüche (Regeltyp 2)

Wenn aufgrund eines Signals ein Zustand angenommen wird (*in*), und sich dieser Zustand auf dem *ok-Pfad* des Prozesses befindet, muss er revidiert werden: es wird ein Widerspruch zum Ausgangsmodell herbeigeführt; z.B.

test(all(P, (in(P, remove, data_exists) imp neg ok(P, remove, data_exists)))):

Der Zustand *data_exists* im Baustein *remove* liegt auf dem *ok-Pfad* des Prozesses. Wenn sich bei der Abduktion herausstellt, daß dieser Zustand für die Erklärung des Signals verantwortlich ist, muß er dort im Gegensatz zur ursprünglichen Annahme fehlerhaft gewesen sein.

Mit den Regeltypen 1 und 2 kann man bis zum *ok*-Pfad gelangen. Es fehlt nur noch die Regel, durch die die Abduktion ausgelöst wird:

VII. Signalabhängigkeiten (Regeltyp 3)

Durch diese Regel wird die Auslösung der Abduktion nach Empfang eines Signals er-möglicht: der erste Fehlerzustand wird ermittelt; z.B.

test(all(P, (proc_zust(P,remove,not_remove_ok) and signal(P,not_remove_ok))

imp in(P,remove,not_remove_ok))):

Wenn der Prozeß P das Signal *not_remove_ok* sendet, muß er dazu im Zustand *not_remove_ok* seines Bausteines *remove* gewesen sein, sofern dieser überhaupt für ihn zulässig ist.

Wenn auf einem Weg Signale ausgefallen sind, sollen sie bei der Diagnose über-brückt werden. Um auf solche Situationen aufmerksam machen zu können, wird der Regeltyp 4 verwendet:

VIII. Überbrückung von Signalen (Regeltyp 4)

Bei fehlerhaften Zustandsübergängen werden die fehlenden Signale automatisch gene-riert; z.B. test(all(P, (in(P,remove,data_exists) imp signal(P,remove_error))))):

Wenn sich der Prozeß im Zustand *data_exists* befindet, kann er das Signal *"remove_error!"* aktivieren, welches dem entsprechenden Pfeil zugeordent ist. Dieses Signal ist demnach für die Diagnose ohne Bedeutung und kann ausgefiltert werden.

Beispiel 3.1: Prozeßinterne Problemsituationen zeichnen sich dadurch aus, daß ihre Erklärungen innerhalb des fehlerhaften Prozesses zu finden sind. Als Beispiel diene nun der Sendeprozeß *vert_snd,* der den Fehler *"no_buffer_data!"* meldet:

kr([signal(vert_snd, no_buffer_data)]).
Kontext - Revision bis Level 50

Prioritätsebenenwechsel:
Prioritätsebenenwechsel

Korr[5].: 1 -> [in(vert_snd, remove, no_data)]

Korr.: 2 -> [in(vert_snd, remove, buffer_exists)]

Korr.: 2 -> [in(vert_snd, remove, remove_begin)]

Prioritätsebenenwechsel:

Korr.: 1 -> [in(vert_snd, remove, no_data)]

Korr.: 2 -> [in(vert_snd, remove, buffer_exists)]

Korr.: 3 -> [signal(vert_snd, empty_buffer), neg ok(vert_snd, remove, buffer_exists)]

 -> Lösung: 99 -> 97

Korr.: 2 -> [in(vert_snd, remove, remove_begin)]

Korr.: 3 -> [signal(vert_snd, no_buffer), neg ok(vert_snd, remove, remove_begin)]

 -> Lösung: 99 -> 96

Resultierende Modelle:

~~~ 97 ~~~

[in(vert_snd, remove, buffer_exists), in(vert_snd, remove, no_data)]

[signal(vert_snd, *empty_buffer*), signal(vert_snd, no_buffer_data)]

~~~ 96 ~~~

[in(vert_snd, remove, no_data), in(vert_snd, remove, remove_begin)]

[signal(vert_snd, *no_buffer*), signal(vert_snd, no_buffer_data)]. (Laufzeit in msec:1450)

Die Kontext-Revision ("kr") wird mit dem Aufruf kr[4](Beobachtungen) aufgerufen.

Es wird immer versucht, die minimalen Annahmen zu revidieren. In diesem Falle muß dazu in die 2. Prioritätsebene gewechselt werden, in der das Prädikat "in" enthalten ist.

Im 1. Schritt wird der Prozeßstatus ermittelt, von dem aus das Signal gesendet wurde (*no_data*).

In der nächsten Such-Ebene (Korr. 2) wird ausgehend von dem in Korr. 1 gefundenen Status weiter in Richtung *ok-Pfad* vorgegangen: die beiden Zustände *buffer_exists* und *remove_begin* werden als nächstes in die Lösung aufgenommen.

Da sie schon auf dem *ok-Pfad* liegen, können die entsprechenden *ok*-Zustände im 3. Algorithmusschritt gemäß Regeltyp 2 revidiert werden. Danach stehen beide Lösungen fest.

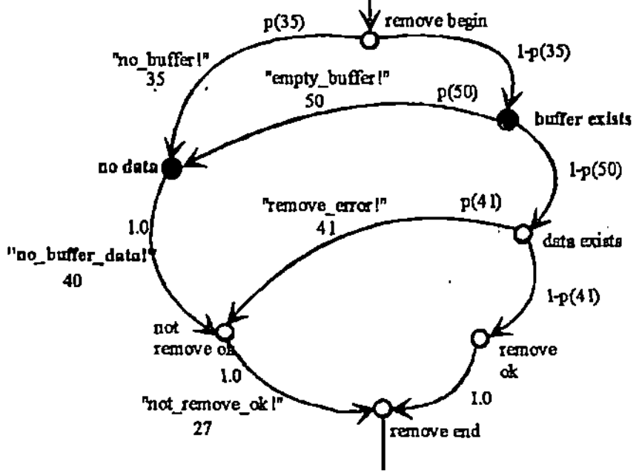

Bild 3.1: Fehler in *buffer_exists*

Der Sender *vert_snd* meldet zusätzlich die Störung *"no_buffer!"*.

---

[4]kr steht für "Kontext-Revision" im Gegensatz zu der später verwendeten "Probabilistischen Revision" (pr)
[5]korr gibt die aktuelle Suchebene an

kr([signal(vert_snd, no_buffer)]).
Kontext - Revision bis Level 50
Prioritätsebenenwechsel:
-> Lösung: 96 -> 95

Resultierende Modelle:

~~~ 95 ~~~

[in(vert_snd, remove, no_data), in(vert_snd,
remove, remove_begin)]
[signal(vert_snd, *no_buffer*), signal(vert_snd,
no_buffer_data)]. (Laufzeit in msec :650)

Durch das neue Signal wird *remove_begin* bevorzugt, weil weniger Annahmen revidiert werden
müssen ⇒ Modell 97 wird zurückgenommen.

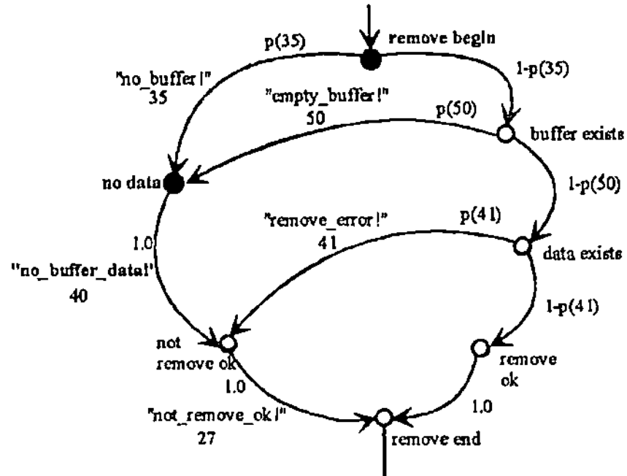

Bild 3.2: Fehler in *remove_begin*

Mit den bisherigen Ausführungen kann man Prozesse definieren. Nun wird vorgestellt,
wie externe Kanten zwischen verschiedenen Prozessen behandelt werden:

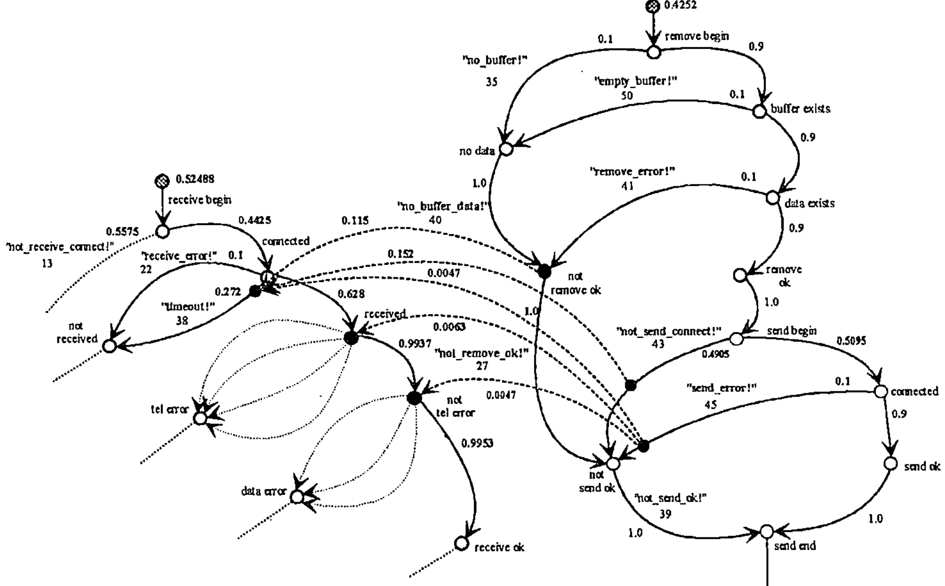

Bild 3.3 : Externe Beziehungen zwischen Empfangs- und Sendeprozeß

IX. Externe Kanten

Analog zu dem beschriebenen Vorgehen für Kanten innerhalb eines Prozesses können
externe Beziehungen zwischen Prozessen behandelt werden. Durch die Einführung des
Prädikats *connected* kann die bestehende Netztopologie im fixen Wissen aufgenommen
werden. Externe "*in*(P1,B1,Z1)→*in*(P2,B2,Z2)"-Übergänge zwischen den Prozessen
P1 und P2 müssen dann um die Zusatzbedingung "*connected*(P1,P2)" erweitert
werden. Dadurch kann bspw. die Beziehung "*in*(*vert_rec,receive,timeout*)→
~~~

in(wvz_snd,send,not_remove_ok)" ausgedrückt werden, die besagt, daß der Empfangsprozeß *vert_rec* mit seinem Baustein *receive* in den Zustand *timeout* gelaufen ist, weil sein Verbindungspartner *wvz_snd* beim Lesen aus dem Sendepuffer Probleme hatte (z.B. *empty_buffer*) und deswegen keine Daten verschicken konnte.

Beispiel 3.2: Der Empfangsprozeß *wvz_rec* ist mit zwei Sendepartnern verbunden (*vert_snd* und *verkehr_snd*). Er erwartet von ihnen in regelmäßigen Zeitabständen Daten. Wenn diese ausfallen, signalisiert er ein *"timeout!"*. Dann hat diese Störung ihre Ursache nicht im Empfangsprozeß selbst, sondern sie ist eine Folge irgendwelcher Unregelmäßigkeiten in einem der beteiligten Sender (bspw. wegen eines *"send_error!"*). Wenn beim Fehlermanager als erstes Signal die Meldung *"timeout!"* vom *wvz_rec* eintrifft, und keine anderen Signale sonst vorliegen, müssen alle möglichen Urfehler untersucht werden. Da nach dieser einen Notifikation der Sendepartner noch nicht eindeutig bestimmt werden kann, werden alle möglichen Sender untersucht, was zu einer Vielzahl von Erklärungen führt. Sie sind in Bild 3.3 für einen der Sender dargestellt. Insgesamt liefert die Diagnose für die beiden Prozesse *vert_snd* und *verkehr_snd* jeweils die Ursachen *"send_error!"*, *"not_send_connect!"*, *"no_buffer!"*, *"empty_buffer!"* und *"remove_error!"* (Laufzeit in msec:29400). Wenn nun zusätzlich das Signal *"send_error!"* von *vert_snd* eintrifft, ist nur noch das Modell für *vert_snd* mit der Ursache *"send_error!"* erlaubt (Laufzeit in msec:900).

X. Integration von Wahrscheinlichkeiten

Um die Revision von weniger sicherem Wissen zu bevorzugen, können Prioritäten vergeben werden. Wenn man sie als reelle Zahlen aus [0,1] verwendet, können damit die Weg-/Erklärungsgewichtungen berechnet werden.

Dazu muß vorausgesetzt werden, daß jeder Wechsel in einen Fehlerzustand durch ein Signal angezeigt wird. Dann kann man die Kantengewichtungen im *remove*-Baustein (Bild 2.1) durch die Bewertung der *signal*-Prädikate in DRUM realisieren:

assert[6](prior[7](signal(_, not_remove_ok),1)), assert(prior(signal(_, no_buffer),0.1)), ...

Die Diagnose und damit auch die Gewichtungsberechnung endet bei Erreichen des *ok-Pfades*. Bis dahin sind lediglich Signal-Gewichte für die Erklärungswahrscheinlichkeit berücksichtigt worden. Da die Ur-Fehler i.a. keine Ur-Ereignisse sind, muß zusätzlich noch eine Ur-Gewichtung verwendet werden, die die Wahrscheinlichkeit für das Erreichen des *ok*-Zustandes angibt:

assert(prior(neg ok(_, remove, remove_begin),1)), assert(prior(neg ok(_, remove, buffer_exists),0.9)),
assert(prior(neg ok(_, remove, data_exists),0.81)), ...

Beispiel 3.3: In diesem Beispiel soll der Schwerpunkt auf die Verwendung der Wahrscheinlichkeiten gelegt werden. Analog zu dem vorangegangenen Fall wird nochmals ein fehlerhafter Pufferzugriff untersucht: Der Sendeprozeß *"vert_snd"* meldet den Fehler *"not_remove_ok!"*:

---

[6]Dieses ist ein DRUM-Prädikat, welches die Prioritätenvergabe zur Steuerung der Revision ermöglicht.
[7]Dieses DRUM-Prädikat definiert die Prioritätsart: in diesem Falle werden Wahrscheinlichkeiten verwendet.

pr([signal(vert_snd, not_remove_ok)]).
Probability - Revision bis Level 50. (minprob: 0.001)
REVISION DES MODELLS: < 99 >

1 -> [in(vert_snd, remove, not_remove_ok)]
2 -> [in(vert_snd, remove, data_exists)]
3 -> [signal(vert_snd, remove_error), neg ok(vert_snd, remove, data_exists)]
 -> Lösung: 99 -> 97
Prod:0.081

3 -> [in(vert_snd, remove, remove_begin), signal(vert_snd, no_buffer_data)]
4 -> [signal(vert_snd, *no_buffer*), neg ok(vert_snd, remove, remove_begin)]
Prod:0.1 P:0.09
*** Neue Lösung ist besser als Modell < 97 > .
 -> Lösung: 97

Die probabilistische Revision ("pr") wird mit dem Aufruf pr(Beobachtungen) aufgerufen. In diesem Beispiel ist die Beobachtung das Signal *"not_remove_ok!"* vom Prozeß *vert_snd*.

Als erste Erklärung wird der Fehler *"remove_error!"* ermittelt, der im Zustand *data_exists* aufgetreten ist. Die Erklärung hat eine Wahrscheinlichkeit von 0.081[8]. Sie wird als momentan beste Lösung festgehalten. Die nächste Erklärung ist *"empty_buffer!"* und wird aufgrund ihres höheren Gewichtes von 0.09 als aktuell beste Lösung geführt.

Nun wird als Erklärung *"no_buffer!"* ermittelt. Sie hat den Wert 0.1 und ist daher wahrscheinlicher als die aktuell beste Erklärung mit 0.09 (*"empty_buffer!"*). Daher wird sie als aktuell beste Lösung akzeptiert.

Die Revision ist beendet, weil es keine weiteren zu berücksichtigenden Erklärungen mehr gibt. Daher ist die zuletzt beste Erklärung (*"no_buffer!"*) die insgesamt beste. (Laufzeit in msec:1580)

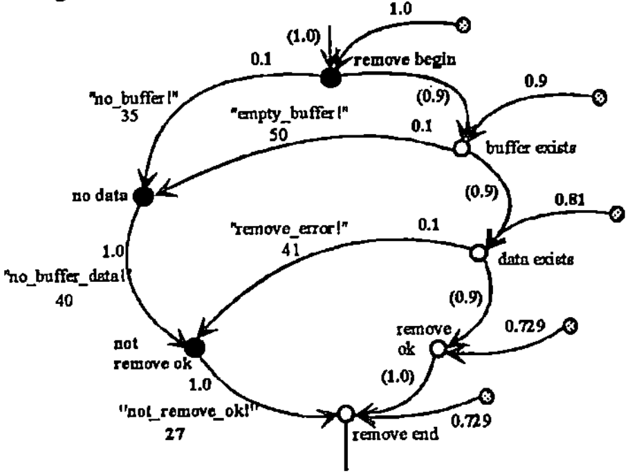

Bild 3.4: 3. und beste Erklärung mit der Wahrscheinlichkeit 0.1.

4. Notifikationsgraph

Aus den Prozeßbeschreibungen in Kapitel 2.2 kann automatisch ein Notifikationsgraph generiert werden, wie in Bild 4.1 am Beispiel des *remove*-Bausteins demonstriert wird. Unter Berücksichtigung dieses Graphen kann das in Kapitel 3 beschriebene Diagnoseverfahren auch durch Graphalgorithmen realisiert werden. Diese kann man dann in Prozeßsysteme mit dynamischer Topologie integrieren.

---

[8]die Berechnung der Wahrscheinlichkeiten wird in Kapitel 2.2 vorgeführt

5. Zusammenfassung

In dieser Arbeit haben wir einen Algorithmus für die modellbasierte Diagnose vorgestellt, der in das Fehlermanagement von Verkehrsinformationsnetzen integriert werden kann. Dabei wurde das Verhalten des gesamten Systems, welches aus vielen autonomen Prozessen besteht, durch endliche Automaten beschrieben. Zur Bewertung der ermittelten Erklärungen wurden Wahrscheinlichkeiten in die Prozeßspezifikation integriert. Die Modelle sind in einem Belief Revision System implementiert worden und können direkt zur Fehlerdiagnose eingesetzt werden. Wir erhalten auf diese Weise die üblichen Vorteile von modellbasierten Diagnosesystemen, wie Modularität, leichte Modifizier- und Erweiterbarkeit und eine deklarative Systembeschreibung, die bei heuristischen Lösungen nur ansatzweise existieren.

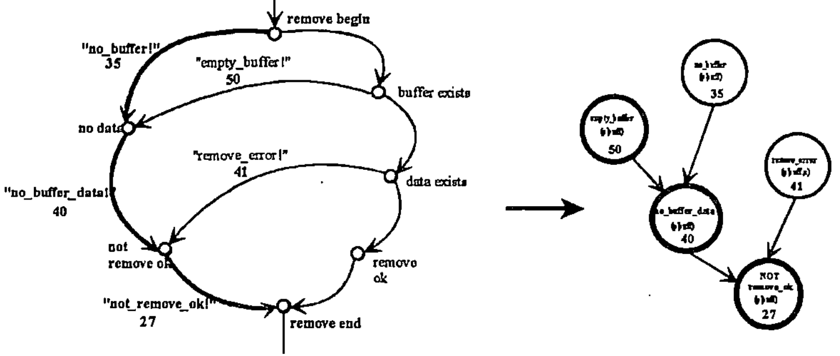

Bild 4.1: Generierung des Notifikationsgraphen

Literatur

[1] S. Brugnoni, G. Bruno, R. Manione, E. Montariolo, E. Paschetta, L. Sisto. *An expert system for real time fault diagnosis of the Italian telecommunications network.* IFIP Transactions C, vol. C-12, 1993.

[2] Bundesanstalt für Straßenwesen. *Technische Lieferbedingungen für Streckenstationen.* November 1992.

[3] R. Deng, A. Lazar, W. Wang. *A probabilistic approach to fault diagnosis in linear lightwave networks.* IFIP Transactions C, vol. C-12, 1993.

[4] W. Hamscher, L. Console and J. de Kleer. *Readings in Model-Based Diagnosis.* Morgan Kaufmann, 1992.

[5] International Organization for Standardization. ISO/IEC 10164-4/5, 10165-1/4, 7498-4.

[6] R. K. Jurgen. *Smart cars and highways go global.* IEEE Spectrum, May, 1991.

[7] W. Nejdl and B. Nedizavec. *DRUM - A belief revision system for reasoning about revision with new information as well as updates caused by actions.* Dutch/German Workshop on Nonmonotonic Reasoning, 1993.

[8] D. Poole. *Probabilistic Horn abduction and Bayesian networks.* Journal of Artificial Intelligence, vol. 64, 1993.

[9] R. Reiter. *A theory of diagnosis from first principles.* Artificial Intelligence, 1987.

[10] M. Riese. *Diagnosis of communicating systems: dealing with incompleteness and uncertainty.* IJCAI, 1993.

[11] D. Schüth. *Interaktives Fehlermanagement in Verkehrsinformationsnetzen.* Diplomarbeit, RWTH Aachen, February 1994.

[12] C. Wang and M. Schwartz. *Fault detection with multiple observers.* IEEE Trans. on Networking, vol.1, no.1, February 1993.

DINO, ein Softwarewerkzeug zur technischen Diagnose - Konzept und erste Erfahrungen

Klaus Dieter Meyer-Gramann
Daimler-Benz AG, Austauschgruppe des Ressorts Forschung und Technik,
70.546 Stuttgart

Stefan Dieter
Bodan InformationsManagement Systeme GmbH, Postfach 1309, 88.671 Markdorf

Zusammenfassung

DINO (*D*iagnosis with *I*ndividual *N*avigation *O*ffering) ist ein Softwarewerkzeug, mit dem man symptombasierte Expertensysteme für die Diagnose technischer Anlagen und Prozesse erstellt. DINO beruht auf Ergebnissen der Daimler-Benz-Forschung. Die Laufzeit- und die Wissenserwerbs-Komponente von DINO werden vorgestellt. DINO bietet dem Fachexperten als Beschreibungssprache die Begriffswelt der technischen Diagnose. Das Wissen wird als semantisches Netz repräsentiert. Die von DINO angewandte Diagnosestrategie wendet Methoden der wissensbasierten Klassifikation an, ist strikt vorwärtsgerichtet und vermeidet im Gegensatz zu Suchbaumverfahren ein "Backtracking". Die Benutzerführung bei der Diagnose ist auf die Wünsche und Anforderungen von Instandhaltungs- und Wartungspersonal zugeschnitten. Beschrieben und diskutiert werden erste Erfahrungen beim Wissenserwerb und bei der Diagnose. Applikationsbeispiel ist ein Groß-Dieselmotor der Firma mtu. Als Ausblick wird dargelegt, wie man auch technische Systeme hoher Variantenvielfalt effizient modellieren kann. DINO ist in der ersten Ausbaustufe seit Mai 1994 kommerziell verfügbar, die Behandlung der Variantenvielfalt wird bis Ende 1994 integriert sein.

0. Einleitung

Die technische Diagnose als klassisches Analyseproblem ist eines der wichtigsten Anwendungsgebiete von Expertensystemen [20]. Fast alle der Expertensysteme für technische Diagnose, die zur Zeit in der Industrie eingesetzt werden, lassen sich als symptombasiert bezeichnen. Der symptombasierte Ansatz wird auch in den nächsten Jahren in der Praxis vorherrschen. Auch wenn die modell- und die fallbasierte Diagnose in den letzten Jahren bedeutende Fortschritte gemacht haben und es erfolgreiche Anwendungen gibt, haben diese Techniken nämlich prinzipielle Grenzen, die ihre Anwendung oft ausschließen:

o Modellbasierte Diagnose ist oft sehr geeignet für technische Systeme mit simplen Komponenten, auch und gerade bei sehr vielen Komponenten. Das klassische Anwendungsgebiet sind daher elektrische Schaltungen. Für andersartige technische Systeme sind die prinzipiellen funktionalen Zusammenhänge nicht genau genug bekannt, oder Modell-Parameter lassen sich nicht bestimmen. Ohne ein zureichend genaues und aussagekräftiges Modell lassen sich aber die klassischen modellbasierten Verfahren, die durch [3], [5], [8], [9], [17] begründet wurden und z. B. in [6] und [13] angewendet werden, nicht anwenden. Häufig läßt sich mit vertretbarem Aufwand nicht einmal ein qualitatives Modell aufstellen, wie es z. B. in [10] und [11] benötigt wird. Solche qualitativen Modelle haben außerdem prinzipiell begrenzte Aussagekraft. Ein weiterer Nachteil modellbasierter Ansätze: Die Auswertung des Modells benötigt zu viel Laufzeit.

o Prinzipielle Grenzen der z. B. in [19] vorgestellten fallbasierten Diagnose sind, daß man oft nicht entscheiden kann, ob der Beispielsatz repräsentativ ist oder das in der Fallwissensbasis gefundene Beispiel, das der aktuellen Symptommenge am nächsten kommt, tatsächlich eine für die aktuelle Situation brauchbare Diagnose liefert. Ein repräsentativer Beispielsatz ist darüber hinaus umfangreich. Erfahrungen mit regelbasierten Expertensystemen, z. B. dem Konfigurierer XCON [16], belegen eindrücklich die Grenzen großer Beispiel- oder Regelsätze.

Aus diesen Gründen wird die symptombasierte Diagnose trotz ihrer Grenzen auch in Zukunft für viele Anwendungsfälle die am besten geeignete Methode sein, ein technisches System wissensbasiert zu diagnostizieren und zu reparieren. Im folgenden stellen wir das Softwareprodukt DINO (*D*iagnosis with *I*ndividual *N*avigation *O*ffering) vor. DINO ist ein Werkzeug zum Bau symptombasierter Expertensysteme für die technische Diagnose. DINO wird z. Zt. von der Bodan InformationsManagement Systeme GmbH (Biodan IMS GmbH), einem zum Daimler-Benz-Konzern gehörenden Softwarehaus, in Zusammenarbeit mit der Daimler-Benz-Forschung entwickelt. Anforderungen, die die Benutzer an das Laufzeitsystem stellen, sowie Anforderungen der Fachexperten an die Wissenserwerbs-Komponente (WEK) wurden identifiziert.

Typische Benutzeranforderungen sind:
o Das Diagnose-Werkzeug diagnostiziert korrekt, schnell und kostengünstig.
o Das Diagnose-Werkzeug erfaßt so viele Symptome wie möglich automatisch über eine System-Schnittstelle.
o Nicht nur Einfach-, sondern zumindest auch Doppel-Ursachen werden gefunden.
o Auch jede Folge-Störung, die durch die aktuellen Ursachen hervorgerufen wurde und die eine eigene Abhilfe erfordert, wird diagnostiziert. Ein Beispiel ist eine durchgebrannte Sicherung als Folge eines Kurzschlusses.
o Eine Diagnose läßt sich auch dann fortsetzen, wenn die aktuell vorgesehene Aktion sich als nicht durchführbar erweist.
o Der Benutzer kann jederzeit einen Verdacht darüber, welche Störung aktuell vorliegt, dem Diagnose-Werkzeug "mitteilen" und dadurch die Diagnose steuern.
o Auf Wunsch wird dem Benutzer nachvollziehbar erklärt, warum eine Aktion von ihm verlangt wird, warum eine bestimmte Ursache gefunden und warum eine andere ausgeschlossen wurde.
o Ein Anfänger wird vom Diagnose-Werkzeug geeignet geführt. Einem erfahrenen Benutzer hingegen bietet das Diagnose-Werkzeug die Möglichkeit, selber die jeweils nächsten Aktionen festzulegen, und unterbreitet ihm Empfehlungen. Dieser Benutzer würde durch eine starre Abfolge von Abfragen "genervt".

Zu den Anforderungen der Fachexperten zählen:
o Die formale Beschreibungssprache, die die WEK bietet, ist einerseits ausdrucksstark genug, andererseits zureichend leicht zu erlernen und zu beherrschen. Ein Wissens-Ingenieur als Mittler zwischen Fachexperten und Rechner ist nicht erforderlich.
o Technische Systeme sind meist modular aufgebaut. Mehrere Fachexperten können gleichzeitig ihr Wissen über verschiedene Module formulieren.
o Der Fachexperte kann Wissen modular aufbauen und derartige "Wissens-Module" wiederverwenden.

o Technische Systeme existieren in verschiedenen Varianten. Die WEK unterstützt die Fachexperten dabei, eine Wissensbasis für eine bestimmte Variante zu erstellen.

o Die WEK unterstützt die Fachexperten dabei, für jeden Benutzerkreis des Diagnose-Werkzeuges eine Wissensbasis zu konstruieren, die auf diesen zugeschnitten ist.

o Erfahrungsgemäß tun sich die meisten Fachexperten mit Zahlwerten schwer, die nicht ihrer Denkwelt entstammen. Daher werden möglichst keine nichttechnischen Werte wie Wahrscheinlichkeiten oder Sicherheitsfaktoren verlangt. Keinesfalls darf ein Diagnoseergebnis von solchen Werten essentiell abhängen.

o Die WEK deckt nicht nur syntaktische Lücken und Widersprüche in der Wissensbasis auf, sondern verifiziert die Wissensbasis auch soweit wie möglich.

Aufgrund dieser Anforderungen wurde entschieden, daß DINO auf dem FACTEDIS-Konzept basiert, das in der Daimler-Benz-Forschung entwickelt und in [7] und [12] vorgestellt wurde. Im folgenden beschreiben wir die Repräsentation von Wissen durch DINO (Kapitel 1), das Vorgehen bei einer Diagnose (Kapitel 2), die Arbeit der WEK (Kapitel 3), erste Erfahrungen mit DINO (Kapitel 4) sowie als Ausblick die Behandlung des Problems Variantenvielfalt (Kapitel 5).

1. Repräsentation von Wissen durch DINO

Die Wissenserwerbs-Komponente von DINO bietet einem Fachexperten als Beschreibungssprache die Begriffswelt der technischen Diagnose. Diese Beschreibungssprache liefert die in Bild 1 veranschaulichten Begriffe und Relationen des semantischen Netzes, im dem der Experte sein Fachwissen organisiert.

Die Beschreibungssprache wird anhand des ersten Applikationsbeispiels erläutert: des Dieselmotors 16 V 396 TE 74 der mtu (Motoren- und Turbinen-Union) Friedrichshafen GmbH. Er wird überwiegend auf Schiffen eingesetzt. Seine Motorleistung beträgt 1680 kW bei 2000 Umdrehungen/min. Seine 16 Zylinder haben einen Hubraum von je 3,96 l.

"Einheit" ist unser Oberbegriff für Komponenten, Teilsysteme und das technische System als ganzes. Da die Hierarchie unter den Einheiten nur ein "Gerippe" ist, um das übrige Wissen zu strukturieren, wird nicht zwischen einer physikalischen und einer funktionalen Untergliederung unterschieden, sondern nur von den "Untereinheiten" einer Einheit gesprochen.

Eine Einheit kann verschiedene Betriebszustände haben. Wir fassen einen Zustand als Wert einer Kenngröße auf; die Werte einer Kenngröße schlioeßen sich gegenseitig aus.
> Die Kenngröße *Betriebszustand des Motors* hat die beiden möglichen Werte *Motor ist in Betrieb* und *Motor steht*. Die Kenngröße *Betriebspause des Motors* hat die Werte *Motor steht seit weniger als einer Stunde*, *Motor steht seit mehr als einer Stunde, aber weniger als einem Tag* und *Motor steht seit einem Tag*.

Zentraler Bestandteil des Experten-Wissens ist Wissen über die kausalen Zusammenhänge zwischen Störungen. Wir unterscheiden zwei solche Zusammenhänge:

- Störung A ist sichere Folge von Störung B.
- Störung A ist mögliche, aber nicht sichere Folge von Störung B.

Beidesmal ist Störung B einer der möglichen Verursacher von Störung A.

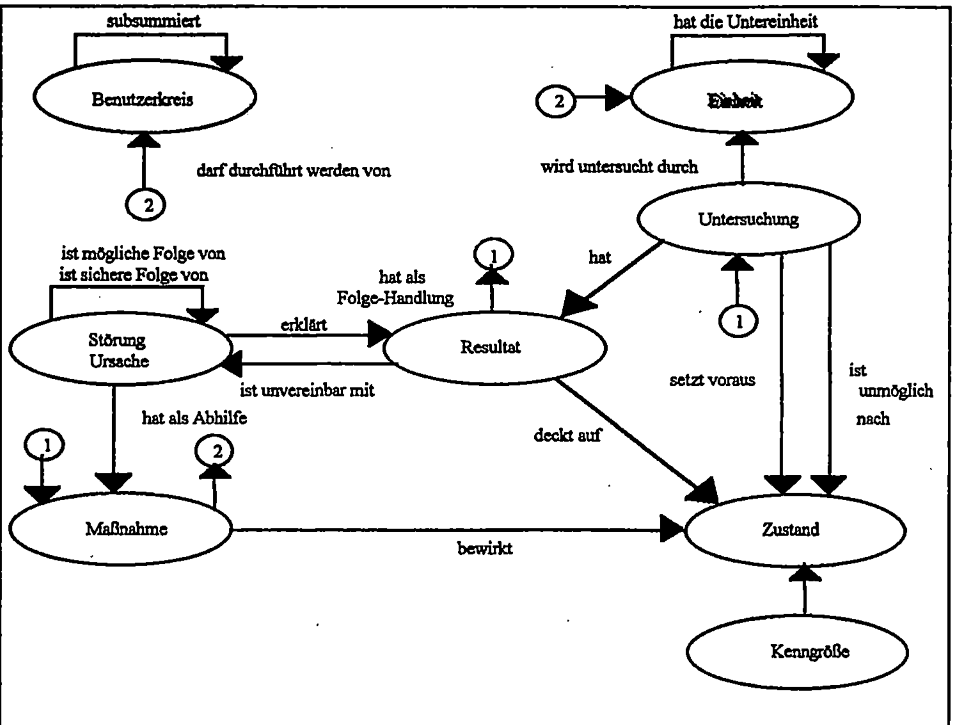

Bild 1 Die Beschreibungssprache von DINO

Die kausalen Beziehungen unter Störungen bilden den "totalen Störungs-Graphen", dessen Knoten für die Störungen an den Einheiten und dessen Kanten für Relationen der Art "ist sichere Folge von" und "ist mögliche Folge von" stehen. Jede Wurzel steht für eine nach außen wirkende Störung am technischen System, jedes Blatt repräsentiert eine Störung ohne Verursacher.

Jeder Ursache, das ist eine Störung ohne Verursacher, ist eine Abhilfe zugeordnet, das ist eine einzelne Maßnahme oder eine Abfolge von Maßnahmen. Einer Ursache können mehrere alternative Abhilfen zugeordnet sein, die absteigend nach Priorität geordnet sind. Läßt sich die Abhilfe höchster Priorität nicht durchführen, so wird versucht, die nächste Abhilfe durchzuführen.

    Die Ursache *Undichte Kraftstoffleitung* hat die alternativen Abhilfen *Kraftstoffleitung ersetzen* und *Kraftstoffleitung behelfsmäßig reparieren.*

Die Resultate einer Untersuchung schließen sich gegenseitig aus. Soll-Resultat heißt das Resultat, das die Untersuchung beim störungsfreien technischen System hätte, die übrigen Resultate sind die Nicht-Soll-Resultate.

Anlaß einer Diagnose ist, daß man ein Fehlverhalten des technischen Systems beobachtete und dadurch Einstiegs-Symptome gewann. Ein Einstiegs-Symptom betrachten wir als Nicht-Soll-Resultat einer Untersuchung, die der Benutzer des technischen Systems (oft unfreiwillig) machte.

Das Einstiegs-Symptom *Motor spring nicht an* ist ein Nicht-Soll-Resultat der Untersuchung *Springt der Motor an?*

Eine Handlung, d. h. eine Untersuchung oder Maßnahme, darf durchgeführt werden, wenn sie nicht an Voraussetzungen geknüpft ist oder wenn mindestens eine ihrer Einzel-Voraussetzungen aktuell erfüllt ist. Eine Einzel-Voraussetzung ist eine UND-Verknüpfung von Zuständen, früheren Maßnahmen und/oder Resultaten früherer Untersuchungen. Außerdem kann für eine Handlung eine Listen von ausschließenden Zuständen definiert sein: Liegt einer dieser Zustände vor, darf die Handlung nicht ausgeführt werden

Die Untersuchung *Wird die Elektronik mit Spannung versorgt, nachdem man die Sicherung xy ersetzt hat* hat die Voraussetzung *Sicherung xy ersetzen*. Diese Maßnahme beseitigt eine mögliche Ursache. Im Zustand *Elektronik wird mit Spannung versorgt* ist die Untersuchung unzulässig, da sinnlos.

Für jede Handlung ist spezifiziert, ob sie vom Benutzer oder automatisch durchgeführt wird, und im ersten Falle festgelegt, welchem Benutzerkreis der Benutzer "mindestens" angehören muß, um die Handlung durchzuführen.

Den *Motorkühlwasserstand kontrollieren* darf ein Kundentechniker selbst, den *Zylinder endoskopieren* darf nur ein mtu-Wartungstechiker. Der Benutzerkreis *mtu-Wartungstechniker* subsummiert den Benutzerkreis *Kundentechniker*.

Eine Untersuchung kann eine Abfolge von vorbereitenden Maßnahmen erfordern.

Die Untersuchung *Welche Beobachtung liefert das Endoskopieren der Zylinderkopfunterseite?* erfordert nacheinander folgende Maßnahmen: *Motor stoppen, Motorstart unterbinden, Zylinderkopfhaube abbauen, Kraftstoffeinspritzventil ausbauen* und *Motordrehvorrichtung anbauen*.

Zentraler Bestandteil jedes symptombasierten Diagnose-Expertensystems ist Wissen darüber, wie Störungen und Indizien zusammenhängen. In der Beschreibungssprache von DINO gibt es dafür zwei Relationen:
- Eine Störung "erklärt" ein Resultat, wenn die Störung für das Resultat verantwortlich gemacht werden kann. Ein Nicht-Soll-Resultat wird im allgemeinen durch mehrere Störungen erklärt. Zu den Erklärungen kann auch eine Mehrfach-Störung gehören, wenn diese, aber keine ihrer Einzel-Störungen das Resultat erklärt. Ein Soll-Resultat bedarf keiner Erklärung.

  Das Nicht-Soll-Resultat *Der Motoröldruck fällt* wird u. a. durch die Störungen *Ein Motor-Öldruck-Ventil defekt* und *Ölkreislauf undicht* erklärt.
- Eine Störung "ist unvereinbar mit" einem Resultat, wenn das Resultat die Störung logisch ausschließt. Diese Relation kann stets gelten oder nur unter der Bedingung, daß bestimmte weitere Störungen nicht aufgetreten sind.

  Das Resultat *Temperatur im Soll* der Untersuchung *Welche Abgastemperatur wird für den Zylinder 5 angezeigt?* ist bedingt unvereinbar mit der Störung *Zylinder 5 verschlissen*, nämlich außer wenn zusätzlich *Temperaturanzeige für Zylinder 5 defekt* aufgetreten ist.

2.   Das DINO-Diagnosekonzept

Eine Diagnose besteht daraus, daß nacheinander die Schritte Fehlererkennung, Fehlerdiagnose und Fehlerbehandlung durchgeführt werden. Bei Bedarf wird diese Abfolge wiederholt.

2.1   Strategie für die Fehlerdiagnose

Bild 2 demonstriert unseren Algorithmus zur Fehlerdiagnose.

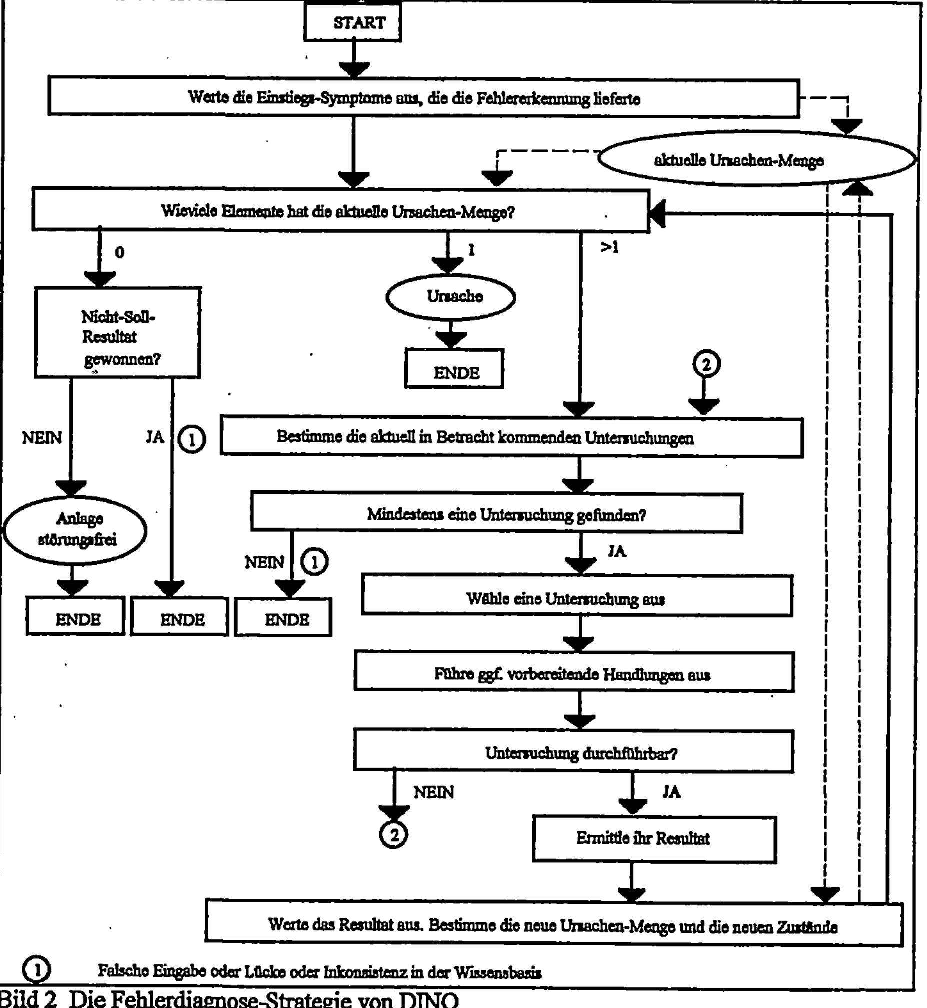

Bild 2 Die Fehlerdiagnose-Strategie von DINO

Wir fassen eine Fehlerdiagnose als Klassifikationsaufgabe auf: Unter den am technischen System möglichen Ursachen sind alle tatsächlich vorliegenden zu bestimmen. Der verwendete Algorithmus verwendet zwar Wissen ähnlich der heuristischen Klassifikation [2], versucht aber, zu jedem Zeitpunkt die Beobachtungen im Sinne der überdeckenden Klassifikation [21] zu interpretieren.

Die aktuelle Ursachen-Menge besteht zu jedem Zeitpunkt aus den Einfach- oder Mehrfach-Ursachen, die aktuell noch möglich sind, da sie alle bisherigen Resultate erklären. Zu Beginn umfaßt diese Menge alle Ursachen, die die beobachteten Einstiegs-Symptome erklären. Gibt es keine Einstiegs-Symptome, so besteht die Ursachen-Menge aus allen in der Wissensbasis berücksichtigten Ursachen am technischen System.

Die aktuelle Ursachen-Menge wird iterativ verkleinert, bis sie
o   aus einer einzigen Ursache besteht - damit ist die Ursache gefunden -
o   oder leer ist - dann ist das technische System störungsfrei, falls im Verlaufe der Fehlerdiagnose kein Nicht-Soll-Resultat gewonnen wurde, ansonsten hat der Benutzer eine falsche Eingabe gemacht -
o   oder es sich als unmöglich erweist, sie auf ein Element zu verkleinern. Dann sind am Ende der Fehlerdiagnose noch mehrere Ursachen möglich, zwischen denen das Diagnose-Werkzeug nicht differenzieren kann.

Die ersten beiden Schlußfolgerungen gelten natürlich nur unter der Voraussetzung, daß die Wissensbasis konsistent und vollständig ist. Falls keine Ursache mehr möglich ist, obwohl ein Nicht-Soll-Resultat gewonnen wurde, so hat der Benutzer einen Fehler gemacht, oder der Fachexperte hat beim Wissenserwerb eine Ursache vergessen, oder eine Relation zwischen einem Resultat und Ursachen ist falsch. Die dritte Schlußfolgerung ist ein Beweis für eine Wissenslücke.

Zu Beginn einer Fehlerdiagnose werden die über eine Systemschnittstelle quasi ohne Aufwand zu beschaffenden Symptome erfaßt und ausgewertet. Danach muß in aller Regel der Benutzer tätig werden. Bei der Bestimmung, welche Untersuchung jeweils als nächstes erfolgt, unterscheidet DINO zwei Modi: Einem unerfahrenen Benutzer stellt DINO eine Reihe von Fragen, bis die Fehlerdiagnose beendet ist. Ein erfahrener Benutzer hingegen wählt selber aus, welche Untersuchung er als nächstes durchführen will. In beiden Modi bestimmt DINO zunächst, welche Untersuchungen aktuell überhaupt in Betracht kommen. Diese Untersuchungen werden anschließend bewertet. Je nach Modus verlangt DINO vom Benutzer dann, die als optimal bewertete Untersuchung auszuführen, bzw. bietet ihm alle in Betracht kommenden Untersuchungen zur Auswahl an, und zwar absteigend nach Nutzen-Aufwand-Bewertung sortiert.

Eine Untersuchung kommt aktuell in Betracht, wenn sie
-   den Benutzer nicht überfordern würde
-   und noch nicht durchgeführt wurde
-   und nicht an eine Voraussetzung gebunden ist, eine ihrer Einzel-Voraussetzung aktuell erfüllt ist oder die Untersuchung zulässig gemacht werden kann
-   und kein sie ausschließender Zustand aktuell vorliegt
-   und eines ihrer Resultate die aktuelle Ursachen-Menge verkleinern würde.

Ein Zustand kann durch eine Maßnahme hergestellt oder durch ein Resultat aufgedeckt sein. DINO protokolliert Wissen über den aktuellen Zustand des technischen Systems und geht davon aus, daß der Zustand solange vorliegt, bis eine Maßnahme oder Resultat einen anderen Zustand derselben Kenngröße herstellt bzw. beweist. DINO trifft keine "Default"-Annahme darüber, welchen Wert eine Kenngröße aktuell hat. DINO führt zur Laufzeit eine rudimentäre Planung durch, um bei Bedarf Untersuchungen zulässig zu machen.

Die *Färbung der Abgase* kann nur bei laufendem Motor ermittelt werden. Steht der Motor, so kann diese Untersuchung durch eine Maßnahme zulässig gemacht werden, die den Zustand *Motor läuft* herstellt - vorausgesetzt, diese Maßnahme hat Erfolg. Ist unbekannt, ob der Motor läuft oder nicht, so bedarf es entweder ebenfalls dieser Maßnahme oder aber eines Resultates, die den Wert der betreffenden Kenngröße aufdeckt.

Damit diese Planung nicht zu aufwendig wird, wurde DINO in der gegenwärtigen Version auf die Suchtiefe 1 beschränkt: Eine Maßnahme, die eine Untersuchung zulässig macht, muß selbst aktuell zulässig sein.

Die Bewertung einer Untersuchung ist das Verhältnis zwischen ihrem aktuell zu erwartenden Nutzen und ihren Kosten. Der Nutzen einer Untersuchung liegt darin, daß die aktuelle Ursachen-Menge durch das Resultat, das die Untersuchung liefert, verkleinert wird. Der Nutzen wird - wie in der Klassifikation üblich [15] - als zu erwartender Informationsgewinn numerisch bewertet, er hängt von der alten Ursachen-Menge ab. Die hierfür benötigten Wahrscheinlichkeiten werden aus groben linguistischen Angaben des Fachexperten über die Auftritts-Häufigkeiten von Ursachen berechnet. Auch die Kosten von Maßnahmen und Untersuchungen werden vom Fachexperten mit groben Angaben bewertet. Viel zu aufwendig erscheint es, beim Wissenserwerb numerische Wahrscheinlichkeiten oder präzise Kostenangaben zu verlangen. Da der Nutzen ein logarithmisches Maß ist, werden die Kosten vom Nutzen subtrahiert.

Im Gegensatz zu anderen Diagnosestrategien erfordert die vorgestellte Strategie zu keinem Zeitpunkt, daß der Benutzer eine Hypothese aufstellt - etwa deshalb, weil die Fehlerdiagnose keine eindeutige Fortsetzung besitzt. Jedoch kann der Benutzer jederzeit dem Diagnose-Werkzeug eine Hypothese "mitteilen", indem er unter den aktuell noch möglichen Ursachen eine als diejenige kennzeichnet, die seiner Meinung nach tatsächlich vorliegt. DINO schränkt dann den Kreis der dem Benutzer angebotenen Untersuchungen ein, nämlich auf diejenigen, die nicht nur gemäß dem gerade geschilderten Kriterium in Betracht kommen, sondern auch noch die Hypothese überprüfen. Eine Untersuchung prüft eine verdächtige Ursache, wenn sie ein Resultat besitzt, das durch die Ursache erklärt wird, und ein anderes, das mit der Ursache unvereinbar ist. DINO verfolgt die Hypothese solange, bis sie bestätigt ist - das ist der Fall, wenn die Hypothese die einzige noch mögliche Ursache ist - oder sie widerlegt wurde oder wenn es keine Untersuchung gibt, die die Hypothese prüft. Im letzten Falle liegt eine Wissens-Lücke vor, und als Notbehelf wird die Hypothese zurückgezogen.

Die Diagnosestrategie von DINO vermeidet jedes Backtracking - auch dann, wenn ein Verdacht des Benutzers widerlegt ist oder zurückgezogen wurde. Damit unterscheidet sie sich von allen Suchbaum-Strategien, z. B. von dem bekannten Vorgehen, einen Fehlerbaum in der Wurzel beginnend abzuarbeiten, bis ein Blatt erreicht und damit eine Ursache gefunden ist. Diese Strategie wendet beispielsweise TestBench [18] unter der Bezeichnung "Navigieren im Fehlerbaum" an. Ein weiterer Vorteil der DINO-

Strategie gegenüber Suchbaum-Verfahren ist: Eine Diagnose mit DINO läßt sich auch dann fortsetzen, wenn eine Untersuchung sich als undurchführbar erweist, ohne daß eine Hypothese aufgestellt und möglicherweise wieder zurückgezogen werden muß.

2.2   Echtzeit-Fehlerdiagnose

Ein Diagnosewerkzeug kann eine Echtzeit-Anforderung erfüllen und damit z. B. einen Prozeß überwachen, wenn es zur Laufzeit einen Entscheidungsbaum abarbeitet: Falls man die Dauer jeder Handlung nach oben abschätzen kann, so kann man eine obere Schranke für die Dauer einer Fehlerdiagnose angeben. In [15] wird ein Überblick über Techniken gegeben, die klassifizierende Entscheidungsbäume erzeugen. Prinzipiell kann auch ein Diagnose-Werkzeug, das einen menschlichen Benutzer berät, einen Entscheidungsbaum abarbeiten. Das Werkzeug wäre aber zu unflexibel, um auf die Anforderungen und Wünsche des Benutzers einzugehen.

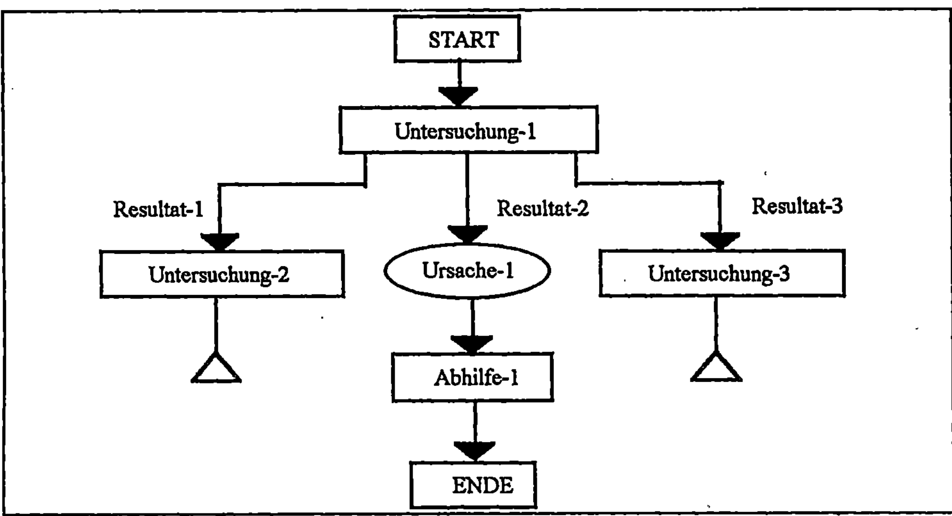

Bild 3 Ausschnitt aus einem Entscheidungsbaum zur Fehlerdiagnose

Auf Wunsch generiert DINO aus einer Wissensbasis einen wie in Bild 3 strukturierten Entscheidungsbaum. Dieser Entscheidungsbaum ist nicht nur zur Diagnose anwendbar, sondern läßt sich auch dazu nutzen, die Wissensbasis zu analysieren, vgl. Abschnitt 3.3.

2.3   Strategie für die Fehlerbehandlung

Falls DINO eine Ursache diagnostiziert hat, so schlägt es dem Benutzer die Abhilfe mit der höchsten Priorität vor bzw. versucht, diese automatisch auszuführen. Ist die Abhilfe aktuell unzulässig, so versucht DINO, sie durch eine Maßnahme zulässig zu machen. Läßt sich die Abhilfe nicht zulässig machen oder erweist sich eine hierfür erforderliche Maßnahme als undurchführbar, so wird in der Wissensbasis nach einer alternativen Abhilfe gesucht. Läßt sich keine Abhilfe durchführen, so ist die Fehlerbehandlung gescheitert.

Falls die Fehlerdiagnose damit endet, daß noch mehrere Ursachen möglich sind, zwischen denen DINO nicht unterschieden kann, so wählt der Benutzer aus, welche Ursache er als nächstes beseitigen (lassen) möchte. Ihm werden die Auftritts-Häufigkeiten jeder Ursache sowie die zu erwartenden Kosten für ihre Beseitigung angezeigt. Denkbar wäre, daß DINO eine Differentialdiagnose stellt und hierfür eine numerische Evidenz für jede noch mögliche Ursache ermittelt. Dies würde aber erfordern, daß jeder Zusammenhang zwischen einer Ursache und einem Resultat numerisch bewertet wird - etwa nach dem Vorbild von MED2 [14] oder CLASSICA [4]. Da der Aufwand beim Wissenserwerb erheblich wäre, wurde auf eine Differentialdiagnose verzichtet.

Sobald alle diagnostizierten Ursachen beseitigt sind, werden die bewirkten Folge-Störungen beseitigt, und zwar nach dem gleichen Vorgehen wie die Ursachen.
Die Ursache *Undichte Kraftstoffleitung* hat die sichere Folge *Luft im Kraftstoffsystem*. Diese Störung zu beseitigen ist erst dann sinnvoll, wenn die Kraftstoffleitung nicht mehr undicht ist.

3. Wissenserwerb

Der Wissenserwerb ist als der "bottle-neck" der Expertensystem-Technik bekannt, daher erspart ein effizienter Wissenserwerb viel Zeit und Geld.

3.1 Gewinnung des für eine Diagnose erforderlichen Wissens

Die gerade vorgestellte Diagnosestrategie nutzt im wesentlichen folgendes Wissen über das zu diagnostizierende technische System:
o Welche Ursachen können überhaupt auftreten und kommen daher als Kandidaten in Betracht?
o Welche Auftritts-Wahrscheinlichkeit hat jede Ursache, und welche zu behebenden Folge-Störungen kann sie hervorrufen?
o Welche Nicht-Soll-Resultate sind Einstiegs-Symptome?
o Welche Untersuchung sind möglich, und welchen Aufwand, welches Soll-Resultat und welche Nicht-Soll-Resultate hat jede Untersuchung?
o Was folgt aus dem gerade gewonnenen Resultat? Hierfür muß bekannt sein:
  - für jedes Nicht-Soll-Resultat: durch welche Ursachen wird es erklärt? Damit ist insbesondere auch bekannt, welche Ursachen die (als Nicht-Soll-Resultate aufgefaßten) Einstiegs-Symptome erklären
  - für jedes Soll-Resultat: Mit welchen Ursachen ist es unvereinbar?

Dieses Wissen ist in der Wissensbasis des Laufzeitsystems abgelegt. Durch "Extrahierung" wird es automatisch aus dem Experten-Wissen, dessen Strukturierung in Kapitel 1 dargelegt wurde, gewonnen. Das vom Fachexperten erworbene Wissen wird also nicht unmittelbar zur Laufzeit genutzt, sondern zuvor zum Zwecke einer schnelleren Diagnose umgeformt.

Die "Extrahierung" besteht daraus, daß die Zusammenhänge zwischen Resultaten und Störungen mit dem totalen Störungs-Graphen (also mit den Zusammenhängen unter Störungen) kombiniert wird, um die zur Laufzeit benötigten Zusammenhänge zwischen Resultaten und Ursachen automatisch zu gewinnen. Angewendet werden folgende plausiblen Grundsätze:

- Eine Störung A erklärt ein Resultat, wenn mindestens eine der Folgen von A eine Störung ist, die das Resultat erklärt.
- · Eine Störung A ist unvereinbar mit einem Resultat, wenn eine Störung, die sichere Folge von A ist, oder jede Störung, die mögliche Folge von A ist, mit dem Resultat unvereinbar ist.

Bild 4 erläutert diese Extrahierung.

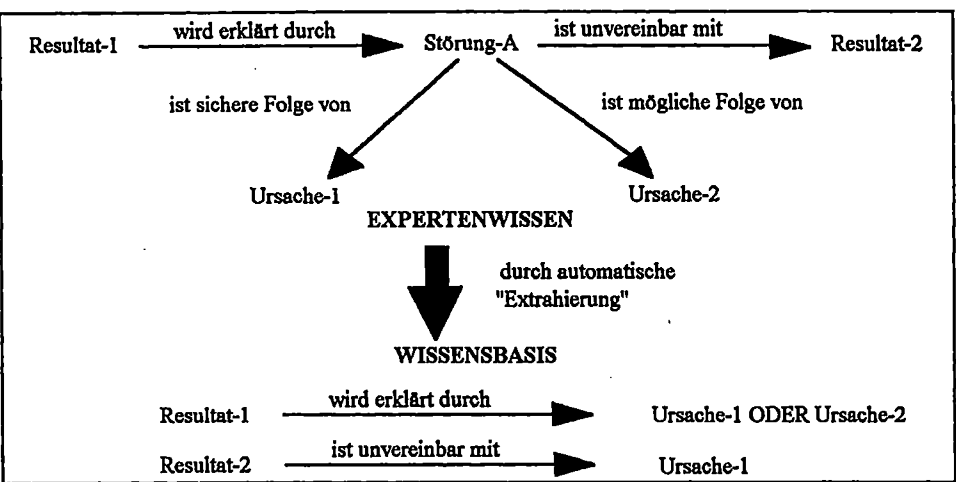

Bild 4 "Extrahierung" einer Wissensbasis aus Experten-Wissen

3.2   Die Wissenserwerbs-Komponente von DINO

Mit der Wissenserwerbs-Komponente von DINO macht ein Fachexperte sein Wissen einem Diagnose-Werkzeug verfügbar, indem er Experten-Wissen formuliert, das wie in Kapitel 1 beschrieben strukturiert ist. Die Wissenserwerbs-Komponente (WEK) "extrahiert" aus diesem Wissen eine Wissensbasis für das DINO-Laufzeitsystem.

Grundsatz beim Wissenserwerb ist, daß der Fachexperte sein Wissen in der von ihm gewünschten Reihenfolge schrittweise aufbauen kann. Zu seiner Unterstützung gibt es zu jeder "einfachen" Relation eine Umkehrrelation. Beispielsweise ist die Umkehrrelation zu der Relation "hat die Folgehandlung", die zwischen einem Resultat und einer Handlung definiert ist, die Relation "wird ausgeführt nach". Der Experte kann Wissen unter beiden Sichtweisen formulieren, also beispielsweise Folgehandlungen eines Resultates festlegen oder umgekehrt bestimmen, nach welchen Resultaten eine Handlung auszuführen ist. Durch Wissens-Propagierung stellt die WEK sicher, daß das aus beiden Sichtweisen formulierte Wissen zueinander paßt.

Die WEK besitzt eine vollgraphische Oberfläche. Die Hierarchie unter den Einheiten sowie der totale Störungs-Graph werden mit je einem Browser dargestellt, der den Graphen "ausgekämmt" als Baum zeigt - ein Objekt mit n Vorgängern tritt n-mal im Browser auf oder öfters, wenn ein Vorgänger seinerseits mehrere Vorgänger hat. Bild 5 zeigt zwei Browser.

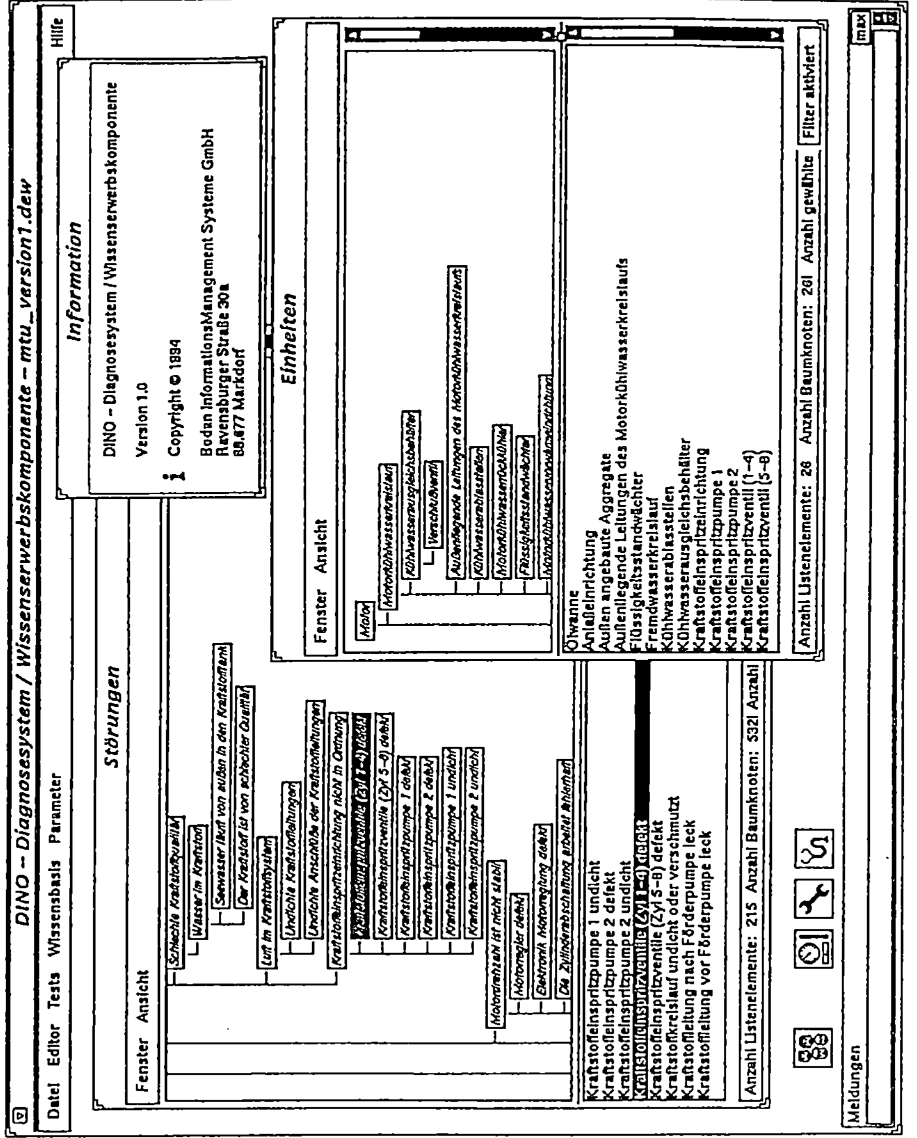

Bild 5 Einheiten-Baum und Störungs-Graph

Die Attribute und Relationen eines Objektes definiert der Fachexperte mit einem Attribute-Editor, der spezifisch für die Klasse dieses Objektes ist. Bild 6 zeigt beispielhaft den Editor für die Maßnahme *Ölabstreifringe ersetzen*.

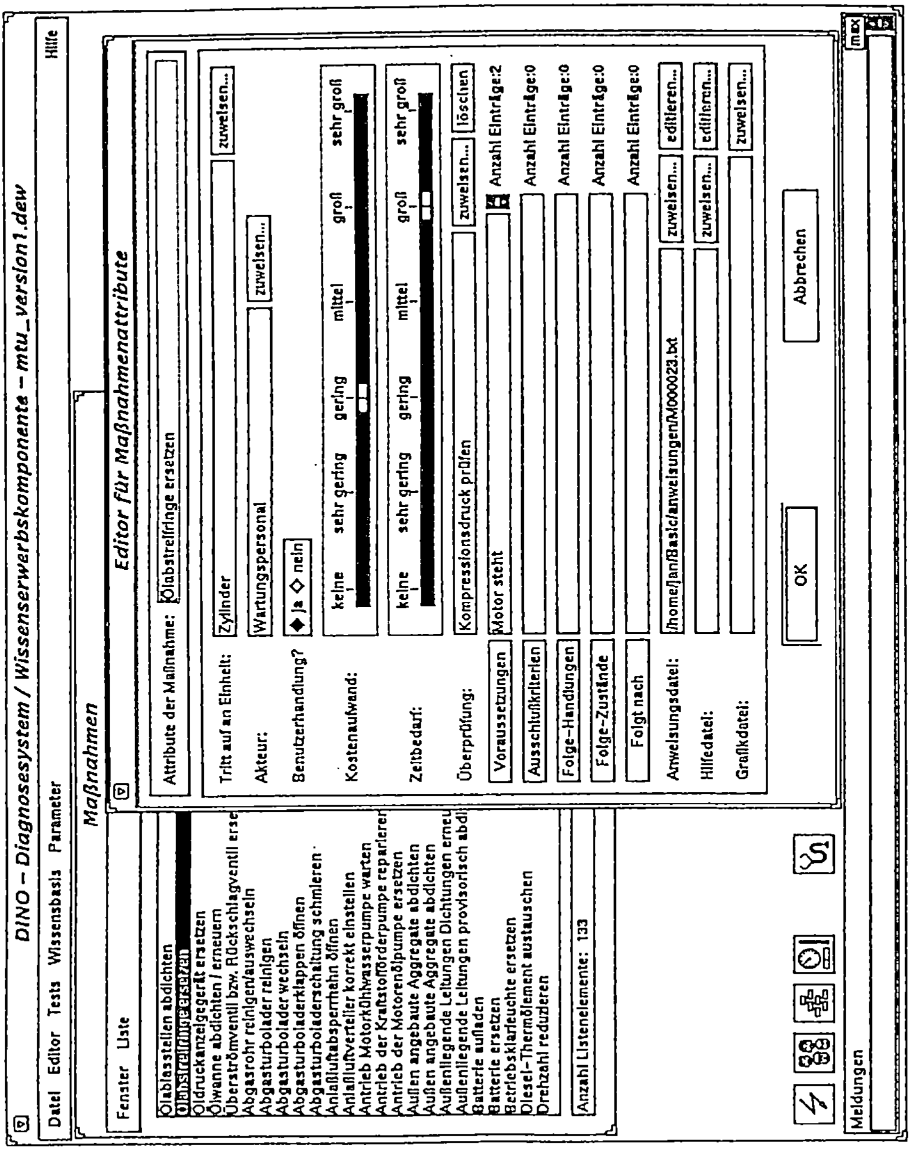

Bild 6 Attribute-Editor für eine Maßnahme

3.3   Prüfung des Experten-Wissens

DINO bietet dem Fachexperten effiziente Werkzeuge an, mit denen er das Wissen auf
Vollständigkeit und Konsistenz überprüfen lassen kann:

o Eine Inkonsistenz liegt beispielsweise dann vor, wenn der Fachexperte eine
   Störung sowohl als Erklärung eines Resultates als auch als mit dem Resultat
   unvereinbar kennzeichnet oder wenn eine Maßnahme sich selbst als Voraussetzung
   hat. Eine solche Festlegung fängt DINO ab und nimmt sie gar nicht ins Experten-
   Wissen auf. Eine andere Art der Inkonsistenz, die DINO aufdeckt und dem

Fachexperten anzeigt: Eine Folge einer Ursache erklärt ein Resultat, eine andere Folge derselben Ursache ist mit dem Resultat unvereinbar.

o Jederzeit kann der Fachexperte das Experten-Wissen auf syntaktische Vollständigkeit überprüfen. Eine syntaktische Lücke liegt z. B. dann vor, wenn für eine Störung weder ein Verursacher noch eine Abhilfe oder für eine Untersuchung weniger als zwei Resultate definiert sind.

DINO verifiziert das Experten-Wissen in drei Schritten: "Extrahierung" einer Wissensbasis (vgl. Abschnitt 3.1), Generierung eines Entscheidungsbaumes (vgl. Abschnitt 2.2) und Analyse dieses Entscheidungsbaumes. Vorhergesagt werden Situationen, in denen eine Fehlerdiagnose kein "voller Erfolg" werden wird:

o Sind einem Blatt noch mehrere Ursachen zugeordnet, so fehlen in der Wissensbasis Untersuchungen, die zwischen diesen Ursachen zu differenzieren vermögen.

o Ist einem Blatt keine einzige Ursache zugeordnet, obwohl der Pfad von der Wurzel zu diesem Blatt nicht der Gutpfad des Baumes ist, so liegt möglicherweise ein Fehler oder eine Lücke in der Wissensbasis vor.

o Jede mögliche Ursache muß diagnostiziert werden können und daher einem Blatt des Entscheidungsbaumes zugeordnet sein. Gibt es für eine Ursache kein derartiges Blatt, so ist die Wissensbasis lücken- oder fehlerhaft.

4. Erste Erfahrungen beim Einsatz von DINO

Als erster Schritt wurde ein Demonstrator für den mtu-Dieselmotor erstellt. Dieser sollte nicht den gesamten Motor in voller Tiefe, sondern einerseits den gesamten Motor oberflächlich und andererseits das Teilsystem *Ölkreislauf* eingehend diagnostizieren. Prinzipiell hätte ein Fachexperte von mtu selbst diesen Demonstrator mit DINO bauen können. Da die mtu-Experten jedoch nicht genug Zeit hatten, tat dies ein Bodan-Mitarbeiter.

Folgende Informationsquellen standen zur Verfügung, um mit DINO einen Demonstrator zu konstruieren, der den mtu-Dieselmotor diagnostiziert: ein "trouble shooting guide", mit dessen Hilfe ein Kunde von mtu selber eine Diagnose auf oberer Ebene durchführt, ein ausführliches Wartungshandbuch für mtu-Techniker und ein menschlicher Fachexperte.

Zuerst wurde der "trouble shooting guide" ausgewertet. Die dort aufgeführten Symptome wurden als Resultate modelliert. Die im "trouble shooting guide" als Ursachen aufgeführten Störungen erwiesen sich als Grobdiagnosen, so daß sie als Folge-Störungen ins Experten-Wissen aufgenommen wurden. Schrittweise wurde dann dieses Wissen um das im Wartungshandbuch abgelegte erweitert und abgeändert.

Bei beiden Schritten erwies sich ein Vorgehen nach einem Phasenmodell als hilfreich: Die Arbeit an einer Phase sollte so weit wie möglich abgeschlossen werden, bevor man zur nächsten übergeht.
Phase 1: Einheiten-Baum
Phase 2: Störungs-Graph, Abhilfen und Zustände
Phase 3: Weitere Zustände, Untersuchungen und Resultate
Phase 4: Störungen und Resultate.

Es gab keine prinzipiellen Probleme, das vorhandene Wissen in der DINO-Beschriebungssprache zu formalisieren und damit einem Demonstrator-Prototyp für das gesteckte Ziel (oberflächliche Diagnose des Gesamtmotors, eingehende Diagnose des *Ölkreislaufes*) zu konstruieren. Das folgende Beispiel erläutert, wie komplexere Zusammenhänge modelliert werden.

Hat man den Verdacht, daß ein Zylinder verschlissen ist, so bleibt oft nur, ihn zu endoskopieren. Diese Untersuchung ist sehr aufwendig, denn sie erfordert eine Abfolge vorbereitender Maßnahmen. Hat man diese einmal durchgeführt, so wird man den gesamten Zylinder untersuchen und dabei stets mehrere Symptome gewinnen. Dieser Sachverhalt wurde durch drei Untersuchungs-Objekte modelliert: *Kolbenboden endoskopieren*, *Laufbuchse endoskopieren* und *Zylinderkopfunterseite endoskopieren*. Jedes Resultat einer dieser Untersuchungen hat als Folge-Handlungen die beiden anderen Untersuchungen; der Algorithmus zur Fehlerdiagnose vermeidet eine Endlos-Schleife zur Laufzeit. Die drei Soll-Resultate haben als Folge-Handlungen die Maßnahmen, die den Zylinder wieder betriebsbereit machen, die Nicht-Soll-Resultate die Maßnahmen, die vor der jeweiligen Abhilfe (z. B. *Kolben ersetzen*) nötig sind.

Erst als dieser Prototyp aufgrund der schriftlichen Unterlagen vorlag, wurde der menschliche Fachexperte zu Rate gezogen, um den Prototypen zum Demonstrator auszubauen. Der Fachexperte testete den Prototyp und unterbreitete Verbesserungsvorschläge. Die Vermutung bestätigte sich, daß die Arbeit mit dem Prototypen den Fachexperten weit mehr motivierte und herausforderte, als wenn man ihn gleich zu Anfang befragt hätte: Seine Verbesserungsvorschläge waren sehr gezielt und zweckmäßig. Es zeigte sich, daß die schriftlichen Unterlagen Lücken aufweisen: Viele für Untersuchungen erforderlichen Betriebszustände werden nicht explizit erwähnt. Für einen einigermaßen erfahrenen menschlichen Diagnostiker mag dieses Wissen selbstverständlich sein, nicht aber einem unerfahrenen Benutzer. In einer Wissensbasis müssen die Voraussetzungen daher explizit modelliert sein.

5.   Ausblick: Behandlung der Variantenvielfalt

Um technische Systeme an die Wünsche der Kunden anzupassen, werden sie typischerweise aus Modulen zusammengesetzt. Bereits bei wenigen Modulen hat man eine gewaltige Zahl theoretisch möglicher Varianten: Bei 10 Modulen mit je 3 Alternativen gibt es bereits $3^{10} = 59.049$ Kombinationsmöglichkeiten.

Der klassische Weg, Expertensysteme zu erstellen, ist bei hoher Variantenvielfalt sehr unwirtschaftlich: Für jede Variante müßte man erneut Wissen erwerben und validieren. Der einzig erfolgversprechende Weg zur Lösung des Problems Variantenvielfalt ist, das Wissen des Fachexperten in einer solchen Weise modular zu organisieren, daß die zur Diagnose einer bestimmten Variante benötigte Wissensbasis sich automatisch aus Wissens-Modulen erzeugen läßt. Für jeden realen Modul-Typ gibt es dann ein derartiges Wissens-Modul. Jedes Wissens-Modul wird so oft kopiert, wie das entsprechende reale Modul im technischen System auftritt, und die Wissensbasis wird aus diesen Wissens-Modul-Kopien zusammengefügt.

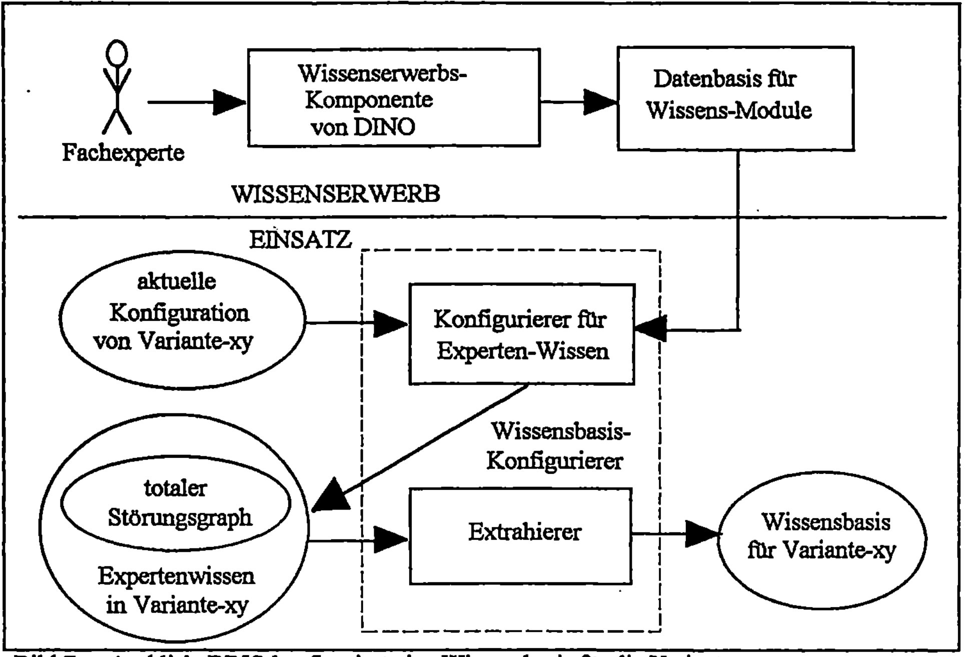

Bild 7   Ausblick: DINO konfiguriert eine Wissensbasis für die Variante-xy

Bild 7 zeigt diese Lösungsidee. Mit welchem Konzept das FACTEDIS-Konzept diese Idee realisiert, wird in [12] beschrieben. Kernpunkt der Lösung ist es, im Wissens-Modul für ein aus Komponenten zusammengesetzten Modul-Typ "Platzhalter" für die Untereinheiten einzuführen. Das Wissen darüber, welche Außenwirkungen eine Komponente hat, wird diesem Platzhalter zugeordnet. Das Wissen über das "Innenleben" der Komponente wird hingegen dem Wissens-Modul für den Komponenten-Typ zugeordnet.

6.   Anforderungen an Hard- und Software, Stand der Arbeiten.

Das Laufzeitsystem ist derzeit auf Workstation und PC verfügbar, die WEK nur auf Workstation. Folgende Anforderungen stellt DINO:
o   auf Workstation:
  - Sun SPARCstation, Graphik- oder X-Terminal, mind. 16 MB Arbeitsspeicher, mind. 30 MB Platte
  - Sun OS 4.1.x, X-Windows, OSF/Motif-Window-Manager
o   auf PC:
  - Graphik-Bildschrim, mind. 8 MB Arbeitsspeicher, mind. 10 MB Platte
  - Windows 3.1.

Sowohl das Laufzeitsystem als auch die WEK wurden in C++ implementiert und benötigen zum Einsatz nur eine der gerade genannten Plattformen und eine Laufzeitlizen von Bodan IMS GmbH. DINO ist in der ersten Ausbaustufe seit Mai 1994 kommerziell verfügbar, die in Kapitel 5 skizzierte Behandlung der Variantenvielfalt wird bis Ende 1994 integriert sein.

Literatur

[1] H.-J. BULLINGER: "Integrationspotentiale von Expertensystemen in der Produktion". Technische Rundschau 31 (1990), S. 14 - 28.

[2] W. CLANCEY: "Heuristic Classification". Artif. Intell. 27, pp. 289 - 350 (1985).

[3] R. DAVIS: "Diagnostic Reasoning Based on Structure and Behavior". Artif. Intell. 24, pp. 347 - 411 (1984).

[4] U. GAPPA, F. PUPPE & S. SCHEWE: "Graphical Knowledge Acquisition for Medical Diagnostic Expert Systems". Special Issue on Knowledge Acquisition, Artificial Intelligence in Medicine (1993).

[5] W. HAMSCHER, L. CONSOLE & J. DE KLEER: "Readings in Model-Based Diagnosis". Morgan Kaufmann Publ., San Mateo, 1992.

[6] S. IWANOWSKI: "Model-Based Diagnosis for Different Time Points". Proceed. 11th Europ. Conf. on Artif. Intell., pp. 28 - 36 (1992).

[7] E.-W. JÜNGST & K. D. MEYER-GRAMANN: "FACTEDIS - a Tool for Generating Real-Time Expert Systems". Proceed. 5th US Postal Service Adv. Technol Conf. (1992).

[8] J. DE KLEER & B. C. WILLIAMS: "Diagnosing Multiple Faults". Artif. Intell. 32, pp. 97 - 130 (1987).

[9] J. de KLEER & B. C. WILLIAMS: "Diagnosis with Behavioral Models". Proceed. Int. Joint Conf. on Artif. Intell. '89, pp. 1324 - 1330 (1989).

[10] S. KOCKSKÄMPER, B. NEUMANN, A. JOSUB & H. MÜLLER: "Die Anwendung modellbasierten Schließens bei der Diagnose schiffstechnischer Anlagen". In: F. PUPPE & A. GÜNTER (Hrsg.): "Expertensysteme 93". Informatik aktuell, Springer Verlag, Heidelberg, 1993, S. 14 - 27.

[11] B. KUIPERS & D. BERLEANT: "Using Incomplete Quantitative Knowledge in Qualitative Reasoning". In: Proceed. AAAI '88, pp. 324 - 329 (1988).

[12] K. D. MEYER-GRAMANN & E.-W. JÜNGST: "Diagnose von modularen technischen Systemen hoher Variantenvielfalt mit FACTEDIS". In: F. PUPPE & A. GÜNTER (Hrsg.): "Expertensysteme 93". Informatik aktuell, Springer Verlag, Heidelberg, 1993, S. 28-41.

[13]: M. PFAU-WAGENBURG, Th. BRUNNER & W. NEJDL: "Process-Oriented Techniques in an Expert System for Power System Diagnosis". Proceed 10th Europ. Conf. on Artif. Intell. (1992), Workshop W9.

[14] F. PUPPE: "Problemlösungsmethoden in Expertensystemen". Studienreihe Informatik, Springer Verlag, Heidelberg, 1990.

[15] S. R. SAFAVIAN & D. LANDGREBE: "A Survey of Decision Tree Classifier Methodology". IEEE Transact. Systems, Man & Cybern. Vol. 40 No. 3, pp. 315 - 320 (1991).

[16] E. SOLOWAY et al.: "Assessing the Maintainability of XCON-in-RIME: Coping with the Problems of a VERY Large Rule-Base". Proceed. AAAI '87, pp. 824 - 829 (1987).

[17] P. STRUß & O. DREßLER: "Physical Negation - Integrating Fault Models into the GDE". Proceed. Int. Conf. on Artif. Intell., pp. 1318 - 1323 (1989).

[18] N. WALESCHKOWSKI: "Implementierung in TestBench". In: W. HERDEN, H.-W. HEIN & H. VOß (Hrsg.): "Realisierung von Expertensystem-Implementierung in fünf Entwicklungsumgebungen". Oldenbourg-Verlag, München, 1992.

[19] S. WEß: "PATDEX - ein Ansatz zur wissensbasierten und inkrementellen Verbesserung von Ähnlichkeitsbewertungen in der fallbasierten Diagnostik". In: F. PUPPE & A. GÜNTER (Hrsg.): "Expertensysteme 93". Informatik aktuell, Springer Verlag, Heidelberg, 1993, S. 42 - 55.

[20] H. WEULE: "Expertensysteme im industriellen Einsatz". In: F. PUPPE & A. GÜNTER (Hrsg.): "Expertensysteme 93". Informatik aktuell, Springer Verlag, Heidelberg, 1993, S. 1 - 12.

[21] YUN PENG & J. REGGIA: "Abductive Inference Models for Diagnostic Problem-Solving". Springer Series Symbolic Computation - Artificial Intelligence. Springer Verlag, Heidelberg, 1990.

Modellbasierte Fehlerdiagnose eines Ballastwassersystems

C. Böttcher, A. Brinkop, M. Zimmermann-Sturm
Fraunhofer Institut für Informations- & Datenverarbeitung (IITB)
Fraunhoferstr. 1
D-76131 Karlsruhe
FRG
{boet,bri,zmn}@iitb.fhg.de

1. Einleitung

Eine der großen Herausforderungen der modernen Industrie ist die ständig steigende Komplexität technischer Anlagen und Prozesse. Die erforderliche Wirtschaftlichkeit und Sicherheit kann nur durch ein hohes Maß an Zuverlässigkeit und Verfügbarkeit erfüllt werden. Der Forschungsbereich "Modellbasiertes Schließen" ist einer der vielversprechenderen Ansätze der KI, die zu rechnergestützten Lösungen dieser Probleme beitragen können. Für eine Reihe von Anwendungsdomänen (analoge Schaltungen, Energieversorgungsnetze) erlauben die entwickelten Techniken zur modellbasierten Fehlerdiagnose bereits die Lösung realistischer Diagnoseprobleme. Doch gerade im Bereich dynamischer Systeme, wie etwa Ballastwassersysteme, sind noch viele Aspekte in Hinblick auf Modellierung des Systemverhaltens und Steuerung der Diagnosestrategie ungeklärt.

Dieser Bericht beschreibt Ergebnisse und Erfahrungen, die im Rahmen des Verbundprojektes BEHAVIOR[1] am IITB bei der Anwendung der Techniken der modellbasierten Fehlerdiagnose auf ein Ballastwassersystem, gemacht wurden. Ziel war es, mit den zur Verfügung stehenden Werkzeugen alle Fehlerszenarien, die laut Anwendungspartner relevant sind ([Rümelin 93]), zu lösen und daraus Rückschlüsse zu ziehen, inwiefern diese Werkzeuge geeignet sind, Problemstellungen dynamischer Systeme zu behandeln.

Die Anwendungsdomäne Ballastwassersysteme und die damit verbundenen Diagnoseprobleme werden in Kapitel 2. beschrieben. Kapitel 3. geht auf hier relevante Aspekte der modellbasierten Diagnose ein, in Abschnitt 3.2 insbesondere auf die Frage der Modellierung für die Diagnose. Modellbasierte Diagnose basiert auf der Zurückführung verletzter Erwartungen auf daran beteiligte Komponenten. Daher ist im Gegensatz zu traditionellen Modellierungsansätzen eine Modularisierung entlang der Komponentenstruktur notwendig. Darüberhinaus muß die Dynamik des Systems angemessen berücksichtigt werden. Die meisten Ansätze haben sich bisher auf Approximationen des Verhaltens durch statische Modelle beschränkt ([Cermignani, Tornielli 93]). Die in diesem Bericht vorgestellte Modellierung nutzt die Dynamik des Systems explizit aus. Unter Verwendung von Rechenmodellen des korrekten Systemverhaltens und von Fehlverhaltensweisen lassen sich alle Fehler in den von den Domänenexperten bereitgestellten Fehlerszenarien ([Rümelin 93]) eindeutig lokalisieren. Die Diskussion der Diagnose der Fehlerszenarien erfolgt in Kapitel 4. Darin eingebettet ist die

---

1. BEHAVIOR ist ein vom BMFT gefördertes Verbundprojekt, PT-FKZ: 01 IW 203 B/8

Darstellung der Modellierung der Anwendung (Kapitel 4.1 und 4.3). Kapitel 5. schließlich skizziert die Architektur des implementierten Prototyps. Der Bericht schließt mit einer Diskussion der Ergebnisse.

2. Das Problem

Ballastwassersysteme finden sich auf Ölbohrplattformen (oder auch auf Schiffen) um trotz Seegang und wechselnder Ladung, die Balance der Plattform zu garantieren. Sie bestehen aus einer Menge von über die Anlage verteilten Tanks, die durch Rohre und Pumpen miteinander verbunden sind. Gemäß den äußeren Anforderungen müssen Ventile geöffnet/geschlossen und die Tanks in angemessener Weise befüllt/entleert werden. Ein konventionelles System besteht aus etwa vierzig Tanks. Es werden aber nur wenige gleichzeitig befüllt bzw. entleert. Eine Minimalkonfiguration von 3 Tanks ist daher bereits kennzeichnend für eine reale Anwendung (siehe Bild 1., siehe [Rüme-

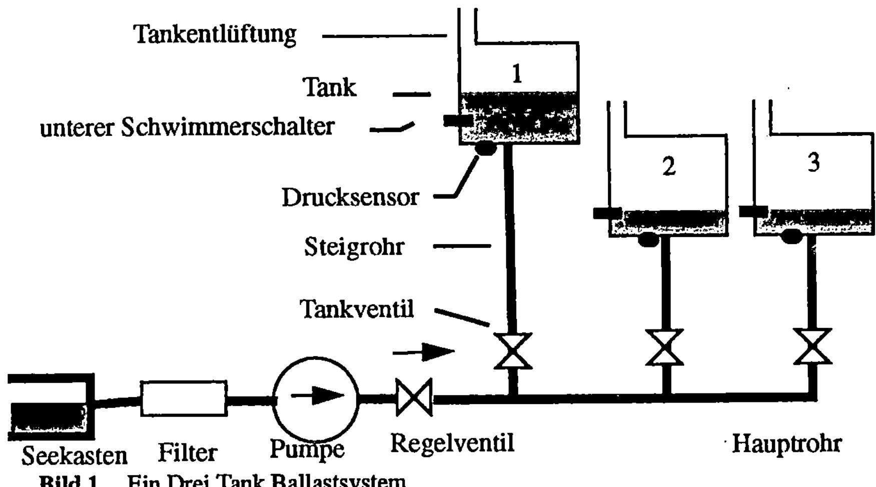

Bild 1   Ein Drei Tank Ballastsystem

lin 92], [Rümelin 93] für weitere Details zur Anwendungsdomäne)

Ballastwassersysteme können in unzähligen Konfigurationen auftreten. Doch im wesentlichen setzen sie sich immer aus den gleichen Grundbausteinen zusammen. Das hier betrachtete System umfaßt die Komponententypen *Tank* einschließlich Lüftungsrohr, *Schwimmerschalter*, *Tankventil*, das sowohl automatisch als auch per Handbetrieb geöffnet/geschlossen werden kann, *Steigrohr*, *Pumpe*, *Filter*, *Drucksensor*, *Rohr*, *Regelventil*, *Pumpenkontrollsystem*, *Pumpenmotor* und *Ventilsteuerung*. Die Hydraulik zur Ansteuerung der Ventile wird hier nicht betrachtet.

Relevante Fehler dieser Komponenten sind laut Anwendungsexperten ([Rümelin 93]) *verstopfte Tanklüftung*, *Luft in der Pumpe*, *verstopfendes Filter*, *Ventilleck*, Drucksensor verklemmt (*Sensor konstant*), Drucksensor falsch kalibriert, d.h. er zeigt einen um einen konstanten Offset verschobenen Wert an (*Sensor Offset*) und *falsche Ventilstatusanzeige*. Diese werden in Kapitel 4. diskutiert.

Als Messungen sind verfügbar der statische Druck am Boden eines jeden Tanks, Signal, ob Maximalfüllstand erreicht ist, saugseitiger Druck an der Pumpe, druckseitiger

Druck an der Pumpe, Ventilstatusanzeige, Meldung der unteren Schwimmerschalter, seeseitiger Druck und Öffnungswinkel des Regelventils.

Zur Vereinfachung der Diskussion wird im folgenden immer von demselben Szenario ausgegangen: Alle drei Tanks sollen gefüllt werden. Dazu werden alle Tankventile geöffnet und die Pumpe in den Pumpmodus gesetzt. Tank1 ist bereits teilweise gefüllt. Die anderen beiden Tanks sind minimal gefüllt (ganz leer dürfen die Tanks nicht sein).

3. Modellbasierte Diagnose

3.1 Konzepte der modellbasierten Diagnose

Bei der modellbasierten Diagnose werden Fehler als Abweichungen von einem *erwarteten* Systemverhalten charakterisiert. Ein explizites Rechenmodell des ungestörten Systemverhaltens wird verwendet, um die Erwartungen zu generieren, indem *relevante* Teile des Verhaltens hergeleitet werden. Die Relevanz bestimmt dabei den Detaillierungs-/Granularitätsgrades des Modells. Im Hinblick auf die Diagnose wird die erforderliche Granularität bestimmt durch die verfügbaren beobachtbaren Systemparameter ("genauer braucht man nicht zu modellieren") und die relevanten Fehler ("so genau sollte man mindestens modellieren").

Diese Erwartungen werden mit dem beobachteten Verhalten verglichen. Werden Inkonsistenzen festgestellt, werden diese zu den an der Vorhersage beteiligten Komponenten zurückverfolgt. Offensichtlich ist mindestens eine dieser Komponenten defekt (siehe [de Kleer et al. 90], [Reiter 87]).

Ein einfacher Weg dieses Verfahren zu realisieren, ist das in [Davis 84] beschriebene *Constraint Suspension*. Jede Komponente wird durch ein *Constraint*, d.h. eine Relation auf den Wertebereichen ihrer Modellgrößen beschrieben ([Sussman, Steele 80], [Murthy, Addanki 86]). Das Gesamtsystem wird durch ein Netz von Constraints beschrieben, wobei Constraints verschiedener Komponenten entsprechend der Systemstruktur durch Identifikation der Modellgrößen miteinander verbunden werden. Wird eine Inkonsistenz entdeckt, ist jedes in der entsprechenden Inferenzkette verwendete Constraint bzw. Komponente verdächtig. Durch sukzessives Deaktivieren der Constraints und erneute Simulation werden die Kandidatenhypothesen getestet. Nach Deaktivierung des entsprechenden Constraints darf keine Inkonsistenz mehr herleitbar sein. Bei Einfachfehlern ist dieses Verfahren linear in der Anzahl der Komponenten. Zur Lösung von Mehrfachfehlern ist die notwendige wiederholte Simulation nachteilig.

Zur Diagnose des Ballastwassersystems haben wir ein der *General Diagnostic Engine (GDE)* verwandtes Konzept verwendet. Die in [deKleer,Williams 87] beschriebene GDE umfaßt ein elegantes Verfahren zur einheitlichen Behandlung von Ein- und Mehrfachfehlern. Explizite Verwaltung aller Inferenzen und ihrer Gültigkeitsbedingungen erleichtert die Wiederverwendung ganzer Inferenzketten und erspart den Hypothesentest durch Constraint Deaktivierung. Dazu wird für jeden Wert propagiert, unter welchen Mengen von Annahmen er gültig ist. Eine Inkonsistenz wird direkt auf inkonsistente Annahmenmengen, *Konflikte*, zurückgeführt, wobei die Menge aller Konflikte durch die Menge minimaler Konflikte charakterisiert wird. Ein Diagnosekandidat wird dann verstanden als eine minimale (bzgl. Mengeninklusion) Menge von Korrektheitsannahmen über Komponenten, die alle Konflikte überdeckt.

Auch bei Verwendung des GDE Ansatzes bleibt der Suchraum exponentiell in der Anzahl der Komponenten. Weitere Maßnahmen zur Aufwandssteuerung sind notwendig.

Durch explizite Berücksichtigung von in der Diagnose üblichen vereinfachenden Annahmen bzw. *Arbeitshypothesen* wie "nur Einfachfehler", "keine sporadischen Fehler" oder "keine unbekannten Fehler" kann der Suchraum in kleinere, leichter handhabbare Teilräume aufgeteilt werden.

Fokussierter Gebrauch der Systemmodellierung bewirkt eine weitere Strukturierung des Suchraumes zur Effizienzsteigerung. Ein entsprechend strukturierter Modellraum erlaubt die gezielte Verwendung geeigneter Teilmodelle, struktureller Aggregierungen (strukturelle Fokussierung) oder Abstraktionen.

Im Laufe des Diagnoseprozeßes werden die entstehenden Teilräume in einer der gegebenen Diagnosesituation angemessenen Reihenfolge durchsucht. Eine bestimmte Diagnosesituation ist dann charakterisiert einerseits durch den Fokus auf die instanziierte Modellierung, andererseits durch die Menge aktiver Arbeitshypothesen, und schließlich durch die Menge an Diagnosekandidaten, die die bei dieser Einstellung interessanten Inkonsistenzen erklären. Dabei ist ein Diagnosekandidat eine minimale (bzgl. Mengeninklusion) Teilmenge der Komponenten, die zur Herleitung *aller* Inkonsistenzen *notwendig* waren. Notwendig heißt hier, läßt man die entsprechenden Komponenten-Modell-Paare aus dem Modellfokus weg, können keine Inkonsistenzen hergeleitet werden.

3.2 Konzepte für die Modellierung

Eine modellbasierte Lösung eines Diagnoseproblems steht und fällt mit der Modellierung. Einerseits soll sie die Erkennung möglichst aller, zumindest jedoch aller relevanten Fehler ermöglichen, andererseits soll die Simulation (eines Modells) möglichst einfach und schnell sein.

In vielen Domänen sind bereits Simulationsmodelle vorhanden. Diese herkömmlichen Modellierungsverfahren beschreiben das Verhalten eines Systems i.a. durch eine Menge von Differentialgleichungen, die den physikalischen Gesetzen entsprechen, denen das Systemverhalten unterworfen ist. Das hier verwendete Verfahren erfordert eine Modellierung, die erlaubt, bestimmte Verhaltensweisen auf die einzelnen daran beteiligten Komponenten zurückzuführen. Bei einer Darstellung durch Differentialgleichung ([Franke 94]) geht die Information über die Komponentenstruktur bzw. der Zusammenhang zwischen einem bestimmten Systemverhalten und daran beteiligten Komponenten verloren. Beim *komponenten-orientierten Ansatz* wird jede Komponente *lokal* in ihren Verhaltensweisen beschrieben bzw. jede Verhaltensweise wird so als Relation auf den der Komponente zugeordneten Modellgrößen beschrieben, daß die Verhaltensweisen anderer eventuell damit verbundener Komponenten nicht vorweg genommen werden.

Diese Modularisierung erleichtert einerseits die Zurückverfolgung hergeleiteter Werte auf die daran beteiligten Komponenten, andererseits die Wiederverwendung der Modelle innerhalb anderer Systeme mit gleichen Komponententypen aber anderer Struktur.

Grundbaustein für die Verhaltensspezifikation ist das Constraint (siehe Kap. 3.1). Um dynamisches Verhalten modellieren zu können, wird ein Constraintbegriff mit Bezug zur Zeit benötigt. Verhalten wird dann als Folge von *Episoden* beschrieben, wobei eine Episode ein Tripel aus Modellgröße, Wert und zeitlichem Intervall ist.

Zur Berechnung des Verhaltens aus den gegebenen Modell-Constraints und beobachteten Werten wird hier ein *Episoden-Propagierer* verwendet ([Guckenbiehl 91b]). Er erlaubt, bestimmte Wertebereiche für Modellgrößen zu definieren und dabei das zu verwendende Gleichheits- bzw. Subsumptionsprädikat explizit zu spezifizieren. Auf diese Weise können zu berücksichtigende Toleranzen aufgrund von Meßungenauigkeiten und Rechenfehlern modelliert werden.

Für jeden definierten Komponententyp können verschiedene Modelle spezifiziert werden. Das Verhalten eines Gerätes kann einmal direkt durch eine Menge quantitativer Constraints beschrieben werden (*Verhaltensmodell*), oder durch Spezifikation seiner Teilkomponenten und der Verbindungsstruktur zwischen diesen (*Strukturmodell*). Eine Reihe von Modellen kann ein Gerät in unterschiedlicher, schrittweise abgestufter Granularität beschreiben. Ein Modellverwaltungssystem erleichtert den Zugriff auf diese Modellvielfalt ([Möller, Zimmermann-Sturm 92]). Dazu beinhaltet eine Modelldefinition zusätzlich zur Constraint-Spezifikation, Information *über* dieses Modell, wie etwa Anwendbarkeitsbedingungen oder ein Attribut "Sicht" um die Perspektive der jeweiligen Modellierung explizit zu repräsentieren (etwa zur Unterscheidung einer Modellierung aus der Sicht der Mechanik gegenüber einer aus der Sicht der Elektrodynamik).

4. Diagnose des Ballastwassersystems

Im folgenden wird die Diagnose der sieben vom Anwendungsexperten spezifizierten Fehlerszenarien (siehe Kapitel 2.) diskutiert. Der erste Schritt des Diagnoseprozesses besteht darin, Erwartungen über das Systemverhalten zu generieren. Zunächst wird vom Diagnosesystem angenommen, daß alles korrekt ist. Es wird ein Modellfokus entsprechend dem korrekten Systemverhalten gesetzt.

4.1 Modellierung des korrekten Systems

Die Modellierung umfaßt alle in Kapitel 2. aufgeführten Komponententypen. Grundlage sind die Gesetze der Hydrodynamik. Ziel ist eine lokale Verhaltensbeschreibung jeder einzelnen Komponente. Bild 2 zeigt einen Ausschnitt aus der Modellierung. Das Verhalten eines Rohrs (oder auch eines Filters) wird bestimmt durch einen Volumenstrom, der durch einen Druckabfall zwischen den Enden bewirkt wird. Charakteristische Komponentenparameter sind die entsprechenden Widerstandsbeiwerte. Bei einem Steigrohr muß zusätzlich der statische Druck, den die im Rohr stehende Wassersäule auf die Grundfläche des Rohres ausübt, berücksichtigt werden. Ein Ventil stellt einen gemeinsamen Druckpunkt zwischen zwei Teilsystemen her, wenn es geöffnet ist, oder hält letztere getrennt. Wenn es geschlossen ist, muß der Volumenstrom gleich null sein. Die grundlegende Aufgabe eines Tanks ist, Wasser zu speichern. Zu diesem Zweck ist er mit einem Einlaß und einer Lüftung versehen. Sein Verhalten wird durch die Füllhöhe charakterisiert. Sie wird durch den Volumenstrom über den Einlaß verändert. Das Lüftungsrohr erlaubt den entsprechenden Druckausgleich im oberen Teil des Tanks. Der statische Druck am Tankboden muß immer direkt proportional zur Wasserhöhe sein. Ein Drucksensor hat die Aufgabe, den statischen Druck am Tankboden zu melden. Eine detailliertere Beschreibung der Modellierung findet sich in [Böttcher, Brinkop 93].

Die Lokalität der im Episoden-Propagierer (siehe Kapitel 3.2) verwendeten Constraint-Propagierungstechnik läßt die Lösung obiger Gleichungen nicht zu.[2] Der Übergang zu einer symbolischen Constraint Propagierung löst das Problem, doch muß man dann hohe Laufzeiten in Kauf nehmen. (siehe [deKleer, Sussman 80], [Cermignani, Tornielli 93]).

Der Formalismus des Episoden-Propagierers und dessen Inferenztechnik des Schließens *über Zeiteinheiten* (oder Intervallen) *hinweg* erlaubt eine Lösung des Problems

<table>
<tr><td>

Tank
Füllhöhe h,
Füllhöhenänderung h'
Volumenstrom i

$$h = \frac{p_{Sensor}}{\rho g}$$

$h(t + dt) = h(t) + h'(t)\, dt$
$i = h'F$

</td><td>

Ventil
status, Kommando,
status-Meldung
Volumenstrom $i_1,\ i_2$
Drücke $p_{unten},\ p_{oben}$
Status = Kommando
$\qquad$ = Status-Meldung

$\begin{cases} i_1 = -i_2 \text{ , falls Status} = \text{:offen} \\ i_1 = 0 = i_2 \text{ und} \\ p_{oben} = p_{unten},\ \text{falls Status} = \text{:zu} \end{cases}$

</td></tr>
<tr><td>

Rohr
Drücke $p_{Ende},\ p_{Anfang}$
Volumenstrom i

$$p_{Ende} = p_{Anfang} + i^2 R_{Rohr}$$

</td><td>

Steigrohr
Drücke $p_{unten},\ p_{oben}$
Volumenstrom i

$$p_{unten} = p_{oben} + i^2 R_{Rohr} + \rho g b$$

</td></tr>
</table>

Drucksensor
Druck p
$p = \;$<Meßwert>

Bild 2   Ausschnitt aus der Verhaltensmodellierung

durch explizite Modellierung der Dynamik auf der Basis der Messung der Tankdrücke zu *verschiedenen* Zeitpunkten:

$$p' = (p(t) - p(t + dt))\,/\,(dt)\ .$$

Auf diese Weise steht auch die Druckänderung als Ausgangsgröße des Drucksensors und als Eingangsgröße für das Tankmodell zur Verfügung, so daß unter Hinzunahme der Gleichung

$$h' = p'_{Sensor}\,/\,(\rho g)$$

eine lokale Verhaltensberechnung möglich ist.

Zur Komplexitätsreduktion wird das System auf zwei Strukturebenen beschrieben. Auf der gröbsten Ebene besteht das System aus vier Teilsystemen: Drei Tanksysteme und ein Pumpensystem. Ein Tanksystem setzt sich zusammen aus einem Tank, einem Steigrohr, einem Ventil, einem unteren Schwimmerschalter, einem Drucksensor und einer Ventilsteuerung. Ein Pumpensystem setzt sich zusammen aus einem Filter, einer

---

2. Beispiel: Gegeben sei ein System von zwei Tanks verbunden mit drei Rohren, jedes Rohr werde lokal durch die Gleichung $p_{out} = p_{in} - i^2 R_{pipe}$, jeder Tank durch $p_{out} = \rho g h$ beschrieben. Sind die Anfangswerte für die Füllstände in den Tanks gegeben, scheint unmittelbar klar, wie das Gleichungssystem zu lösen ist: Eine Gleichung wird nach dem Strom i aufgelöst und dann entsprechend in eine andere Gleichung eingesetzt. Die Implementierung eines derartigen Schlußfolgerungsvorgang erfordert die Propagierung symbolischer Ausdrücke und ihre analytische Behandlung.

Pumpe, einem Regelventil, einem Hauptrohr und einer Pumpensteuerung (siehe Bild 3, die schraffierten Kästen entsprechen einem Teilsystem).

Zur Vereinfachung des Modells werden die Zwischenrohre zwischen den Teilsystemen vernachlässigt[3], d.h. alle Teilsysteme sind in einem Knoten verbunden (Bild 3).

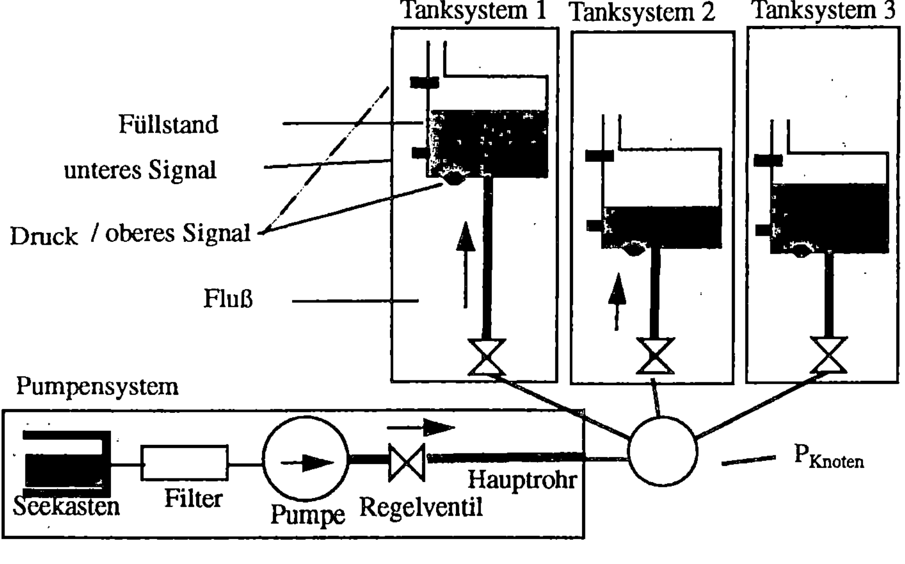

Bild 3   Vereinfachung der Struktur

Im wesentlichen lassen sich zwei Teilaspekte in der Modellierung unterscheiden.

- Druckkonsistenz
  Ausgehend von der Änderungsrate des Tankdruckes, der durch den Sensor beobachtet wird, kann der Volumenstrom in einem Tanksystem berechnet werden. Aus diesem Strom und dem Druck, der vom Sensor gemeldet wird, kann der Druck am Fuße eines Tanksystems berechnet werden. Ist das Tankventil geöffnet, muß dieser Druck gleich dem sein, der durch die anderen angekoppelten Teilsysteme in diesem Knoten bewirkt wird. Auf diese Weise werden implizit die Druckwerte aller Sensoren paarweise auf Konsistenz geprüft.

- Flußkonsistenz
  Das Kontinuitätsgesetz für den Fluß besagt, daß die Summe aller in einem Knoten zusammenkommenden Ströme gleich 0 sein muß. Diese Regel erlaubt, die aus den Druckänderungsraten bestimmten Ströme auf Konsistenz zu prüfen.

4.2   Diagnose mit dem korrekten Modell

Die Diagnose beginnt mit einem Modellfokus auf der gröbsten Strukturebene. Um überhaupt Inferenzen machen zu können, muß das Inferenzsystem mit Eingangsgrößen und Messungen versorgt werden. Da Inferenzen über die Zeit erforderlich sind, werden

---

3. Laut Anwendungsexperten sind die entsprechenden Rohrwiderstände vernachlässigbar gegenüber den übrigen Widerstandswerten im System.

die Messungen über einen gesamten Vorgang hinweg in den Episoden-Propagierer eingelesen. Wie bereits in Kapitel 2. erläutert, wird im folgenden immer ein Füllvorgang aller Tanks betrachtet.

Ein *Leck des Tankventils* macht sich erst bemerkbar, wenn das Ventil geschlossen wird. Dann meldet die Ventilstatusanzeige "geschlossen". Unter Verwendung des korrekten Modells wird geschlossen, daß der Strom gleich 0 sein muß. Doch da das Ventil leckt, wird trotzdem eine Druckänderung beobachtet (siehe Bild 4., ein Pfeil markiert, welche Größen zwischen den Constraints transportiert werden, die Färbung markiert den Gültigkeitskontext): Inkonsistenz! Die Komponenten, die innerhalb des schraffierten

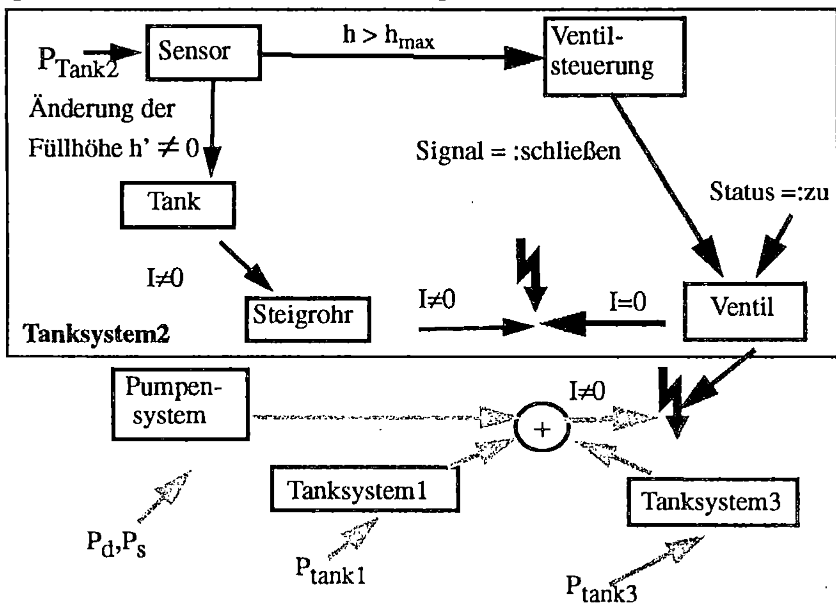

Bild 4   Leckes Ventil

Bereichs dargestellt sind, treten auf der gröbsten Strukturebene noch nicht explizit auf. Die Inkonsistenz ist lokal zum defekten Tanksystem. Das heißt, als einzige Diagnose wird {Tanksystem2 defekt} berechnet. Als nächster Schritt bietet sich die genauere Betrachtung der Struktur von Tanksystem2 an. Der Modellfokus wird geändert. Anstatt eines Verhaltensmodells wird jetzt ein Strukturmodell eingesetzt um das Verhalten des Teilsystems darzustellen. Nun wird sichtbar, daß die Komponenten {Sensor, Tank, Steigrohr, Ventil} an der Inferenz dieser Inkonsistenz beteiligt waren. Darüberhinaus läßt sich jetzt feststellen, daß die Berücksichtigung der übrigen beobachteten Druckänderungen auch auf einen Strom in Tanksystem2 ungleich null schließen läßt. Diese Inferenz war zuvor durch die lokale Inkonsistenz in {Tanksystem2} verdeckt, da Konflikte durch minimale Konflikte charakterisiert werden und diese Inferenz zusätzlich die übrigen Teilsysteme umfaßt hätte. In der detaillierteren Strukturebene führt diese Überlegung zu der Inkonsistenz {Ventil, Tanksystem1, Tanksystem3,Pumpensystem}. Die einzige Einfachfehler-Diagnose, die beide Inkonsistenzen erklärt, ist {Ventil defekt}. Alle anderen Hypothesen sind Mehrfachfehler. Das heißt, allein aufgrund der Betrachtung des erwarteten Verhaltens kann der Fehler lokalisiert werden!

Ähnlich einfach können die Fehlerfälle Filter verstopft und Luft in der Pumpe behandelt werden. *Verstopft das Filter,* vergrößert sich der Widerstand, was zu einem Abfall des saugseitigen Druckes führt. Das Modell berechnet diesen Druckabfall lokal auf der Basis des seeseitigen Druckes und des saugseitigen Pumpendruckes. Ist der tatsächliche Widerstand größer als modelliert[4], berechnet das Modell hier einen anderen Wert als beobachtet. Daraus ergibt sich eine Inkonsistenz, die zunächst lokal zum Pumpensystem bestimmt wird und bei Betrachtung der Struktur des Pumpensystems lokal zum Filter ist. Das heißt, das Ergebnis der Diagnose ist das Filter. Analog wird beim Fehler *Luft in der Pumpe* lokal eine Inkonsistenz zwischen dem saugseitigen und dem druckseitigen Pumpendruck bezüglich des erwarteten Systemverhaltens hergeleitet, was zur eindeutigen Lokalisierung des Fehlers führt.

Die übrigen Fehler können nicht allein aufgrund des erwarteten korrekten Systemverhaltens eindeutig lokalisiert werden. Ist die *Lüftung eines Tanks verstopft* (etwa Tank2), wird durch das ansteigende Wasser die eingeschlossene Luft zusammengedrückt. Dieser Gasdruck wirkt zusätzlich auf den Drucksensor. Als Folge entspricht der angezeigte Druck nicht mehr direkt dem Füllstand des Tanks. Genau davon wird jedoch im Modell ausgegangen. Das heißt, berechnet man auf der Basis der beobachteten Druckänderung den Strom und verwendet diesen Strom zusammen mit dem Druckwert um den Druck auszurechnen, der an der Verbindung zu den anderen Tanksystemen herrschen müßte, und vergleicht diesen Wert mit jenen, die auf der Basis der übrigen Sensoren hergeleitet wurden, bekommt man Inkonsistenzen. Bild 5 veran-

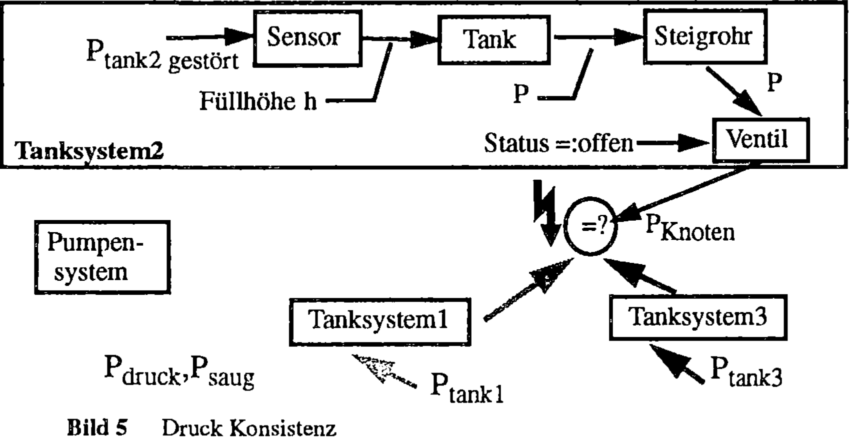

Bild 5   Druck Konsistenz

schaulicht die Berechnung dieser Inkonsistenzen. Zunächst ergeben sich die drei Inkonsistenzen {Tanksystem2, Tanksystem1}, {Tanksystem2, Tanksystem3} und {Tanksystem2, Pumpensystem}. Diese werden erklärt durch die minimalen Diagnosekandidaten {Tanksystem 2 defekt} oder {Tanksystem1, Tanksystem3, Pumpensystem defekt}. Im allgemeinen wird man eine *Einfachfehlerhypothese* immer einer Mehrfachhypothese vorziehen. Daher bietet sich als nächster Schritt die genauere Betrachtung der Struktur von Tanksystem2 an. Dann ergeben sich die Inkonsistenzen {Ventil,

---

4. Da ein Filter die Aufgabe hat, größere Verunreinigungen aus dem Ballastsystem herauszuhalten, ist ein gewisser Verstopfungsgrad auch beim ungestörten System zu berücksichtigen bzw. zu modellieren.

Steigrohr, Tank, Sensor, Tanksystem1}, {Ventil, Steigrohr, Tank, Sensor, Tanksystem3} und {Ventil, Steigrohr, Tanks, Sensor, Pumpensystem} und daraus die Einfachfehlerkandidaten {Tank}, {Sensor}, {Steigrohr} und {Ventil}. Hier sind weitere Diskriminierungsschritte notwendig.

Die Fehler *"Sensor offset"* und *"Sensor konstant"* führen analog zu Inkonsistenzen und ergeben daher die gleichen Kandidaten.

4.3 Modellierung von Fehlverhaltensweisen

Die in Abschnitt 4.1 skizzierte Modellierung grenzt den Diagnosesuchraum ein auf wenige Kandidaten. Um in allen Fällen eindeutig zwischen den sich ergebenden Diagnosekandidaten differenzieren zu können, sind weitere Maßnahmen notwendig. Üblicherweise wird zur Diskriminierung nur die Akquisition weiterer Meßwerte oder die Anwendung weiterer Testvektoren vorgeschlagen. In unserer Anwendung stehen keine weiteren Meßpunkte zur Verfügung. Auch "Testvektoren" (z.B. gezieltes Öffnen/ Schließen von Ventilen) sind hier nicht anwendbar. Ein anderer Weg besteht darin, zusätzlich Wissen über die Verhaltensweisen der Komponenten im Fehlerfall in Form von *Fehlermodellen* auszunutzen

Der Fehler *"offen verklemmte Ventilstatusanzeige"* des Ventils z.B. läßt sich sehr einfach beschreiben durch Änderung der Zuweisung an die Größe *Status-Meldung* in "Status-Meldung = :offen" und Beibehalten der übrigen Constraints (siehe Ventil Modell in Bild 2).

In vielen Fällen ist die Modellierung von Fehlern schwieriger als die Beschreibung des korrekten Verhaltens. Die Fehler verstopfendes Filter, Sensor Offset, Sensor verklemmt oder Tank Lüftung verstopft z.B. entsprechen jeweils einer Klasse von Verhaltensweisen. Ein Filter kann auf vielerlei Weise verstopfen, ein Sensor bei fast jedem Wert verklemmen und das Verhalten eines verstopften Tanks ist abhängig von der jeweiligen Füllhöhe zum Zeitpunkt der Verstopfung. Das Fehlermodell muß jeweils alle Ausprägungen umfassen. Dabei ist für die Fehlersuche der eigentliche Verstopfungsverlauf, Offsetwert oder Verstopfungszeitpunkt irrelevant. Es interessiert, ob es bei gegebener Situation konsistent ist, den Fehler zu hypothetisieren.

Charakteristisch für den Fehler *Sensor Offset* z.B. ist, daß der effektive Druck den gleichen Verlauf hat, wie der gemeldete (d.h. die Ableitungen dieser Verläufe sind gleich),doch der Abstand ist ungleich Null. Ist die *Tanklüftung verstopft*, steigt/fällt der Druck beim Füllen/Leeren drastisch. In Abhängigkeit von der Pumpenleistung kann bestimmt werden, welcher Druckgradient maximal durch einen Volumenstrom bewirkt werden kann. Nur bei einer verstopften Tanklüftung kann ein größerer Gradient beobachtet werden.

Andere Fehler, wie z.B. *"Luft in der Pumpe"*, sind analytisch nicht beschreibbar. Grob läßt sich dieser Fehler beschreiben als Störung der Pumpencharakteristik. Bei Betrachtung der Meßkurve des Pumpendruckes läßt sich ein drastischer Druckabfall erkennen. Auch hier kann unter Verwendung der Kurvendiskussionstechniken der Mathematik eine qualitative Approximation des Verhaltensverlaufes spezifiziert werden.

Zu diesem Zweck wurde ein Werkzeug QQM ([Brinkop, Sutschet 92]) entwickelt, das erlaubt mit Hilfe partieller Funktionen, charakterisiert mit den Mitteln der Kurvendiskussion der Mathematik, und qualitativen Zeitrelationen ([Allen 83]) zwischen diesen Funktionen Klassen von Funktionsverläufen zu spezifizieren. Bei der Analyse werden alle Zeitintervalle bestimmt, in denen ein gegebener Funktionsverlauf einer gegebenen Klassenspezifikation entspricht.

Mit Hilfe dieser Technik werden die Fehlermodelle für die Fehler "Luft in der Pumpe", "verstopfender Filter", "Drucksensoranzeige verklemmt", "Tanklüftung verstopft" und "Drucksensoranzeige konstant versetzt" beschrieben. Problematisch bei dieser Technik ist jedoch das Einhalten des Lokalitätsprinzip der Diagnose.

4.4 Diagnose mit Fehlermodellen.

Zur Diskriminierung der Kandidaten, die nach Analyse des korrekten Modells noch übrig sind, wird jetzt betrachtet, wie sich Komponenten überhaupt im Fehlerfall verhalten können. Durch Einsetzen eines Fehlermodells einer Komponente in den Modellfokus wird überprüft, ob es konsistent mit den Beobachtungen und den anderen Komponentenmodellen ist, den Fehler anzunehmen. Kennt man für eine Komponente alle Fehler und sind die aktuellen Beobachtungen und der aktuelle Modellfokus für die übrigen Komponenten inkonsistent mit allen diesen Fehlern, wird die Komponente in Bezug auf diese Situation als Kandidat ausgeschlossen (Diese Form der Inferenz entspricht dem Verfahren des "Physical Negation" wie es in [Struß, Dressler 89] beschrieben wird).

Z.B. im Fall *verstopfte Tanklüftung* muß zwischen den Kandidaten {Tank}, {Sensor}, {Steigrohr} und {Ventil} diskriminiert werden. Für das Steigrohr sind keine Fehler bekannt. Es wird eine explizite Annahme in die Menge aktueller Arbeitshypothesen eingeführt, um diesen Kandidaten zu streichen. Für den Sensor sind die Fehler "Sensor konstant" und "Sensor Offset" bekannt, für das Ventil die Fehler "Leck" und "falsche Statusanzeige" und für den Tank "Lüftung verstopft". Der Fehler "Sensor konstant" kann sofort widerlegt werden, da eine Druckänderung zu beobachten ist. Bei dem Fehler "Sensor offset" wäre lediglich die Abbildung zwischen Füllstand und statischem Druck um einen Faktor verschoben. Das Verhalten entspräche sonst dem korrekten Modell. Dadurch können nicht alle Inkonsistenzen erklärt werden. Ventilfehler werden erst beobachtbar, wenn die Ventile schalten. Die Inkonsistenzen treten aber schon vorher auf. Beim Fehler "Lüftung verstopft" muß das Constraint gelockert werden, das den Füllstand mit dem statischen Druck im Tank in Beziehung setzt. Nunmehr kann nur noch gesagt werden, daß bei einem positiven Strom eine positive Druckänderung zu beobachten ist, bzw. daß eine lineare Füllstandsänderung eine überlineare Druckänderung bewirkt, wobei diese Druckänderung über dem normalen Maximalgradienten liegen muß. Nur dieses Modell "Tanklüftung verstopft" kann alle Beobachtungen erklären.

5. Implementierung

Bild 6 zeigt die Architektur der Implementierung des Diagnoseprototyps. Als Diagnoserahmensystem diente der Diagnoseassistent MuDia (Multiple Models in Diagnosis [Böttcher 91]). MuDia ist als Experimentierwerkzeug konzipiert. Es erlaubt dem Benutzer den aktuellen Modellfokus und die aktuelle Menge an Arbeitshypothesen nach Belieben zu setzen (siehe Kapitel 3.) Das System stellt eine Reihe von sogenannten Diagnoseaktionen zur Verfügung ("acquire observations", "generate candidates", "change focus", "fault analysis", etc.), durch die der Modellfokus und die Arbeitshypothesen in bestimmter Weise verändert werden und aus denen eine der gegebenen Situation angemessene Strategie realisiert werden kann. Als zusätzliche Unterstützung zur Strategiewahl steht eine Methode "evaluate actions" zur Verfügung. Die Methode berechnet für jede Diagnoseaktion eine Bewertung ihrer Nützlichkeit in Bezug auf die aktuelle Diagnosesituation.

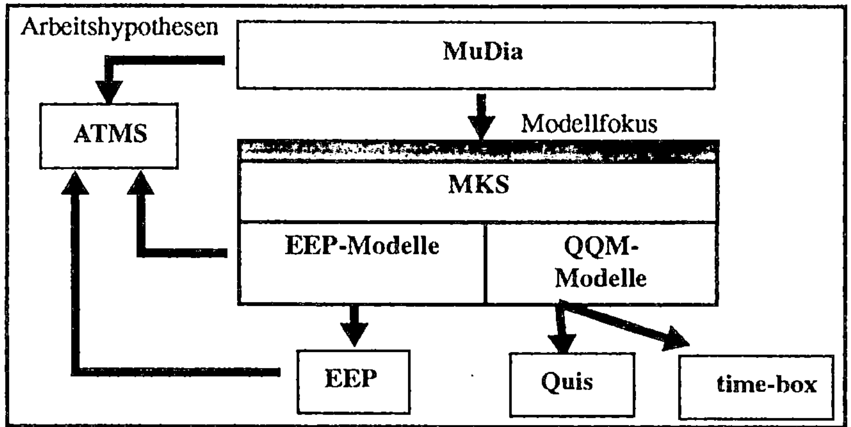

Bild 6   Überblick über die Systemarchitektur

Die in Kapitel 4. diskutierten Fehlerszenarien können im wesentlichen durch die folgende Aktionsfolge diagnostiziert werden:

- "acquire observations" und "generate candidates", um Messungen einzulesen und anfängliche Kandidaten zu generieren

- "change focus", um für eines der Teilkomponenten das Verhaltensmodell gegen ein Strukturmodell auszutauschen

- "test candidate fault", "physical negation", um zwischen Kandidaten durch Betrachtung von Fehlermodellen zu diskriminieren

Der Zugriff und die Auswertung der verschiedenen Modelle (siehe Kapitel 3.1) wird durch das Modellverwaltungssystem MKS (Modellierung komplexer Systeme [Möller, Zimmermann-Sturm 92]) koordiniert. MKS ermöglicht durch explizite Modellierung der entsprechenden Ontologien verschiedene Inferenzmechanismen miteinander zu integrieren. Für die Diagnose bleibt verborgen, welcher Modellierungsformalismus zur Analyse eines bestimmten Komponentenmodells jeweils benötigt wird.

Wie in Kapitel 4. beschrieben, werden zum einen Modelle auf der Basis von Episoden verwendet. Diese werden durch den Episoden-Propagierer EEP ausgewertet. Zum anderen wird zur Spezifikation von qualitativen Charakterisierungen von Fehlern das Werkzeug QQM ([Brinkop, Sutschet 92]) verwendet. Dabei stellt das Werkzeug QUIS die Sprachmittel der mathematischen Kurvendiskussion zur Verfügung und die "time-box" die Auswertung qualitativ zeitlicher Relationen.

Alle Werkzeuge sind in Allegro Common Lisp implementiert und laufen auf SUN Sparc Workstations.

6. Diskussion

Mit der hier vorgestellten Arbeit ist das Problem der modellbasierten Diagnose dynamischer Systeme sicher nicht gelöst. Doch anhand einer prototypischen Lösung der Diagnoseprobleme eines derartigen Anwendungsbereiches konnte gezeigt werden, daß modellbasierte Techniken für Problemstellungen dynamischer Systeme geeignet sein können.

Auf der Basis einer komponenten-orientierten, vorwiegend quantitativen Modellierung des korrekten und gestörten Systemverhaltens konnten alle Fehler eines Ballastwassersystems eindeutig lokalisiert werden. Eine komponenten-orientierte Modularisierung erleichtert zum einen das Zurückverfolgen hergeleiteter Werte auf die daran beteiligten Komponenten und darüberhinaus die Wiederverwendung der Modelle für die Modellierung von Systemen mit gleichen Komponententypen aber anderer Struktur.

Durch Inferenzen über die Zeit, bzw. durch explizite Modellierung der Dynamik wird ein System simultaner Gleichungen lokal gelöst. Dazu müssen allerdings alle Messungen über einen Beobachtungszeitraum hinweg verfügbar sein.

Bild 7. gibt einen Überblick über die Ergebnisse, die wir mit der vorgestellten Model-

Fehler Szenario	Ergebnisse
verstopfte Tanklüftung	S,V,T,Ap
Sensoranzeige konstant	S,V,T,Ap
Sensoranzeige Offset	S,V,T,Ap
Ventil Leck	V
Falsche Ventil Status Anzeige	V,S
Luft in der Pumpe	P
verstopftes Filter	F

wobei S = Drucksensor, V = Ventil, T = Tank, Ap = Steigrohr, P = Pumpe, F = Filter

Bild 7 Ergebnisse der Diagnose mit der quantitativen Modellierung des OK-Verhaltens

lierung erzielen konnten. Die Tabelle zeigt für jedes der diskutierten Szenarien, welche möglichen Fehlererklärungen übrig blieben, nachdem ein Modell des ungestörten Verhaltens des Systems mit den Beobachtungen verglichen wurde. Bei zusätzlicher Verwendung von Fehlermodellen lassen sich alle Fehler eindeutig lokalisieren[5].

In Abhängigkeit vom Fehlerfall dauert die Diagnose 5-50 Minuten[6]. Zum einen sind diese Laufzeiten auf die prototypische Implementierung zurückzuführen. Ein weiterer Grund liegt in der Art der expliziten Modellierung der Dynamik. Einerseits erweitert sie die Mächtigkeit der Modellierungssprache[7], andererseits ist mehr Rechenaufwand erforderlich. Der Episoden-Propagierer leitet innerhalb eines Beobachtungszeitraumes alle möglichen (Variable, Wert, Zeit) Tripel *über die Zeiteinheiten hinweg* einschließlich *aller Gültigkeitskontexte* her. Zur Zeit wird als Beobachtungszeitraum immer ein gesamter Füll- bzw. Leervorgang gewählt. Bei genauerer Betrachtung der Ergebnisse zeigt sich, daß zur Detektion der relevanten Inkonsistenzen jeweils ein Zeitraum über zwei Zeiteinheiten ausreichend ist. Schränkt man den Beobachtungszeitraum entsprechend ein, wird die Dauer der Diagnose reduziert. Für eine allgemeine Lösung sind

---

5. In [Böttcher, Brinkop 93] findet sich eine ausführlichere Darstellung Modellierung und Fehlerdiskussion.
6. Das Füllen eines Tanks dauert realiter anderthalb Stunden.
7. Sie ermöglicht z.B. die Erfassung zeitverzögerter Fehler.

Strategien zur Wahl eines adäquaten Zeitraumes in Abhängigkeit von der Anwendung, der Modelle und des gegebenen Fehlerfalles erforderlich.

Alternativ könnte eine qualitative Abstraktion des Modells verwendet werden[8]. Dabei werden die Wertebereiche der Modellgrößen in eine kleine Anzahl Intervalle unterteilt, die jeweils qualitativ gleiche Werte zusammenfassen. Dadurch vereinfachen sich einerseits die notwendigen Berechnungen, andererseits können sehr viel mehr Zwischenergebnisse wiederverwendet werden, da sich ein System qualitativ sehr viel langsamer ändert als bei Betrachtung der reellen Meßwerte. Diese Beobachtungen werden in [Dressler,Freitag 94] für ein sehr effizientes Monitoringverfahren genutzt. Durch geschicktes Cashing wird die wiederholte Berechnung eines stationären qualitativen Modells über einen Zeitraum hinweg erheblich beschleunigt.

Unter Verwendung eines qualitativen Modells und dem in [Dressler,Freitag 94] beschriebenen Verfahren läßt sich die Diagnose einiger Fehler erheblich beschleunigen. Andere jedoch erfordern eine geschickte Erweiterung des qualitativen Modells. In [Rümelin 94] wird der hier vorgestellte Diagnoseprototyp evaluiert und einer auf einer qualitativen Modellierung basierenden Lösung gegenübergestellt.

Der kritische Punkt einer Modellierung ist die Wahl des Granularitätsgrades. Für die Diagnose wird sie durch die verfügbaren Meßpunkte und relevanten Fehler bestimmt. Strebt man ein qualitatives Modell an, ist die offene Frage, wie man zu einer hinreichend vollständigen Erfassung relevanter, qualitativ unterschiedlicher Systemzustände kommt. Für einige Fehler wird ein grobes Modell ausreichen. Andere jedoch sind bei Verwendung eines zu groben Modells nicht unterscheidbar oder werden gar nicht erst entdeckt. In [Dressler et al. 93] wird ein Konzept zur integrierten Verwendung von qualitativen *und* quantitativen Modellen vorgestellt, mit dem man dieser Problematik in Teilen begegnen kann.

Langfristig ist eine engere Verzahnung der Modellentwicklung für die Diagnose mit der Entwicklungsphase eines technischen Systems anzustreben. Dies ermöglicht frühzeitige Rückmeldungen über die Diagnostizierbarkeit eines neuen Systems (Design for Diagnosis, optimale Sensorplazierung), sowie eine Erleichterung der Auswahl der relevanten Verhaltensweisen und damit der Granularitätswahl beim Diagnosemodell.

7. Danksagung

Wesentliche Beiträge zu dieser Arbeit verdanken wir T. Guckenbiehl (EEP), G. Sutschet, (QQM), J. Möller (MKS) und H.W. Früchtenicht, durchseine Unterstützung in allen Fragen der Physik. Ohne sie sähe das Ergebnis sicher ganz anders aus. Weiterhin danken wir allen unseren Mitstreitern aus dem Behavior Projekt für zahlreiche stimulierende Diskussionen.

8. Literatur

[Allen 83] J.F. Allen "Maintaining *Knowledge about temporal intervals*", CACM 26, pp. 832-843 1983

---

8. Laut [Struß 92] gilt, wenn ein Modell M eine Abstraktion eines anderen Modells M' ist, kann jede Inkonsistenz, die mit M hergeleitet wurde, auch mit M' hergeleitet werden. Das heißt, Diagnosen, die unter Verwendung des abstrakten, einfacher zu simulierenden Modells berechnet wurden, sind auch Diagnosen unter dem detaillierteren Modell. Aus diesem Grund ist eine vollständige Aufzählung des Verhaltens eines Systems zum Zweck der modellbasierten Diagnose nicht notwendig.[Struß 92] gibt eine formale Charakterisierung der Modellierung für die Diagnose mit multiplen Modellen

[Böttcher 91] C.Böttcher:*"Die Verwendung mutipler Modelle in der modellbasierten Diagnose"*, Diplomarbeit, Universität Karlsruhe, 1991

[Böttcher, Brinkop 93] C. Böttcher,A.Brinkop: *"Diagnosing the three tank ballast system*, Behavior-Memo[9] 12-93, Karlsruhe,1993

[Brinkop, Sutschet 92] A. Brinkop, G. Sutschet:*"The use of qualitative information for discriminating fault models"*, Behavior-Memo[9] 15-92, Karlsruhe, 1992

[Cermignani, Tornielli 93] S. Cermignani, G. Tornielli: *Model-based diagnosis of continuous static systems*, Artist Bericht, erhältlich über CISE, Milano,erscheint in: Annals of Mathematics And Artificial Intelligence, Spezialausgabe *Model Based Diagnosis*, vol. 11, nr.1-4, 1994 .

[Davis 84] R. Davis, *Diagnostic-reasoning Based on Structure and function*, in:"Readings in Model based Diagnosis", Hamscher, Console,de Kleer (eds.) Morgan-Kaufmann, 1992

[de Kleer et al 90] J. de Kleer, A. Mackworth, R. Reiter, *Characterizing Diagnoses,*in "Readings in Model based Diagnosis", Hamscher, Console,de Kleer (eds.) Morgan-Kaufmann, 1992

[deKleer,Williams 87] de Kleer J., Williams B. *Diagnosing Multiple Faults,*in "Readings in Model based Diagnosis", Hamscher, Console,de Kleer (eds.) Morgan-Kaufmann, 1992

[deKleer, Sussman 80] J. de Kleer, G.J. Sussman: *Propagation of constraints applied to circuit synthesis*, in: Circuit theory and applications. 8, pp. 127- 144, 1980

[Dressler et al. 93] O. Dressler, C. Böttcher, M. Montag, A. Brinkop: *"Qualitative and Quantitative Models in a Model-based Diagnosis system for Ballast Tank Systems"* in: Proc. Tooldiag 93, Toulouse, April 1993

[Dressler, Freitag 94] O.Dressler, H. Freitag: *"Prediction Sharing accross time and contexts"* , erscheint in Proc. AAAI 94, Seattle (WA), August 1994

[Frank 94] P.M. Frank: *"Diagnoseverfahren in der Automatisierungstechnik"*, at 2/94, Februar 1994.

[Gallanti et al.89] M.Gallanti, M. Roncato, A. Stefanini, G. Tornielli: A Diagnostic Algorithm based on Models at Different Level of Abstraction,Proc IJCAI 89,Detroit,1989, pp.1350-1355

[Guckenbiehl 91b] T. Guckenbiehl, *An Extended Episode Propagator - Version 2* FhG-IITB, interner Bericht, 1991

[Möller, Zimmermann-Sturm 92] J. Möller, M. Zimmermann-Sturm: *Specification of the MCS Environment*, Version 1, Behavior-Memo[9] 14-92,1992, Karlsruhe

[Murthy, Addanki 86] S.S. Murthy, S. Addanki: *"PROMPT: An Innovative Design Tool"*, Proc. 6th AAAI, Seattle (WA), 1986

[Reiter 87]Reiter R.*: A Theory of Diagnosis from First Principles*, in "Readings in Model Based Diagnosis" Hamscher, Console, deKleer(eds.), Morgan-Kaufmann, 1992

[Rümelin 94] W. Rümelin: *Evaluierung der BEHAVIOR-Diagnosesysteme am Beispiel des Ballasttanksystems,*Behavior-Memo[9], STN Hamburg, 1994

[Rümelin 93] W. Rümelin:*Daten und Fakten über das Ballastssytem,* Behavior-Memo[9] 02-93, STN Hamburg,1993

[Rümelin 92] W. Rümelin: *Systemanalyse des Dreitank-Ballastsystems,* Behavior-Memo[9] 11-92, STN Hamburg, 1992

[Struss 92] Peter Struss:*"What's in SD?"*, in "Readings in Model based Diagnosis", Hamscher, Console,de Kleer (eds.) Morgan-Kaufmann, 1992

[Struß, Dressler 89] P. Struß, O. Dressler: *"Physical Negation" - Integrating Fault Models into the General Diagnostic Engine*, Proc. 12th IJCAI, 1989, S. 1318 - 1323

[Sussman,Steele 80] G.J. Sussman, G.L. Steele: *CONSTRAINTS -A language for expressing almost-hierarchical descriptions*, Artificial Intelligence, 14(1), 1980

---

9. interner Bericht,erhältlich über FhG-IITB, Karlsruhe

HYPERCON: Ein Konsultationssystem zur Hypertonie auf der Basis modular organisierter Wissensbestände

Barbara Heller, Josef Meyer-Fujara, Sonja Schlegelmilch, Ipke Wachsmuth

Technische Fakultät, Universität Bielefeld, Postfach 10 01 31, D–33501 Bielefeld

Abstract.
Das wissensbasierte System HYPERCON zur Konsultation für die Diagnose und Therapie der Hypertonie wird vorgestellt. Zunächst wird der Einsatzkontext und die abzubildende Domäne beschrieben. Es folgt das erarbeitete Konzept zur Modularisierung, die Aufteilung der Wissensdomäne und die zugrundeliegende Systemarchitektur. Am Beispiel eines authentischen Patientenfalles wird der Schlußfolgerungsprozeß unter Fokussierungs- und Granularitätsaspekten illustriert.

1 Einführung

Bluthochdruck (Hypertonie) ist eine chronische multifaktorielle Erkrankung des Herz-Kreislaufsystems. Sie gehört in den Industriestaaten zu den häufigsten Erkrankungen und geht mit einem deutlich erhöhten Mortalitätsrisiko einher. Ihre vielfältigen Ursachen und Wechselwirkungen mit anderen Erkrankungen, z.B. Diabetes, sind nur teilweise erforscht. Bei mehr als der Hälfte der Bluthochdruckpatienten wird die Krankheit nicht angemessen behandelt.

Vor dem Hintergrund dieser drängenden medizinischen Motivation wird im HYPERCON-Projekt[1] ein Konsultationssystem zur Unterstützung bei der Diagnose und Therapie der Hypertonie erstellt, das die Entscheidungsgrundlagen objektivieren und durch umfassenderes Wissen verbessern soll. Im angestrebten Einsatzszenario für das entwickelte System HYPERCON (HYPERtension CONsultation) [15] wird die Wissensbasis interaktiv von Ärzten, also sachkundigen Benutzern, konsultiert. Es liefert keine endgültige Diagnose oder Therapie, sondern stellt problem- und fallbezogen Wissen bereit, u.a. über epidemiologische Studien, Leistungsfähigkeit und Risiken möglicher Untersuchungsverfahren, über konkurrierende Diagnosen, zu beachtende Kontraindikationen und Prädispositionen. Die Initiative für den Wissensabruf liegt weitgehend beim Benutzer; er bleibt für die sich daraus ergebende Intervention verantwortlich. Interesse an der Nutzung wurde von theoretischen Medizinern, von niedergelassenen und von Klinikärzten bekundet. Zunächst ist der offline-Einsatz in einer Klinik vorgesehen, wo Ärzte in der Ausbildung sich im Dialog mit dem System auf die Patientenvisite vorbereiten und im Anschluß Diagnose und Therapie im Bezugsfeld ähnlicher Fälle und aufgearbeiteter Literatur vertiefen möchten.

---

[1] Das Projekt wird vom nordrhein-westfälischen Ministerium für Wissenschaft und Forschung unterstützt (Fördernummer IVA6-400 015 92). Wir danken den medizinischen Experten Prof. K. Kauffmann, Prof. H.-D. Faulhaber und Dr. U. Müller-Kolck für ihre Geduld bei der Erklärung medizinischer Sachverhalte sowie unseren Studenten Ch. Dücker, J. Hamann, A. Möller, Ch. Scheering and J. Stoye für ihre Mithilfe.

Das Schwergewicht des Projekts liegt in der Aufarbeitung des medizinischen Wissens zum Bluthochdruck und der Entwicklung einer leicht erweiterbaren und aktualisierbaren Wissensbasis. Aus informatischer Sicht wurden dazu Grundlagen zur Konzeptualisierung und Strukturierung schwer überschaubarer Wissensdomänen erforscht, die sich in einer Modularisierung auf der Wissenebene ("knowledge-level modularization") niederschlagen [8]. Das System bildet zunächst den wichtigen Teilbereich der durch Nierenerkrankungen und durch endokrine Störungen verursachten Hypertonie ab.

2 Überblick über die Domäne

Als Hypertonie wird eine dauerhafte Erhöhung des Blutdrucks[2] im arteriellen Gefäßsystem bezeichnet, die unbehandelt zu typischen Komplikationen z.B. an Gefäßen, Herz, Niere und Gehirn führt. In Deutschland wird die Hypertoniehäufigkeit auf 12% der Gesamtbevölkerung geschätzt, für die Altersgruppe über 45 Jahren wird eine Häufigkeit von 25% angenommen [7]. Die Hypertonie wird aufgrund ihrer Entstehung in primäre und sekundäre Formen eingeteilt.

Die primäre (essentielle) Hypertonie, die mit ungefähr 90% den Hauptanteil der Bluthochdruckerkrankungen stellt, ist ätiologisch bisher nicht aufgeklärt, während die sekundären Hypertonien auf ein Grundleiden von Niere, Hormonsystem, Herz-Kreislaufsystem oder Nervensystem zurückgeführt werden können.

Das System bildet zunächst die Diagnose und Therapie der *renalen Hypertonien* ab, da eine *primäre* Hypertonie nur nach Ausschluß sekundärer Hypertonieformen angenommen werden kann, unter denen die renale Hypertonie die weitaus häufigste ist. Diese kann bedingt sein durch:
— angeborene oder erworbene Veränderungen des Nierengewebes (renoparenchymatöse Hypertonie),
— eine Einengung der Nierenarterien (renovaskuläre Hypertonie).

Umgekehrt ist Hypertonie ein häufiges (50-60%) Begleitphänomen von Nierenerkrankungen und kann sogar – vor allem bei renovaskulären Störungen – das *Hauptsymptom* einer Nierenerkrankung sein. Daneben gehen zahlreiche Allgemeinerkrankungen mit einer Nierenstörung einher und verursachen somit eine renale Hypertonie (z.B.: Diabetes mellitus, Gicht, Lupus erythematodes). In Anbetracht der vielfältigen Ursachen hat schon die anamnestische Befragung eines Hypertoniepatienten ein breites Symptomspektrum zu berücksichtigen. Während einige der o.g. Erkrankungen dabei mit einem typischen Erscheinungsbild einhergehen, fehlen bei anderen ebenso wie bei der primären Hypertonie häufig charakteristische Hinweise.

Für die Diagnose und Therapie der Hypertonie ist insgesamt Wissen verschiedener Teilbereiche der Medizin erforderlich: über Häufigkeit von Krankheiten und Symptomen, Prädisposition und Vererbung (Epidemiologie), über die Durchführung von Befragungen und Untersuchungen (Anamnese, körperliche Untersuchung, Labor, diagnostische Verfahren), über die Systematik der Krankheiten, ihre Entstehung, ihre Erscheinungsformen (Nosologie, Ätiologie, Klinik), über die normalen und krankhaften Zustände und Regelungen wesentlicher Parameter wie des Blutdrucks (Pathophysiologie), über die makroskopischen und mikroskopischen Strukturen des Körpers (Anatomie und Histologie) und schließlich über Therapie (z.B. Pharmakologie).

---

2 gemäß der Definition der WHO (World Health Organization) entspricht dies einem durchschnittlichen Blutdruckwert von 160/95 mmHg und darüber.

Die Komplexität der Zusammenhänge wird exemplarisch bei Bluthochdruck durch eine Verengung der Nierenarterie deutlich: Diese führt zu einem lokalen Blutdruckabfall in der Niere. Darauf reagieren mikroskopische Teile der Niere, die juxtaglomerulären Apparate, mit der Ausschüttung des Hormons Renin, das über Zwischenstufen in Angiotensin II verwandelt wird. Dieses führt zur Zusammenziehung der Blutgefäße und damit zu hohem Blutdruck. Eine Klasse von Medikamenten, die ACE-Hemmer, wirkt gerade durch die Blockade der Umwandlung in Angiotensin II. Einer der Zusammenhänge zum Diabetes besteht darin, daß Diabetes Arteriosklerose und damit Verengungen der Nierenarterie begünstigt.

Die Vielfalt der Einflußgrößen sowie kausal-physiologischer Zusammenhänge macht es besonders dringlich, das relevante medizinische Wissen *transparent* aufzubereiten, um eine gute Differenzierung zwischen verschiedenen Ursachen der Hypertonie (Differentialdiagnostik) zu erreichen.

3 Wissensakquisition

Vor Projektbeginn waren bereits Vorgespräche mit Medizinern unterschiedlicher Ausrichtung geführt worden, um den möglichen Nutzen eines Systems festzustellen und um sich der Mitarbeit mehrerer Experten zu versichern. Als Experten stehen ein niedergelassener Facharzt für Innere Medizin sowie Professoren an der Franz-Volhard-Klinik und am Max-Delbrück-Centrum für molekulare Medizin in Berlin-Buch sowie am Deutschen Institut für Bluthochdruckforschung in Heidelberg zur Verfügung. Das Projektteam besteht aus Informatikern (darunter eine Medizininformatikerin), die – teilweise aus der Industrie – bereits Erfahrung mit der Erstellung wissenbasierter Systeme haben, sowie aus Informatikstudenten als Hilfskräften.

Die Wissensakquisition erfolgte aus einschlägigen Lehrbüchern, aus Datenbanken und über etwa 20 Experteninterviews. Die Interviews bezogen sich zunächst auf die Struktur des Gebiets, dann auf die günstigste Ausrichtung des Systems, anschließend auf das diagnostische Vorgehen und schließlich auf die Betrachtung authentischer Fälle, an denen zum einen das entwickelte Vorgehensmodell überprüft und zum anderen detailliertes Wissen erhoben wurde. Ein Schwerpunkt war dabei die quantitative Festlegung der qualitativen Begriffe, die in Büchern und Artikeln die Basis der Beschreibung bildeten. Die Interviews wurden mit Video- und Tonbandgeräten aufgezeichnet; anhand begleitend geführter Protokolle wurden die zu transkribierenden Teile bestimmt. Eine volle Transkription aller Interviews erwies sich als zu aufwendig für die vorhandenen Personalressourcen (zeitlicher Multiplikationsfaktor 8). Die transkribierten Fallbeispiele wurden nach einem aus dem Vorgehensmodell abgeleiteten, einheitlichen Schema aufbereitet.

Datenbanken wurden für die Bestimmung von Begriffsstandards und für die Suche nach epidemiologischen Studien und Beschreibungen authentischer Fälle (Kasuistiken) herangezogen. Die beschriebenen Fälle betrafen jedoch überwiegend seltene Kombinationen von Hypertonie mit anderen Krankheiten, deren zusätzliche Abbildung im System den gegebenen Projektrahmen überschritten hätte. Der ursprüngliche Plan, die Datenbank der Klinik über behandelte Patienten als Falldatenbank heranzuziehen, wurde aufgegeben, da er eine unvertretbare Erweiterung der Datenbank hinsichtlich erfaßter Details erfordert hätte, die erst mit einem voll installierten Krankenhausinformationssystem möglich scheint.

Als Lehrbücher wurden von den Experten empfohlene aktuelle Werke verwendet. Für die nicht medizinisch vorgebildeten Projektmitarbeiter war es zunächst eine schwierige Aufgabe, bei der Aufbereitung der Interviewfälle die Grenzen des für das System noch relevanten Wissens zu bestimmen. Schwierigkeiten bereitete auch die unterschiedliche Nomenklatur und die je nach Blickwinkel unterschiedliche Einteilung von Krankheiten in spezifischere Formen.

Modell des diagnostischen Schlußfolgerns. In den Experteninterviews wurde in mehrfacher Iteration das in Abb. 1 dargestellte Modell des diagnostischen Schlußfolgerns erarbeitet.

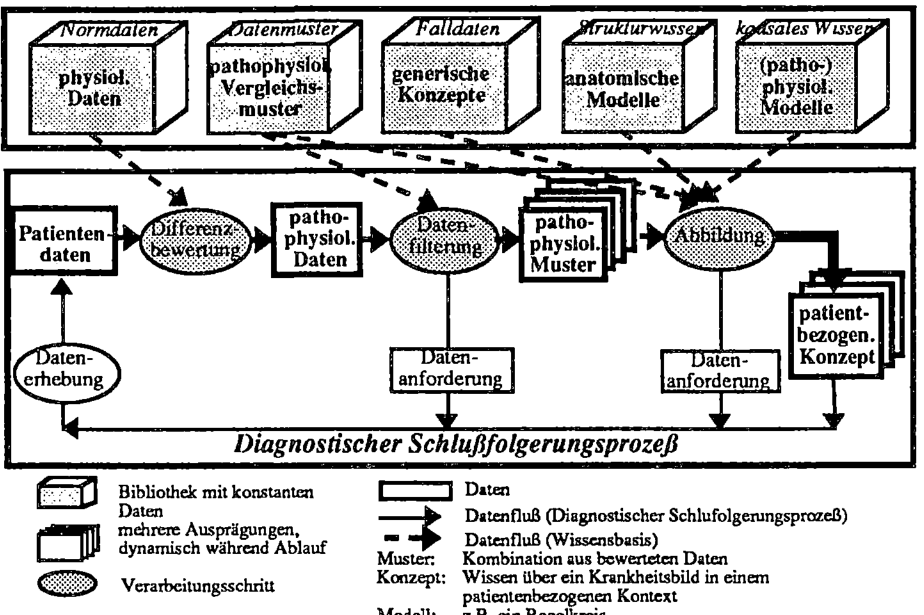

Abb. 1. Modell des diagnostischen Schlußfolgerns (weitere Erläuterung im Text)

Zunächst werden *Patientendaten* erhoben (*Datenerhebung*). Im ersten wesentlichen Schritt ihrer Verarbeitung (*Differenzbewertung*) werden sie mit den Normwerten (*physiologische Daten*) verglichen und als physiologisch bzw. pathologisch klassifiziert: *pathophysiologische Daten*. Es ist wichtig, Daten im Normbereich nicht einfach zu ignorieren, da gerade die Kombination aus physiologischen und pathologischen Patientendaten aufschlußreich sein kann. Die pathophysiologischen Daten werden anschließend mit bekannten Symptommustern von Krankheiten (*pathophysiologische Vergleichsmuster*) verglichen; aus der Menge dieser Muster werden durch *Datenfilterung* die wiedererkannten herausgefiltert: *Pathophysiologische Muster*. Die Krankheiten, auf die erkannte Muster hinweisen, werden näher betrachtet: zu ihnen gehörige Symptommuster, Krankheitskonzepte (*generische Konzepte*) und, falls erforderlich, Modelle ggf. pathologisch veränderter Körperstrukturen, Zustände, Vorgänge und Regelungen (*anatomische, pathophysiologische Modelle*) werden für den speziellen Patienten angepaßt (*Abbildung*) und ergeben zusammen *patientenbezogene Konzepte*. An mehreren Stellen dieses Prozesses kann eine *Datenanforderung* erzeugt werden, die zur Erhebung weiterer Daten führt.

4   Modularisierung

Eine wichtige Beschränkung der Anwendbarkeit wissensbasierter Systeme liegt noch immer im beschränkten Umfang beherrschbarer Wissensbasen. Viele Anwendungsbereiche erfordern den Umgang mit komplexen – d.h. großen und diversen – Wissensbeständen. Wie im vorausgehenden Abschnitt dargestellt, ist das beim Patientenmanagement von Hypertonie in besonderem Maße der Fall. Komplexe Wissensbestände können nur arbeitsteilig, in Teamarbeit, erhoben, implementiert und gewartet werden (vgl. [14]). Teammitglieder aber müssen ihre Aufmerksamkeit auf einen *Teil* des Gesamtwissens einschränken können. Auch der Problemlöser kann nur dann effizient sein, wenn er jeweils nur die Teile des Wissens fokussiert, die *aktuell relevant* sind. Gebraucht wird also eine *Modularisierung* wissensbasierter Systeme. Sie kann nicht auf einer lediglich technischen Ebene geleistet werden, sondern muß sich am Inhalt des Wissens orientieren, also semantische Abgrenzungen vornehmen. Die Aufgabe liegt damit auf der Wissensebene (im Sinne von Newell, [11]), es geht um *"knowledge-level modularization"* [18]. Eine solche Modularisierung wirft Fragen auf, nach welchen Kriterien modularisiert wird, wie das jeweils relevante Wissen bestimmt wird und wie der Zugriff darauf organisiert wird.

Die bisherigen Modularisierungsansätze haben sich neben den technischen Aspekten (Regelgruppen, Kontexte und Welten) mit inhaltsbezogener Steuerung durch Metaregeln [1,5] und mit der Aufteilung von Wissen hinsichtlich seiner Verwendung befaßt, z.B. für Problemlösung bzw. Erklärung [2]. Die übliche Unterscheidung zwischen Domänen- und Kontrollwissen ist in KADS [19] durch die Aufteilung auf verschiedene Ebenen eines konzeptuellen Modells verfeinert worden. Soloway et al. [14] schlagen domänenspezifische "buckets" vor, hierarchisch organisierte Problemräume, die darin verfolgten Zielen entsprechen. Ziel und Inhalt ("topic") werden auch bei Clare [3] betont. Die im "Knowledge Sharing Effort" – vgl. [4,10] – angestrebte Wiederverwendbarkeit bereits existierender Wissensbasen betrifft automatisch auch die Frage nach einer Aggregation großer Wissensbasen aus bibliotheksmäßig gesammelten oder inkrementell entwickelten Teilen, die dort durch Standardisierungsbemühungen angegangen wird. Schließlich hat die Beobachtung, daß spezielle Wissenselemente (wie Frames und Regeln) beim Menschen in Clustern gebündelt vorliegen und zur Problemlösung herangezogen werden, zum Vorschlag partitionierter Wissensbasen mit dynamischen Zugriffsbedingungen geführt [16,17]. Die grundlegenden Prinzipien betreffen Inhalt und Spezifität als strukturierende Aspekte und schlagen vor, Wissen in geschichteten, evtl. überlappenden *Wissenspaketen* zu organisieren, deren Inhalt nur betrachtet wird, wenn ein Paket als aktuell relevant eingestuft wird.

4.1   Ansatz in HYPERCON

Unsere Analyse des diagnostischen Vorgehens (vgl. Abb. 1) legt zunächst eine Aufteilung in Datenerhebung, Diagnosebestimmung und Therapie nahe, die idealisiert Phasen entsprechen, in realistischen Fällen aber iterativ durchlaufen werden. Eine Verfeinerung entsprechend dem üblichen Vorgehen des Arztes führt zu folgenden inhaltlich abgeschlossenen Struktureinheiten, *Wissensmodule*[3] genannt.

---

[3]   Dabei umfaßt Anamnese die Erhebung von Vorgeschichte und subjektiven Beschwerden der Patienten, klinische Untersuchung einfache körperliche Untersuchungen wie Abhorchen, Blutdruckmessen und Augenhintergrund ansehen, diagnostische Verfahren z.B. EKG und Ultraschallbild, Nosologie die systematische Lehre von den einzelnen Krankheiten und Pathophysiologie die Beschreibung der normalen und krankhaften Vorgänge wie etwa der Blutdruckregelung.

Akquisitionsmodule: Anamnese, Klinische Untersuchung, Labor, Diagnostische Verfahren,
Diagnostische Module: Hypothesengenerierung, Hypothesenverifikation,
Therapiemodule: Medikamentöse Therapie, Nicht-Medikamentöse Therapie, Invasive Therapie, Operative Therapie.
Bibliotheksmodule: Nosologie, Anatomische und Pathophysiologische Modelle,

Die Module umfassen abgeschlossene spezifische Wissensbereiche und sind durch spezielle Interfaces mit einer zentralen Kommunikationskomponente verbunden. Mit Ausnahme der Bibliotheksmodule ist stets nur ein Modul aktiv.

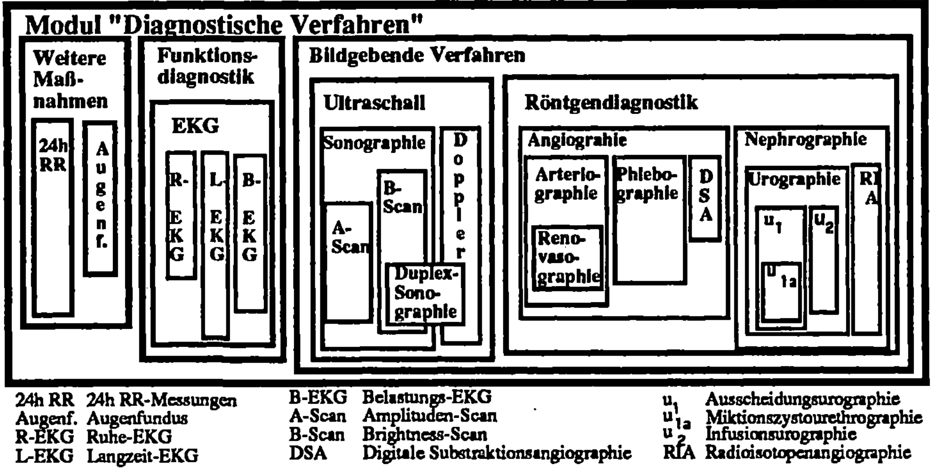

24h RR 24h RR-Messungen
Augenf. Augenfundus
R-EKG Ruhe-EKG
L-EKG Langzeit-EKG
B-EKG Belastungs-EKG
A-Scan Amplituden-Scan
B-Scan Brightness-Scan
DSA Digitale Substraktionsangiographie
u_1 Ausscheidungsurographie
u_{1a} Miktionszystourethrographie
u_2 Infusionsurographie
RIA Radioisotopenangiographie

Abb. 2. Ausschnitt aus der Paketstruktur des Moduls "Diagnostische Verfahren"

Die Wissensmodule sind ihrerseits in *Wissenpakete* unterteilt – Kollektionen von Wissenselementen, die vom Problemlöser gemeinsam fokussiert werden. Wissenselemente in einem nicht fokussierten Paket sind für die Inferenzmaschine unsichtbar, um irrelevantes Wissen von Suche und Musterabgleich auszuschließen. Ein Ausschnitt der Paketstruktur des Moduls "Diagnostische Verfahren" ist in Abb. 2 gezeigt. Dabei dürfen nebeneinanderliegende Pakete alternative Sichten oder konkurrierendes Wissen enthalten. Die gesamte Wissensbasis ist auf ca. 250 Wissenspakete aufgeteilt.

4.2 Abgrenzungskriterien für Wissenspakete

Analog zur Kohäsion [20] im klassischen Software-Engineering ist das wichtigste Kriterium der inhaltliche Zusammenhang des Wissens eines Wissenspakets. Als Prüfkriterien können dabei gemeinsame zeitliche Verwendung, gemeinsame benötigte Daten, ähnliche Spezifität, ähnlicher Detaillierungsgrad und einheitliches Gesichtsfeld (s.u.) dienen. So gibt es ein Paket über die bei Systemstart zu erfassenden Stammdaten von Patienten und eines über Muster, die Krankheitsverdachte aus anamnestischen Daten generieren. Wissen über Diagnose und Folgen von Verengungen der Nierenarterie wird in einem (relativ unspezifischen) Paket gehalten; erst in einem Unterpaket werden spezifische Merkmale beschrieben, die abhängig von der Ursache der Verengung sind. Wissen über häufige Krankheiten wird getrennt von Wissen über extrem seltene gehalten, da letzteres nur in Ausnahmefällen überhaupt in Betracht gezogen zu werden braucht.

161

Entsprechendes gilt über seltene Konstellationen, wie Patienten, denen eine Niere fehlt. Der Detaillierungsgrad wird sowohl in taxonomischer als auch in kompositionaler (mereologischer) Hinsicht berücksichtigt: die Klassifikation der Nierenerkrankungen und die der membrano-proliferativen Glomerulonephritis werden ebenso in unterschiedlichen Paketen dargestellt wie die makroskopische Aufteilung der Niere einerseits und die Aufteilung ihrer mikroskopischen Bausteine andererseits. Zu einem Paket sollte möglichst ein einheitliches Gesichtsfeld gehören, es sollte also nicht gleichzeitig Merkmale des Bluts und des Urins beschreiben – schon um die Eindeutigkeit von Namen wie Kreatiningehalt und der Einschätzungen eines Meßwerts zu gewährleisten, ohne zu umständlichen Namensergänzungen (Normwert-Kreatiningehalt-im-Blut) greifen zu müssen. Für Vergleiche ist von dieser Regel abzuweichen.

Da das Kontrollwissen zu einem bestimmten Bereich nur gleichzeitig mit dem entsprechenden Domänenwissen relevant ist, werden Kontroll- und Domänenwissen jeweils im gleichen Modul bzw. Paket gehalten, darin aber in Anlehnung an KADS auf unterschiedliche Ebenen aufgeteilt, die in Abschnitt 4.3 beschrieben werden.

Eine angemessene Größe für Wissenspakete festzulegen ist nicht einfach; sie liegt wohl dort, wo weitere Unterteilungen künstlich wirken. Leider ist die von Expertensystemtools angebotene Notation so weit von der Ebene des Expertenwissens entfernt, daß die zu wünschende Überschaubarkeit des Textes eines Paketes auf dieser Sprachebene schwer erreichbar scheint. Die Analogie zur Forderung funktionaler Kohäsion im klassischen Software Engineering bestünde für Pakete darin, daß weitere Unterteilungen keine sinnvolle, eigenständig nutzbare Funktionalität mehr zulassen.

4.3 Fokussierung von Modulen und Wissenspaketen

Die umfangreiche zugrundeliegende Domäne macht es notwendig, die Wissensbasis so zu strukturieren, daß situationsbezogen nicht die ganze Wissensbasis, sondern nach Möglichkeit nur derjenige Wissensausschnitt betrachtet wird, der für die jeweilige Aufgabenstellung relevant ist.

Globale und lokale Fokussierungskomponente. Der Aufbau der Wissensbasis aus Modulen und Paketen erfordert die Konzeption zweier Komponenten: der globalen Fokussierungskomponente (GF) und der lokalen Fokussierungskomponente (LF). Während die GF die Auswahl eines geeigneten Moduls zum Ziel hat, entscheidet die LF über das Paket, dessen Wissen aktuell heranzuziehen ist. Die Struktur der Fokussierungskomponenten ist – unter Bezugnahme auf KADS [19] – durch fünf Ebenen gekennzeichnet (s. Abb. 3).

<table>
<tr><td>Strategieebene</td><td colspan="3">Problemklassen   Problemlösungsmethoden   globale Pläne   globale Strategien</td></tr>
<tr><td>Taskebene</td><td colspan="3">Klassen von Aufgaben, Teilaufgaben, Unteraufgaben</td></tr>
<tr><td>Taktikebene</td><td>situationsabhängige Pläne</td><td>alternative Pläne
konkurrierende Pläne</td><td>ergänzende Pläne</td></tr>
<tr><td>Inferenzebene</td><td colspan="3">Regelgruppen zur Beschreibung von atomaren Inferenzschritten im Problemlösungsprozeß,
Regelgruppen für die situativen Pläne, Metaregeln</td></tr>
<tr><td>Bereichsebene</td><td colspan="3">Moduln</td></tr>
</table>

Abb. 3. Ebenen der Globalen Fokussierung (GF)

Auf der *Strategieebene* sind Problemklasse (in unserem Beispiel die Diagnose und Therapie) und Problemlösungsmethode (im Beispiel "Heuristische Klassifikation") durch die Systemausrichtung vorgegeben.

Ausgangspunkt für eine effiziente Wissensfokussierung sind die globalen Strategien, die durch die globalen Pläne beschrieben werden. Die Strategien geben ein globales Vorgehen beim Schlußfolgern an und entsprechen Abstraktionen unseres diagnostischen Schlußfolgerungsmodells. Neben strikten Plänen gibt es auch Pläne, bei denen ein vorübergehender Wechsel zu einem anderen Plan in sogenannten Akutsituationen oder ein vollständiger Ausstieg zu anderen Plänen, bspw. von heuristischem zu modellbasiertem Vorgehen, möglich ist.

Die *Taskebene* beschreibt die auszuführenden Aufgaben (z.B. generiere oder verifiziere Hypothese), die ihrerseits in verschiedene Teilaufgaben und Unteraufgaben gegliedert sind.

Aus Gründen einer spezifischeren Fokussierung und vor dem Hintergrund einer modularen Wissensbasis wurde in unserem System als Erweiterung zu KADS eine *Taktikebene* eingeführt. Eine Taktik beschreibt eine Methode zur situationsabhängigen Anwendung von Inferenzschritten und zur Fokussierung entsprechender Pakete unter Berücksichtigung der Ziele, die mit Teilaufgaben verbunden sind. Eine Taktik ist somit nicht von der übergeordneten Strategie oder der allgemeinen Task abhängig. Die Taktikebene unterstützt als Bindeglied zwischen Task- und Inferenzebene die Transparenz beider Ebenen und erlaubt deren kontrollierte Erweiterung.

Auf *Inferenzebene* sind neben Meta-Regeln und atomaren Inferenzschritten auch Regelgruppen zur Ausführung der verschiedenen Taktiken ("Taktikgruppen") modelliert.

Die unterste Ebene, die *Bereichsebene*, umfaßt bei der GF die bekannten Module. Bei der LF beinhaltet sie Konzepte und Objekte der Domäne eines Moduls, Relationen zwischen ihnen und schließlich Metawissen über den Objektbereich.

Um das bereichsspezifische Wissen eines Moduls, das auf globaler Ebene ausgewählt wurde, fokussieren zu können, muß eine geeignete Schnittstelle zwischen der GF und der LF des Moduls bestehen. Die Schnittstelle sieht die Übergabe folgender Inhalte vor:

- globale Situation (bestehend aus Task und Subtask und Taktikgruppe)
- Patientenkonzept (bestehend aus den aufbereiteten Patientendaten und bisher erzielten Ergebnisse (z.B. erkannte Muster, Hypothesen, ...)
- fokussierter Bereich (bestehend aus einem der Wissensbasismodule)

Über diese Schnittstelle wird die LF aktiviert. Die lokale Strategie- und Taskebene der LF entsprechen einer Abstraktion bzw. einer Verfeinerung tiefer liegender Ebenen der GF in Abhängigkeit von der jeweiligen inhaltlichen Zuständigkeit eines Moduls (Beispiel einer Instantiierung der LF eines Moduls s. [8]).

5   Systemarchitektur

Die Architektur von HYPERCON wurde erstellt, um eine maximale Flexibilität und Erweiterbarkeit des Systems zu gewährleisten. Ihre wesentlichen Komponenten sind die globale Fokussierungskomponente (GF), die Wissensbasis-Komponente (WB) mit mehreren Wissensmodulen und die Koordinationskomponente (KO) (s. Abb. 4).
Eine wesentliche Voraussetzung für die wissensbezogene Modularisierung war die softwaretechnische Modularisierung des Systems selbst, der eine Verteilung von "wissensbezogenen" und "systemtechnischen" Aufgaben zugrundegelegt wurde. Die Interaktion der Komponenten sowie die Datenübermittlung basieren auf vereinheitlichten Schnittstellen [6].

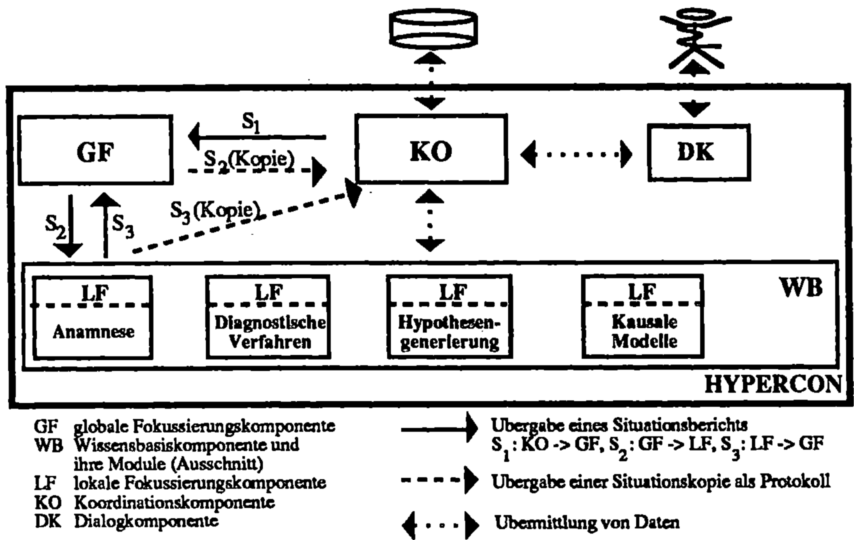

GF globale Fokussierungskomponente
WB Wissensbasiskomponente und
     ihre Module (Ausschnitt)
LF lokale Fokussierungskomponente
KO Koordinationskomponente
DK Dialogkomponente

Übergabe eines Situationsberichts
S_1: KO -> GF, S_2: GF -> LF, S_3: LF -> GF

Übergabe einer Situationskopie als Protokoll

Übermittlung von Daten

Abb. 4. Die Systemarchitektur und ihre Komponenten

Systemkomponenten und Schnittstellen. Als wissensbezogene Komponenten werden die GF und die WB bezeichnet. Die GF koordiniert, wie in Abschnitt 4.3 beschrieben, die Aktionen der Module. Sie führt den globalen Plan aus, indem sie der aktuellen Situation des Schlußfolgerungsprozesses entsprechend sukzessive Module aktiviert, ihre Ergebnisse evaluiert und den Plan modifiziert und/oder entsprechend weiterverfolgt.

Die WB besteht aus Modulen (s. Ausschnitt in Abb. 4), die je eine lokale Fokussierungskomponente (LF) zur Auswahl von Paketen und Unterpaketen besitzen.

Die KO ist für die technische Koordination der Abläufe im System zuständig. Sie verwaltet u. a. die globale Datenbasis des aktuellen Patientenfalles und die protokollierten Interaktionen zwischen der GF und den Modulen.

Die globale Datenbasis strukturiert akquirierte Patientendaten, Hypothesen und Therapievorschläge, die von mehreren Modulen benötigt werden. Zur strukturunabhängigen Übermittlung von Daten stellt die KO allen Komponenten standardisierte Transferfunktionen bereit.

Die Interaktion der Komponenten beruht gleichfalls auf einer einheitlichen Schnittstelle. Sie ist durch das Konzept "Situationsbericht" realisiert, das von der KO an die GF und zwischen GF und LF eines Moduls übergeben werden kann. Ein Situationsbericht bezeichnet den globalen Status, der Information über die aktuelle Situation enthält, in der sich der Schlußfolgerungsprozeß befindet. Zudem führt er zu seiner chronologischen Einordnung eine Kennung. Jeder Situationsbericht wird als Protokoll in die KO kopiert, um die spätere Wiederaufnahme einer Konsultation zu unterstützen. Beispielhaft ist ein Situationsbericht angeführt, der von der GF an die LF des Moduls Anamnese (LF(M_A)) übergeben wird (vgl. in Abb. 4: Situationsbericht S_2):

S_2: ist-ein: situationsbericht
      sender: GF
      empfaenger: LF(M_A)
      hat-globalen-status: neuer-patient-mit-unbekannter-anamnese
      hat-kennung: 2

Über den globalen Status und die Kennung wird eine Konkretisierung des Situationsberichts zugänglich, die von LF(M_A) verarbeitet werden kann:

neuer-patient-mit-unbekannter-anamnese-2:
    konkretisiert: S_2
    hat-statusspezifikation: generiere-hypothese
                              patientendatengesteuert

Durch die Statusspezifikation der Konkretisierung übergibt die GF den Ausschnitt ihrer Ebeneninstantiierung (s. Abschnitt 4.3), der für die Strategie und den Plan der LF maßgebend ist. Dies veranschaulicht auch das Beispiel in Abschnitt 6.

Realisierungsplattform. Zu Projektbeginn wurden mehrere markteingeführte Entwicklungswerkzeuge evaluiert [12]. Als Auswahlkriterium für HYPERCON standen weniger die zu erwartende Effizienz des Systems als vielmehr die Vielfalt und Domänenangemessenheit der Repräsentationskonstrukte und Inferenzmechanismen im Vordergrund. Das System wird auf SUN Sparc 10 Workstations unter Unix realisiert. Als Entwicklungswerkzeug wird die lispbasierte hybride Software "Knowledge Craft" (KC) eingesetzt, die u. a. eine mächtige Repräsentationssprache besitzt und ihren Regelverarbeitungsmechanismen OPS5 sowie Prolog zugrundelegt.

6 Beispiel

Am Beispiel eines authentischen Patientenfalles werden die Kommunikation zwischen den einzelnen Systemkomponenten, die dynamische Fokussierung von Modulen und ihren Paketen sowie Granularitätsaspekte beschrieben. Aus Gründen der Übersichtlichkeit werden nur die Ergebnisse der Module aufgeführt; mit Ausnahme der Schritte (1) und (2) wird auf eine explizite Schnittstellenspezifikationen verzichtet.

Folgender medizinischer Fall ist gegeben: Ein Internist wird von einer neuen Patientin mittleren Alters wegen plötzlicher Schmerzen in Brust und Hals sowie verschwommenen Sehens konsultiert.

Beim Start des Systems erstellt die Koordinationskomponente (KO) einen Situationsbericht für die globale Fokussierungskomponente (GF), die das erste zu fokussierende Modul auswählen muß.

(1) **GF:** Für die GF wird ein Schema instantiiert, das die aktuelle Einstellung der Kontrolle auf den jeweiligen Ebenen beschreibt. Es hat angesichts bisher fehlender Daten und Hypothesen die Gestalt
    globale Strategie: *heuristische Klassifikation*
    globaler Plan: *Default-Plan*
    Haupttask: *etabliere Hypothese*
    Subtask: *generiere Hypothese*
    Taktik: *patientendatengesteuertes Vorgehen*

Wir nennen es auch kurz *Instanz der GF*. Aufgrund des instantiierten Default-Planes und der Subtask sowie des im Situationsbericht als "neu" ausgewiesenen Patientenstatus fokussiert GF nun das Modul Anamnese. Die GF übergibt einen Situationsbericht (beinhaltet die Werte der GF-Instanz) an die lokale Fokussierungskomponente des Moduls Anamnese (LF (M_A)). Die Werte der GF-Instanz auf den unterschiedlichen Ebenen werden dabei konkretisiert:

(2) LF(M_A):Wie für die GF wird auch für die LF ein Schema instantiiert, das die aktuelle Einstellung der Kontrolle beschreibt. Dabei werden Werte der GF-Instanz auf andere Ebenen übernommen.

lokale Strategie:	*generiere Hypothese*
lokaler Plan:	*Default-Plan*
Haupttask:	*Musterbildung*
Subtask:	*Datenbewertung*
Taktik:	*Datenerhebung,-vergleich und -interpretation*

Unter Berücksichtigung der aktuellen Situation (Taktiken) werden die entsprechenden Wissenspakete (hier Regelklassen) aktiviert. Die im Situationsbericht enthaltene Information führt zu einer feineren Fokussierung auf einzelne Pakete innerhalb des Moduls. Zunächst werden die Anamnesedaten (Alter, Geschlecht, o.b. Beschwerden) der Patientin erhoben und ggf. qualitativ eingeschätzt. Danach werden die qualitativen Daten unter Berücksichtigung von physiologischem und pathologischem Hintergrundwissen des Anamnesemoduls gefiltert, und ggf. vorhandene Muster werden erkannt. Der Abarbeitungsprozeß des lokalen Planes hängt von den Gegebenheiten auf Subtask- und Taktikebene des lokalen Situationsberichts ab.

Ergebnis-Ausgabe des Moduls "Anamnese":
>Ein Muster einer Akutsituation wurde erkannt. Es weist folgende Akutsymptome auf:
>plötzliche Schmerzen in Brust und Hals einhergehend mit verschwommenem Sehen.
>Eine umgehende klinische Untersuchung mit Blutdruckkontrolle ist indiziert!

Diese Ergebnisse werden in einem Situationsbericht aufbereitet, in der KO protokolliert und der GF übergeben. Der Inhalt "Akutsituation" des Situationsberichtes führt zu einem Wechsel innerhalb des globalen Planes, d.h. die GF wechselt vom Default-Plan zum Akut-Plan und fokussiert entsprechend das Modul "Klinische Untersuchung" (M_{KU}). Für M_{KU} wiederholt sich Vorgang (1) und (2).

(3) LF(M_{KU}): fokussiert das spezifische Paket "Blutdruckmessung" – die Messung ergibt 240/120 mmHg – und anschließend das Paket "Blutdruckeinschätzung".

Ergebnis-Ausgabe des Moduls "Klinische Untersuchung":
> Es liegt der Verdacht auf eine schwere Hypertonie mit
> sehr hohem diastolischem Wert vor. Eine Akutsituation kann vorliegen.

(4) GF: fokussiert aufgrund der bestätigten Akutsituation und des verwendeten Akutplanes das Modul "Hypothesengenerierung" (M_{HG}). LF(M_{HG}) fokussiert sofort das Paket "Akut-Hypothesen".

Ergebnis–Ausgabe des Pakets "Akut-Hypothesen":
> Es besteht ein starker Verdacht auf eine Hypertone Krise. Bitte Therapie einleiten!

(5) GF: fokussiert aufgrund der Hypothese das Modul "Medikamentöse Therapie". Entsprechend der übergebenen Akutsituation fokussiert LF(M_{MT}) dort das Paket "Therapie bei Hypertoner Krise".

Ergebnis-Ausgabe des Pakets "Therapie bei Hypertoner Krise":
> Da wahrscheinlich eine Hypertone Krise vorliegt,
> wird folgende Therapie vorgeschlagen: Nitrolingual zur Entlastung des Herzens,
> Calciumantagonist zur Senkung des hohen Blutdrucks.

Bisher ist das folgende Patientenmodell aufgebaut worden:
Patientenmodell 1:

Anamnese:	weiblich, mittleres Alter (60 Jahre), plötzliche Schmerzen in Brust und Hals, verschwommenes Sehen
Klinische Untersuchung:	Grad der Hypertonie: schwer (RR 240/120 mmHg)

Nach erfolgter Therapie hat sich der Zustand der Patientin weitgehend stabilisiert. Es kann nun mit der Ursachenabklärung bzgl. der Akutsymptome begonnen werden. Dazu werden weitere Patientendaten in einem zweiten Patientenmodell erfaßt.

Patientenmodell 2:

Anamnese: aktuell o.B.[4]

Klinische Untersuchung: (umfaßt Gewicht, Körpergröße, Auskultation des Herzens und der Lunge, Erhebung des Pulsstatus, Bauchstatus)

Labor: (umfaßt großes Blutbild, Leberprofil, Nierenprofil, Fettprofil, Urinstatus)

Die KO bildet nun, unter Berücksichtigung der in der Vergangenheit protokollierten bewerteten Patientendaten, Situationsberichte und neu hinzugekommenen Patientendaten (s. Patientenmodell 2), einen Situationsbericht, den sie der GF übergibt. Die GF interpretiert die bisherigen Konsultationsergebnisse und die aktuellen Patientendaten. Auf dieser Basis werden globaler Plan, Task, Subtask und spezifische Taktik festgelegt und nacheinander die Module "Klinische Untersuchung" (M_{KU}) und "Labor" (M_L) ausgewählt; darin werden die entsprechenden Werte erhoben und eingeschätzt.

(6) LF(M_{KU}): fokussiert nacheinander die spezifischen Pakete "Grundmeßgrößen", "Herz-Kreislaufstatus" und "Übriger-Status".

Ergebnis-Ausgabe des Moduls "Klinische Untersuchung":

> *Grundmeßgrößen o.B. Der Herz-Kreislaufstatus weist ein Systolikum[5] von 2/6 auf,*
> *der übrige Status ist o.B.*

(7) LF(M_L): fokussiert zuerst das spezifische Paket "Serum-Laboruntersuchung" mit den Unterpaketen "Blutbild", "Gerinnungsstatus", "Leberprofil", "Fettprofil" und "Serum-Nierenprofil". Des weiteren wird das Paket "Urin-Laboruntersuchung" mit den darin enthaltenen Paketen "Urin-Stoffwechselprofil", "Urin-Sediment", "Urin-Elektrolyte", "Urin-Nierenprofil" und "Urin-Hormone" fokussiert.

Ergebnis-Ausgabe des Moduls "Labor":

> *Serum-Cholesterin erhöht, ansonsten alle Laborwerte o.B.*

Aufgrund entsprechender Situationsberichte fokussiert nun die GF das Modul "Hypothesengenerierung"(M_{HG}).

(8) LF(M_{HG}): fokussiert zunächst die Pakete "Hypothesengenerierung KU", "Hypothesengenerierung L" und anschließend das Paket "Hypothesengenerierung KU $\cup$ L", jeweils bezogen auf die nach Pathologie gefilterten Patientendaten.

Ergebnis-Ausgabe des Moduls "Hypothesengenerierung":

> *Verdacht auf Infarkt aufgrund von sehr hohem Blutdruck,*
> *plötzlichen Schmerzen in Brust und Hals, Systolikum 2/6 und erhöhtem Cholesterin.*
> *Abklärung der Hypertonie (sekundär versus primär) notwendig.*

Alle Patientendaten sind qualitativ bewertet und gefiltert; es wurde jedoch kein pathophysiologisches Muster erkannt. Der vorliegende Verdacht ist zu vage, um eine Hypothese etablieren zu können, d.h.: die globale Task "etabliere Hypothese" ist noch nicht abgearbeitet. Aus diesem Grund wird im globalen Plan der GF nach einem alternativen Weg gesucht. Der globale Plan sieht an der aktuellen Stelle vor, das Modul "Diagnostische Verfahren" (M_{DV}) zu konsultieren. GF übergibt nun die relevanten Patientendaten und die generierte Hypothese "Verdacht auf Infarkt" an LF(M_{DV}).

---

[4] ohne krankhaften Befund
[5] Systolikum von 2/6: anomales Herzgeräusch bestimmter Lautstärke

(9) LF(M$_{DV}$): fokussiert zunächst das Paket "Bildgebende Verfahren" mit den Unterpaketen "Röntgen-Thorax", "Echokardiographie-Herz", "Sonographie-Niere" und die Unterpakete "Ruhe-EKG", "Belastungs-EKG" des Pakets "Funktionsdiagnostik" zum Ausschluß der Infarkthypothese. Des weiteren wird das Paket "Weitere Maßnahmen" mit dem Unterpaket "24h-Messungen" zur Abgrenzung zwischen primärer und sekundärer Hypertonie fokussiert.

Ergebnis-Ausgabe des Moduls "Diagnostische Verfahren":
> *Verdacht auf möglichen Infarkt konnte nicht bestätigt werden, da Röntgen-Thorax,*
> *Ruhe-EKG, Belastungs-EKG o.B., Echokardiographie des Herzens o.B.*
> *Sonographie war ebenfalls o.B.*
> *Eine primäre Hypertonie kann aufgrund der unauffälligen Blutdruckmeßergebnisse*
> *(mittlerer RR-Wert von 152/85 mmHg, maximaler RR-Wert von 160/93)*
> *der 24h-Messungen nicht bestätigt werden.*

Die bisher durchgeführten diagnostischen Untersuchungen ergeben keine pathologischen Befunde. Aus Platzgründen erfolgt die weitere Darstellung in komprimierter Form.

Da der Verdacht auf Infarkt verworfen wird und keine pathologischen Befunde vorliegen, kann die Hypertone Krise der Patientin bisher nicht erklärt werden. Im Modul Hypothesengenerierung werden deshalb weitere mögliche Ursachen einer Hypertonie fokussiert, u.a. Nierenkrankheiten. Da die Standarduntersuchung (Sonographie) keine Hinweise geliefert hat, müssen belastendere diagnostische Verfahren in Betracht gezogen werden. Für die zunächst fokussierte speziellere Krankheit "Verengung der Nierenarterie" (Nierenarterienstenose) kommt in erster Linie die Digitale Subtraktionsangiographie (DSA) in Frage [13; S. 14.10]. Sie wird dem Benutzer vorgeschlagen. Für das Verständnis des bei Durchführung einzugebenden Befundes wird Wissen über die Anatomie gebraucht; ein entsprechendes Paket des Bibliotheksmoduls "Anatomische Modelle" wird fokussiert. Sein Umfang ist durch eine Granularitätsanalyse [9] bestimmt worden: das Gesichtsfeld schließt neben der Nierenarterie die Nachbarorgane ein, insbesondere die Niere und die Aorta. Die Auflösung der DSA liegt im Millimeterbereich, dementsprechend enthält das Paket keine Information über den Feinbau der Arterien oder gar über mikroskopische Strukturen. Eine erkannte Verengung kann jedoch hinsichtlich ihrer Lokalisation (z.B. aortennahes Drittel der Arterie) und ihrer Form beschrieben werden. Bei der Patientin wird eine perlenkettenförmige Stenose im mittleren Drittel der Arterie beobachtet. Zu deren Verständnis wird ein weiteres Paket "Anatomiewissen-Gefäße" gebraucht, das die Struktur der Arterienwand beschreibt.

Als wahrscheinliche Hypothese kommt in diesem Falle eine Nierenarterienstenose durch fibromuskuläre Dysplasie in Frage. Diese wird, bevor sie an den Benutzer ausgegeben wird, durch das Modul "Hypothesenverifikation" (M$_{HV}$) verifiziert. Dieses Modul enthält Wissen über konkurrierende Krankheitsbilder, die dann dem Benutzer zusammen mit der verifizierten Hypothese angezeigt werden.

Im Anschluß an die Hypothesenverifikation ist der globale Plan bzgl. "Hypothesenetablierung" abgearbeitet. Daraufhin wird der globale Plan für die *Therapiegenerierung* unter Berücksichtigung der etablierten Hypothese instantiiert.

(11) GF: fokussiert aufgrund der verifizierten Hypothese das Modul "Invasive Therapie" (M$_{IT}$). Des weiteren wird das Modul "Nicht-Medikamentöse Therapie" (M$_{NMT}$) konsultiert.

(12) LF(M_{IT}): fokussiert zunächst das Paket "Dilatation Gefäße" und dort das spezifischere Unterpaket "Nierenarterien".

Ergebnis-Ausgabe des Moduls "Invasive Therapie":
> *Mögliche Therapie: Dilatation der Arteria renalis während angiographischer*
> *Untersuchung oder operative Korrektur.*
> *Hinweis: Die Erfolgsaussichten bzgl. Dilatation lassen sich durch seitengetrennte*
> *Nierenvenenreninbestimmung genauer abklären. Weitere Information auf Anfrage.*

(13) LF(M_{NMT}): fokussiert die Unterpakete "Diätplanung" und "Blutdruckkontrollen".

Ergebnis-Ausgabe des Moduls "Nicht-Medikamentöse Therapie":
> *Es wird eine eiweiß- und kalorienreduzierte Diät und*
> *aufgrund der Patientendisposition zu möglichen weiteren Stenosen werden*
> *regelmäßige Blutdruckkontrollen im Abstand von 4 Wochen empfohlen.*

7 Zusammenfassung und Kritik

In diesem Papier haben wir zunächst den Anforderungen an ein Konsultationssystem zur Hypertonie und die Herausforderung der Aufbereitung des relevanten medizinischen Wissens dargestellt.

Unser Vorgehen zur Wissensaufbereitung stützte sich entscheidend auf ein in Experteninterviews erarbeitetes Modell des diagnostischen Schlußfolgerns, das sowohl die Wissensakquisition als auch die Wissensaufteilung leitete. Unser Konzept für die Modularisierung der Wissensbasis setzt auf der Wissensebene an und sieht eine Partitionierung in Module und feiner in Pakete vor. Diese Pakete können teils unter- und übergeordnet sein, teils als alternative oder konkurrierende Pakete nebeneinander liegen. Ihre Fokussierung schließt außerhalb gelegene Wissenselemente von der Betrachtung aus.

Die Architektur erlaubt durch eine zentrale Koordinationskomponente und standardisierte Transferfunktionen eine unabhängige Wahl von Repräsentationsformaten in den einzelnen Modulen. Die globale Fokussierung wählt zu aktivierende Module aus, wohingegen die lokale Fokussierung innerhalb eines Moduls über das Paket entscheidet, dessen Wissen aktuell heranzuziehen ist. Als Abgrenzungskriterien für Wissenspakete wurden inhaltliche Kohäsion und u.a. Ähnlichkeit in Spezifität und Detaillierungsgrad sowie textuelle Überschaubarkeit herangezogen.

Schwierigkeiten bestehen noch in dem großen Abstand, der die Sprache des benutzten Expertensystemwerkzeugs KC von der der Experten trennt; das macht sich insbesondere bei der Übersichtlichkeit des formalisierten Wissens bemerkbar.

Der Zufriedenheit mit der framebezogenen Repräsentationsmächtigkeit und der vergleichsweisen Offenheit von KC steht ein Mangel an Komfort und Effizienz der Regelkomponente gegenüber. Diese Schwierigkeit dürfte sich jedoch durch eine spätere Reimplementation mit einem C-basierten Werkzeug verbessern lassen.

Hinsichtlich des Entwicklerteams ist dafür zu sorgen, daß bei einer Aufteilung von Arbeiten zwischen Wissenserhebung und systemtechnischer Realisierung jede Seite guten Einblick in die Anforderungen bzw. Möglichkeiten der anderen hat.

Unser Ansatz ist in einer medizinischen Domäne erarbeitet worden. Da er sich dort trotz ihrer extremen Verflochtenheit bewährt hat, halten wir ihn erst recht für tragfähig in anderen, stärker trennbaren Bereichen.

8 Literaturangaben

1. Bocionek, S.: *Modulare Regelprogrammierung*. Braunschweig: Vieweg (1990)
2. Clancey, W.J.: The Epistemology of a Rule-Based Expert System – a Framework for Explanation. *Artificial Intelligence* 20 , 215-251 (1983)
3. Clare, M.: When Information Engineering Meets Knowledge Management. *Proceedings AAAI Workshop Modelling in the Large*, Washington (1993)
4. Czedik, D.: Status Quo der Wiederverwendbarkeit von Wissensbasen. *KI* 6 (1), 27-32 (1992)
5. Davis, R.: Generalized Procedure Calling and Content-Directed Invocation. *SIGPLAN Notices* 12, 8, 45-54 (1977)
6. Heller, B. & Schlegelmilch, S.: Modularization of Knowledge: A Competence-Oriented Approach. *Proc. AAAI Workshop Modelling in the Large*, Washington (1993)
7. Meurer, K.A.: Arterielle Hypertonie. In W. Siegenthaler et al. (Hrsg.): *Lehrbuch der Inneren Medizin*. Stuttgart: Georg Thieme Verlag (1992)
8. Meyer-Fujara, J., Heller, B., Schlegelmilch, S. & Wachsmuth, I.: Knowledge-Level Modularization of a Complex Knowledge Base. *Wissenschaftliche Konfererenz KI-94*, Saarbrücken (1994)
9. Meyer-Fujara, J.: *Granularitätsanalyse für die Modellierung renal bedingter Hypertonie.* Technischer Bericht (1993)
10. Neches, R. et al.: Enabling technology for knowledge sharing. *AI Magazine* 12 (3), 37-56 (1991)
11. Newell, A.: The Knowledge Level. *Artificial Intelligence* 18, 1-20 (1982)
12. Schlegelmilch, S., Heller, B., Linke, T., Meyer-Fujara, J.: *Evaluation hybrider Expertensystemtools*. MOSYS-Report 13, Universität Bielefeld, Technische Fakultät (1993)
13. Siegenthaler, W. & Kuhlmann, U.: Hypertonie. In W. Siegenthaler (Hrsg.): *Differentialdiagnose innerer Krankheiten*. Stuttgart: Thieme Verlag (1988)
14. Soloway, E., Bachant, J. & Jensen, K.: *Assessing the Maintainability of XCON-in-RIME: Coping with the problems of a VERY Large Rule-Base*. AAAI-87 (1987)
15. Wachsmuth. I., Heller, B. & Meyer-Fujara, J.: HYPERCON: *Modulare Wissensbasen für Hypertonie-Konsultation*. MOSYS-Report 10, Universität Bielefeld, Technische Fakultät (1992)
16. Wachsmuth, I. & Gängler, B.: Knowledge Packets and Knowledge Packet Structures. In O. Herzog & C.-R. Rollinger (eds.): *Text Understanding in LILOG: Integrating Computational Linguistics and Artificial Intelligence*, Berlin: Springer (1991), pp. 380-393
17. Wachsmuth. I. & Meyer-Fujara, J.: Adressing the Retrieval Problem in Large Knowledge Bases (Summary). *Proc. 3rd Conf. Computational Intelligence (CI-90)*, Milano (1990)
18. Wachsmuth. I.: *Modularisierung Wissensbasierter Systeme*. MOSYS-Report 1, Universität Bielefeld, Technische Fakultät (1989)
19. Wielinga, B., Schreiber, A. Th. & Breuker, J.: KADS: a modeling approach to knowledge engineering. *Knowledge Acquisition* 4, 5-53 (1992)
20. Yourdon, E. & Constantine, L.L.: *Structured Design – Fundamentals of a Discipline of Computer Program and Systems Design*. Englewood Cliffs: Prentice-Hall (1979)

Synthesis of Knowledge Based Methodology and Psychology for Recruitment and Training of Salespersons

Rajiv Khosla[1], Tharam Dillon[2] and Ajeet Parhar[3]

Expert and Intelligent Systems Laboratory,
Applied Computing Research Institute,
Department of Computer Science and Computer Engg.,
La Trobe University, Melbourne, Victoria-3083, Australia

Abstract. In this paper we address two important sales management issues, namely, recruitment and training of salespersons. We describe an Intelligent Assistant for Improving Sales Performance(IAISP) which can assist the management in recruitment of salespersons. IAISP can also assist a freshly recruited salesperson in improving their inter-personal skills in their day to day interactions with customers. IAISP aware of any such existing system which is based on such a synthesis. We particularly concentrate in this paper on the knowledge acquisition and analysis which brings about the synthesis between deep knowledge in the form of a a behavioral model and shallow knowledge in the form of knowledge and experience of the sales managers. IAISP has been field tested and the results are encouraging.

1   Introduction

Sales management among other responsibilities includes forecasting demand (sales), managing salespersons, and establishing sales quotas. Managing salespersons involves such activities as recruitment and training of salespersons, supporting the salespersons in their work, meeting with customers, establishing territories and evaluating performance. Recruiting the right type of salesperson who match the organizational needs and ingraining them with proper selling attitude has a critical impact on the performance of the sales force, sales manager, and the organization as a whole. The existing recruiting and training procedures though useful, have met with limited success. The high salesperson turnover and stress levels on sales managers while on job are good indicators of limited success of these procedures. Development of IAISP is an attempt to enhance the margin of success of these procedures.

IAISP combines deep knowledge in the form of a behavioral model and shallow knowledge in the form of knowledge and experience of the sales managers in order to achieve the above objectives. The knowledge-based methodology has been used as it facilitates such a synthesis between the heuristics used by the sales managers (domain experts) and the research done by behavioral scientists in assessing selling and buying behavior.

In this paper we will concentrate on the knowledge acquisition and analysis of selling behavior knowledge and buying behavior knowledge which has resulted in such a synthesis . It was also the most time consuming and difficult task in the development of IAISP.

In order to do this, the paper is organized in 8 sections. Section 2 outlines the the existing problems in recruitment and training of salespersons. Section 3 briefly describes the reasons for using a behavioral model as a starting point for knowledge acquisition. Section 4 outlines the areas related to selling and buying behavior knowledge which form the basis of knowledge refinement and analysis. Section 5 briefly describes steps undertaken for knowledge refinement Section 6 describes the analysis of the selling and buying behavior knowledge respectively. This analysis is used as a basis for categorization of salesperson's selling behavior and customer's buying behavior. Section 7 outlines the adaptive knowledge used for giving advice to the the salesperson. Lastly section 8 outlines the implementation.

2 Existing Issues with Recruitment and Training of Salespersons

Most organizations rely on interview as the main strategy for recruiting salespersons. Product knowledge, verbal skills, hard work, self-discipline, and personality are generally assumed to be well taken care of in the interviewing process. However, a) the sales manager and the top management spend limited time with the salesperson during the interview. In this limited time, it is difficult to realistically assess all the factors which affect the selling behavior of a salesperson, and b) the sales manager and the top management view the selling behavior of the salesperson based on their traits, experience and knowledge in this area and human interaction in general. Thus a subjective element is introduced in the process. This subjectivity is ideally supposed to reflect the organization's needs/marketing strategy. However, it is accepted that the difference between the expected performance levels of some of the successful candidates at the recruitment stage and those delivered in real work situations are enough to cause worry.

Customers are motivated to buy by their task and personal needs as shown in Fig. 1. Task needs can vary from cars to mainframes to courses in baking pasteries. Customer's personal needs can be inferred from observation of customer's behavior, and through successful communication[1, 8].

Most salespersons are led by intuition and their past experience in dealing with different types of customers. Very few of them make a serious effort to get beneath the surface and a) diagnose what makes customers behave differently from one another, b) understand why they get along with certain customers and do not get along with others, and c) how they should adapt their selling behavior to the customer's buying behavior in order to maximize sales results. The two sources which help them to develop the above attributes are the training programs and their superior/sales manager. Though both these sources serve a

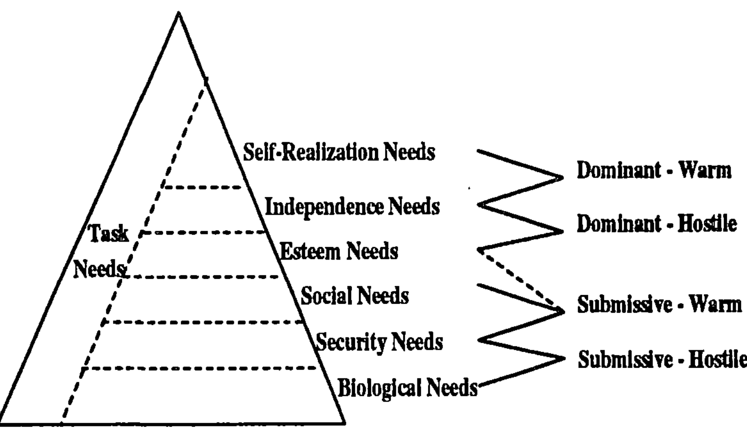

Fig.1: Maslow's hierarchical model of human needs and task needs

useful purpose, some of their limitations are a) training programs are generally condensed four to five day affairs; these programs cannot guarantee assimilation of ideas to effect positive behavioral changes, because behavioral changes occur over a period of time and these training programs fall far too short to bring about the necessary changes; b) training programs do not guarantee uninhibited participation; c) training programs are expensive; d) sales managers generally feel highly pressured for time to prepare individual advice recipes for different salespersons in the sales force; and e) sales managers have to repeatedly start from scratch with every new recruit thus making the training exercise a boring and monotonous one. The above issues related to recruitment and training indicate that to a large extent the problem lies not in the knowledge but the constraints of time under which it is applied and the way it is applied. These two constraints are the major motivation for developing IAISP.

3   Behavioral Model

One way of determining behavior [1] knowledge qualitatively is to observe the sales managers (chosen as domain experts) at work and discuss in detail with them as to how they identify the varying personal needs of the salespersons and customers and deal effectively with them. In other words, this would involve grouping similarities in selling behaviors of salespersons and buying behaviors of customers into different categories.

However, it was felt that it would be better to use the independent research findings of the behavioral scientists as a starting point. To some extent this would eliminate the subjectivity (which may limit IAISP's applicability) that would creep in if the behavioral model were to be developed otherwise. Then we can couple or modify the results of this model with the interviews/discussions

---

[1] The word behavior is implied to mean selling and/or buying behavior as is applicable and is in context of inter-personal behavior

held with the domain experts in order to make the system more realistic and useful.

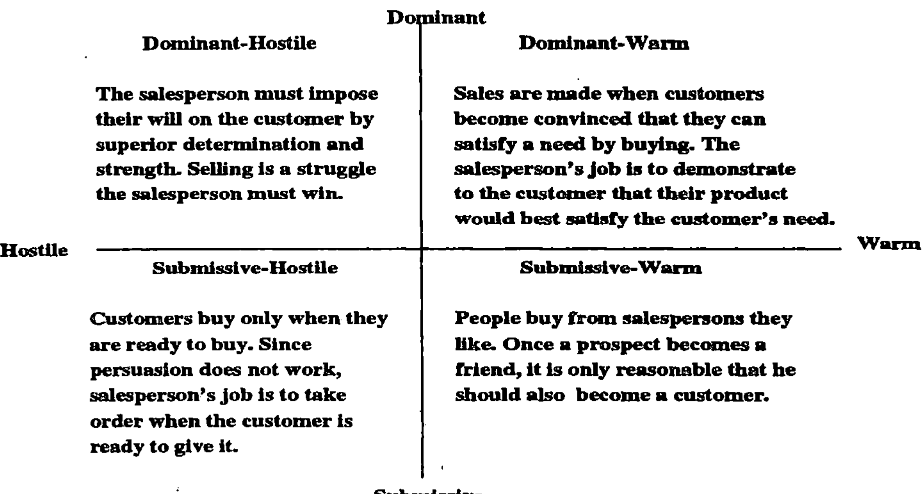

Fig.2: Salesperson behavior profile

Though quite a bit of work has been done in modeling salespersons and customer behaviors [6, 7, 8], the behavioral model[1] used is shown in Fig. 2 and 3 respectively. The reasons for using this model are a) the domain experts found it less complex, b) they found it easy to relate with as it mimicked their way thinking for typifying/categorizing salesperson and customer behaviors and, c) they found this model close to sales training programs they had undergone. The behavioral model used here has two dimensions namely, "warm ——hostile and submissive———dominant" . Warmth is regard for others. A warm person is optimistic and willing to place confidence in others. Hostility is lack of regard for others, the attitude that other people matter less than oneself. A hostile person rarely trusts others. Submission is the disposition to let others take the lead in personal encounters. It includes traits like dependence, unassertiveness, and passiveness. Dominance is the drive to take control in face-to-face situations. It includes a cluster of traits like initiative, forcefulness, and independence. For more details see [1, 2].

The behavioral model is related to Abraham Maslow's model (Fig.1) of human (personal) needs. The thickness of each layer in Fig.1 can vary depending upon the intensity of the personal need represented by each layer. The two dimensions "Submissive———Dominant" and "Warm——Hostile" are the two most significant dimensions in which selling and buying behavior is expressed. These two dimensions give rise to four broad groups of salespersons and customers, i.e., Dominant-Hostile(DH), Submissive-Hostile(SH), Submissive-Warm(SW), and Dominant Warm(DW). There are more dimensions like IQ, need for achievement, etc which could be associated with the model. However, it was felt a) it would

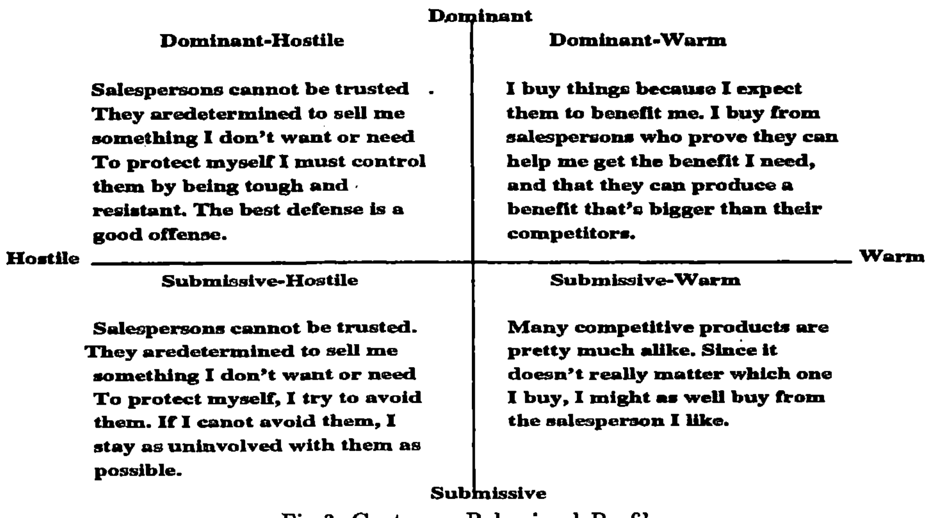

Fig.3: Customer Behavioral Profile

make the model more complex, b) marginalize distinctions between salesperson/customers and make documenting the knowledge more difficult, and c) it would be better develop a subsystem, with only these additional dimensions and put the conclusions of the two systems together. As per the behavioral model, salesperson's or customer's behavior is governed by their lowest unfulfilled personal need. Each of the above four categories is related to one or more personal need. Some of the characteristics [1, 2] of the four salesperson types and of the four customer types are shown in Fig. 4 and 5 respectively.

What has been described in Figs. 2 to 5 relates to primary or usual behavior of the four types. However, salespersons and customers also exhibit secondary and masked behaviors. Secondary behavior is an automatic, unconscious shift in behavior to overcome frustration. It is not planned or contrived. Whereas masked behavior is a deliberate response to external pressures. All the four types of salespersons and customers exhibit secondary or masked behaviors. For example, if DH salespersons become frustrated in what they want, or if they are deprived of a reward/promotion they feel is due and apparently they cannot do anything about it, they will adopt a passive behavior and become withdrawn like SH salespersons. On the other hand, they may deliberately don a mask of an easy going and friendly person (SW) if they find that the customer has "freezed up" because of their aggressive attitude.

IAISP takes into account the effect of secondary and masked behaviors in order to bring out the primary behavioral strategy of the salespersons and customers as will be shown in section 6.

3.1   Some Observations on the Behavioral Model

Various questions arise in the mind about the behavioral model like why these two dimensions?, why four categories? etc.. Few of them are addressed below.

Areas	DH	SH	SW	DW
General Attitude	Aggressive and manipulative	Cautious and careful	Friendly and easy going	Engaging, warm and assertive
Selling	Provides fast money. You have got what it takes.	Just like any other job	Provides opportunities to socialize with people.	Provides opportunities to transform your potential into actuality. Provides growth.
Success and Failure	Find very hard to digest failure. Must achieve success by any means.	Cover their back. Blame company for failures.	Believe people are more important than success and failure	Learn from their failures. People are important upto a point. Success is ultimate goal.
Decisiveness	Apparently decisive. Many times in self-doubt.	Indecisive. Lets things take their own shape.	Likes to be led in making decisions.	Decisive and cool headed. Never in self-doubt.

Fig.4: Some characteristics of salesperson types

Areas	DH	SH	SW	DW
Communication	Indulges in monologue Boastful tone. Impatient listener.	Keeps words to minimum. Responds in grunts and nods.	Socializes. Indulges in small talk. Gullible listener.	Engages in dialogue. Patient and purposeful.
Buying Priorities	Argues in challenging manner positive features of product. Goes into trivialities.	Changes existing suppliers only if circumstances force change	Buys from salesperson he likes rather than on product benefits.	Demands relevant information. Wants proof that purchase will benefit him.
Opinions and Feelings	Guided more by offering resistance than for making any rational contribution.	Unwilling to reveal opinions or feelings.	Invariably an endorsement of those of the salesperson.	Has a rationale behind them. May or may not be in line with those of salesperson.
General Attitude	I know best	Leave me alone	Nice guy	Net gain, businesslike.

Fig.5: Some characteristics of customer types

- The two dimensions shown in Figs. 2 and 3 are the two most significant dimensions in gauging the selling and buying behaviors of salespersons and customers respectively. These two dimensions are intuitive to selling, as salespersons and sales managers express the behavior of customers and salespersons respectively in terms of these two dimensions in their everyday conversation. So it is more practical and realistic to use these two dimensions. Further these two dimensions help one to examine the salesperson, and the customers on variety of topics related to selling and buying.
- The above model is interactional. The above two dimensions are are in terms of what happens between people. The idea of warmth or hostility has no meaning apart from interaction. Selling is an outcome of interaction between two or more individuals and these two dimensions help one to express the behavior of one individual with respect to the other explicitly.
- The idea of using the above model is not primarily to establish four categories of salespersons and customers but to use these categories to determine the predominant or lowest unfilled personal need which motivates the persons in these categories to behave the way they behave.
- Very few salespersons or customers in the real world could be expected to be perfect fits in any category. In fact the behavioral profile of most of them will have parts in each category. Thus although the behavioral model can provide us some basis for distinction, it cannot be used as a conclusive proof of a salesperson's primary selling behavior or a customer's primary buying behavior[2] . It is here that the *role of the domain experts* becomes extremely important. How do they use this knowledge in a manner which helps them to deal effectively with salespersons and customers. What areas they feel are important for gauging selling and buying behavior? What areas are overlooked or considered unimportant?. Answers to these questions would provide us the heuristics used by the sales managers for categorizing salespersons and customers. These heuristics when combined with the behavioral model will allow IAISP to determine the primary predominant category of a salesperson's selling behavior and a customer's buying behavior. Primary predominant behavior category is the category which determines a salesperson's selling behavior in most salesperson-customer interactions. It further establishes their lowest unfilled personal need.

4 Areas Related to Selling and Buying Behavior

In order to determine the answer to the questions outlined in the previous section, it is important to focus on the factors which affect the selling behavior of salespersons and buying behavior of customers.

Accordingly, in the knowledge acquisition exercise different areas for gauging salesperson's selling behavior and customer's buying behavior were determined (see Fig.6) based on the discussion with sales managers and knowledge available in the literature[1, 7, 8]. The number of customer areas is limited because the

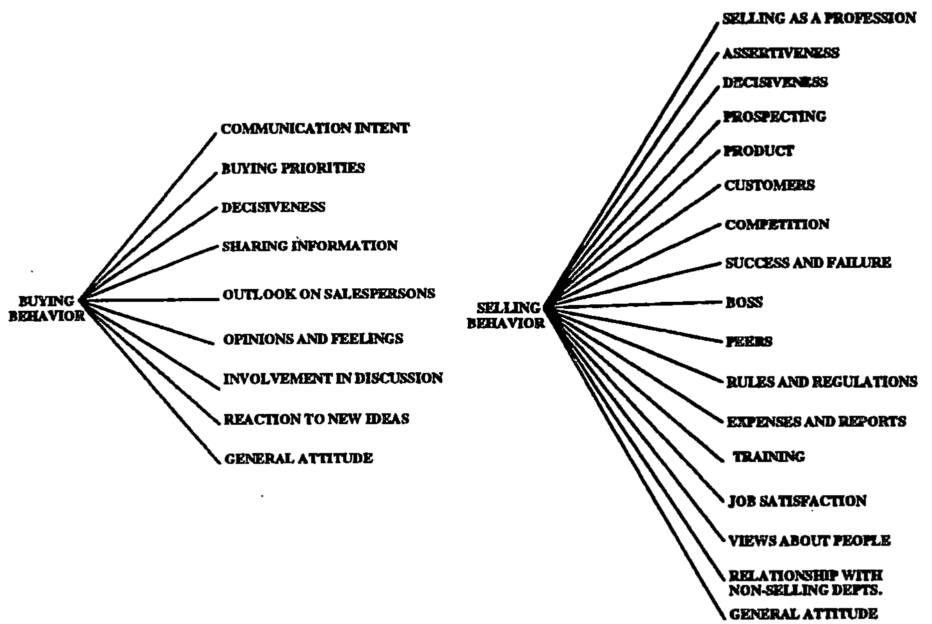

Fig.6: Related areas for gauging selling and buying behaviors

feedback on the customer has to be taken from the salesperson and the limited
duration of the salesperson-customer interaction. In order to quantify the varying degree of importance attached to the different areas of selling and buying
behavior by the domain experts, weights have been assigned to them on a scale
of 1 to 10.

After determining the different areas and their weights, attributes related
to each of these areas with respect to different behavioral categories have been
determined. The attributes of each of these areas have been designed in the form
of questions. For each area there are at least four questions (one belonging to
each behavior category). The questions are designed with five answer options to
provide for snap answers. The other parameters which have been kept in view
while designing the questions are a) What is going to be the tone of various
questions? b) What is going to be the length of each question? c) What is going
to be the total number of questions? d) What is going to be the ordering of the
five answer options? e) What is going to be the pattern of questions?

The latter question is likely to get more affirmative answers from DH salespersons than the former. The questions for customers have been designed on
similar lines except that questions are more direct. This is so because the feedback given by the salesperson is related to a third person.

5 Refining Selling and Buying Behavior Knowledge

For the purpose of improving the qualitative (questions) and quantitative (weights)
knowledge, salesperson and customer questionnaires were developed [2] . Feed-

back was taken from salespersons on themselves and on their interactions with customers through these questionnaires and personal interviews. This process of developing questionnaire and getting feedback was repeated several times. The final salesperson and customer questionnaires contain 76 and 60 questions respectively. The number of questions had to be thus limited because the salespersons said that they could not maintain their concentration towards the end and their answers are likely to be misleading. The feedback also prompted us to have questions contradicting each other wherever possible, in order to ascertain commitment and consistency in answers. Thus the questionnaires and feedback helped us to a) mimic the way in which IAISP takes information from the salesperson, b) refine all aspects of questions as listed out in section 4, c) refine the weightages, d) derive the heuristics required for determining the primary behavioral category of the salesperson's selling and customer's buying behavior, and e) determine heuristics for pruning out contradictory(secondary or masked) and superfluous answers. Superfluous answers are those answers which relate to a personal need level higher than the lowest unfilled need.

6 Selling and Buying Behavior Analysis

Understanding the analysis done by the sales manager on the various factors is one matter, expecting an interactive system to do a reasonably accurate analysis of salesperson and customer behavior based on these factors is another.

6.1 Selling Behavior Analysis

Selling behavior analysis was carried out on the feedback given by the salesperson on themselves. This analysis was carried out to determine the primary behavioral category of the salesperson. An answering pattern was determined based on accumulated answer score to all the questions in each behavioral category. The accumulated answer score of a salesperson in each behavioral category on all the questions was calculated using the formula

$$\Sigma_{i=1}^{i=17}[AreaWeight_i * AnsweringOptionPercentageWeight]$$

The selling behavior analysis of a typical salesperson has been done in two parts.

Firstly, the initial predominant category is determined based on a set of heuristics (typical one shown in Fig.8) which are derived from the answering patterns of salespersons on themselves and the feeling (opinion) of the sales manager (domain expert) who deals with or supervises the salespersons giving feedback. A detailed discussion on analysis of the feedback patterns is given in [2].

Once the initial predominant category has been determined, it is necessary to prune out the contradictory answers to clearly establish the primary behavioral category of the salesperson. The four criteria chosen for pruning out the contradictions and masked answers are. a) personal need level (based on Abraham Maslow's model), b) salesperson's initial predominant category, c) domain

```
IF
        max (score DH,  score SH,  score SW,  score DW) = score DW
    AND
        score DW / Total score  < 0.65
THEN
        Pursue  max ( score DH,   score SH,   score SW, )

IF
        Pursued category  = DH
    AND
        score SH  / score DH    > 0.6
        score (SW + DW) / score (DH + DW)   <= 0.9
        score (SH + SW) / score (DH + DW)   >= 0.7
THEN
        Pursue  max (score SH,  score SW)
```

Fig.8 : A typical salesperson categorization heuristic

expert's feeling on what sorts of contradictory answers, salespersons with a particular initial predominant category engage in, and d)account for secondary or
masked behavior (based on the behavioral model).

```
"In sales law of the jungle prevails. It's you or the competitor. You relish
 beating your competitor with every available weapon."
(DH Category)
            Answer - Yes
"You do not believe in being aggressive towards you competitors. Competitors
 are people like you and there is room for everybody."
(SW Category)
            Answer - Yes
"You may not be aggressive otherwise. But when it comes to competition you are
 just the opposite. You spend good deal of your time to explain to the customer why
 he should not buy from the competitor."
(SH Category)
            Answer -  No
"You cannot take your place for granted nor can you apply the 'law of the jungle'
 principle. The best hope to outsell competitors is by keeping abreast of competitive
 activity, and demonstrating the net gain the customer will derive from buying your product."
(DW Category)
            Answer - Yes
```

Fig.9: An example of contradictory answers on Salesperson categorization

An example shown in Fig.9 in the area of competition will explain the use of
the above mentioned criteria.

Assume the salesperson has been initially predominantly categorized as DH
type. The affirmative answer to the SW question is a clear contradiction to the
affirmative answer to the DH question. Since the salesperson has been initially
predominantly categorized as a DH type, the affirmative answer to the SW

question is a masked answer based on the behavioral model and is pruned out from the salesperson's score in the SW category. However, if the answer to the SH question had been 'Yes', then the affirmative answer to the DH category would have been treated as a masked answer and pruned out; this would have resulted in lowering the score of the DH category. This is so because the domain experts feel that such salespersons are not intense DH salespersons and have a substantial element of SH category in their behavior which should be reflected by such a pruning.

The personal need level of a DH type is lower than a DW type. The affirmative answer to the DW question is thus a superfluous answer since if a lower need level is unfilled then upper need level is likely to be unfilled too. Hence, the DW answer is pruned out of a salesperson's score in the DW category.

In case, the salesperson had answered 'No' to the DH question and 'Yes' to others, the answer with the lowest need level (i.e. SH) would have been considered as the correct answer, and the other answers pruned out.

The extent or range of pruning varies from 70% to 100% according to the area the question belongs to and according to the extent of contradiction which has been achieved between the set of questions in that area. The pruning process only considers the 'Yes' and 'To a large extent yes' answers. It is possible that after pruning out the contradictions the scores of two adjacent categories may lie close to each other. This reflects the transitory nature of the need level. For example, scores of SH (security needs) and SW (social needs) category may lie close to each other.

6.2 Customer Buying Behavior Analysis

When asked about themselves, the salespersons come across as complex beings, but when asked their opinion on a third person, they are likely to come out with clear and decisive answers. For this reason, the customer analysis proved a lot more straightforward.

There are fewer heuristics involved in establishing customer's initial predominant category as compared to the ones used in the initial predominant categorization of salespersons.

Since it is difficult to ascertain from the feedback whether the contradiction in the answers is due to secondary or masked behavior of the customer or confusion in the mind of the responding salesperson, here we have relied on the customer's initial predominant category and the personal need level for pruning.

Based on the selling and buying behavior analysis, unpruned and pruned salesperson and customer behavioral profiles are shown by IAISP to the user Typical salesperson and customer behavioral profiles are shown in Figs. 10 and 11 respectively.

7 Adaptive Knowledge

The pruned salesperson and customer behavioral profiles provide a clear picture to the salesperson on their and customer's primary behavioral category.These pruned behavioral profiles are also shown in the form of a probability chart (Fig. 12) to help the salesperson make the decision on the salesperson-customer combination they would like to pursue. Based on a particular combination, general and specific advice is given to the salesperson to adapt their selling behavior.

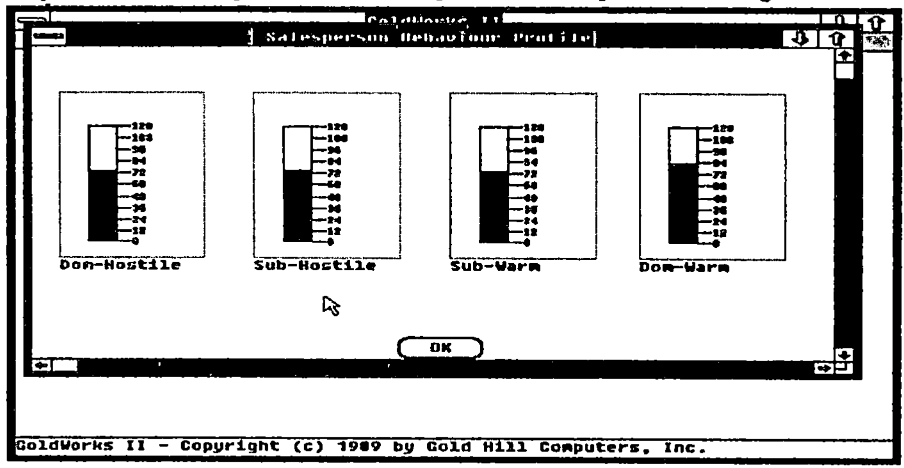

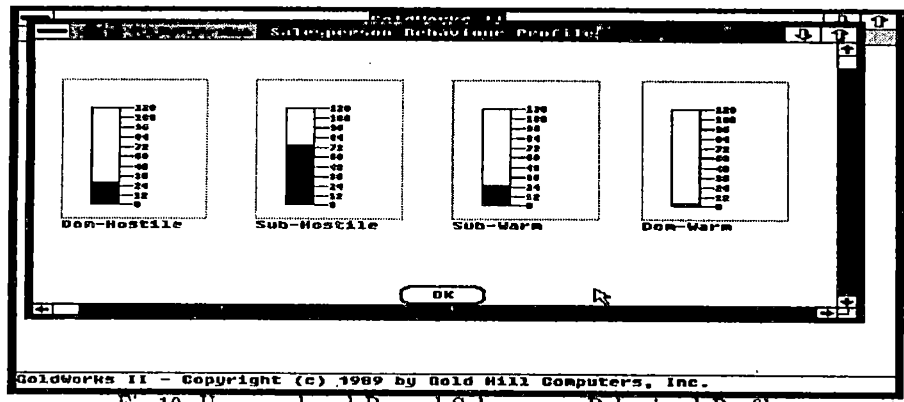

Fig.10: Unpruned and Pruned Salesperson Behavioral Profile

The general recommendations include i) general characteristics of a particular customer type; ii) how a particular customer type expresses his needs ,and iii) in general, how to establish benefits with a particular customer type.[2] The specific recommendations are given for each affirmative answer given by the salesperson while giving feedback on the customer for questions which are related to customer's primary behavioral or predominant category. The general and specific recommendations are expected to give enough information to the salesperson not only on the 'why' of customer's buying behavior but also on how to adapt to that buying behavior to maximize sales results.

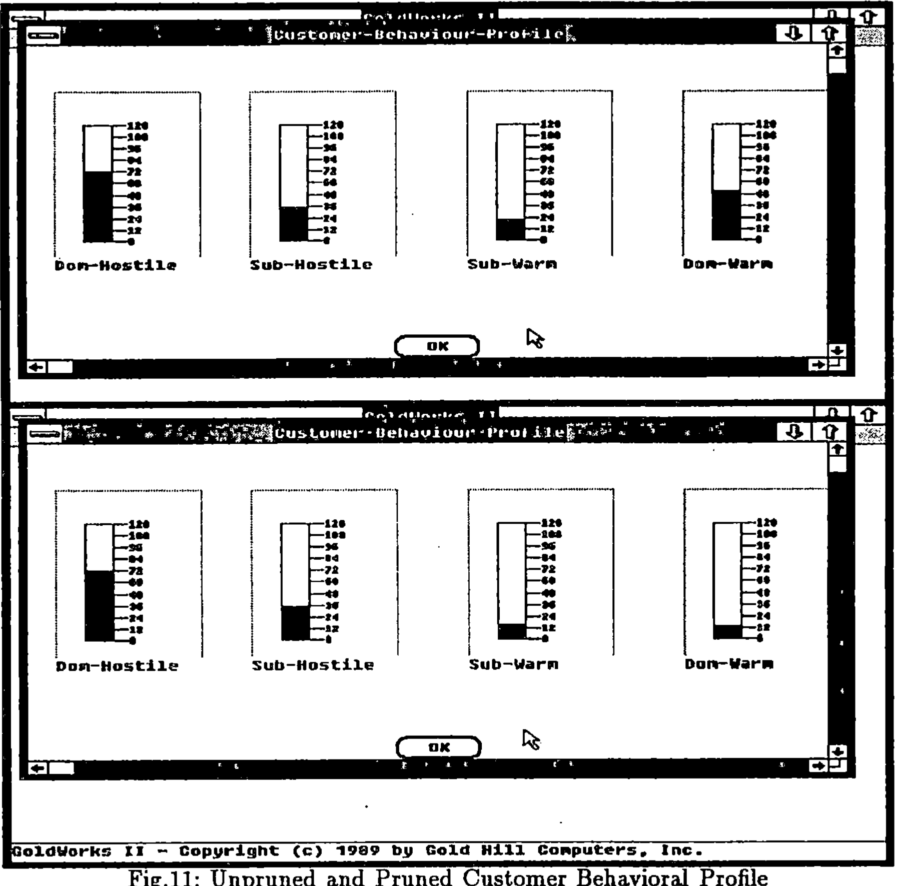

Fig.11: Unpruned and Pruned Customer Behavioral Profile

8 Implementation

Goldworks II, an expert system shell with hybrid(frames and rules) representational environment, written in common Lisp has been used for building IAISP. There are about 40 frames and 500 rules written in 20 different rule sets or groups. Forward chaining is adopted as the inferencing as it mimics the processing of information by the domain experts and the salespersons.

For the purpose of taking information from and having an interactive dialogue with the salesperson, various types of popup menus like confirm, choose, ask user and, text menus(about 200 in all) have been built. Knowledge explanation mechanisms have also been built. For more implementation details see[3, 2].

A flow chart of a typical interactive session between a salesperson and IAISP is shown in Fig.13. For recruiting purposes steps 1 to 4 will be followed where the candidate salesperson will only go through steps 1 and 2. The information related to steps 3 and 4 will be provided to the management as an independent feedback prior to or after the interview. Thus, the management has additional information based on variety of factors to enable it to improve quality of its

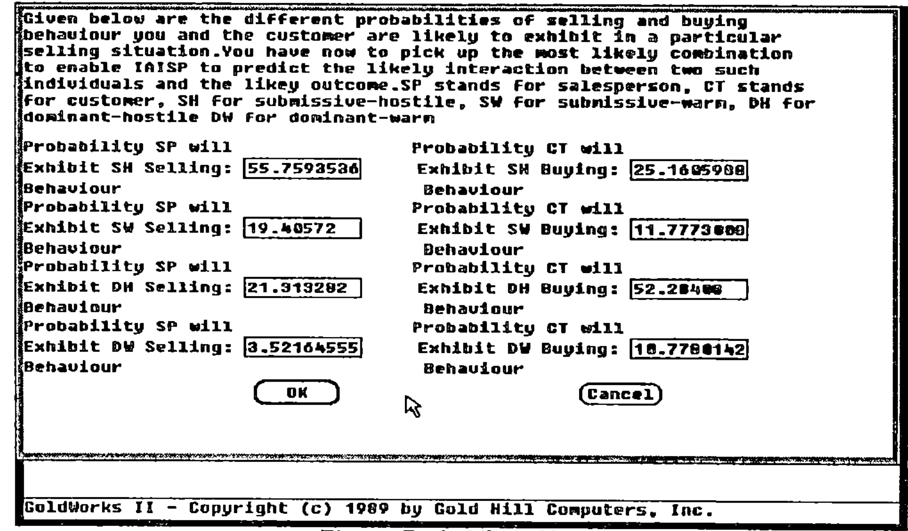

Fig.12: Probability Chart

recruiting decision. For purpose of training, steps 1 to 12 will be followed by the salesperson. In case salesperson has previously categorized themselves, they can start from (at their option) step 6.

9 Conclusion

In this paper we have reported on various aspects of the knowledge acquisition and analysis which have gone into the development of IAISP. We have shown how the synthesis of the knowledge engineering techniques and psychology can be effectively used to improve the quality of decision making for recruiting salespersons and also assist in training salespersons. Such a synthesis can be also be used in other domains where human behavior forms an important component of decision making or job performance. Up to now IAISP has been field tested on about 80 salespersons. The results are encouraging. About 80 percent of categorizations of salespersons done by IAISP have been correct. In the balance 20 percent the pruned profiles lay too close between two categories (possibly indicating transitory nature of the need level) for the IAISP to decide on one. In no case to date has the pruned profile been off the mark. The categorization has been validated with the salespersons themselves and their sales managers (wherever possible). Industry stands to benefit from using IAISP in the following ways a) It can be used to assist the interviewing process for recruitment of salespersons. It can give an independent feedback to the management on the selling behavior and training needs of the salesperson. It will bring uniformity in application of recruitment procedures and improve the quality of decision making, b) IAISP can be used as a desk tool by salespersons(especially in remote locations) for improving their interpersonal skills. Repetitive and uninhibitive use of IAISP will ingrain these special skills in the salesperson and will shorten the training cycle, c) Because of the nature of the problem it deals with, IAISP has an extremely wide application base, d) IAISP can be integrated with any system which configures task needs and provide comprehensive support to the

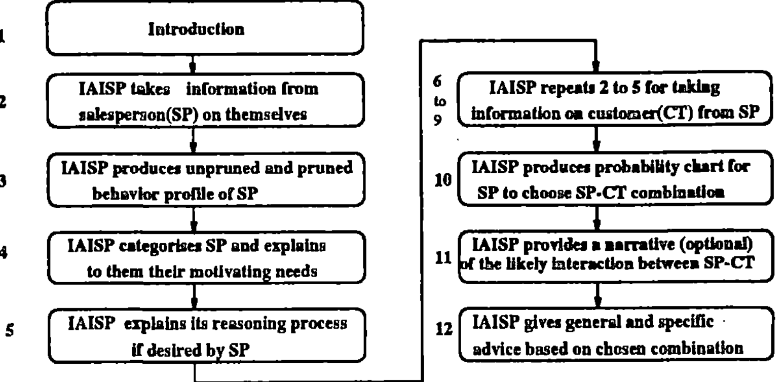

Fig.13: Typical Interactive session with a salesperson

salesperson at the personal and task need level. Besides being used interactively, it can be used for building up a historical database on personal needs of different customers for future use, and f)] When put together, the benefits above can improve the effectiveness of the sales/service and support management functions and can help organizations gain a competitive edge.

Acknowledgments

The authors thankfully acknowledge the active support for this project of Mr. Ray Horton, Sales Manager, Siemens Ltd., Mr. Doug Donovan, Sales Manager, President Ford Pty. Ltd(Ford Car dealer), and Hewlett Packard, based in Melbourne, Australia.

References

1. Buzzotte, V. R., Lefton, R. E., Sherberg, M., Effective Selling through Psychology, Psychological Associates, New York, 1981.
2. Khosla, R., "An Intelligent Assistant for Improving Sales Performance", Masters thesis: Department of Computer Science and Computer Engineering, La Trobe University, Melbourne, Australia, June 1991.
3. Khosla, R and Dillon, T, "An Intelligent Assistant for Improving Sales/Customer Service Performance" - IEEE Workshop on Customer Service and Support, San Jose, California, U.S.A, July 1992.
4. Meng, L. S., Busch, P. S., and Roedder, D., "Knowledge Bases and Salesperson's Effectiveness", Journal of Marketing Research, pp. 164-78, May 1989.
5. Oppenheim, A.N., Questionaire Design and Attitude Measurement, Heinemann Educational Books, London, 1966.
6. Sujan, H., Sujan, M., and Bettman, J., "Knowledge Structure Differences Between More Effective and Less Effective Salespeople", Journal of Marketing Research pp. 81-86, 1989
7. Szymanski, David M., (Nov. 1988), "Determinants of Selling Effectiveness: The Importance of Declarative Knowledge to the Personal Selling Concept". The Journal of Marketing Research, pp. 64-77.
8. Weitz, B. A., Sujan, H. and Sujan, M., "Knowledge, Motivation and Adaptive Behavior: A Framework for Improving Selling Effectiveness", Journal of Marketing Research, pp. 174-91, 1986.
9. Goldworks II Manual, GoldHill Computers. Masachusetts, U.S.A., 1989.

PEMOSYS - ein validiertes hybrides Expertensystem zum Pflanzschutzmittel-Monitoring

J. Zhao[*], M. B. Wischnewsky[*], K. Wang[*], I. Novopashenny[*],
W. Pestemer[**], P. Günter[**]

[*] KI-Labor der Universität Bremen
FB Mathematik/Informatik
Bibliothekstr. (MZH)
D-28359 Bremen, FRG

[**] Institut für Ökologische Chemie
Biologische Bundesanstalt
Königin-Luise-Str.
14195 Berlin-Dahlem

Zusammenfassung: Dieses Papier beschreibt die Vorgehensweise und Erfahrungen bei der Entwicklung des hybriden Expertensystems PEMOSYS. Ausgehend von der Charakterisierung der Domäne wird über die Wissensrepräsentation, Systemarchitektur, Integration verschiedener Problemlösungsmethoden, Implementierung und Validierung detailliert diskutiert. Verwendet werden in PEMOSYS modellbasierte, regelbasierte, fallbasierte und tabellengesteuerte Techniken.

1. Einleitung

Unter den derzeitigen ökonomischen Rahmenbedingungen intensiver Pflanzenproduktion kann auf den Einsatz von *Pflanzenschutzmitteln* (=Herbizide, Fungizide, Insektizide und sonstige, Abk.: PSM) in der Landwirtschaft kaum verzichtet werden. Aus ökologischen und ökonomischen Gesichtspunkten ist eine *bestimmungsgemäße* und *sachgerechte* Anwendung von PSM gefordert, um die Ertragsleistungen der Landwirtschaft sicherzustellen und zugleich mögliche Nebenwirkungen auf den Naturhaushalt, eine Schädigung von Nachbaukulturen oder einen potentiellen Eintrag in das Grundwasser zu verhindern. Ausgehend von dieser Situation wurde von dem KI-Labor der Universität Bremen und der Biologischen Bundesanstalt ein Expertensystem zum Pflanzenschutzmittel-Monitoring **PEMOSYS** (**PE**stizid-**MO**nitorings**SYS**tem), entwickelt, das Hilfen zu Auswahl und Einsatz von PSM und zur Beurteilung des Abbau- und Einwaschungsverhaltens sowie Auswirkungen der Rückstände im Boden auf Nachbaukulturen geben soll.

Nach der Vorstellung der *"Guten Fachlichen Praxis"* beinhaltet ein umweltvertretbarer Einsatz von PSM u. a. die Nutzung von Schadenschwellen und einen systemati-

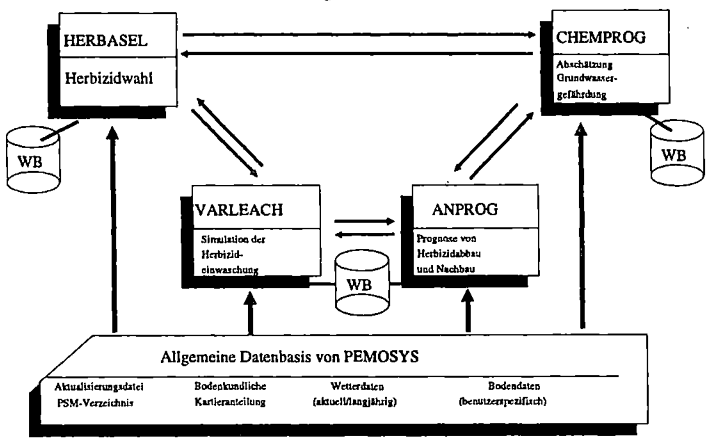

Abb. 1: Die Teilsysteme von PEMOSYS

schen Wirkungswechsel. Eine situationsbezogene, flexible Applikation am jeweiligen Standort ermöglicht eine Optimierung der Anwendertermine und Minimierung der Aufwandmengen. Durch Nutzung von Expertensystemen können dem Anwender Entscheidungshilfen angeboten werden, in denen strukturelles (z. B. Fakten, Regeln, Modelle) und strategisches Wissen (z. B. Erfahrungen, Bewertungsskala, Suchverfahren) bereitgestellt werden. So sollte mit dem Expertensystem PEMOSYS ein Beratungssystem entwickelt werden, das die verschiedenen Aspekte der Beratung, wie

- PSM-Auswahl,
- standortspezifische Abschätzung der Grundwassergefährdung,
- Prognose von PSM-Abbau und Nachbausicherheit sowie
- Einwaschung im Bearbeitungshorizont,

in die Teilkomponenten HERBASEL, CHEMPROG, ANPROG und VARLEACH gliedert (sh. Abb. 1).

2. Architekturen der wissensbasierten Module

Aufgrund der unterschiedlichen Charaktere von Problemstellungen sind zwangsläufig *hybride* Paradigmen zu verwenden. Für die Teilsysteme ANPROG und VARLEACH ist das Wissen weitgehend modellbasiert: Differentialgleichungen beschreiben die (verteilten) Abbauprozesse. Mit Methoden der numerischen Simulation lassen sich die (verteilten) Abbaukurven numerisch ermitteln.

2.1 ANPROG und VARLEACH

Die Systemarchitektur und Bildschirm-Layout von ANPROG und VARLEACH zeigen die Abbildungen 2 und 3.

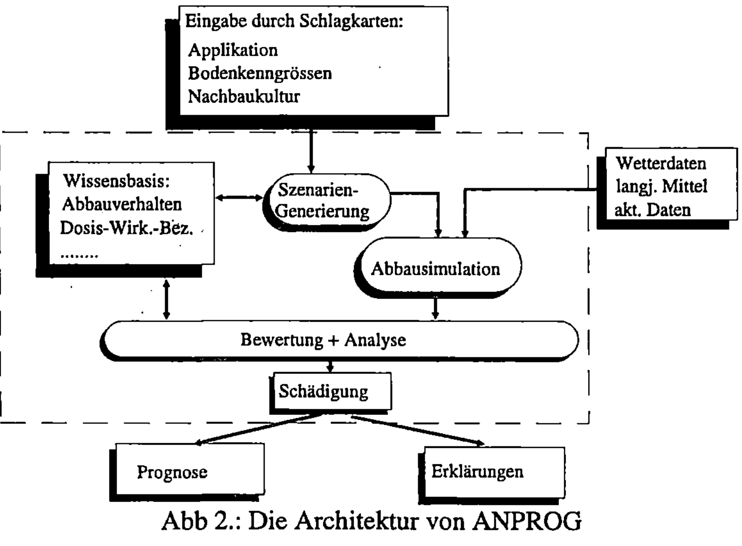

Abb 2.: Die Architektur von ANPROG

Die Prognose des PSM-Abbaus erfolgt mit dem von [WALKER und BARNES 1981] beschriebenen PSM-Abbausimulationsmodell (einem linearen Differentialgleichungs-

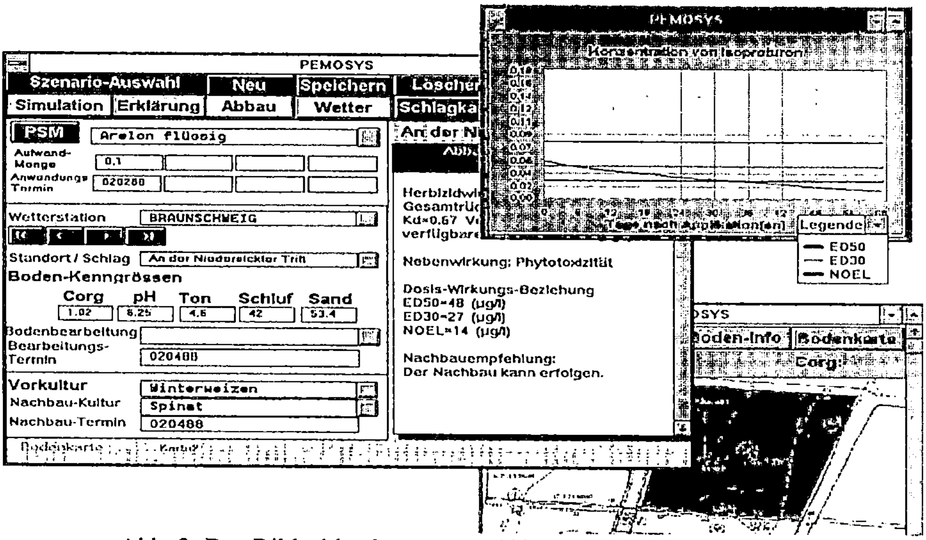

Abb. 3: Das Bildschirmlayout von ANPROG und VARLEACH

system, sh. [Zhao et. al. 1992]). Die Linearität besagt, daß die Multiplikation eines konstanten Faktors mit dem Systeminput auch zu einer Veränderung des Outputs um den gleichen Faktor führt. Diese Eigenschaft kann zu unterschiedlichen Fragestellungen: Input (I)/Output (O)-Mustern, führen (sh. Tab. 1).

Vorgabe	Antwort
feste Vorgabe: PSM-Wahl Applikationsdatum	
Aufwandmenge, Nachbautermin Nachbaukultur ⟶	Nachbauprognose Ertragssicherheit
Aufwandmenge Nachbaukultur ⟶	Prognose des frühest möglichen Nachbaus, Berücksichtigung der Praxisanbautermine
Aufwandmenge, Nachbautermin ⟶	Auswahl d. zu diesem Zeitpunkt sicher anzubauenden Kulturen
Aufwandmenge ⟶	Angabe der sicheren Nachbau- termine für die verschiedenen Nachbaukulturen, Berücksichti- gung der Praxisanbautermine
Nachbautermin Nachbaukultur ⟶	Verringerte Aufwandmenge, bei der keine Schädigung zu erwarten ist
Nachbautermin ⟶	Nur Abbausimulation ohne Nachbauprognose

Tabelle 1: Verschiedene Fragestellungen in ANPROG

Die errechneten Rückstandsgehalte, sowie die errechneten Bodenfeuchtigkeits- und Bodentemperaturwerte werden für jeden Tag des Simulationszeitraumes in einer externen Datei gespeichert und können vom Benutzer über die verschiedenen Output-Optionen von PEMOSYS (Graphik, Text, Farben in der Schlagkarte) ausgegeben werden.

Generierung von Simulationsszenarien in ANPROG und VARLEACH

Vor dem Aufruf des Simulators werden die Eingangsdaten (Abbauparameter, standortspezifische Daten) mit Hilfe der *fallvergleichenden Klassifikation* ermittelt.

Die fallvergleichende Klassifikation unterscheidet sich prinzipiell von allen anderen Wissensarten, da ihr Wissen weniger auf einer Abstraktion von Fallwissen beruht, sondern ein neuer Fall direkt mit abgespeicherten Fällen einer Datenbank verglichen wird ([PUPPE 1990]).

Die bekannten Fälle enthalten jeweils Merkmalausprägungen und die zugehörige Lösung. Entsprechend den Merkmalausprägungen wird mittels einer Distanzfunktion mit einem Matching-Verfahren der ähnlichste Fall in der Datenbank gesucht und dessen Wert zur Lösung des anstehenden Problems (z. B. geeignete Simulationsparameter) übernommen. Zur Festlegung der Ähnlichkeit ist ein Ähnlichkeitsmaß und im allgemeinen Zusatzwissen erforderlich.

Bei der fallvergleichenden Klassifikation ist ein Optimierungsprozeß eingebettet, denn das Ähnlichkeitsmaß induziert eine zu optimierende Zielfunktion, die die Lösungsmöglichkeiten anordnet.

Beispiele: Parameterwahl in ANPROG

Aus den Literaturdaten (z. B. [PESTEMER und AUSPURG 1987]) sowie Untersuchungen der Biologischen Bundesanstalt (BBA) wurden bisher für ca. 30 PSM bei mehr als 90 verschiedenen PSM-Bodenkombinationen Abbauparameter (E_a, A, B) für das Simulationsmodell zusammengestellt. Mit den wichtigsten Daten über Eigenschaften und Zusammensetzung der Böden (Gehalt an organischem Kohlenstoff [C_{org}], pH-Wert [pH], Tongehalt [Ton]), in denen die Abbauparameter ermittelt wurden, sind die Abbauparameter in einer Datei in Faktenform

$$EAB(PSM, C_{org}, Ton, pH, E_a, A, B)$$

gespeichert.

Liegen mehrere Abbaukonstanten für ein PSM vor, werden anhand der Bodenparameter aus dem vorhandenen Datensatz die E_a-, A- und B-Parameter der entsprechenden PSM-Bodenkombination ausgewählt, bei der sich die Böden - in dem die Konstanten ermittelt wurden und für den die Simulation durchgeführt werden soll - am ähnlichsten sind.

Bei der Auswahlstrategie wird zunächst eine Teilmenge M aus dem Datensatz der Wissensbasis - orientiert am PSM-Wirkstoff - gebildet:

$$M = \{EAB(H[PSM], C[C_{org}], T[Ton], P[pH\text{-Wert}], E_a, A, B)|H = Wirkstoff\}.$$

Mittels einer gewichteten Distanzfunktion, bei der der Tongehalt und der Gehalt des Bodens an organischem Kohlenstoff als wichtigste Auswahlgrößen definiert sind, werden die Abbaukonstanten nach dem Kriterium der geringsten Abweichung der Parameter (C_{org}, Ton, pH) ausgewählt:

$$Minimum [d((C_{org}, Ton, pH), (C, T, P))$$
$$= 0{,}3 * abs((C_{org} -C)/C) + 0{,}6 * abs((Ton - T)/T) + 0{,}1 * abs((pH - P)/P)].$$

Mit unterschiedlichen Gewichtungsfaktoren wird die gleiche Methode auch bei der Auswahl von Sorptionskonstanten (K_d-*Werten*) angewendet, aus denen die potentielle Pflanzenverfügbarkeit der PSM-Rückstände abgeleitet wird.

2.2 CHEMPROG

Das Modul CHEMPROG führt für die ausgewählten PSM eine Abschätzung der potentiellen Grundwassergefährdung durch. Die Bewertung erfolgt durch eine *Scoring-Klassifikation*, d. h. Symptome oder Merkmale - in diesem Fall physikalisch-chemische Kenndaten der Wirkstoffe und deren Verhalten im Boden - werden den Auswertungspunkten zugeordnet. Diese Punkte werden zur Diagnose durch die jeweiligen Bewertungsverfahren verwendet, die mittels Klassifikationsregeln repräsentiert sind (siehe Abbildung 4). Eine Scoring-Klassifikation eignet sich für Klassifikationsprobleme, bei denen fundiertes (statistisches) Erfahrungswissen verfügbar ist.

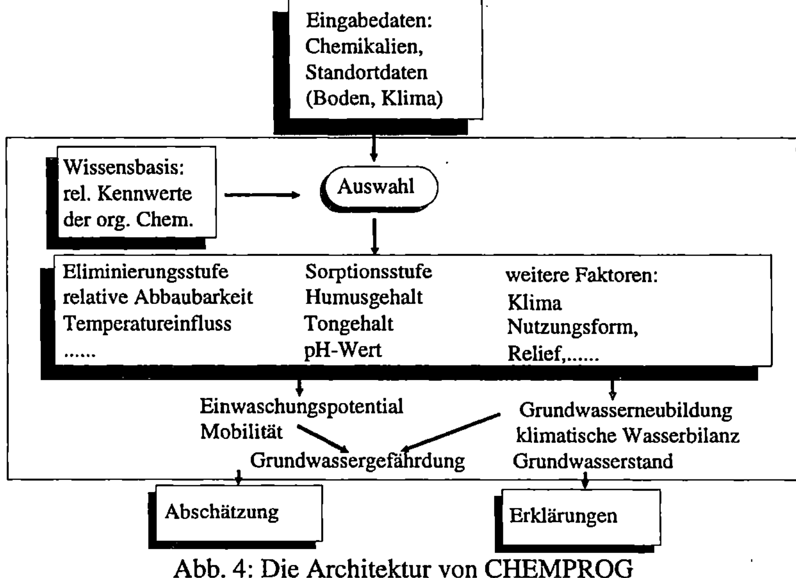

Abb. 4: Die Architektur von CHEMPROG

Zur Überprüfung bzw. Verfeinerung der Diagnose wird die Scoring-Klassifikation in CHEMPROG durch die Teilkomponente VARLEACH - eine Simulation des Einwaschungsverhaltens von PSM mit dem von [WALKER 1987] modifizierten Einwaschungsmodell (CALF, **Calculation Flow**) - ergänzt. Dieses Leaching-Modell ermöglicht eine numerische Berechnung der zeitlichen und vertikalen Rückstandsverteilung von PSM im Bodenprofil.

2.3 HERBASEL

Das *PSM-Selektionsmodul* HERBASEL bietet dem Landwirt nach seinen speziellen Anforderungen (Suchbedingungen) eine Liste von zugelassenen Präparaten, Tankmischungen und Splitting-Verfahren zur Auswahl an. Die Suchbedingungen können durch die *Kultur, Anwendungszeiten, Einschränkungen* (z. B. Wasserschutz-gebiet), *zu bekämpfende Unkräuter*, aber auch eine allgemeine *Strategie* kombiniert werden. Die PSM-Daten werden in einer relationalen Datenbank abgespeichert und zur Aktualisierung von fachspezifischen Experten (Herbologen) verwaltet. Alle wichtigen fachkundigen Informationen (Eigenschaften) über ein PSM werden in entsprechenden Feldern repräsentiert. Diese Datenbank dient zur effizienten Repräsentation von Faktenwissen über PSM und gleichfalls als Schnittstelle zu anderen Anwendungen. Das zentrale Problem ist die Kopplung dieser Datenbank mit Inferenzmechanismen.

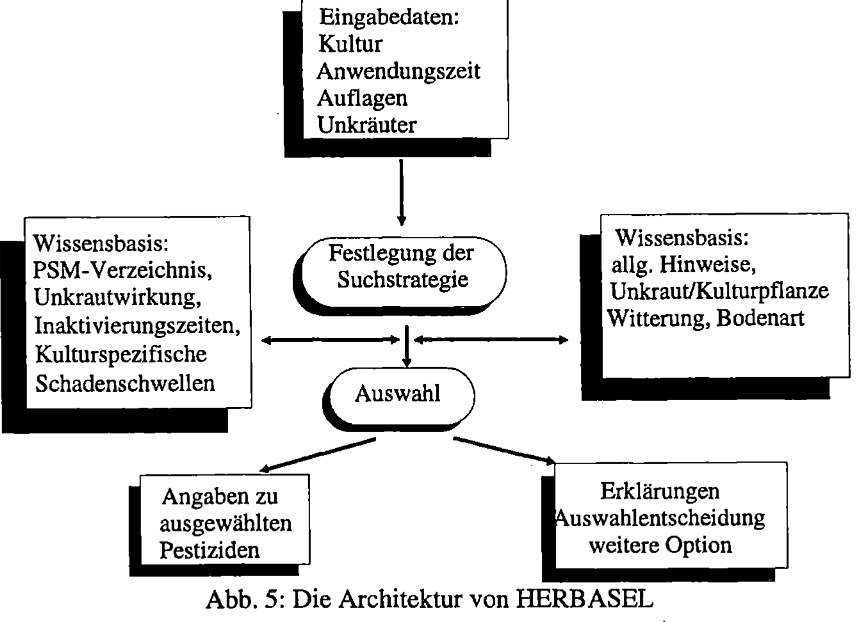

Abb. 5: Die Architektur von HERBASEL

Die in HERBASEL benötigte Inferenzstrategie besteht hauptsächlich aus einer unifikationsbasierten Rückwärtsverkettung. Hier wird die Aufgabe für die Unifikationen von dem Pattern-Match in der Datenbank übernommen. Zur Effizienzsteigerung werden einige Felder in der Datenbank indiziert, damit bei der Datenbank-Kopplung die Inferenzzeit nicht zu sehr belastet wird. Grundsätzlich lassen sich bei der Verbindung relationaler Datenbanken mit KBMS zwei verschiedene Ansätze bezüglich der Kopplungsrealisierung unterscheiden (vgl. [Karagiannis 94]): der Assoziierte Ansatz und der Integrative Ansatz.

Für die Datenbank-Kopplung in HERBASEL wurde der Integrative Ansatz verwendet. Bei der Implementierung unterscheidet man lose Kopplungen (Loose Coupling) und enge Kopplungen (Tight Coupling). Eine lose Kopplung kann dann erfolgreich angewandt werden, wenn sich ein Vergleich zwischen dem zur Verfügung stehenden Arbeitsspeicher und der aus der Datenbank zu extrahierenden Datenmenge durchführen läßt. Da sich diese Anforderung im praktischen Einsatz von PEMOSYS nur schwer erfüllen läßt, haben wir bei der Implementierung von HERBASEL eine enge Kopplung bevorzugt, die erst dann Bestandteile der Datenbasis anfordert, wenn diese zur Beweisführung benötigt werden.

Zur Situationsunterscheidung dient die *gesteuerte Suche*, d. h. die Suche nach PSM kann durch verschiedene Strategien gesteuert werden.

Als Beispiele solcher Suchstrategien mögen folgende Verfahren dienen:

- Zur Suche nach ähnlich wirkenden PSM müssen alle wichtigen Eigenschaften der Präparate verglichen werden.

- Zur Suche nach Präparaten, die die vom Benutzer vorgegebenen Restriktionen erfüllen, müssen diese Restriktionen bei der Suche strikt eingehalten werden.

Nach der Situationserkennung wird jeweils ein zutreffender Suchalgorithmus aktiviert. Nach Festlegung der Suchstrategie durch Eingabedaten zu Kultur, Anwendungszeit, Einschränkungen und von maximal fünf Unkräutern erfolgt die Auswahl der PSM bzw. Mischungen aus der Datenbasis. Die Auswahl von Präparaten bzw. der Kombinationen, die die Unkräuter am effizientesten bekämpfen, geschieht mit Hilfe der *kombinatorischen Optimierung*. Eine Funktion bewertet die Bekämpfungseffizienz. Das Wissen über die Bekämpfungseffizienz von PSM gegenüber verschiedenen Unkräutern wurde in der Form einer Präparate/Bekämpfungsgrade-Matrix mit dem normierten Wertebereich in [0,1] repräsentiert. Die Elemente der Matrix bilden die Bekämpfungskoeffizienten. Die Zielfunktion ist die Summe der Effizienzfaktoren bezüglich der gesuchten PSM zur Bekämpfung der angegebenen Unkräuter.

Beispiel (PSM-Auswahl)

Die Suchbedingungen werden durch die Einschränkungen definiert:

Kultur:	Winterweizen
Anwendungszeit:	Nachauflauf
Einschränkungen:	237 (Keine Anwendung in Zuflußbereichen von Grund- und Quellwassergewinnungsanlagen, Heilquellen und Trinkwassersperren sowie sonstigen grundwasserempfindlichen Bereichen.)
Unkräuter:	Windhalm, Kamille

Mit der Berücksichtigung des Schadenschwellenprinzips wird eine nach Bekämpfungskoeffizienten angeordnete Präparate-Liste erzeugt. **Tolkan Super (X)** steht an der Spitze.

2.4 Anwendung von Hypermedia-Techniken in PEMOSYS

Konventionelle Umgebungen für die Wissensrepräsentation erlauben die Eingabe von Wissen in Form von Symbolen. Diese Eingabe hat zwei Arten von Semantik (sh. [Karbach/Linster 90]):

- das Verständnis desjenigen, der mit dem System arbeitet (Experte, Knowledge Engineer und Benutzer) und der gewisse Erwartungen mit der Benennung der Symbole verknüpft, und

- die Benutzung der Symbole durch den Rechner, d. h. das, was das System mit den Symbolen macht.

In der Wissensakquisition beschäftigt man sich im wesentlichen mit der Kodierung von Wissen in Symbolen.

Da Experte und Benutzer in der Regel nicht dieselbe Person sind, wird bei der Benutzung des Wissens häufig die Frage gestellt, welches Wissen durch diese Symbole dargestellt wird. Der konventionelle Weg besteht darin, diese Unklarheit durch sogenannte in-line-Dokumentation zu beseitigen. Allerdings hat dies ([Karbach/Linster 90]) zwei wesentliche Nachteile:

- die in-line-Dokumentation ist auf recht knappe Texte beschränkt,
- der Anschluß zu dem Wissen, das die Grundlage für die Regel war, ist verlorengegangen, insbesondere wenn dieses Wissen in Form der Graphiken, Bilder oder Filmsequenzen vorhanden war, bevor es für das Expertensystem kodiert wurde.

In PEMOSYS wurde diese Problematik bei der Phase Wissensakquisition aufgegriffen. Z. B., für die Erkennung von bestimmten Unkräutern sind symbolische Regeln allein nicht ausreichend. Dies motivierte uns, bei der Repräsentation von Wissen auch zusammenhängende Informationsblöcke wie Schlagkarten, Diagramme und Bilder von Unkräutern als Informationsknoten in einer Datenbank abzulegen.

3. Integration von Problemlösungsmethoden in PEMOSYS

Die o.g. vier wissensbasierten Komponenten werden mit einer Architektur der Gleichordnung miteinander verbunden (Abb. 6).

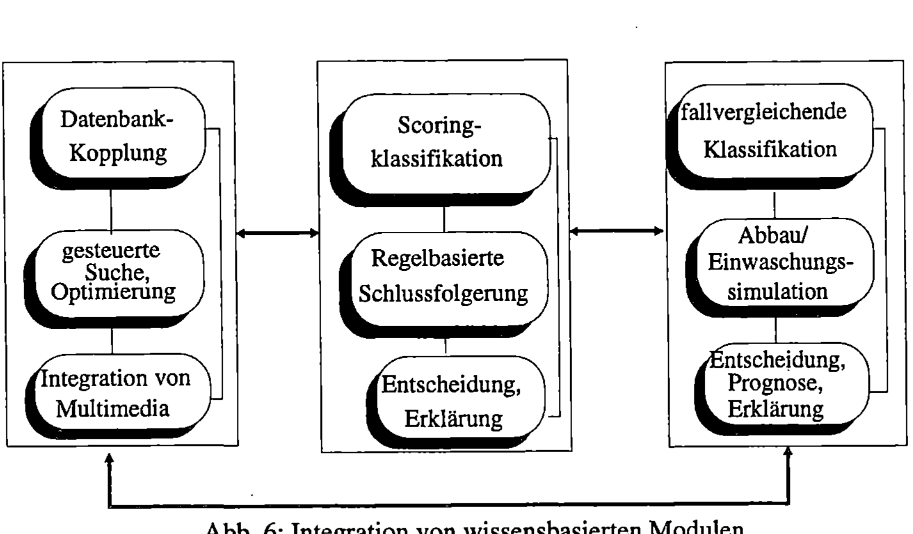

Abb. 6: Integration von wissensbasierten Modulen

Bei der wechselseitigen Ergänzung der Problemlösung wurde der *kooperierende Ansatz* gewählt, d. h. *"das Gesamtsystem zerfällt in unterschiedliche Teilprobleme, die am zweckmäßigsten mit verschiedenartigen Problemlösungsmethoden (regelbasiert, modellbasiert,...) behandelt werden"* (vgl. [Puppe 90]).
Dieser Ansatz gilt teilweise auch für verschiedene Problemlösungsphasen innerhalb einer gleichen Problemklasse. Z. B. werden bei der Problemklasse Klassifikation die Verdachtsgenerierung heuristisch und die Verdachtsüberprüfung (mit Simulationsmethoden) modellbasiert gelöst. Aus den Resultaten einer Problemlösungsstrategie ergeben sich häufig die Eingangsdaten für die nachfolgende Problemlösungsphase.

Wie man in Abb. 2 sieht, entspricht die Architektur von ANPROG und VARLEACH der eines Intelligent Front Ends (IFE) (vgl. [Mertens 92]).

Ein IFE ist eine benutzerfreundliche Oberfläche zu einem Softwarepaket. Diese Benutzeroberfläche sollte zur Reduzierung der Diskrepanz zwischen der Aufgabespezifikation durch den Benutzer (Front) und dieser von dem Softwarepaket (Ends) dienen. Insofern wird ein IFE selbst oft als ein Expertensystem oder zumindest als eine wissensbasierte Komponente betrachtet.

Ein IFE besteht aus einem *Zugangssystem*, einem *Simulator* und einem *Abgangssystem*. Das Zugangssystem bildet ein Modell für den Benutzer-Dialog. Als eine wissensbasierte Komponente *(fallvergleichende Klassifikation)* generiert das Zugangssystem geeignete Szenarien, die geeignete Simulationen auslösen.

Ein Simulator als ein eigenständiger Prozeß hat lediglich die Aufgabe, einen gegebenen Anfangszustand des Modells mittels einer Simulation in einen Endzustand überzuführen, wobei eventuell zusätzliche Datenaufzeichnungen und Protokollierungen von Zustandsübergängen während des Ablaufs der Simulation notwendig sind.

Die Simulationsergebnisse werden an das Abgangssystem weitergeleitet, das diese Ergebnisse intelligent auswertet und interpretiert. Dieses Abgangssystem entspricht in PEMOSYS einer *Erklärungskomponente*. Diese Komponente dient zur *qualitativen Erklärung*, die die numerischen Simulationsergebnisse in die übliche fachkundige Umgangsprache umwandelt (numerische Daten werden in qualitative Fachausdrücke abgebildet). Zusätzlich werden zur Unterstützung der *quantitativen Erklärung* Text- und Graphikdarstellungen zur Rechtfertigung der Ergebnisse verwendet.

4. Blackboard-Architekur des Gesamtsystems

Die Basiskomponenten eines Blackborad-Modells sind bekanntlich (sh. z.B. [Fathi 94]):

- die Wissensquellen: Das für die Lösung eines Problems notwendige Wissen ist in funktional unabhängige Module, die Wissensquellen (ANPROG, VARLEACH, HERBASEL und CHEMPROG), unterteilt. Dies impliziert eine modulare Architektur von PEMOSYS.

- die Blackboard-Datenstruktur: Die Daten und Informationen zum Zustand der Problemlösung werden in einer globalen, strukturierten Datenbasis, dem Blackboard, verwaltet. Die Wissensquellen verändern die Einträge des Blackboards und erzeugen so schrittweise eine Problemlösung. Das Blackboard ist einziges Kommunikationsmedium der Wissensquellen. Der Austausch von Informationen zwischen Wissensquellen erfolgt ausschließlich indirekt über das Blackboard.

In PEMOSYS werden Lösungen einer Wissensquelle über das Blackboard in andere Wissensquellen hineinfließen. Z.B. die in HERBASEL gefundenen PSM werden in ANPROG übernommen. Nach der Prognose der Nachbaurisiken (ökonomischer Aspekt) wird CHEMPROG zur Überprüfung der Umweltverträglichkeit (qualitativer Beurteilung) des PSM-Einsatzes und ggf. auch VARLEACH zur quantitativen Überprüfung aktiviert (ökologischer Aspekt). Wenn negative Beurteilungen vorliegen, werden wieder in HERBASEL entsprechende Alternativen gesucht.

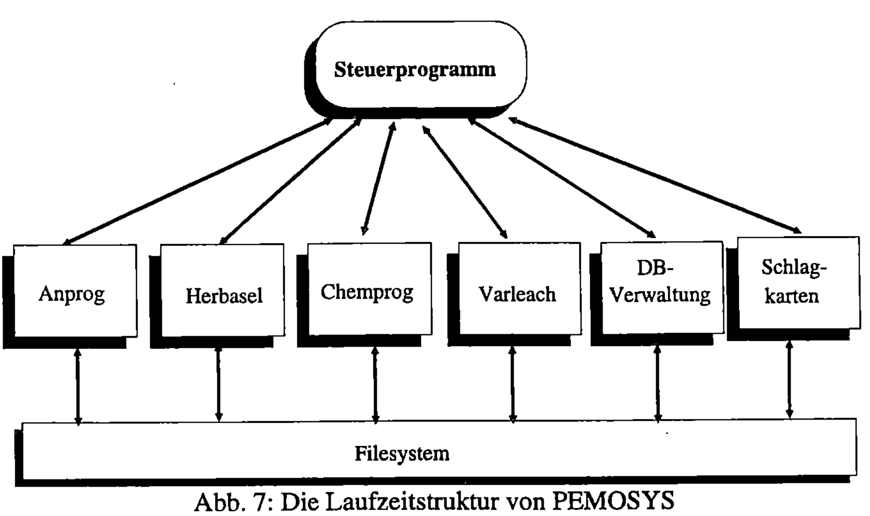

Abb. 7: Die Laufzeitstruktur von PEMOSYS

5. Implementierung

Das Expertensystem PEMOSYS gehört zur Klasse hybrider Expertensysteme, in der mathematische Simulationsmodelle und wissensbasierte Programmiertechniken verknüpft werden. Erst derartige Hybridmodelle, die Datenbanken, wissensbasierte Komponenten und Algorithmen kombinieren, können in der Praxis die Anwendbarkeit von Prognosemodellen wie hier in der landwirtschaflichen Beratung gewährleisten.

PEMOSYS wurde in den Programmiersprachen Prolog und C++ unter MS-Windows geschrieben.

Die Wissensbasis in PEMOSYS beinhaltet Fakten, Regeln, Tabellen und prozedurales Wissen (Integrator einer Differentialgleichung). Das Regelwissen läßt sich mit Hilfe der deklarativen Programmiersprache Prolog gut repräsentieren. Die Fakten dagegen wurden in externen Datenbanken abgelegt. Hierbei ist auf die möglichen Kopplungsarten der Datenbanken mit den Inferenzmechanismen zu achten (sh. 2.3). Die Simulationsmodelle in PEMOSYS sind im Gegensatz zu den oben genannten Wissensobjekten typisch prozedurales Wissen von algorithmischer Natur. Dieses läßt sich mit einer prozeduralen Programmiersprache wie C++ einfacher und zeit- und raumeffizienter realisieren. Da die Modelle mehrere I/O-Muster haben können, wurden diese in mehreren, bis auf die Suffixnumerierung, gleichnamigen C-Funktionen geschrieben und beim Linken zu Prolog-Objekten als globale Prolog-Prädikate deklariert. Somit verhält sich das Simulationsmodell wie ein Prolog-Prädikat.

Die Benutzung der Sprache Prolog und C++ sowie zusätzlich die Verwendung einer Datenbankabfragesprache spiegelt unsere Überzeugung wider, daß ein unter den vielfältigen Umwelteinflüssen in der landwirtschaftlichen Praxis funktionierendes Expertensystem normalerweise sowohl (oft heuristisches) Regelwissen (Oberflächenwissen) als auch prozedurales Wissen (Tiefenwissen) enthalten muß. Biologische Prozesse zu beschreiben ist aufgrund von Wissenslücken über die Vorgänge in der Natur immer mit Unsicherheiten behaftet, die nur durch Abschätzungen von Experten in einem derartigen System zu repräsentieren sind.

Damit ist zwangsläufig eine breite Palette von Programmiersprachen, Wissensrepräsentationsmechanismen aber auch eine umfangreiche Sammlung von technisch aufwendigen Konzepten (Beispiel: Kopplung von Inferenzmechanismen und externen Datenbanken) anzuwenden.

Die Implementierung wird in Abb. 8 dargestellt.

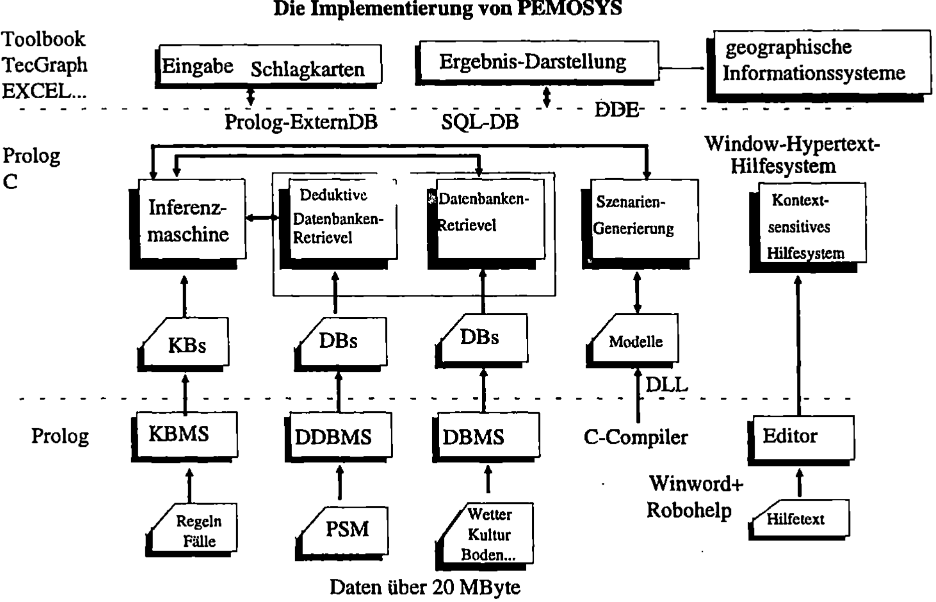

Abb. 8: Die Implementierung von PEMOSYS

6. Validierung von PEMOSYS

6.1 Technikbewertung

- **Die Wartbarkeit**

Aufgrund der modularen Systemarchitektur wird die Systemwartung bzw. -pflege sehr erleichtert. Die Arbeit der Systemwartung wird hauptsächlich von Domänen-Experten der Biologischen Bundesanstalt übernommen. Die Domänen-Experten geben an die Systementwickler (KI-Labor der Universität Bremen) Rückkopplungen bezüglich

» der Korrektheit des Systems (sh. 6.2),

» neuer Vorschläge zur Verbesserung der Funktionalität und des Laufzeitverhaltens und der

» Verbesserung der Bedienungen für fachliche Praxisanforderungen.

Darüber hinaus ist der Domäne-Experte zuständig für die Aktualisierung

» der Datenbanken (neu zugelassene PSM oder Verbot eines PSM) sowie

» der Wissensbasen (neue Modelle, neue Erkenntnisse aus der Forschung).

Dies ist eine wichtige Voraussetzung für die Anwendungsbreite.

- Die Transferierbarkeit

des Systems wird ebenfalls durch die modulare Architektur unterstützt:

» In PEMOSYS kann man die gewünschte Ländersprache wählen. Z. Zt. gibt es Versionen in Englisch, Deutsch und Chinesisch. PEMOSYS kann leicht an andere Sprachen angepaßt werden.

» PEMOSYS ist z. Zt. in 56 Pilotinstallationen weltweit getestet oder eingesetzt (z.B. Deutschland, Österreich, China, USA, Neuseeland und Australien).

- Die Effizienz

des Systems wird aufgrund der realzeitigen Simulationsmodelle gewährleistet. Eine entsprechende MS-DOS-Version von PEMOSYS ist selbst auf einem AT-286 lauffähig. Zu empfehlen ist jedoch ein Rechner mit einem Prozessor ab 80386 (Windowsversion 80486 66 MHZ).

- Die Portierbarkeit

von PEMOSYS ist durch die Unterstützung von standardisierten Schnittstellen gegeben. So läßt sich PEMOSYS z.B. leicht mit dem landwirtschaftlichen Expertensystem PRO_PLANT (Auswahl von Fungiziden, sh. KI-3/93) koppeln.

- Ergonomische Aspekte

» Dialogführung: Eine große Klasse von Benutzern von PEMOSYS sind Landwirte, die in der Regel kaum über EDV-Kenntnisse verfügen. Daher ist PEMOSYS in seiner Bedienbarkeit sehr einfach konzipiert und implementiert und verfügt über umfangreiche Online-Hilfen zur Handhabung und zur Beantwortung von Fragen.

» Die Benutzeroberfläche berücksichtigt die wichtigsten Konventionen von graphischen Benutzeroberflächen (sh. z.B. SAA 91).

» Die Erklärungen von Ergebnissen können sowohl graphisch als auch in natürlicher Sprache dargestellt werden. Die Anwendung von multimedialen Techniken erhöht die Akzeptanz von PEMOSYS in fachlicher Praxis.

» Durch die Unterstützung des Dynamic Data Exchange (DDE) können Daten von PEMOSYS ggf. an andere kommerzielle Softwares übergeben werden. Z.B. die graphische Darstellung von Kurven kann in MS-EXCEL erfolgen. Dies führt zur Verbesserung der Kosten/Nutzen-Relation bei der Systementwicklung.

6.2 Validierung der Funktionalität

6.2.1 Qualitative Validierung von PEMOSYS durch Field Tests

PEMOSYS befindet sich seit Anfang 1991 im praktischen Test. Die Beteiligten umfassen ein breites Anwenderspektrum: Pflanzenschutzämter, Berater von landwirtschaftlichen Genossenschaften, Industrieberater und Forschungsinstitute. Die Datenpflege der Wissensbasen erfolgt für die jeweiligen Anwendungsbereiche.

In Untersuchungen der BBA zum Nachbau verschiedener Kulturen nach Einsatz von PSM wurden Simulationsrechnungen zum Abbau sowie Prognosen der Nachbausicherheit durchgeführt und diese mit den ermittelten Praxisergebnissen verglichen.

PSM	Nachbaukultur	prognostizierte Nachbauschädigung	ermittelte Nachbauschädigung
pendimethalin	Spinat	x	+/-
	Flachs	+/-	+/-
	Flachs	+/-	+/-
	Spinat	xxx	xxx
	Flachs	+/-	+/-
	Spinat	xxx	xxx
methabenzthiazuron	Flachs	+/-	+/-
	Flachs	xxx	+/-
	Flachs	xxx	+/- bis x

Tabelle 3: Gemessene und simulierte Rückstandsgehalte von Atrazin in der Boden-schicht (0-10 cm) und ermittelte Schäden und Prognose der Nachbausicherheit. -- =kein Nachbau; +/- = sicher; x = leichter Schaden; xx = signifikanter Schaden; xxx = schwerer Schaden.

Eine statistische Analyse ergab, daß die prognostizierte Nachbauschädigung fast immer auf der sicheren Seite steht ([GOTTESBÜREN 1991]).

6.2.2 Quantitative Validierung von PEMOSYS

Mit dem in ANPROG implementierten Modell von [Walker & Barnes 1981] wurden unter Verwendung standortspezifischer Witterungsdaten der Abbau von PSM-Wirkstof-fen simuliert und die Ergebnisse zu den gemessenen Rückstandsdaten in Beziehung gesetzt.

Aus den Vergleichen von Simulationsergebnissen mit gemessenen Rückstandsverläufen einiger Wirkstoffe sollen die generellen Tendenzen der Validierung des Simulationsmo-dells dargelegt werden.

Die quantitative Validierung erfolgt im Projekt PEMOSYS durch die Euklidische Norm. Da die beobachtete Realausgabefunktion $y(t)$ nur an verschiedenen Zeitpunkten verfüg-bare Werte $t_0 < t_1 < ... < t_n$ hat, wird die Euklidische Norm dementsprechend angepaßt,

$$d_0^2(y,y') = \frac{\sum_{i=1}^{N}(y(t_i)-y'(t_i))^2}{N}$$

wobei $y(t_i)$ der gemessene Rückstandgehalt am Tag t_i und $y'(t_i)$ der aus dem Abbaumo-dell errechnete Rückstandgehalt sind. $y(t_i)$ und $y'(t_i)$ sind normierte Werte, d. h. das Maximum von den jeweiligen Reihen ist 1.

Es wurden in der BBA zu verschiedenen Wirkstoffen umfangreiche Messungen und Vergleiche durchgeführt. Hier sei stellvertretend das Ergebnis für den Wirkstoff *Ethof-umesat* dargestellt.

Versuchsbezeichnung	Jahr	r^2 Anpassung
ET-4	1988	0,945
ET-6	1988	0,869
ET-7	1989	0,917
ET-9	1990	0,978
ET-10	1990	0,954
ET-11	1990	0,937
ET-13	1990	0,965
ET-14	1990	0,887
ET-15	1990	1,000

Tabelle 4: Übereinstimmung zwischen simulierten Abbaukurven und gemessenen Rückständen von Ethofumesat in Freilandversuchen nach dem Maß $r^2 = 1\text{-}do^2(y,y')$

7.2.3 Literaturhinweise auf Ergebnisse der Validierung

Die Ergebnisse der Validierung von PEMOSYS sind in einer Reihe von Veröffentlichungen enthalten:

- Rückstandsverhalten und Prognose der Persistenz von PSM mit ANPROG und VARLEACH

  Das Rückstandsverhalten von PSM wurde sowohl in Kleinparzellenversuchen als auch auf Versuchsflächen der BBA und in verschiedenen Praxisbetrieben untersucht. Zur Validierung der Modellansätze wurden Simulationsrechnungen durchgeführt und die gemessenen Rückstandswerte mit den berechneten verglichen. Die Ergebnisse wurden in [Gottesbüren 1991] dargestellt.

- Abschätzung der potentiellen Grundwassergefährdung mit CHEMPROG

  Wegen einer geringen Anzahl von zur Verfügung stehenden Versuchsergebnissen wurde zur Kalibrierung ein zusätzlicher Vergleich der Abschätzung der potentiellen Grundwassergefährdung mit einem einfachen Screening-Verfahren nach RAO et al. (1985) durchgeführt (siehe auch [Gottesbüren 1991]).

- Validierung von HERBASEL

  Bislang wurden in HERBASEL starre Schadensschwellenrichtwerte verwendet, die als quantitative Orientierungshilfen für die Beurteilung der Bekämpfungswürdigkeit einer Verunkrautung dienen. Häufig wird vom Landwirt nur eine qualitative Bestandsaufnahme der Zusammensetzung der Unkrautflora vorgenommen, seltener erfolgt zusätzlich noch die genaue Auszählung der Unkrautdichte oder Schätzung des Unkrautdeckungsgrades, wie sie bei der Verwendung von Schadensschwellen erforderlich ist. Die Richtwerte der Schadenschwellen erscheinen daher in ihrer Genauigkeit ausreichend, zumal aufgrund der Variabilität verschiedener Einflußfaktoren die tatsächliche ökonomische Schadensschwelle erst nach der Ernte berechnet werden kann. Problematisch erscheint bei dem hier gewählten Ansatz die Einzelbeurteilung der Unkräuter auf Bekämpfungswürdigkeit, denn es fehlen noch überprüfte Werte zur Beurteilung verschiedenartiger Mischverunkrautungen (siehe [Heiermann et al. 92]).

Literatur

Fathi-Torbaghan, M. und A. Höffman: Fuzzy Logik und Blackboard-Modelle in der technischen Anwendung, Oldenbourg, 1994

Gottesbüren, B. 1991: Konzeption, Entwicklung und Validierung des wissensbasierten Herbizid-Beratungssystems HERBASYS, Dissertation, Uni. Hannover.

Heiermann, M., W. Pestemer, B. Pallutt, K. Wang, M.-B. Wischnewsky und J. Zhao 1992: Einbildung von Herbizid-Wirkungsgraden und nichtchemischen Verfahren in das Expertensystem HERBASYS, Zeitschrift für Pflanzenkrankheiten und Pflanzenschutz, Sonderheft, XIII, 337-344, 1992.

Karagiannis, D. 1994: Wissensbasierte Datenbanken, HdI 8.2, Oldenbourg Verlag, 1994.

Karbach, W. und Linster M. 1990: Wissensakquisition für Expertensysteme, Carl Hanser Verlag, München/Wien, 1990.

Mertens, P. 1992: Zugangssysteme ("Intelligent Frond-Ends"), Wirtschaftsinformatik 34 (1992) 3, S. 269ff.

Pestemer, W., B. AUSPURG 1987: Prognose - Modell zur Erfassung des Rückstandsverhaltens von Metribuzin und Methabenzthiazuron im Boden und deren Auswirkungen auf Folgekulturen. Weed Res. 27, 275-286.

Pestemer, W., V. Radulescu, A. Walker, L. Ghinea 1984: Residualwirkung von Chlortrianzin - Herbiziden im Boden an drei rumänischen Standorten. Teil I: Prognose der Persistenz von Simazin und Atrazin im Boden. Weed Res. 24, 359-369.

Puppe, F. 1990: Problemlösungsmethoden in Expertensystemen, Springer-Verlag 1990.

Rao, P.S.C., HORNSBY, G. & JESSUP, R.E. 1985: Indices for ranking the potential of pesticide contamination of groundwater. -Soil and Crop Science Society of Florida, Proceedings, 44, 1-8.

Walker, A., A. Barnes 1981: Simulation of herbicide persistance in soil: a revised computer model. -Pesticide Science, 12, 123-132.

Walker, A., R. Allen 1984: Influence of soil and environmental factors on persistance. -BCPC Monograph No. 27, 89-100.

Zhao, J., K. Wang, M. Wischnewsky, B. Gottesbüren, W. Pestemer 1992: Einbindung eines Simulationsmodells zum Herbizidabbau in ein Expertensystem zur Herbizidberatung (HERBASYS), in Hrsg: O. Günther et al., Informatik Fachberichte 301, Springer-Verlag, 1992.